ALL GONE TO LOOK FOR AMERICA

D1584088

PETER MILLAR was born in Northern Ireland and educated at Magdalen College, Oxford. He has worked as a journalist for Reuters, the *Daily* and *Sunday Telegraphs*, and *The Sunday Times* based in London, Brussels, Berlin, Warsaw and Moscow. He was named Foreign Correspondent of the Year for his coverage of the Fall of the Berlin Wall in 1989. He is the author of two novels, three translations from the German and one book of oral history, and is popular fiction critic for *The Times*.

He is married with two sons and lives in the beer-drinking idyll of Hook Norton, Oxfordshire, when he is not sitting with his eyes closed and fingers crossed in the North Stand of The Valley, Charlton Athletic's South London football ground.

ALL GONE TO LOOK FOR AMERICA

Peter Millar

ARCADIA BOOKS

Arcadia Books Ltd
15–16 Nassau Street
London W1W 7AB

www.arcadiabooks.co.uk

First published by Arcadia Books 2009

ISBN 978-1-906413-02-6

Typeset in Arno by MacGuru Ltd
Printed in Finland by WS Bookwell

Arcadia Books gratefully acknowledges the financial support of Arts Council England.

Arcadia Books supports English PEN, the fellowship of writers who work together to promote literature and its understanding. English PEN upholds writers' freedoms in Britain and around the world, challenging political and cultural limits on free expression.
To find out more, visit www.englishpen.org or contact
English PEN, 6-8 Amwell Street, London EC1R 1UQ

Arcadia Books distributors are as follows:

in the UK and elsewhere in Europe:
Turnaround Publishers Services
Unit 3, Olympia Trading Estate
Coburg Road
London N22 6TZ

in the US and Canada:
Independent Publishers Group
814 N. Franklin Street
Chicago, IL 60610

in Australia:
Tower Books
PO Box 213
Brookvale, NSW 2100

in New Zealand:
Addenda

Contents

Acknowledgements

FIRST AND FOREMOST I would like to thank the friendly people at Amtrak who helped me organise my trip, fixing reservations when I needed them and organising a timetable across a continent on trains that mostly run only once a day. The US railroad system has its drawbacks but few of them are the fault of the enthusiastic, cheerful people who run it. They operate the legacy of one of the world's great transport systems; maybe the need for greener forms of travel will one day see it restored to its former glory. But unless Barack Obama really surprises us, not any time soon.

Also thanks to my wife Jackie for putting up with my absence (not that much of a hardship) and for providing me with my one luxurious night in a grand hotel in Chicago.

And finally, but not least importantly, all those great musicians and songwriters who accompanied me on my iPod and in my head, providing a soundtrack both essential and inescapable to a country that has given the world so much of its popular music. I hope I have given all of them due recognition, but I owe a special debt to Paul Simon whose music haunts so many American locations, and which gave me inspiration for my title.

Peter Millar, Hook Norton, December 2008

Prologue

I COULD HAVE BEEN BORN an American. Almost. My mother emigrated there from Northern Ireland after the Second World War, but while her brother remained in the country she returned home. Like many British and Irish people, I have American relatives and have visited them. Because of that, and its familiarity from Hollywood and television, America is a country most of us feel we know well, but which can still surprise us by being disconcertingly foreign.

Many people in Europe instinctively love America or hate it: for having rescued us in the Second World War, and for never letting us forget it. The phenomenon of anti-Americanism has always – certainly in Britain – been part envy of America's wealth and power, part resentment at how it throws its weight around. Yet there is an irony that almost precisely at the moment of the Cold War 'victory' which seemingly secured global dominance, America started to look more vulnerable. Over the past two years we have seen something remarkable: Americans asking questions about their own country and giving a political answer almost no one had thought possible outside the realms of Hollywood and television: the first black president.

New York is the modern Rome. When Mayor Rudy Giuliani claimed after the attacks of 11 September 2001 that New York was the 'capital of the world', he wasn't kidding. He was, of course, pandering to its citizens' concept of their own status, but also expressing a metaphorical truth. New York is the ultimate expression of the city as we know it at the close of the twentieth century, which began with the high point of the British Empire and may have ended with the high point of America's.

They have never called it an empire. It was our – British – empire which they still pride themselves on escaping. In films such as *Star Wars* the 'empire' is always bad while the good guys always fight for the 'republic' (even if it has princesses). But that is not such a difference as you might think. Augustus, the first Roman emperor, presented himself as the restorer of the 'republic', with himself as merely its 'first citizen', and his wife the 'first lady'. A little hypocrisy has always gone with the territory.

The cosmopolitan, financial and cultural powerhouse of New York, with its instantly identifiable architecture and boundless self-confidence, has for the last hundred years personified America. Yet visiting it today, after the outrage of 9/11, I can't help wondering if this is what it was like to visit Rome at the end of the fourth century, still the metropolis at the centre of the turning world but, having suffered indignity at the hands of invading barbarians, no longer invincible. The eternal city, but no longer immortal. It is a sobering thought.

The great difference, of course, is that America is a proud democracy – as it has just resoundingly proved – but beyond that the similarities are marked. The USA is not just a vast territory in its own right, but the world's pre-eminent military power with a sense of mission and a firm belief that to shape as much of the world as possible in its image is a good thing. The Romans would have understood.

It might not have been that way. And almost certainly wouldn't if it hadn't been for the railways. When the Golden Spike was tapped into a polished laurel wood tie at Promontory Point, just north of the Great Salt Lake in Utah at 11:00 a.m. on the morning of 10 May 1869, the single world 'Done' was flashed by telegraph to a waiting nation. A nation, that in truth was not yet wholly convinced that it was a nation.

One of the great wonders of the world had been accomplished, and the dream of Thomas Jefferson, third president of the fledgling coastline country called the United States of America, was fulfilled. The project which had begun when he sent explorers Meriwether Lewis and William Clark with barely a dozen men to find a way overland across an unexplored continent had become known as America's 'Manifest Destiny'. That dream was a United States that would stretch 'from sea to shining sea', a nation on a continental scale, and not, as had seemed extremely possible only a brief few years earlier, a continent made up of half a dozen political entities – nation states, colonies and tribal homelands – with different flags, different laws and customs and perhaps even different languages. It was an invention only in its infancy towards the end of Jefferson's long life that made his dream possible: the railroad.

Without the railroad, the United States of America, global military and economic superpower, would never have existed in the form we know (and love or hate) today. Without a means of transport that 90 per cent of Americans nowadays never use, the South might have succeeded in seceding, California and Texas might have been independent countries, part of a greater Mexico or independent Spanish-speaking nations (less hard to imagine these days than a few decades ago). Alaska would have remained part of Russia, the Indian nations might just have survived – think North American equivalents of Paraguay or Bolivia speaking English or French alongside their native tongues. Utah would have been a polygamy-practising sovereign Mormon nation. The prime reason a breakaway British colony on the eastern coast came to span a continent comes down to the humble railway train.

America is what it is today not least because it is a country the size of a continent. So what better way to explore it than by the engine that created it. It was not as easy as it might seem. The railway may have given birth to the USA but modern America has since abandoned it. Today Promontory Point, Utah, is not even on a line. Nor is Cheyenne, Wyoming, once one of the biggest railway junctions on earth. You can no longer get to Chattanooga on a choo-choo. America's railroads today – long in decline – are at a turning point which might just see them revived and revitalised as a more environmentally friendly form of transport, or abandoned forever as an outmoded curiosity. Yet for now at least you can still use them to travel from coast to coast, from the Canadian to the Mexican borders. I was determined not only to 'ride The City of New Orleans', but to take those other trains that still bear such evocative, romantic names – Hiawatha, The Empire Builder, The Coast Starlight and The Southwest Chief – to see where they took me and what they told me about America today.

In little over a month, taking advantage of a roamer ticket only available to foreigners, I crisscrossed the continent travelling by train alone, in a route that – with regrettable omissions, such as New England or Florida, the latter for reasons that will become clear – encompassed as much of America's magic as possible: the metropolises of New York and Los Angeles; the jaw-dropping natural splendours of Niagara Falls and the Grand Canyon; the casinos of Las Vegas's little sister Reno in the empty Nevada desert, and the beautiful wild wastelands of Montana littered with bones of dinosaurs that once roamed an inland sea; the surprisingly similar homes of Elvis Presley in Memphis, Tennessee, and Bing Crosby in remote Spokane, Washington; the chilled-out, hi-tech city of Seattle, home to Starbucks and Microsoft, the laidback, hurricane-damaged Big Easy of New Orleans and the home of the Mormons in Salt Lake City; my first baseball game and David Beckham's vain attempts to coax Americans to watch proper football.

This is not a trainspotter's book: those who want details of engine sizes or horsepower will have to look elsewhere (there are, in any case, only two real workhorse engines and sets of rolling stock on the whole of the Amtrak network). Nor is this a work of political or socio-cultural analysis except insofar as such observations fall within the framework of reportage. This is my view: opinionated, muddle-headed maybe, but always honest. In that respect it has one very American quality: I tell it the way I see it. As often as not over a beer and with a song rattling away in the back of my head. Modern America has rediscovered the microbrewery, and I defy anyone to travel anywhere in this country without its music jangling in the mental background.

The USA today is a nation not quite as easy with itself as it likes to be, still tied into a war that lacks popular support and a fast-growing population for whom English is not the native language and who, for the first time in US history, do not feel particularly compelled to learn it. Now it has in the remarkable and charismatic Barack Obama not just the nation's first black president but a man to whom it looks for miracles that may yet, in a time of financial crisis and economic downturn, prove more than he can achieve.

But for all that, American remains an empire unto itself, the global power *sans pareille.* Yet times are changing, fast. India and China are rising to the challenge, while a revived capitalist Russia is a rogue card in a deck being rapidly reshuffled. George W. Bush's neo-conservatives laid out a route map for a 'new American century', yet like imperial Great Britain so secure in its global hegemony just a hundred years ago, ended up heading for a train wreck. Whether Barack Obama can put the locomotive back on track remains to be seen.

This does not aspire to be a definitive picture of the United States: what could be? It is a subjective snapshot in time of one man's trip around a great country at what may yet come to be seen as the apogee of its power. For better or worse.

Smile please, America.

Click.

x

1

Manhattan Transfer

YOU KNOW YOU CAN ONLY be in New York when within five hours of landing, you've been held up by Presidents George W. Bush and Mahmoud Ahmedinejad, caught up in a media scrum around a pouting Paris Hilton, and watched some bloke prepare to jump over six yellow taxis on a quad bike. All before dinner.

If, to much of the world, New York City *is* America, to most Americans it feels like somewhere else entirely. Somewhere they, like the rest of us, know mostly from the movies. A huge number of them have never been there. To many New Yorkers, on the other hand, 'America' is that place beyond the Hudson River, where they sometimes go at weekends but rarely visit. To those who live on the long thin island at its heart, Manhattan is a world of its own. In some ways indeed it is *the* world in microcosm, fond of dressing up to show the visitor different faces, yet beneath it all brashly itself.

The New York experience begins in the arrivals hall at JFK airport, with the stewards in the long line at immigration telling you in that broad nasal twang that in itself sets New York apart from the rest of the country, to wait until the 'awwfissa' calls you forward. With a population drawn from most other cities on the planet, New York when it wants to can resemble any one of them: on this particular day the arrivals hall at JFK is doing a very good impression of Tel Aviv. In the queue in front of me are lines of orthodox Hasidic Jews: pale faces with trailing ringlets under black hats and in long black coats. Many of the women have their hair covered with scarves. It is to be one of my more unexpected experiences that although the United States has a growing Muslim population the only women I encounter covering their hair for religious reasons are either orthodox Jewish or fundamentalist Christian.

On the shuttle minibus into Manhattan, sitting up front next to the driver is in itself a lesson in the 'global city's' evolving ethnicity. Dark-skinned, with

1

a baseball cap on backwards – men's headgear I am also going to discover is a more important social marker in America than women's – jeans, a T-shirt and sneakers, I have the driver marked out as an unremarkable African-American. I'm amused by his native New York savvy as we negotiate the concrete barriers and bollards between the terminals – partly there as security measures but primarily because most of the airport, as always, is a construction site in a state of Third World confusion – and he nods to the first cop, a freckle-faced, red-haired man, with a 'Thanks, pal', while the second, a swarthier type with a neat moustache, gets a '*Muchas gracias, amigo*'. Then as we bounce up onto the freeway he picks up his mobile phone and reveals his native language to be Arabic. 'I'm from Morocco,' he tells me in the brief seconds during the whole 90-minute journey when he is off the phone long enough for me to ask.

The journey is 90 minutes rather than the usual 45 because almost as soon as we reach Manhattan – the astounding skyline even without the Twin Towers still as iconic of the twentieth century AD as the Roman Coliseum was to the first or the pyramids of Giza to the twentieth BC – the traffic closes around us in absolute gridlock. It had not dawned on me, as I suspect it had not on most people, that this is 'UN Week', the opening of the United Nations' annual General Assembly session, the occasion of choice for national leaders with an urge to grandstand to the world. This was the forum at which Nikita Khrushchev banged his shoe on the rostrum and told America 'We will bury you', where Che Guevara and Fidel Castro accused America of imperialism and terrorism, while making the most of New York's capitalist comforts. Today it is the turn of the White House's *bête noire* of the moment, the president of Iran, to declare he will continue to flout American power by developing nuclear power. If the UN does nothing else, as George W. Bush in these waning days of his presidency certainly believes, it is nonetheless remarkable that it can bring him and Ahmedinejad together in one building, even if all they do is trade insults.

The other thing this deadly duo do, of course, is cause traffic mayhem, as limousines with motorcycle outriders rush hither and thither between the riverside UN building and the offices of their permanent missions (it requires a mental double-take at times to remember that New York is not the capital of the USA and therefore has no embassies). Meanwhile, we sit stuck in the bus, now on the Upper East Side looking out at backstreet lots between apartment buildings in brownstone or brick, with teenagers playing in basketball courts, for all the world like a scene out of *West Side Story* (east side or west side, there are few cheap parts of modern Manhattan), and then we shunt along a few blocks and are dwarfed by the soaring commercial office blocks and hotel sky-scrapers, then at last to the Upper West Side where I clamber out and look with no little apprehension at the towering old and rather dilapidated building where I am to spend the next three nights.

I'm not sure I can really say now precisely why I decided to stay at the YMCA. I'd love to say it was nothing to do with the song. But the image of the Village People in those costumes – fireman's uniform, Indian headdress, cowboy hat etc. – is too ingrained in my generation's consciousness not to think of it every time I hear the initials. There is simply no way to shake loose a song that has been parodied, spun off and imitated more times than any, other than Tony Christie's 'Amarillo', and yes, I'd thought of asking the way there too.

Of course, the world – and the YMCA – has moved on a lot since the seventies. It is some time since it has been used by gay men as a cover for cruising, which is not my intention. The 'Y' has long been open to both sexes and used by families and student groups as budget accommodation. That, plus a relatively cheap rate for New York City and a nice-looking picture of a single room on their website, meant I'd hardly considered anywhere else. There was also the idea that next time it hit the jukebox I could sing along as someone who'd actually been there, even if not quite done that. The sad truth, though, I can say with hindsight, is: it's NOT fun to stay at the YMCA.

If you're used to dormitories or are a teenager in a school group from Germany, as most of the inmates seemed to be, maybe it's not absolute hell. But having been advised – by an internet travel site – to ask for an 11th floor room with a view of the park, I end up in an 11th floor room with a view of the central heating system boilers. In fact, most of the building seems to be dominated by pipework and other industrial equipment, the 11th floor in particular. The 'Y' was in the midst of an extensive and much-needed renovation programme that meant parts of internal walls were missing and the corridors carpeted with soggy cardboard. I may be doing this trip on a budget, not least because I want to see real America, not be cocooned in Holiday Inn uniformity, but there is the middle-aged male bladder to consider and this is what I'm going to have to pad along for a pee in the middle of the night. My accommodation looks not so much like the small but cosy single-bedded room on the website, as a one-up, one-down at Her Majesty's Prison Wormwood Scrubs, though at least that would have had a toilet in the corner. The sleeping facilities in my spartan white-walled cell amount to a set of iron-framed bunks against one wall. At least there's nobody in the other one. Yet. But what the hell – they've already got my money (no refunds available) and I'm not here to watch cable TV.

Unlike most of America, Manhattan is a pedestrian's city. The West Side YMCA is on West 63rd St, a short walk from Central Park, the city's great green lung and one of the finest city parks on the planet which has long outlived its once dangerous reputation. I'm told that over two decades New York has meta-morphosed from the murder capital of the world to one of its safer cities, at least as far as street crime is concerned. Even so, I'm wearing my cash in a well-concealed money belt, not the most comfortable thing given that according to a temperature sign by Columbus Circle it is 86 degrees Fahrenheit, which a few seconds later thankfully translates to 30 Celsius. Older Britons may cling to Fahrenheit and love the Americans for preserving it, but a scale that goes from 32 to 212 rather than zero to 100 has always seemed doomed to me.

This is maybe the fourth time in my life that I have been to New York and I'm trying hard to be blasé. It doesn't work. It never does. There is only one thing constant about New York: the sheer, awe-inspiring, jaw-dropping, colos-sal, cluttered, sky-clogging, perpetually self-reinventing vibrant immensity of the place. From Columbus Circle down towards the insane, pulsing, tourist-ridden, high-tech, low-life, urban jungle arena that is Times Square, New York is so in your face you can hardly step back and see it properly. I know from my minimal experience that this is the best time to confront it, in early evening when the heat is beginning to subside, the day turning quickly to a violet dusk as the kaleidoscope of neon and whirling promotional projections start to wheel across the soaring, jutting, idiosyncratic façades of the sky-scraping (think what a good phrase that was when it was first coined) architecture, fusing them surreally with the onrushing night. You can't do Times Square without thinking they should never even have attempted to make Piccadilly Circus emulate it. Except perhaps as a focal point for tourists, the garish little clutch of neon lights around the statue of Eros never was and never will be on a par. It looks today much as Times Square did on my first visit: and that was as a child in 1968. Forty years ago.

The truth is that Times Square has never been a place on the ground so much as a space in your head. A commercial space at that. One that has far, far less in common with the quaint concept that we still call 'the bright lights' and far more to do with Ridley Scott's vision of future Los Angeles in *Blade Runner* (in fact far more than Los Angeles). This is a sea of architecture in motion awash with moving faces and shimmering images. The buildings – themselves ever-changing over the decades as stone, brick and concrete have yielded to steel, glass and carbon fibre, rising and falling and rising ever higher in tune with the demands of the commercial property market – are just the backdrop.

The Times Square–Broadway interface is a figment of a fevered imagination enacted fleetingly in real life and constantly subject to reinterpretation, as the neon yields to laser, hologram and HD digital projection.

Even before I reach what passes for the 'square' itself, on the corner of 53rd Street and Broadway, crash barriers have been erected to cordon off a whole section of street and hay bales positioned around a half dozen trademark New York yellow taxis parked in close order next to one another. At one end there is a ramp and beyond it a man in padded clothing is revving a high-powered quad bike, clearly with the intention of driving it up the ramp in an insane Evel Knievel attempt to jump over the cabs. This is too potty, too archetypal 'Noo Yoik' nuts not to stop and watch, except there is nothing much to watch. He is spending a lot of time not actually doing it, just sitting there revving his engine, spewing clouds of noxious diesel into hot night air that already reeks of engine fumes. Meanwhile the film crews bustle here and there, as if they aren't really sure when or if he's going to do it or if, improbably, the whole set-up is about to be moved 50 or 100 yards in one direction or the other. But then they aren't really there for him at all, it appears, as a surreally-stretched limo glides in from the far end of the street, through the hastily opened barriers. And in between a couple of burly black-suited minders, a pretty, bottle-enhanced blonde in a tiny black dress, steps out and heads for a door in the wall.

It's the first time I've noticed the door or the fact that a sign above it says 'Ed Sullivan Theater' and realise this is the stage door for one of America's most famous venues, long-time home of the show hosted by the eponymous Ed but for the past decade and a half the setting for the *Late Show* with David Letterman. As to the leggy luvvy stepping out of the limo I'm not left long in the dark about her identity as a vast scrum of hacks armed with microphone booms and television cameras crushes against the crowd barriers and begins calling, 'Paris, Paris, over here, over here.' For it is she, the Hilton heiress, famous for being infamous – and of course rich – primarily because thanks to her ex-boyfriend Rick Salomon, several million people on the internet have watched intimate details of her having sex. And also because she has been jailed for drink driving, discovering God in prison (amazing how many people bump into Him there) and emerging to declare herself ready to work for peace in Rwanda. Rwanda, I am sure, is thankful.

'Paris, Paris, talk to us, we've been with you through all your trials and tribulations,' shouts one overly devoted member of the media (though both trials and tribulations there have been in her silly pampered artificial existence). She trips across and trots out what I take to be the usual platitudes – I'm not close enough to hear and really couldn't care less – and then trots off through the stage door out of our lives and into those of the millions watching Mr Letterman on TV. The minders scowl at the disassembling press pack and disappear after her. Exit pursued by bears.

And then all is dark again, or at least relatively so in the absence of the television arc lights, and the other bear-like figure, the man in the padded jacket on the quad bike, has climbed off and is lighting up a cigarette by the hay bales, clearly in search of some alternative means of living dangerously. The one he had previously anticipated, it is rapidly becoming clear, is no longer on the cards, as the ramp is being dismantled by stage hands and a lorry has backed into the street where the limo was, ready to be loaded with the bales. I am left there in a state of some confusion and minor disappointment: had I missed the show? No, there was no sign of any previous attempt. Had he simply changed his mind? Seemed unlikely. I asked one of the hired hands, who just shrugged in a very Noo Yoik way and said, 'I guess it was just in case ...' 'In case of what?' I asked. But he just waved his hand at the stage door and got on with shifting bales of hay.

I'm not about to hang around to see Paris flounce out again though. I'm hungry. And I need a bit more New York inside me before I return to the spartan comforts of the 'Y'. On the advice of an English friend who used to live in New York I'm heading away from the neon bustle of Times Square for the bohemian delights of 'the village'. Greenwich Village, that is, though for those of us who actually live near the original Greenwich village in south London, the expression always sounds odd. Time to find myself an entrance to the Tube!

No, I know I can't call it that. The movies have fixed 'subway' so firmly in the collective English-speaking consciousness that I know even Londoners who see a sign above stairs leading under the street marked 'Subway' and almost subconsciously assume it is referring to the Underground (which it often also leads to), when actually it just refers to the underpass to cross the street. And yet, as I am to discover in other cities, we are completely wrong to think therefore that 'subway' is American for what we call 'the Tube' or, officially, the 'Underground'. In most of America, if you ask someone where the 'subway' is, they'll direct you to the nearest branch of a takeaway chain selling giant sandwiches. This is not just because very few American cities actually have underground railway transportation systems, but also because those which do call it the 'metro'. Don't ask me how the French won this battle behind our backs, but believe me, outside New York, they did.

Just to make the point, a ticket on the New York subway is called a 'Metro' card. I buy mine and load it up with enough dollars to cover a three-day stay and head down into the bowels of Manhattan. 'Veins' might be a better word as the subway lies literally just below the surface. The days are long gone when the Manhattan Transport Authority was famed only for the risk of being mugged in its stations and rattling trains so covered in spray-painted graffiti that there was even a fashion for praising them as urban artwork in an attempt to make light of their awfulness. Mugging is a relative rarity and if the trains still rattle they are remarkable nowadays for the pristine silver sheen of their metal exteriors. That said, by European standards it's still a useless system shuttling up and down beneath the avenues like a glorified underground bus service, replicating rather than complementing the pattern of the streets above.

But it gets me downtown, beyond the grid, into 'the village' the city established before the planners took control of it, where haphazard European-style street patterns predominate and probably perversely, we Europeans somehow find it easier to find our way around. Down here the streets are of average length and not anything up to five miles long, so if you get yourself to the right one at least you know you're probably within walking distance and not about to discover that it's still a cab ride away. Down here street numbers might run to 200 or 300 but never to 2300. Even so, it doesn't always mean you get where you want to, or rather in a city with an evolutionary churn like New York's that the place you were aiming for is still there. That's why with detailed internet instructions to hand to find one of the city's more recondite but supposedly convivial drinking establishments, I still find myself walking in circles around a small block even though I'm certain I'm in the right place. It turned out I am, but just at the wrong time. Two blokes sitting on steps of a nineteenth-century tenement that probably cost a king's ransom, confirm, 'Oh yeah, that place, it was neat, but it's gone. They might reopen it though, but not yet.'

Which was how two hours later than intended I finally find myself tucking into a burger in a half-empty bar picked at random. But in the funny way fate has of throwing bad luck and good luck at you alternately it turns out to be a great burger, served as I'd asked, medium-rare, still pink in the middle and oozing just the tiniest trace of blood along with flavour. The waitress is cute and sassy in that New York way that makes you feel like you're flirting when you're just ordering a meal and makes you fork out the outrageous amount of tip she's expecting without feeling a victim of extortion.

And the beer is excellent, in the way only modern American microbrewed beer can be, gassy for British tastes but tasting of hops and malt rather than

7

the weak rancid rat's piss their big brewers now try to sell to susceptible Brits. This particular beer, however, comes from one of America's oldest breweries but has still kept its taste and tradition. Even the name makes me smile, a typically American fusion of English and German that manages to look and sound Chinese: Yuengling. Once upon a time it would have been written Jüngling, and been German for 'youngster', until the Anglos – perhaps some immigration officer out on Ellis Island – wrote it down the way it sounded, with the result that most bartenders today pronounce it 'Ying Ling', as if it was made by Bruce Lee's cousin.

And then there's the muzak. If I have any residual religion, which I'd prefer to think I haven't, it is a quasi-pagan, wholly superstitious ingrained belief in the divine power that governs incidental music, or to give it a name, the 'small god of the iPod'. Maybe it was the waitress who had programmed the jukebox, or else my minor deity really had tickled the laws of chance to produce as background buzz, Lou Reed's proto-heavy-metal anthem of Big Apple street life, 'Waiting For My Man', followed seamlessly by Sting's rendition of 'Englishman in New York'. I'm not really an Englishman, of course, but it's the thought that counts. For a blissful moment or two, as the clocks tick heedlessly past 11:00 p.m., still chucking-out time even in most post-licensing-liberalisation England, and the waitress brings me another Yuengling with a wink and a smile, I felt totally at home.

Cool.

Jesus Christ, I'm even learning the language.

My first thought on waking next morning is to get out of the squalor of the 'Y' to find some breakfast and an internet connection to start sorting out some of the basics needed before undertaking an odyssey across an alien continent: like a mobile phone that works on America's quirky network, and a new pair of shoes, having discovered in barely 18 hours on the ground that the clunky trainers which are all I've packed are far too heavy and far too hot to cope with this semi-tropical climate and my feet are not just sweating but turning wrinkly.

The 'Y', needless to say, doesn't offer wi-fi internet access but that doesn't mean it isn't available, right outside the front door, I gather, spotting half a dozen kids with open laptops perched at various levels up and down the external iron fire escape, 'air-surfing': piggy-backing on someone's unsecured wi-fi connection. In a city like this, surrounded by apartment blocks and offices, there are bound to be at least a couple of them. I try asking one of them, a girl in her twenties staring intently at her notebook about five feet above my head on the first landing of the fire escape.

'Excuse me,' I ask her politely, 'but have you got a wi-fi connection there?'

In return I get a blank stare. I hadn't said something accidentally obscene, had I? You never know in another country. Maybe Americans didn't use the expression 'wi-fi' but that seemed a bit unlikely; it's one of those phrases that had 'made in America' stamped all over it. Perhaps she was a deaf mute. Perhaps she just didn't like strange men asking her questions. I reckon it's worth one more try:

'Do you have a wi-fi, a wireless internet connection?'

Another blank look, but not quite as blank as first time around. She looks at least moderately interested in my question. And then all of a sudden her face brightens up and she exclaims with a smile, '*Ahhhh, weefeee. Internyet. Da, da.*' We used to fear the Russians were coming. Today, they're already here. Everywhere.

Even so, I think better of opening up my laptop and fighting for a space on the higher rungs of the fire escape and decide instead to try the easier, if more expensive, option of the nearby Borders bookshop. It has the advantage of comfy seats and, American bookshops being what they are, I can have breakfast at the same time. Breakfast in New York means bagels which are eaten by everybody, and come both savoury and sweet, but best of all warm with cream cheese and a decent cup of coffee. I may complain – and I will – about the Americanisation of Britain but I have to add that in New York there is almost no such thing as a bad cup of coffee and we have Americans to thank for transforming the watery bitter brew that even our old Italian delis had degenerated into producing, before Starbucks mugged them. The Borders bagel is excellent, warm as a puppy dog and almost as comforting, with a consistency like thick dough which sounds nasty but is actually delicious.

But there's a pilgrimage to be made. In the summer of 2001 on a flying visit to New York we chose to take the children up the Empire State Building rather than the World Trade Center – luckily, you might say, since it could have been that August day rather than three weeks later on September 11 – that the suicide attacks took place. We made the choice because the Empire State was more iconic, from its starring role in *King Kong*. Had 9/11 not happened the World Trade Center might have garnered similar cult status with the release of *Spider-man 2* in which the baddies' helicopter got trapped in a web strung between the towers. Under the circumstances, obviously, the plot had to be rewritten* as video of the towers attained iconic status for altogether more tragic reasons.

Now I have no alternative but to go and see Ground Zero, worried slightly that it might be ghoulish behaviour, but consoling myself that it's no more so than visiting Auschwitz: the scene of an atrocity of historical dimension. There is also an added, personal if rather venal, advantage: right next to Ground Zero is the biggest budget footwear shop in New York. In the inferno of 9/11 when the Twin Towers collapsed, weakening the structure of half a dozen surrounding buildings to the extent they required demolition, they left the budget shoe superstore next door unmarked. And when I say next door, I mean right next door, as I discover when I emerge from the subway. The blue hoardings that keep the public back from what is still the world's biggest urban hole in the ground stand just feet from the front door of the Century21 discount clothing store. It is sobering to think that those who might have escaped certain death at their office desk that morning could have done so because they had nipped out to buy a cheap pair of sneakers or a new pair of tights.

But then there are few things that need sorting more urgently than your feet. I've already decided what I want to replace my waterproof, weatherproof, but totally unwearable trainers with: Converse sneakers. The one thing troubling me about this is that I have only remembered their existence because the British press has highlighted them as the casual footwear of choice of David Cameron, leader of the Conservative Party. You have to understand what an existential trauma this is. I have never before coveted the footwear of a Tory leader. Or indeed any politician. Cameron's Converses, on the other hand, I immediately recognised with a swallow of nostalgia as the 'baseball boots' of my youth. In the early 1970s these imports from America became an overnight sensation that made anybody wearing the previously commonplace white plimsolls – 'guttees' in our charming Northern Irish patois – hopelessly out of touch. It's only now I realise how out of touch we were, seeing my fondly remembered 'baseball boots' correctly labelled as the 'classic basketball shoe'.

Buying them isn't that easy though. First of all you have to find them, and then make them fit. Okay, I've known for years – in theory at least – that Americans are uniquely like Russians in not having a concept of 'ground floor'. But that doesn't stop me seeing on the store index that what I want is on the first floor and then start climbing the stairs to get to it. It's not much better when I

---

*The trailer for the original plot line, including the spectacular shot of the web between the towers is on YouTube at http://www.youtube.com/watch?v=F2-DS5lgyXc

come back down again and try them on. Those 'imperial' British stalwarts who think that the Americans will preserve their 'non-continental' measures for them – like Fahrenheit – rejoice in the fact that American sizes – 8 or 9 rather than 42 or 43 – seem the same as British ones. They aren't. In the same way – sort of, I'm not sure where the correlation is – that you can order a pint of beer in an American bar but you won't get one. Not a British one. The US pint is 16 fluid ounces rather than 20; in fact it's pretty much half a litre. So American shoe sizes are – to use an old English expression that will only complicate the issue – not quite the full shilling. If you wear a British 8 (42) you really need to buy an American 9. This would be well and good, in an unsatisfactory sort of way, if you could a) remember it, and b) rely on it. And most importantly of all, c) the people who actually make the shoes either knew or cared about it. They don't.

The fact is that 90 per cent of all footwear these days is made in China, India or other Asian countries where they churn them out to what they think are global standards. That means if you pick up a 42 or a 43, you have at least a fair chance of getting what it says on the insole. The same goes if you pick up an 8 or a 9, and are American. But if you are a Brit, and seriously think that the vast shoe manufacturing sweat shops of the developing world are going to remember that there is one tiny part of the Anglo-Saxon world that has measurements just ever so slightly out of synch with its big brother, then you are probably one of those that thinks 50 per cent of the world map is still painted pink. And after nearly half an hour of trying to squeeze my size 9 (43) feet into relatively forgiving size 9 Converse sneakers (which proclaim on the label that they are 9 – UK), I finally give up and buy size 10. But at least my feet are no longer hurting as I go outside to face the aftermath of Armageddon.

Ground Zero, I'm afraid, is deeply underwhelming. I don't know quite what I had expected: some vestige of the destruction, says the ghoul, some quietly imposing memorial, says the human being. But seven years after the disaster this is still one of the world's biggest building sites. Plagued by souvenir hawkers, even though signs expressly forbid them. I'm ambiguous as to whether or not they're in bad taste. What most offer are sets of high quality photographs of the attacks and their aftermath, not charred bodies but the twisted upright metal girders amid the wreckage that became such an iconic image of the destruction and I, for one, thought sure to be preserved as part of any memorial. These photographs or ones very similar can be bought in books all over the city, indeed all over the world. I can understand that perhaps the commerce of selling them on the site may seem dubious but here in the capital of capitalism, when all the industry in the great hole behind the hoardings is dedicated to recreating commercial space and has been the subject of unseemly argument since almost the day after the atrocity, it does not seem totally out of place. Nor, despite the signs forbidding his presence, can I find fault with the guy selling bottles of ice-cold water. I need one, and buying and selling is better than begging. And already the one thing that has shocked me in less than 24 hours on the streets of America is the number of beggars. In the richest society on earth, it is one hell of a long way from the top to the bottom.

Apart from the flying flags around the boarded-off construction site, there is – until the memorial in the footprint of the felled towers is complete – precious little to commemorate the disaster. The most poignant thing is a plaque erected when the Twin Towers were still standing, giving their vital statistics. They still make awe-inspiring reading, from the nearly one billion dollars they had cost to build by the time the first tower was opened in 1972, to the 1.2 million cubic yards of earth and rock excavated and dumped in the Hudson River to form the hardcore base for the Battery Park City housing development. The towers contained 200 lifts serving 40,000 square feet of office space on each of the 102 floors. And being built in the early seventies they also had a virtual monopoly on one of the lingering images of the time: polystyrene ceiling tiles. The Twin Towers incorporated seven million square feet of them. There were also 1,200 'restrooms', a statistic that produces a sad little laugh: one of the most lasting images of the Twin Towers was the *Simpsons* episode when Homer, desperate to take a leak, dashes to the toilet at the top of one of the towers, only to find a sign saying, 'Closed, try next door'.

As it happens, the real memorial to that terrible day is virtually next door – just beyond the budget clothing warehouse: St Paul's church, built in 1766, is the oldest building still standing in Manhattan. Its graveyard abuts Ground Zero. The church itself served as a place for firemen and others to rest during and after the rescue operation, and has become the atrocity's de facto shrine. Next to the carefully preserved pew once used by George Washington are stands displaying tokens of sympathy and encouragement from around the world, most touchingly several thousand origami cranes folded by the schoolchildren of Hiroshima and Nagasaki. A genuine gesture of sympathy and at the same time a point most elegantly unstated

2

A Whole New Ball Game

I AWAKE NEXT MORNING on a mission from god – the god of small cuddly toys. I'm going to spring an English hero from Guantánamo Bay. Or the next best thing. For longer than my lifetime, Winnie-the-Pooh, that arch icon of English childhood, along with his 'collaborators', Eeyore, Kanga, Tigger and Piglet, has been held hostage in a foreign land for 60 years and for the last 20 – contrary to the Geneva Convention? – put on public display by their captors in the New York Public Library. I had been warned about this. They are not in the grand Beaux Arts building on Fifth Avenue despite the famous lions standing guard at the entrance, but located in an altogether more discreet uptown branch: the Donnell Centre at 20 West 53rd Street, clearly a case of 'extraordinary rendition'.

The building itself is anonymous, as you'd expect a detention centre holding some of the literary world's greatest celebrities to be. After passing through security – well, having my bag checked – I make my way to the fourth floor. And there they are, peering out woefully at me from within their cage, looking nothing like themselves. Instead of those familiar figures in the prime of their youth cavorting around the hundred-acre wood, here are a collection of worn-out old has-beens, displayed in a nondescript wooden case that would not have looked out of place in the Victorian halls of the Egyptian Museum in Cairo. I think briefly about a smash-and-grab and a dash for freedom, but it's not just the thought of the bulky security woman on the door downstairs that deters me. Just one look at Eeyore and I realise that such an adventure would knock the stuffing out of him, while Piglet, even more diminutive now in his advanced age is far too frail to survive even being crammed into a pocket. And then Pooh, God bless him, looks after all like just any old teddy bear, rather than the rotund, pointed-nose-in-hunny-jar hero of his youth, EH Shephard's imagination and the Disney films. These blokes are just not up for the great escape.

13

And then, as the sound of children singing nursery rhymes wafts in from the reading room beyond the lifts and my eyes run down the vast list of names in the visitors' book – several dozen this week alone – I realise I'm far too late anyway. Like many a hero before him and since, Pooh has been sold out by the men in charge. Taken to America and left with AA Milne's publishers in 1947, he was moved to the children's section of this library 40 years later. Pooh might not quite have gone native, but he is by now a settled expat happy with his lot, the Alastair Cook of cuddly toys. In retirement.

The Pooh that lives on in celluloid is the Pooh whose soul was sold to the Walt Disney corporation, which has since indulged in various, high-profile, expensive, protectionist scraps with other claimants, including an American lawyer, Winchester School and London's Garrick Club. Ask most people about Winnie-the-Pooh these days – even in Britain – and the image they'll conjure up is the brightly coloured Disney version talking with an American accent rather than Shephard's understated line drawings and Milne's uncompromisingly English prose.

And then I realise that there is not a mention of Disney here, not a cartoon image nor a single reference to 'A Blustery Day', just the original animals – loved half to death – and the original books. Ditto. And there are children round the corner reading together and singing nursery rhymes in a traditional manner I fear rarely happens in modern Britain.

Maybe Pooh and chums are perhaps better off here after all. He wouldn't like being stuck in the Garrick Club. There are enough stuffed shirts there already.

I have one more British icon whose Manhattan shrine needs to be visited: Dylan Thomas, that great Welsh windbag and wordsmith who wowed America and accidentally drank himself to death here. And that means a pilgrimage to an institution of an altogether different ilk, the White Horse Tavern, famously frequented by Jack Kerouac, who was thrown out, and Thomas who downed his last drink there in 1953. At the post-mortem it was disappointingly discovered that the actual cause of Thomas's death was pneumonia, exacerbated by emphysema, caused in turn by heavy smoking and use of morphine. To the astonishment of all concerned, his liver was found to be surprisingly healthy. I can't think of anywhere better to have a few beers to round off the evening, and step boldly out into the road to hail a cab.

14

New York's yellow cabs are as much an institution as London's black ones, their low-slung shape as distinctive as our upright square boxes, the difference being that they never considered having to accommodate a gentleman wearing a top hat. The iconic cab was originally made by the Checker company back in the 1950s – the term 'Checker cab' refers to the brand, and not as I long thought to a former cross-hatching 'chequered' paint job The last was only replaced in 1999. Most New York cabs today are Ford Crown Victoria saloons, a line that has been running since 1992, but to climb into one you could be forgiven for thinking it is a good 30 years older. Certainly this one, driven by a genial Indian bloke, looks as if it's been in service since the Cuban revolution. I know what I am talking about here. I have been to Havana and had the dodgy delight of travelling in one or two of the ancient pre-Castro Lincolns and Dodges that the locals lovingly patch up with whatever they can get hold of. And I have seen several in a lot better condition than this. Electrical wires hang down below the steering column held together with gaffer tape, the suspension has gone and so have the springs in the back seat, as well as most of the ripped and torn leatherwork. This isn't a beaten-up exception; it's the rule of thumb. I wind one window down – manually – to let the warm breeze in as we cruise off into the sticky Manhattan night.

When I give him my destination we convincingly turn sharply and head uptown, except that I know that is totally the wrong direction. That's the moment I realise that my cab driver has no more than the vaguest notion of where I want him to take me. We're 'downtown' here, but in New York City the expression has a totally different meaning to what it has in every other city in America. Out there – across the inland empire – 'downtown' means the city centre; here it means the bottom end of the island – Lower Manhattan – the oldest part of the city, where the streets meander and taxi drivers despair. Your typical New York cabbie, like most New Yorkers themselves, save for the elite little clan who actually inhabit one of the 'villages' downtown, navigates by the grid, and the grid alone. He can cross-reference streets and avenues, knows on which streets the traffic runs east-west and on which it runs west-east (it's supposed to alternate but doesn't always), but ask him to take you off the grid and he's guessing.

I know the White Horse is at 567 Hudson Street, but whereas a London cabbie would know which end of the street that was nearest and where best to turn on to it, my guy hasn't a clue. He wants an intersection and that's a problem because down here the streets don't go east-west, or rather some of them do and some of them don't and there aren't any north-south avenues, or at least not very many and those that do have a disconcerting tendency to change their names to streets and often change direction too. I tell him it's near West 11th Street, but this is a problem because when it gets far enough west, West 11th Street does something New York streets aren't supposed to: it bends, which throws my driver completely. In the end he drops me on an intersection where five roads meet – which is clearly more than he can cope with – and tells me he reckons one of Lower Manhattan's most celebrated pubs 'oughta be around here somewhere'.

With a little bit of observation I work out I'm at the bottom end of Eighth Avenue which splits into the diverging Hudson Street and Bleecker Street with Bank Street and Bethune Street going off at other angles – proper names, you see, not just numbers. The White Horse turns out to be about 100 yards away. It's unmistakable: a proper English Victorian boozer, at least from the outside, and inside too with moulded plasterwork ceilings and a great gin-palace-inscribed mirror behind the dark mahogany bar. The only difference is the ceiling fans, more suited to New York's climate than London's, and the brace of televisions displaying the inevitable baseball game. And of course, the life-size – or probably slightly larger – black-and-white portrait of the great Welsh windbag himself pontificating, glass in hand, carried away by the effortless brilliant breeze of his own tale-twisting words. For a moment I almost fear that the White Horse has betrayed Thomas's legacy to it by becoming a theme pub in his honour, but nobody pays it any heed; they're all too busy drinking, which is, after all, what the great man would have wanted.

The crowd in here could be the crowd in any central London pub: mixed ages, mixed sex, a slight preponderance of young, metrosexual types, a studenty element, earnest conversations, noisy banter and serious chatting-up going on in equal proportion. There are a few blokes standing at the bar, chatting or watching the baseball. I find a space and order a pint of ESB – not from the London brewery Fuller's but from west coast brewery Red Hook. It's a rich, malty beer and once you've got used to the fact that American beer is kegged, and therefore carbonated, it's a fine drink. Standing there sipping, soaking in the atmosphere, and wondering how different it would have been in the fifties when Thomas and Kerouac and crew hung out here, I can't help noticing that the two televisions are showing different baseball games, and that both give the impression of being broadcast live which is mildly surprising seeing as it's gone 10:30 p.m. Even under floodlights, most British evening sport is finished by 10:00 p.m. at the latest.

I mention this, casually, in a sort of friendly, bloke-at-the-bar, stranger-in-a-strange-land, kind of fashion to the middle-aged man next to me who's been paying attention to one of the games rather than the other. He give me an odd look for a moment and then realises that I am obviously an alien, and explains: one television is showing the New York Mets game and the other the New York Yankees, and yes, of course they're still going on, why wouldn't they be, they're not over yet. I realise this is sort of obvious as it seems is my follow-up question: so what time do they finish. This gets an incredulous, not to say sceptical look, and the reply, 'When they're over,' which does me no good at all, and then the explanatory, 'When one team wins.' As a football fan where 0–0 is sometimes not even a disappointing score, and aware than even cricket occasionally ends in a draw, it had simply not occurred to me that baseball doesn't: it's not over until one team wins.

This certainly seems to explain why the games on TV are still going on at a time when anyone sensible would be down the pub – so, even though I'm not exactly fascinated by the topic but am enjoying having a conversation with a native, I ask him to explain. I won't bore you with the details – primarily because I didn't really understand beyond the fact they play nine innings and if it's a draw keep going until the next run, a sort of 'golden goal' situation – but what struck me was how initially reluctant he was to tell me. Normally asking most blokes about their favourite sport is like pleading to be bored to death for the next hour, just try asking about the offside rule in football next time you're down the pub after a game. But after bursting into a brief explanation, he suddenly clams up and retreats into his pint. Realising I may have pushed the social niceties a bit far somehow or other, I say thanks and by the way, my name's Peter. He gives me a perfunctory nod back and says nothing. Fair enough, I think, man doesn't want to be bothered by strange character at bar who doesn't know the most elemental rules of the national sport, and order another ESB.

A few minutes later, however, he turns to me and says, 'Sorry, my name's Laurence, by the way.' And goes on to explain the 'golden goal' bit in more detail than I ever needed (see what I mean). It just gradually dawns on me that rather than just talking to a bloke at the bar, as you might do in London, we have been going through a strange sort of courtship ritual here. And then almost simultaneously when he makes a vivid point of ogling a girl in a tiny halter top, I realise that I am both right and incredibly wrong. He has just been fencing around to check whether I might be gay, not because he is, but because he isn't and before he gets into a conversation he wants to make sure he isn't just responding to a pick-up line. Which seems a good time to tell him I'm a football fan but my wife isn't, just to indicate that she exists really. He nods and tells me that his ex couldn't stand baseball – which I am beginning to think may have been a prime factor in their divorce.

Over the next half hour I learn more than I ever need to know about Red Sox and Black Sox, about how the Yankees are the Bronx and the Mets Queens, why there are two leagues – the National and the American – and that means it's okay for there to be a World Series in a sport which only a handful of countries play and in any case doesn't include them, being restricted to the winners of the two leagues. I also discover that Laurence is a university lecturer in English, a factor in his oblique attempt to explain why there's no point in telling me the rules of baseball when I've never even been to a game: 'You can read *Bleak House*, for example, and you'd know the story but you can't really understand it unless you know the semiotics of Victorian literature.' This loses me somewhat so I change tack and ask him if Dickens is his speciality.

'No, not really,' he replies. 'I did my dissertation on Thomas Hardy, the Wessex novels.'

'So you've been to England, then?'

'No, never been there. Read all the books, know some of them by heart, but never been there at all,' he says in that sort of tone of mild but relieved regret that betrays the fact that, though probably only in his late forties, he has no idea of ever going there. Laurence is a New Yorker born and bred and can't imagine ever living anywhere else, not abroad and certainly not anywhere else in America which he refers to with a mildly patronising scorn.

'They're all fat out there. You'll see.'

I smile, nervously: it's a stereotype of middle America I hadn't intended to raise.

'No really, look about. You don't see many fat women here in New York City.' I look about and realise he's right, in fact I've been noticing since my arrival that there aren't as many fat people as our European stereotype of modern Americans suggests.

'It's just New York,' he adds. 'Sex and the city, people here care. They work out, look after themselves. Out there,' and he waves a hand vaguely in the direction of the Hudson River, 'they are all lard-asses, you'll see.'

Laurence is proud of his own physique, 'keeping in shape' and no less proud of his sexual conquests, including several of his former students. He's starting to remind me of Malcolm Bradbury's sexual predator university lecturer in *The History Man*. But he is also inordinately proud of being a regular in the White Horse Tavern in particular, and a resident of Greenwich Village in general.

'This bar preserves a sort of bohemian alternative lifestyle in the village. But we're getting Starbucks coming in now, and once you get Starbucks, it's the death of the community.'

There's an irony here that laid-back Seattle-founded Starbucks probably sees itself as 'community-creating' with its sofas and iTunes and internet, but it's not what he means. He means the eccentricity and diversity of a neighbourhood in which the shops are owned by individuals, not licensed by franchises. What he means is the little mama-and-papa Anglo-Italian coffee bars I was sniping at earlier, the ones that grew up in London in the 1950s, in Soho particularly. I point out the parallel.

'Your Soho, in London. Oh yeah, I forgot about that,' he says.

I laugh, though he doesn't understand why: having a district named from an old fox-hunting cry from the days when it was a game preserve rather than a mesh of congested streets may sound silly but surely it is at least more real than naming one SoHo in imitation just because it is 'south of Houston Street'. He at least has the good grace to laugh in acceptance, and goes on to list a whole cluster of New York's daffy acronyms invented by gentrifying communities eager for a bit of self-definition: TriBeCa (the triangle beneath Canal Street), NoLIta (north of Little Italy). Could that make the area to the left of Little Italy possibly LoLIta, I ask? He reckons it will as soon as it gets smart enough and somebody thinks of it. You will, Laurence, you will.

'Didn't the East Village used to be a predominantly Jewish neighbourhood?' I ask, trying to show at least a minimal grasp of New York ethnography.

'This is New York. It's all Jewish. I'm Jewish.' And I laugh with him: after all the bagel is the city's breakfast and there is surely a remnant of central European – perhaps mixed with a smidgeon of Irish – in that nasal Noo Yoik accent.

But the whole historic, cosmopolitan, eccentric, and diverse melting pot is all, according to Laurence, perpetually at risk. Greenwich Village is a threatened anomaly in a country that has been bought by big business and sold as suburbia, repackaged and franchised. The book I need to read, he tells me, hell, the book all city officials throughout America need to read, should be ashamed for not having read, is *The Death and Life of American Cities* by Jane Jacobs. I confess my ignorance, and Laurence explains that Jacobs, who died in 2006, was the only reason Greenwich Village still exists in anything like its old form. She was the sworn enemy of Robert Moses, the man who more than any other is responsible for the way most of the rest of New York looks today. She accused him of turning streets over to cars rather than people, of neglecting public transport and of championing the concept of 'urban renewal' in terms of zoning that separated out commercial, industrial and residential neighbourhoods and as a result created isolated, unnatural urban spaces and stripped communities of their uniqueness. Curiously, as I am to discover over the next couple of weeks, New York is perhaps the one city in America to which Moses' ideas were applied least. Others have all but been destroyed by them. I would soon discover that for myself.

Laurence brings the conversation full circle, blaming Moses for causing two of New York City's most famous baseball teams to decamp. The Brooklyn Dodgers, he says, moved to Los Angeles because Moses wouldn't let them build a new stadium in the site they wanted – which he had earmarked for a parking garage – followed by their traditional rivals, the New York Giants, who relocated to San Francisco, partly because the league required at least two major teams in close proximity to one another. Baseball plays the same role in American society that football does in Britain – more even than their football, it is the true national sport. But to date we have had only one movable franchise: created when Wimbledon F.C. departed south London for the new town of Milton Keynes, giving themselves the very American-sounding name MK Dons. But they had to surrender most of their history, handing their trophies back to Wimbledon borough. For a British club to transform itself from a local team with roots deep in the community to a movable 'business franchise' remains anathema, though with growing American (and other foreign) investment in the game and huge armies of fans in Asia who support English clubs, the risk is growing.

I try to make the comparison to Laurence, eager to show how much I have understood the 'semiotics', as he might put it, of his argument, but I might as well be talking about quidditch to someone who has never read Harry Potter: 'We just don't have an affinity with soccer. It'll never catch on.' And who knows, on the evidence – including that of my own eyes a few weeks later – he might well be right.

○

It seems only proper that before leaving New York, I remedy my ignorance about this vital part of American life and go to see 'a ball game'. A ball game in America is only ever baseball. American football and basketball – the other two great, but lesser passions – may also be played with a ball, but a 'ball game' only means baseball. It started out as the New York Game, first referred to in records from 1792 as being played just outside the city, on land that is today Greenwich Village.

The most surprising thing to me is the fact that I can get a ticket at all, especially given that the two New York teams both had home games last night. Unlike our football – or theirs – baseball games are played in series, like cricket test matches, over several days. There's a 'ball game' on virtually every day of the season, and for those teams that do well enough, on into post-season and the World Series. Today is officially the last day of the season and will decide which teams go through, but even so there's no problem at all getting a ticket, I'm told on the phone. But then maybe it's not all that strange when every game is also shown live on television.

The game it's easiest to get to is the Mets at Shea Stadium, the legendary venue where back in the sixties the Beatles pioneered the use of giant outdoor venues for pop concerts. They allegedly played only 25 minutes and the screams of adolescent American girls were so loud and their amplifiers so small nobody could hear them. But it's one of those events in rock history that made the venue famous. Best of all, I can get there by boat, up the East River. The Mets Express leaves Pier 17 at 5:00 p.m., more than two hours before the game and has a scheduled return time of 10:30 or '20 minutes after the end of the game'. Tricky thing organising transport for an event that is open-ended.

A brochure at the 'Y' lists Pier 17 as 'the historic heart of New York's seaport district offering fine views of the Brooklyn Bridge'. The latter at least is true, and the big old bridge, famous from a million movies and the longest suspension bridge in the world when it was completed back in 1870, is an impressive site seen from below, hanging there against an azure, almost tropical, sky that still seems wrong to me for early autumn. But South Street Seaport is a sorry disappointment; like so many 'historic' sites in America its preservation has meant its Disneyfication, old warehouses being transformed into bijou boutiques catering almost exclusively for tourists lured there – like me – by advertisements in brochures.

The one consolation however is that it does have a branch of the Heartland Brewery, New York City's new and so far only micro, which offers a welcoming place for late lunch and cold beer on a sweltering afternoon. I opt for their 'taster' tray of tiny glasses of half a dozen ales and something that calls itself 'popcorn shrimp': scampi you eat with your fingers. Coming soon to a franchise near you! It's okay, but the beers are better, particularly one in the distinctive dry, hoppy English IPA style called – with a better than average attempt at humour – India(na) Pale Ale.

The meal is marked only by a moment of embarrassment when two Irishmen come in and sit up at the bar next to me. They order fish and chips and large cokes and wolf them down. But when it comes to paying, despite the waitress's silken-tongued service manner and her obliging help in explaining how they needed to use a different area code to call Brooklyn on the younger one's mobile phone, they make the classic foreigner's error. As they hand over the $30 for their two meals and giant cokes, the older one, as if an afterthought, turns and adds a tip: a single dollar. To her everlasting credit, the waitress smiles and says, 'Thank you,' and the pair grunt and nod as if they've done her a service, both blissfully unaware that they've just committed a major faux pas.

The American service economy's reliance on tipping is inexplicable to most foreigners but an attempt to subvert it by undertipping is as likely to succeed as an attempt to destroy London's overpriced taxi system by refusing ever to get into one. It is also not just incalculably rude to waiting staff who really do offer 'service with a smile', even if it is for mercenary gain, it is also threatening their livelihood. Waiting staff are paid wages that are in European terms derisory. The government recommends a minimum wage but it is not compulsory and many states have none, leaving employers to offer pay rates on a 'take it or leave it' basis. Kansas has a near criminal minimum wage of $2.65 per hour, while New York with a cost of living equal to London's sets a minimum of only $7.15, only slightly above what we are allowed to pay schoolboys on paper rounds, and even with exchange rates distorted by the fall of sterling, lower than the average British legal minimum for adults. Waiters and waitresses rely on generous tipping to earn a basic living. The cheap mobile phone I've just purchased to avoid the punitive rates of using a British mobile over here, includes a 'tip calculator' function, which lets you decide between a 10 per cent, 15 per cent, 20 per cent and 25 per cent level. New Yorkers will leave up to 30 per cent and anything less than 15 per cent is considered an insult to the staff and you'd be advised not to eat there again. The same goes for drinks too, which is a radical culture shock for those Brits and Irish who are used to taking every last penny or cent back from their barman, in exchange for maybe buying him one later in the evening. But when in Rome … like I said, just because they sort of speak the same language, it doesn't mean you automatically understand them.

By now 5:00 p.m. has rolled around, time to board the Mets Express, a cheery launch sporting blue team colours. The round trip price is an even $20 which is a lot more than I'd have paid on the subway but then it's a treat of a trip on a warm evening with the sun slowly lowering behind the skyscrapers. They sell cans of beer from an ice-filled cooler at a bar in the cabin, not the good beer from the modern microbreweries, but the thin, tasteless stuff Americans put up with for years from the mass manufacturers, Anheuser-Busch, Coors and Miller. Ball game beer. I buy one anyhow. It's cold liquid on a hot evening and hey, I'm going to a ball game.

The ride upriver, away from Manhattan to where the stadium is located in the northern part of Queens borough (actually the southwest end of Long Island) is strangely reminiscent of that downriver from Westminster and central London to Greenwich and the old docklands. The familiar landmarks recede to be replaced by a widening waterscape bordered by rusting remnants of industrial decay. Except that there is no sign here of the renovation that has marked eastern London, led by financial services and now spurred on by the upcoming Olympics. This part of Queens is bleak and abandoned, rusting frames all that remain of old waterside warehouses. And then the great bulk of the stadium rears up, and behind it, squatting in the old parking lot like a cuckoo in the nest, the soaring skeleton of its successor waiting for flesh to be put on its bones for an expected opening in 2009.

As we step off onto the jetty there is a great roar overhead as a passenger aircraft drops into its approach pattern to land at LaGuardia airport, New York's domestic terminal. Before adjustments were made to the flight paths, games at Shea frequently had to be halted while an incoming aircraft passed low overhead, though I am not sure whether this was just because of the horrendous noise or because they feared some hard-hitting batsman could knock a Boeing out of the sky. As predicted I have no difficulty getting a ticket: Shea can seat 55,000 and has rarely been as full as it was when the Beatles played. The cheapest seats, right up high, cost little over five dollars, but I splash out on one lower down, closer to the action at $21 which these days works out at half what I pay to watch even a game in the second tier of English football, let alone the extravagant cost of watching Chelsea or Arsenal. The ticket salesman tries to coax me into a $35 seat, lower down and in a 'better position'. But as I haven't much idea of what goes on and can't quite see myself sticking it out for the full three and a half hours or more, he's on a no-win.

The arena itself is impressive – as big sports stadia are – but seems curiously incomplete with the seating on just two sides behind the batsman (called 'the batter'), so that when he hits a six – or whatever they call it – he is unlikely to kill anyone (inside the stadium at least). This has at least one clear advantage over cricket, where to avoid risk of injury a live audience has to be so far back as to need binoculars to see much of the action. With the words of Laurence from the night before in my head I am very much aware that all this speaks to the American soul like a cricket pitch or a football ground does to most English-men. Indeed, Roger Kahn, the dean of American sports writers, goes further: 'The ball field itself is a mystic creation, the Stonehenge of America.' Heavy.

Then everybody stands up, and they play the national anthem. I wasn't expecting that, and it's not the last time American patriotic displays will take me by surprise. We only play the national anthem at international games. Here they play it before every game, the way they fly the Stars and Stripes all year round. They did it before 9/11, but they do it even more now. Most of the crowd sing along, some with their hands on their chests. I stand and smile and remind myself that over here we Brits can rely on a residual goodwill towards us as a 'loyal ally', even those of us who thought all along Bush's war in Iraq was cynical, stupid and probably illegal, and Tony Blair weak and foolish to go along with it. I remind myself I'm just here to watch the baseball.

As the two teams are introduced individually on huge billboard-sized screens opposite, they don't just tells us their names, they give us little behav-ioural tips too, like: 'If you throw things onto the pitch, you will be arrested' (fair enough, should be made more clear at football games too) but I can't see 'Don't use bad language!' getting anything but a 'Bronx cheer' from a footie crowd in Britain, the origin of that little expression (the noise of disapproval made by New York Yankees fans) showing that baseball fans at least once upon a time had attitude too. The English-speaking players' words are subtitled in Spanish, and one or two of them even add a *gracias* after their 'thank you'. Span-ish-speaking players speak Spanish, with subtitles in English! And even the coach finishes off with a spoken, 'Thanks, *gracias*.' *De nada, de nada*. America is slowly imperceptibly mutating from within.

One element of its soul, however, remains unchanged: an unrestrained commitment to commercialism. The loudspeakers have not long finished introducing the teams and the first innings is just getting underway when they burst into life again: 'Congratulations to the hungry fans in row 115 who've all won vouchers for Bubba Burger. Just take your tickets to the franchise to claim!' Note, now, this is during actual play. Do that in a cricket game in England and people would tut-tut alarmingly at the bad manners, do it in the middle of a football match and, far from queuing up for 'Bubba Burgers' the crowd would probably hurl food at the screen. That is if they noticed at all. Because that's another thing: at a soccer game – there, okay, I said the funny 's' word – fans are committed; apart from the few wallies up in the corporate entertainment seats, everyone in the ground is concentrating on the game, their only diversion being to sing or chant in support of their own team and occasionally hurl taunts at the opposing supporters. There's a chant here – 'Let's go, Mets!' – but it's pre-recorded and booms out to a rhythmic beat from the loudspeakers at sporadic intervals in a mostly vain attempt to get the supporters to join in. And parents may approve, but it lacks the irony-laden exchanges familiar to British football: 'You're supposed to be at home', and the retort, 'We forgot that you were here', not to mention that Falstaffian old favourite, 'Your support is fucking shit.'

Here, with seating intermingled, few people in team colours and in fact few travelling fans – understandable for some of the vast distances involved, but this team are from Washington, just down the road – it's hard to tell who's who and most people seem to spend more time eating, drinking and chatting to one another than actually watching the game. For a start, for large periods of time not a lot is actually going on down there: the pitcher pitches, the batter bats – or tries to and if he misses three times he's out, the 'three strikes' being at least one concept of this game that has gained global recognition. Innings are short – they need to be, there are nine of them! – and unless you're avidly following proceedings it seems half the time the teams are changing over, not that I saw anyone avidly following the proceedings for more than a few minutes at a time. How could they? The seating may provide a great view of the pitch but every two minutes there's somebody waving a huge tree of candy floss ('cotton candy') in front of you, or getting in your line of vision with a cool box full of beer cans on their head, or warming tray full of hot dogs around their neck. But even bringing all this food and drink to the punters in their seats isn't enough to keep most people seated for long: there is a never-ending flow of people wandering up and down the stairs, between seats and out into the concourses. 'Baseball isn't a sport, it's the national pastime,' my naturalised cousin would tell me later.

And he's right. It's more like a shopping trip combined with three hours of eating and drinking with a bit of sport in the background. The pitcher walks up to the mound, assumes that strange, contorted, standing on one leg, other knee raised high, body twisted to the side, both hands polishing the ball and then the loudspeakers boom out, 'Soft hands, smooth play! Palmer's cocoa butter', and a bar of soap appears on the screen behind him, and I fall off my seat laughing, but no one else even notices. It's as if the adverts were part of the game, an intrinsic part of the whole culture, like eating and drinking, rather than just a way of bringing in revenue that the sport needs but we'd all rather do without. I'm beginning to understand how commerce, the business of buying and selling, doesn't just intrude into every aspect of American life, but actually constitutes the American way of life. This is capitalism in the raw; in Europe we just have a pale processed and pre-packaged version. It's a bit like offering a cave-aged Roquefort to a supposed cheese fan who's only ever tasted Laughing Cow. It may be the more genuine article, but the taste takes some getting used to, and I'm not at all sure which I prefer.

The one thing I am sure of is that after an hour or so sitting watching men hit balls and blokes run around trying to catch them with giant gloves to make it easier – at least cricketers use their bare hands – I have well and truly had my fill of baseball. The endless adverts and the smell of hot dogs and beer have worn me down. I know, I know, I haven't really given it a chance and maybe – just maybe – if I got 'into the stats', which is what Laurence in the pub told me is half the fun of following baseball, I'd finally get something out of it, though I've never been much of a fan of football 'stats' either: I don't care how many failed shots on goal we've had so I'm damn sure I wouldn't care what percentage of home runs Babe Ruth scored. The simple truth is that, in the man's own words, I don't have 'an affinity' with baseball. And that's that. Besides I'd get fat.

Time for bed. Tomorrow I've got a train to catch.

NEW YORK TO NIAGARA FALLS

TRAIN: Empire Service
FREQUENCY: up to 8 trains a day
DEPARTS NEW YORK, NEW YORK: 1:20 p.m. (Eastern Time)

via
Yonkers, NY
Croton-Harmon, NY
Poughkeepsie, NY
Rhinecliff-Kingston, NY
Hudson, NY
Albany-Rensselaer, NY
Schenectady, NY
Saratoga Springs, NY
Amsterdam, NY
Utica, NY
Rome, NY
Syracuse, NY
Rochester, NY

ARRIVE NIAGARA FALLS: 10:45 p.m. (Eastern Time)
DURATION: approx 9 hours, 35 minutes
DISTANCE: 460 miles

3

Grand Departures

HUNKERED DOWN in neoclassical splendour by the junction of Vander-bilt (named for Cornelius, king of the railroad tycoons) and 42nd Street (hub of theatreland), Grand Central Station with its great bronze eagle, clustered flags flying and great marble halls lit by myriad chandeliers, is the world's most perfect departure point for a transcontinental railroad.

On the 'dining concourse' downstairs, the famous Oyster Bar and elegant cocktail lounges offer upmarket sustenance for the well-heeled voyager; to the east Grand Central Market is a food hall to put Harrods to shame with its cornucopia of fresh seafood – yellow-fin tuna, Maine lobster, heaps of shining fruit – glistening papaya, burnished Connecticut apples, piled high European cheeses and the most tantalising charcuterie that Little Italy can offer. In the main concourse all the stars of the constellations, painted in gold on a vaulted sky of purest pastel blue look down in benefaction on the passengers descend-ing the cream marble steps. All in vain. Long distance trains don't go from here.

They once did of course. When the current building, properly known as Grand Central Terminal opened on 2 February 1913 it was the focal point of a redevelopment of central Manhattan, creating some of the most expensive real estate on earth. The station itself, served by new electric trains, was intended to be a continental terminus to outclass anything in Europe, leaving Paris's Gare de l'Est distinctly in the shade, never mind any of London's relatively regional terminals. Even today only Kazan Station in Moscow, departure point for the Trans-Siberian, even remotely stands comparison.

As far as its owners, the New York Central Railroad, were concerned, its main domestic purpose was to outclass the terminal of their rivals the Penn-sylvania Railroad, which only makes its eventual fate more ironic. When the station opened, its most famous train, the 20th Century Limited, was already famous worldwide for first class service and for 65 years, from 1902 until 1967,

28

made the journey of just under 1,000 miles to Chicago in 16 hours. To emphasise the status of the train and its passengers a thick red carpet was routinely laid out to take them to the train, giving the world the phrase 'red carpet treatment'.

In 1947 some 65 million people, the equivalent of 40 per cent of the population of the entire United States travelled through Grand Central Station. But if that was its proudest year, it was also the beginning of its long decline as America's new love affair with the automobile and the airplane caused the railways gradually to be abandoned like a jilted bride. Only two years earlier Elizabeth Smart had written her semi-autobiographical, poetic novel entitled *By Grand Central Station I Sat Down and Wept*. A sweeping, romantic, self-pitying yet magnificent tale of adultery and lost love it became immediately notorious. No one noted at the time that it might have been a metaphor for the fate of the station itself.

Already by 1954 there were the first plans to demolish it and build an 80-storey skyscraper that would be 500 feet taller than the Empire State Building (ironically it would have been the first major commission for Chinese-American architect I.M. Pei who went on to design the Louvre's famous glass pyramid and so might have ended up a landmark in its own right). The plan was shelved but as the New York Central Railroad's decline continued plans for the station's demolition multiplied. In 1968 the company finally merged with its once hated rivals, now similarly ailing. Their own, in many eyes, equally magnificent Pennsylvania Station, had been demolished amid an international outcry in 1964, its proud pink granite columns replaced with the concrete slab that holds the sports arena known as Madison Square Garden.

The new railway, then known as Penn Central, submitted plans to treat Grand Central the same way and build a new skyscraper office block on the site, only to find itself facing opposition led by a no less iconic figure than Jacqueline Kennedy Onassis who pleaded with New Yorkers not 'to let our city die by degrees'. Grand Central survived – after a 1978 court case fought by New York City against Penn Central, by then a moribund freight company. The passenger division had been ended by bankruptcy as early as 1970, a cathartic moment for the whole US passenger rail network which ended with government intervention and the creation of Amtrak, effectively as a rescue vehicle, in 1971. Grand Central's survival in the end played its part in the destruction of the company that created it, an old lady ruined by an excess of youthful vanity.

Today Grand Central is simply the world's grandest commuter hub, but long-distance trains continued to roll in until 1991 when a new line linked tracks from Canada and upstate New York into the underground mire of modern 'Penn Station'. And that, regrettably, in an anodyne underground concourse that has more in common with a provincial airport terminal, is where I have to start my journey. At 10:00 a.m. Penn Station concourse is awash with people bustling from the subways, consuming coffee in litre-size cardboard cups at takeaway stalls, flicking through magazines at news stands or feeding their faces with huge 'deli' sandwiches. I should feel exhilarated; in fact I feel rather ill.

I had vaguely hoped for some sense of occasion, even the noisy echoing grime of London's Paddington or King's Cross if not the restored Victorian splendour of St Pancras. At least some sense of echoing train shed and, however restricted, a view into the distance, light at the end of the tunnel. Instead I have a few airport armchairs in the middle of an underground shopping mall, an escalator disappearing into the floor and an electric sign saying Train 283 will depart on time at 10.45 a.m. It would be nice if they even called it by its name 'The Empire Service'. But there is nothing imperial as we queue up to have our tickets checked and descend the escalator disappearing into the floor of the concourse.

The platform is dark and the train scarcely more impressive than a subway train; the locomotive itself is invisible in distant darkness beyond the platform end. I clamber aboard trying to inspire a spring in my step but at least breathe a sigh of relief to see that the seating, even in coach class, has been designed with the average girth of the normal – non-Manhattan – native in mind, and is therefore more than ample for a middle-aged European with middle-aged spread. Unless of course, a larger than average native takes the seat next to you. But out of high season the train – in blessed comparison to the overpriced, overstuffed cattle cars that run on some British lines – is barely one-third full. Perhaps the only noticeable disadvantage is that the windows are slightly grubbier and not quite as large as the camera-toting traveller would like.

Fellow passengers include an elderly couple who look for a moment worryingly English – he is wearing shorts and knee socks while she has one of those faces like a trout that's just realised it's beginning to go off. Curiously she adds to this disconcerting impression over the next half hour by consuming copious quantities of ripe orangey-pink melon that gives off a cloyingly sweet smell uncomfortably reminiscent of putrefaction. The cardboard ticket the conductor attaches to the luggage rack above their heads says they're going to Rome. I hastily check my ticket to ensure I'm on the right continent. Just in front of them a group of four seats arranged in facing pairs is almost completely taken up by an extremely large black man in jogging pants and a baseball cap. It is only when he pulls out a mobile phone and launches into what you just know is going to be an extremely lengthy conversation that I realise from his voice that he is, in all probability, a woman.

It is a less than encouraging prelude to my first long American rail journey, but all of a sudden my concerns are immediately pushed to the back of my mind as the dispatcher on the platform cries, 'All Aboard' – they really do – and the driver toots his horn expansively, even underground. I am quickly to discover that American trains toot a lot, almost incessantly at certain times, as if they know it's expected of them, like chewing gum or wearing baseball caps backwards – and we pull out smoothly through underground tunnels and steep cuttings, urban gorges cut through Harlem, to creep as unnoticed as a worm out of the Big Apple. Crossing the Harlem canal we finally enter what snooty New Yorkers call, almost disparagingly, America.

The difference, when the train at last emerges definitively from the underworld, is more dramatic than you might expect. The skyscrapers are gone, vanished, nowhere to be seen, not even in the receding distance. Instead, here we are trundling along the leafy banks of the vast, wide Hudson, until after about 20 minutes we slow down to stop at the delightfully named Yonkers, a wholly unremarkable piece of small-town provincial America, famed only for the fact that one day back in 1853 a local lad called Elisha Otis invented the emergency brake that for the first time made elevators safe and thereby at a stroke made possible the whole mad megalopolis just a few miles down the river.

With sailboats bobbing gently against the steep rocky bluffs on the far bank of the Hudson, on both sides at one point as the train rolls over a causeway between islands, the whole thing seems an implausible rural idyll so close to such adrenalin-pumping urban insanity. And then the sight of white-painted guard towers on the left brings back a touch of more brutal reality. There are no visible signs to say so but this is Sing Sing 'correctional facility', one of America's oldest prisons, where convicts are still sent 'up the river' to do time. Like 'the Clink' in London this is a jail that has given the English language an expression.

The country that surrounds it though, is affluent. Elegant nineteenth-century houses perch on the hills overlooking the river amid thick deciduous forests that only now in late September are beginning the extraordinary metamorphosis from green to gold, crimson and just about everything in between that the New England 'fall' is famous for but 'upstate' New York exhibits every bit as well.

I try to snatch a few pastoral photographs as we trundle along at speeds of perhaps 50–60 mph, tree colours, groups of swans basking in the sunshine, but the train guard, a jovial pot-bellied man whose bald head is set off by a magnificent flowing white goatee beard, is unimpressed: 'Did you get the barge turned over back there?' I hadn't, hadn't even spotted it in fact. 'Pity. That'd have been good.' He also takes the time to explain to me patiently that in America they don't call him a guard, but a conductor. This seems like hair-splitting to me, which earns me a serious lecture in American railroad language. For a start this is a car we're sitting in, not a carriage. Secondly, and clearly most importantly, the conductor on an American train is anything but a ticket collector; he has subordinates for that. The conductor is the man that matters, the man who tells the engineer – never call him a 'driver' – when to proceed, how fast to go and who makes sure that the points are properly set and the train runs in an orderly fashion.

I make clear that I have learned my lesson and give him his proper respect. Happily I also have the chance to change the subject as we round a bend in the river and come across a great pink stone ruined medieval castle complete with remnants of turrets and drawbridge across a moat. It looks like it ought to belong on the Rhine rather than the Hudson, squatting on an island in the middle of a narrow section of river funnelled between two escarpments. The conductor, as I now know to call him, tells me the rugged crags on either side are called Storm King and Breakneck Ridge, the fortress-like ruin is called Bannerman's Castle and was indeed intended as a fortress, a folly built in 1900 that housed a private arsenal. The American right to bear arms – as we know – often takes extreme forms. The reason it is a ruin is not hard to guess: the ammunition dump exploded.

Stroking his impressive beard learnedly the conductor has clearly now settled into the role of professorial travel guide to this simple foreigner and takes the opportunity to impress me further with his knowledge of our route by pointing out that although there was nothing much to see, we have just passed West Point, the US Army's equivalent of Sandhurst and legendary military academy that has trained just about every US general you've ever heard of, from those grizzled civil war veterans Ulysses S. Grant and Stonewall Jackson to more recent warriors such as Dwight Eisenhower and 'Stormin' Norman Schwarzkopf. Another alumnus was General George Custer – he of the last stand; what were reputed to be the few identifiable bits of him are buried there.

Next stop is Poughkeepsie, an Indian name, but originally a settlement that like much of New York – state and city – was founded by the Dutch (Amsterdam is still to come) in the late seventeenth century. Today it is mostly renowned for making ball bearings and cough drops. We rattle rapidly out of town past mansions that belonged to F.D. Roosevelt and the same railway rogue Vanderbilt who gave his name to the avenue next to Grand Central.

If certain aspects of European history had taken an only slightly different turning in the middle of the seventeenth century, all of this area would still be speaking Dutch or German – settled as it was in the days when even we British didn't differentiate much between the two ('Dutch' is an anglicisation of 'deutsch'). My Rhine mirage of just a little back suddenly doesn't seem so bizarre after all. The next stop here is called Rhinecliff while the laden orchards we pass are centred on Germantown.

This is the beginning of the Catskills, where the legendary Rip Van Winkle (now I understand the conductor's beard) fell asleep for a hundred years. For much of this route, I realise, the 'Empire Service' is very like European trains in that it makes fairly frequent stops at places not far enough apart for a flight; here, unlike in most of the continental USA, the railway remains a relatively economic and convenient mode of transport and as a result trains are relatively frequent. There are up to eight a day on this line, which is more – far more – in some cases, as I am to find out – than there are in a week on lines further west.

The sprawling Hudson River on our left is omnipresent, placid and wide as we pull into the little town that the Dutch once called Claverack Landing for the fields of clover all around but since 1785 it too has been named after Henry Hudson. The station is a little clapboard single storey building with a corrugated iron roof, the whole thing painted deep russet red. A few locals are sitting on a bench outside to watch us pull in and out again. Obviously not a lot happens in Hudson.

Not much happens in Albany either, even though this sleepy little mix of modern high-rise and Victorian classical is the capital of New York State. Forever doomed to be eclipsed by its humongous alter ego – which without even thinking about it subsumes the rest of the state within its 'New York, New York, so good they named it twice' sobriquet – Albany reached its apogee in the late 1820s when the Erie Canal and the first steam train arrived within a couple of years of each other marking a brief boom in its life as a river port.

Our departure from Albany is marked only by the passage through the compartment of the ghost of Casey Jones, the legendary American engine driver who I am to encounter again – or at least a lookalike ghost: a huge portly man in his fifties with a single earring and bushy grey beard, dressed in the legend's trademark blue and white dungarees.

But before I can work out whether he really is a Casey fan or the resemblance

33

was just coincidental – as you on rare occasions see eccentric elderly English gentlemen who could do a good stand-in for WG Grace without being cricket fans – we are already ploughing through the General Electric-dominated outskirts of Schenectady. Known to its inhabitants as the 'the city that hauls and lights the world', the town's exotic name is actually a Mohawk phrase meaning 'through the open pines' which came to be applied to a Dutch fur trading post set up in 1661. But it was the late nineteenth century which improbably put Schenectady on the global map.

The local locomotive works was already taking care of the haulage when a young local lad got his first job with the railway's caterers selling sweets to passengers. With the money he made he bought a couple of chemistry sets and then, having that sort of inquiring mind, experimented building his own version of a telegraph system out of bits of scrap metal. Being a bit tight on space for all these hobbies he decided to set up one of his chemistry sets in a baggage car which had the temporarily unfortunate result of losing him his job, not wholly unreasonably as one of his experiments that went wrong ended up setting fire to the train.

Undeterred, however, this bright spark continued his scientific tinkering and in time Thomas Edison went on to invent the electric light bulb, power stations that would provide the necessary electricity and played a major role in the development of the telephone, cinema camera, phonograph, typewriter, dictation machine and even the humble cement mixer. By the end of his life this ambitious young upstate New Yorker had laid a substantial number of the building blocks of the twentieth century (and therefore foundations of the twenty-first). By the end of his life he had been granted no fewer than 1,093 patents. The company he started went on to become General Electric, a global giant that remains the major employer of the citizens of his home town, Schenectady.

A few miles further on I get the first inkling of just why our driver blows his horn quite so often as the train grinds to a complete halt in an area with nothing but woodland on one side and the flat motionless expanse of the Erie Canal on the other. For a few minutes I suspect a signalling problem but then slowly, lumberingly, a huge, rusting hulk of yellow machinery with what looks like chimney sweeps' brushes sticking out of it at various angles pulls up on the track alongside us, coming in the opposite direction, and stops. After about 10 minutes the driver makes an announcement: it appears there is a crew working on the line next to us – the hulking piece of rusty machinery is some form of track-cleaning equipment – and they have left a substantial amount of their kit on the line in front of us. It would appear that, despite this being – in Amtrak terms – a relatively well-used route, they have somehow not been expecting us.

Happily – whether or not it was down to the horn-blowing – disaster has been averted: we were only doing about 50 mph anyhow but it still would not have been nice. Now all we have to do is wait for the crew to move their kit off the line so we can continue. In the event it takes no more than some 15 minutes before we are ready to move off again. As we do several of the crew clamber on top of their big yellow rail-cleaning machine. One of them waves cheerily; another pulls out a digital camera and takes a picture of us. I am left wondering how often these railroad workers actually come across a moving train.

On through Amsterdam – a small town famed only for being the home of the company that makes Cabbage Patch dolls – and we are rolling through some of the richest, greenest pasture land in America. This part of New York State is littered with dairy farms producing a disproportionate amount of the country's milk and cheese. No wonder the Dutch felt so at home. Unfortunately for most of the twentieth century much of the cheese produced here was disconcertingly similar to the more bland products of the modern Dutch dairy industry: mild – and mildly rubbery – blubber of the Edam/Gouda variety. Only in recent years has there been a movement towards traditional, organic, artisan cheeses. The future is still in the balance.

Gradually now, as we have parted company with the Adirondacks route that heads up into New England, the forest has thinned out. Quaint pastel-painted clapboard houses line the track on the west as we pull out of Utica. Utica used to have the more comprehensible – if more cumbersome – name of Old Fort Schluyer until it was renamed after somewhere in North Africa. Why Utica when it could have been Cairo or Alexandria is for the moment beyond me. Somebody later tells me it was pulled out of a hat. When you remember that there is a town in New Mexico which changed its name from Hot Springs to Truth or Consequences after a radio broadcaster promised to present the next episode of his show from any town that changed its name to that of the programme.

Meanwhile, our next stop is, after all, Rome. A bulky bald conductor who has replaced the one with the Rip Van Winkle beard comes through and bellows it, like a latter-day praetorian looking for gladiators to enter the arena. The little old couple opposite are the only takers.

Somewhere back along the tracks we have obviously passed an invisible marker beyond which the founding fathers in this relatively ancient part of inhabited North America had a classical education. After Rome comes

Syracuse. A young mother with two small children who replaced the mobile phone-addicted hermaphrodite and has been struggling for the past several hours to both entertain them and keep as much as possible of their collection of teddy bears, colouring books, combs and flip-flops in more or less one part of the carriage, asks the praetorian if there is a 'car' to be had at Syracuse. Or if someone could phone ahead.

This seems like a reasonable enough question. I have no idea how big a place Syracuse might be and whether or not they have a taxi rank or car hire office at the station. The praetorian, however, is shaking his head as if informing a pagan mob that there were no Christians and lions on the day's agenda: 'I'm awful sorry, ma'am, but there's no baggage assistance at Syracuse.'

At this point the penny drops and I realise that once again the supposedly common language is proving to be a treacherous friend. What she is really asking for is a 'cart', by which she means a trolley for her luggage.

'I realise that,' she is meanwhile telling the praetorian with remarkable forbearance, 'I just wanted to know if there are carts available on the platform.'

'Well,' he draws out the pause, painfully, 'there is one. But it's kept locked up, for the night shift to use.'

This seems to me as strange a set of priorities as it clearly does to the woman with the children, who has begun to look despairingly at the ever-widening circle of clutter her kids have spread around the carriage. I'm wondering how she's even going to get it all packed again, never mind cope with getting it off the train and to wherever she's going. But the praetorian has a soft heart and comes back a few minutes later to tell her he's rung ahead and they'll 'see what they can do'.

We roll into Syracuse through a building thunderstorm which provides suitable rolling grey rain clouds to accompany the industrial wasteland of brand new breeze blocks, grey corrugated iron factory sheds, an electric power substation and acres of monotone abandoned and decaying structures that were once what we would call fixed caravans, and what Americans know as the lowest level of housing – trailer homes. And this is where they come to die.

In fact Syracuse is mostly known for its salt. Mines here were for years the main source of the town's income and the seasoning Americans in their millions poured on their food until the health lobby in the late twentieth century finally realised how much harm it was doing. The Amtrak station is nearly 10 miles out of the modern city centre, where the tracks were laid to be close to the industrial zone. The otherwise grim vista is allayed for alighting passengers – if you can call it that – by a new out of town retail park, which masks much of the decay. The mother with the small children struggles off the train with most of their baggage piled onto an unfolded pushchair, which means of course that its intended occupant has to walk – or rather toddle – behind. The praetorian's call ahead has somehow failed to persuade the guardians of Syracuse's sole cart to yield it up for the use of a passenger.

But then sympathy for one's fellow passengers on long-distance rail journeys can wear thin, I quickly realise. We are all familiar with the curse of the mobile phone on commuter trains – the endless 'I'm on the train, darling' conversations – and already on my first few hours on Amtrak I'd experienced one serial call-maker, but I had not been prepared for a whole new encounter with the digital age's most useful and annoying invention. The phone as vanity accessory was new to me.

Already by the outskirts of Amsterdam I'd been getting mildly irritated by the series of beeps at irregular intervals coming from the seat behind me, but assumed the big white man dressed all in black with an iPod in one hand and phone in the other was playing some game on the latter and I had done my best to maintain a façade of good humour on my first US rail journey by not even suggesting he might seek out the 'mute' key.

It's only after leaving Syracuse, with the now rather monotonous landscape fast fading beneath a blanket of rain that I decide to switch seats. My new position, across the compartment, doesn't exactly remove me from the noise, but for the first time it enables me to see what he was doing to cause it: he's been taking photographs of himself!

That was one possibility that had simply not occurred to me, but there he is, turning the phone away from himself, in order to face its camera, adjusting his profile this way and then that to present a variation of noble poses reminiscent of Roman emperors perhaps – still in classical mode here – or perhaps Mafiosi *capi*, just to update the Italian theme. After each little flash he turns the phone back round, takes a thorough look at his own likeness and then presses a button which makes the little bleeping noise that's been driving me absolutely potty for hours: whether the bleep is made by him saving or deleting the image I have no idea, but I do know that over the past two to three hours, he has probably taken his own photograph more than 100 times. Whether he's taking his own picture just for fun, to set as his background on his phone or – just conceivably – to send to a loved one, this is a guy clearly concerned about his image. Amused by his vanity, I'm sorely tempted to get a teeny touch of revenge by letting him see me chuckle next time he does it, but when instead he actually uses the phone to make a call, producing a 'Hey, how ya' doin'?' in a gruff New Jersey accent distinctly reminiscent of Tony Soprano, I think better of it and let the moment pass.

In any case he, like almost everyone else on the train is getting off at Buffalo. That includes Casey Jones, rematerialised now in the line of passengers waiting to 'detrain' – this is another word from American locomotive language I have had to learn – with a row of pens, screwdrivers and torch in the front chest pocket of his striped dungarees. I can now see that these cover a grey T-shirt depicting a vintage steam engine that might or might not be the Cannonball Express.

He's also carrying a CSX tool bag identifying him as an employee of the freight lines: a man not necessarily impersonating a legend so much as living his dream; for some people 'workin' on the railroad' is just a job, for others it's a way of life. Back in England he'd be frustrated by dull diesels and short-haul routes and would spend his weekends with other enthusiasts tinkering with vintage steam trains at Didcot Railway Museum. Here the distances are vast and the boundaries between the romance and reality of rail just that little bit more blurred.

Blurred, that is, unless you're a middle-aged, well-to-do couple, originally from New York, trying the great American rail system for the first time on a trip from Baltimore to Toronto. Sandra and Ben, almost my only remaining fellow passengers for the last slow crawl of the journey along the shores of Lake Erie to Niagara Falls, are decidedly unimpressed.

'We've been on these goddamn trains all day,' he fumes in something extremely close to exasperation, barely concealing one of those 'whose idea was this anyway' hints of marital tension.

I can sort of see his point. It's 7:30 in the evening, dark outside, and we've little more than 30 miles or so to go, but according to the conductor it's going to take at the very least another hour to get there. The problem is that there's only one track up here near the frontier and the great long freight trains have priority over our by now very much reduced little four-coach passenger train with fewer than a dozen paying customers. Not normally the most placid of travellers – I can get annoyed with the best of them at unexplained endless delays at airports – I find myself showing a surprising element of British stoicism here: after all the timetable says we don't get in until 8:50 p.m. and at present it looks like we're going to be early.

Ben, however, isn't impressed by the inexorable logic of iron roads that don't allow for overtaking, and his mood is not improved when, staring out into dark freight yards of heavy duty rolling stock, he gradually perceives that we're going backwards. The concept of reversing into a siding to change loco-motives is new to him. And not welcome.

'Come on, honey,' says Sandra gamely, smiling at me for encouragement. 'You agreed to stop off and see Niagara Falls.'

'I didn't know what I was getting into,' says Ben tetchily, obviously regret-ting it. 'I'm a Noo Yoiker,' he says, lapsing into the Big Apple's unmistakable drawl: 'I don't do this stuff. It's like the Statue of Liberty and the Empire State Building. It's for people from other countries.'

Meanwhile our little train is creaking and rattling its way towards what – it occurs to me Ben might possibly have forgotten – actually is another country. It's raining and it feels later than it is, and I realise I have been here before. Not literally, but on a similar slow empty train to the edge of the world: as a student in the 1970s returning home to Northern Ireland at the end of term in Oxford, sitting in a cold railway carriage with worn shabby seats and flickering lights crawling along the bleak and all but invisible Lancashire coast towards the tiny seaport of Heysham and the docks for a soon to be scrapped overnight ferry service to Belfast.

Our all but empty Amtrak service creeping along past dark riverbanks and derelict factories towards the Canadian frontier doesn't exactly have carriages still scuffed by boots of wartime servicemen 30 years earlier and the power at least is consistent, but there's still a feeling of terminal melancholy about it. Something relentlessly soul-sapping about spending a long time on a dark wet night going nowhere fast.

At last we pull in, though it feels more like a siding than a station, as the con-ductor bellows, 'Niagara Falls, New York, end of the line.' Which is precisely what it feels like. As we climb down the high steps to the platform I realise my instinct was right and this is indeed a siding: a little line sprung out on its own on the edge of a vast freight yard, next to a small redbrick building where a single fluorescent strip light burns in an empty room. On a weed-fringed strip of tarmac a couple of motley taxis stand with their lights out.

I watch as the conductor helps Sandra out with her suitcases and she turns her head apprehensively towards Ben who adjusts his thick-rimmed glasses on his nose before declaring: 'Jesus fuckin' Christ, is this it?'

I hope whatever Ben and Sandra have come to Niagara Falls for, it isn't a second honeymoon.

4

Close to the Edge

THERE IS NOTHING quite like the anticlimax of arriving at one of the world's greatest tourist attractions to find it shut.

Not that you can actually shut something like Niagara Falls, pouring more than 25 million gallons of water per minute from one Great Lake towards another for tens of thousands of years. Niagara at night ought to be a spell-bindingly romantic location, and maybe it is if you're in the right mood with the right company and at the right moment, with the moon out and a balmy breeze wafting through the trees. But watching water churn towards a preci-pice you know is there but can't see – which is what you essentially have at city level on the American side of the falls – is weird enough at the best of times. Wandering out alone in the dark with a cold damp drizzle in the air that is almost certainly spray from thundering rapids but feels like a damp dank English autumn evening with the roar of heavy traffic in the background, it seems best to look for entertainment elsewhere and wait for morning. I mean, one of the most famous honeymoon destinations in the world has to have a nightlife. Or then again, maybe not!

One way or another, 10:00 p.m. sees me heading out from my motel room (which costs less than the YMCA and in comparison, with king-size double bed, television and en-suite bathroom feels like the Savoy) across a wilder-ness of parking lots in a blustery drizzle looking for something to eat and maybe a drink and some company. It was the Canadians who first realised that having got the punters into town to see the falls, there ought to be more ways to take money off them than just providing boat trips and viewing platforms. Their first attempt was a 'futuristic' observation tower that now protrudes into the night sky above their side of the falls, rather ruining the impact of a natural wonder, but nowhere near as much as their second, and far more suc-cessful when it came to taking in the money, attempt: several huge, neon-lit multistorey casinos. The skyline of Niagara Falls, Ontario, therefore, as seen from Niagara Falls, New York, gleams surreally out of the night fog like a set from a low budget 1960s sci-fi film. When the 'Skylon' tower and its like were built (1964) – and it is amazing how many of them were – architects had a vision of the future based on Superman comics and imagined that by the twenty-first century we'd all be jetting around in hovercars wearing one-piece figure-hugging jumpsuits. Luckily for carbon emissions and the general shape of the American public, neither of these predictions has proved true.

But they do explain the strange case of one-upmanship that has led the otherwise still small town of Niagara Falls, New York, to erect a 20-storey sky-scraper with an ethnic-tribal symbol in blue and green neon flashing up and down its face. Peeved by the Canadians hogging the lion's share of the tourist income, not least because they also claim that the best view of the falls is from their side, the Americans decided to fight fire with fire and build a casino of their own. Or rather, the Native Americans have. Or sort of, as I shall find out slightly later. Signs proclaim it to be the property of the 'Seneca clan of Iroquois Indians'.

Casinos aren't really my thing, so for the moment I leave it alone and head towards the small row of single-storey buildings that would appear to be what passes for 'Main Street'. I'm just musing on the fact that the Seneca refer to themselves as 'Indians' rather than the now accepted and politically correct Native Americans, when as if conjured up by the power of association (another one of those small gods) I run across the Taste of India restaurant, quickly followed by the Bombay Cuisine, the Sirdhar Sahib and the Punjabi Dhaba, more Indian restaurants in a short stretch than you're likely to find in Leicester or Bradford, and that's saying something. For a moment the thought whizzes through my head that maybe some large group of migrants from the subcontinent heard a rumour that things were going well these days for the Indians up in Niagara and misunderstood. I put it to the back of my mind for the moment as strange but unlikely and forage on.

It quickly becomes clear that the nightlife in Niagara, like many small towns in America, particularly those with a large transient or tourist population, is chiefly made up of rows of identical dark bars with multicoloured neon signs in the window advertising cheap 'domestic' beer – Coors, Bud Lite, Miller – and blaring almost identical music. Kids lurch in and out of them, most repeatedly having to produce picture identity cards to the doorman to prove they are over 21, though such is the practised hypocrisy of absurd drinking laws which even the president's daughters break, that both parties are happily aware they are

41

fake. Doormen examine IDs chiefly in the hope of eliciting cute smiles or a peck on the cheek from pretty girls or for an excuse to turn away 20-year-old men they don't like the look of. Either way, I'm not in the mood for mingling with a load of drunk kids.

The hotel tourist map marks 'Wine on 3rd' which might be worth one final investigation before giving up altogether and admitting defeat to the drizzle before an early night and an early morning start to the sightseeing. I have just about decided that 'Wine on 3rd' is probably a euphemism for the closed 'liquor store' on 3rd Street, when I spot the establishment in question a few doors further along. To my total amazement it is a bright, airy, almost modern minimalist decorated wine bar, with just a few customers of mixed age sitting conversing in civilised fashion at the bar. Too good to miss. And it proves to be better still when the barman – who insists on being known only as JB – turns out to be an authority on something I didn't even know existed: New York wine!

I don't know why – I have had white wine from Herefordshire and red wine from Gloucestershire, English counties far from the sunny climes of the Mosel or Gironde – but New York just didn't chime with wine. On sudden reflection, though, I realise I have actually tasted a wine made in upstate New York: a kosher wine. It had been made from original pre-phylloxera American grapes and then been pasteurised to ensure it would retain its religious authenticity even when served by gentiles, and it tasted like rather manky grape juice. This recollection almost immediately dampens my euphoria at the promise of oenophile delight, particularly as the last thing I want to do in a strange bar in a strange city at night is to offend anybody's religious sensitivities.

My fears could not have been more unfounded. Over the next hour or so the knowledgeable man behind the counter introduces me to a whole new wine landscape: the Finger Lakes of upstate New York and wineries with names ranging from the distinctly Hispanic-sounding Casa Larga from Fairport to the very Anglo-Saxon Heron Hill from Hammondsport. The former produces an interesting variant on the Viognier grape which has so entranced the world since taking off from its niche home at Condrieu on the Rhone (though no one has yet equalled the original), the latter a wholly unexpected mature full-bodied 2004 red, marketed under the brand name Eclipse but full enough of Merlot, Cabernet Sauvignon and Cabernet Franc to pull its weight in any backwater around Bordeaux if not exactly the grand cellars of the Médoc.

A Chardonnay that could have blagged me into thinking it was a Chablis, comes from the Vinifera cellars of Dr Konstantin Frank, a Ukrainian who arrived in the US in 1951 and almost single-handedly created the Finger Lake – and hence New York state – wine industry. The most remarkable thing about that achievement, was that his fluent command of six European languages had one notable omission: English. The winery, also in Hammondsport, is run today by his grandson Frederick, who presumably speaks English fluently and also produces an excellent Riesling.

I could have gone on all evening tasting the wines of upper New York with such a knowledgeable host – this, you remember, on an evening when I had been expecting no more entertainment than a few bottles of Miller Lite in a bar playing The Eagles at 200 decibels – when my sophisticated wine connoisseur bartender unpredictably decides to demonstrate another side to his character. To be fair, the blame probably lay with his assistant barman whose iPod plugged into the stereo system has up until now been providing a background of discreetly subdued classic rock songs. But just as I'm about to say something erudite on the almost Alsatian attributes coaxed by the Frank family into that most German of grapes, the Riesling, the track changes and JB suddenly abandons his sommelier stance for one of raving lunatic: turning up the volume and singing along in a spontaneous karaoke version of Jimi Hendrix's 'All Along the Watchtowers'. Accompanied by some quite spectacular air guitar.

As you can imagine this is followed by something of a pregnant pause in the conversation. I mean, it's sort of hard to get back to discussing poncy points of oenophilia with someone who's just splattered testosterone all over the walls. So under the circumstances I do the only thing any self-respecting Brit would do in my situation, I turn the conversation to the weather. This at least has the benefit of drawing someone else into the discussion, even if not in the way I had quite anticipated.

'Say that again, what you just said. I really *lurvve* your accent,' says the extremely good-looking 30-something woman with long blonde hair who for the past hour has been sitting a few feet away with a bloke old enough to be her father.

'I said it was really hot in New York City,' I say, repeating myself in embarrassment and knowing what's coming. The terrible trouble here, and it is mine particularly, is that I have always had something of an affinity for foreign languages and accents, possibly out of an only-child shyness which made me overly anxious to fit in and therefore eager to adapt any accent that happens to be around me. This is, I have been told, a formidable advantage insofar as I don't feel silly putting on a 'funny' accent if it is the way other people around me are speaking.

The other side of that coin is that, especially in other English-speaking countries, I have a tendency to adopt over-readily the native accent, which of course makes me seem like a complete dork to friends from home if I happen to be travelling with any. There is also the danger – I'm thinking primarily of Scotland here – of ending up doing what is perceived to be a very poor imitation of the locals' accent, which in Glasgow especially is a recipe for ending the evening in the Royal Infirmary, with what the locals term 'yer heed in yer hands'. Try it. I have.

Then, of course, you get the situation, as here, when I have managed not to succumb to local peer pressure and am talking in what I consider to be my normal accent and all of a sudden someone next to me declares it to be the funniest thing she has ever heard. In the nicest possible way. At which point I start thinking about the sound of the words and can, at worst, become horribly confused. Right at this moment, however, I am doing my level best to repeat the words I had just said in exactly the same accent; an attractive young woman, after all, had just said she 'lurrrrved it'.

'Hoht,' she says. 'I just lurrv that. Hoht. You mean "hat".'

'No,' I reply, playing the game because I'm not sure I can take more air guitar, 'that is something you put on your head.'

This causes a fair amount of merriment, including from the older chap next to her. 'That's "het",' she erupts. (I should point out I am doing my best here to render this as it sounded to me at the time; if you are American, of course, it's all going to seem the wrong way round and you won't have a clue what I'm on about, but the only alternative would be to use the international phonetic alphabet, which would come out with things like 'ha]t' and 'hæt' that wouldn't help any of us.)

Anyhow, much to my relief – I could see this going on all night and getting sillier and sillier until one of us took offence – a bloke on my other side taps me on my other shoulder and says, 'I hear you're from London?' I nod, and he continues with: 'Did you just drive down this evening.' Now this has got me puzzled, there being the not insignificant obstacle of the Atlantic Ocean in between, until he catches the accent and says, 'Oh, London, England?' It turns out he thought I had driven from London, Ontario, which it seems is not too far away. 'Like all the Injuns,' he adds, which has got me puzzled again until I realise he means the Indian Indians, of which it seems London, Ontario, has a goodly number. 'Thousands of 'em,' he says, in a tone of voice that leads me to suspect there may be a few racial tensions lurking under the bland friendly face most of us conjure up when we think of Canada. 'They come down here in their thousands too, don't know why. All feel they have to see the falls.' I'm about to mention that a fair few other folk do and that tourist dollars must provide the main source of income around here, when he adds the obvious, 'That's why there's all them restaurants. Don't see any of 'em in the American bars.'

At this point I decide it might be as well to deflect the topic of conversation and tell him that when he said 'Injuns' I had thought he meant the ones that own the casino. That gets a bit of a laugh all round, including from the older bloke with the young woman who turns out to be something of an apologist for the Native American cause. He laughs when I ask him how come the Seneca clan came to still own such a prime chunk of land in the middle of town: 'They gave it to 'em,' he says. 'If you can call it giving to them when they stole it from them in the first place.'

The story of the casino, it appears, is that the town's desire to have one to combat their Canadian competition wasn't received quite so simply down in distant Albany, home of the New York state legislature. There were questions asked, problems posed about moral issues, general doubts about how to go about partially legalising gambling in just one part of the state while it is illegal in the rest. At which point a deal was cut with elders of the Seneca tribe to declare a chunk of downtown Niagara Falls, including a moribund convention centre, tribal territory, in theory making it a 'sovereign nation'. The convention centre was then transformed into a casino with adjoining hotel, using money and expertise put together by a gambling magnate close to Donald Trump and a Chinese billionaire, whose takings theoretically benefit the Seneca. They also, not incidentally, benefit the state to the tune of some $38 million a year in tax. According to my new acquaintance, whose name is Dan and is a college professor – the younger woman being an ex-student – state legislatures purport to uphold a prudish public morality worthy of their Puritan forebears but are happy to let the Indians do the 'dirty work' for them, while the people who run the casino actually make most of the profits. Nobody seems to know quite how much the Seneca Indians actually make out of it, although they are supposedly entitled to a fixed percentage. 'They have a shop in there that sells trinkets,' says Dan with an ironic smile.

On the way back to my motel I decide to take a look inside out of curiosity and there indeed in the marble halls of the lobby is a shop, closed at this time of night, but selling ceremonial tomahawks, coloured blankets and various bits of Indian jewellery. There is also a plaque giving the names of the elders of the Seneca nation in whose name the casino is operated. But it all seems a bit peripheral to the main business which even near midnight is clearly thriving, with lines of decidedly pale faces sitting in rows feeding dollar bills into slot machines. This in itself is new to me: not slot machines but ones that take notes rather than coins, especially notes as low in value as one dollar, which these days can be incredibly grubby considering how many of them you need to buy almost anything. But the single dollar bill is such an intrinsic essential element in American culture that the idea of phasing it out in favour of coins (which would be worth only some 50 pence each, a tenth the amount of the smallest British note) remains unimaginable. Most players in fact feed in larger denominations, fives, tens or even twenties and get proportionately more pulls of the handle, pushes of the button, or electronically-dealt hands of cards.

With twinkling chandelier lights above the flashing electronic lights of the machines and girls in skimpy costumes meandering between them serving drinks, the atmosphere is calculated to eliminate any concept of time of day. I wander over to the circular raised bar in the centre and decide to have just the one more, as a nightcap, especially as they are serving Yuengling, and more particularly because on a small circular stage at head height in the centre of the bar itself there is a saxophone player knocking out a slow cool rendering of the Grover Washington standard 'Just the Two of Us' from his classic album *Winelight*. An almost perfect way to end an evening.

There is just the one of me, however, and as I sip at my beer I can't wholly manage to ignore that built into the bar is an electronic poker machine. Every time I set my pint down after a sip there is a deck of cards underneath it, displaying aces and deuces and inviting me to have a go, just a quick game of blackjack or poker to pass the time. And you think – or at least I do, just as I'm supposed to – hey, why not, and slip a five-dollar note into the inconspicuous slot in the perspex of the bar counter. Five quick games of blackjack; what harm can it do? Within 10 minutes or so, playing cheap at 10 cents debit a hand, my $5 is a princely $7.50, and the music is still playing and I'm quite enjoying myself and the beer is only $3.50 which is the cheapest I've found so far, so what the hell, I have another one, rack up to a dollar a game – big rollers are us – and see if I can break the bank before bedtime.

You can guess the rest. My $7.50, through some incredible unpredictable bad luck with the cards, rises to $11 before dwindling to nothing. At which stage I decide to just play a couple more to make back my initial stake. By the time I leave I am $25 poorer (plus another $12 for three beers plus tip) and as I wander out wearily into the night I realise I have sat there for more than an hour and a half, though it seemed like 20 minutes at most. For the first time

I realise that my residual feeling that supercasinos in Britain would not be a good thing and end up more like an extra tax on the poor and gullible is right on the money, to coin a phrase. Wandering across the parking lot in the rain I feel deeply aggrieved, not at the loss of the money but at the waste of time. Never before have I felt life sucked away quite so meaninglessly as in the past mindless 90 minutes of mental masturbation. Never again, I tell myself as my head hits the pillow. Ha! Ha!

Next morning, the excesses of the night before notwithstanding, 8.45 a.m. sees me standing damp and bedraggled in the continuing drizzle outside the ticket office for the Cave of the Winds reading a sign that warns 'waterproofs should be worn at all times' and doesn't open for another 15 minutes. I had thought the receptionist at the motel might have known this – what time do the various attractions open being a not totally ridiculous question for a tourist to ask at a tourist resort – but she had blithely assured me that everything was up and running by 8:00 a.m. This matters more than you might think to a man travelling on an Amtrak schedule. There are only three trains a day to Buffalo, from where I am intending to catch the Lakeshore Limited to Chicago; one leaves in the middle of the night, one at dawn and the last at 12:35 p.m., which means I have to get my 'falls experience' in sharpish!

In theory that ought not to be such a tall order, especially as I have planned what I want to do. This is not my first visit to Niagara. I came here once before, admittedly some time ago, at the age of 12 in a family group, all packed into my American uncle's enormous 1960s Lincoln Continental car which was like the one JFK had been assassinated in, had reverse opening 'suicide doors' and seemed to me as far removed from my father's Hillman Imp as the Starship Enterprise did from the Boeing 707 we had crossed the Atlantic on. We did, of course, what the clever Canadians had programmed us all to do, and went to see the 'better' view of the falls from the Canadian side. There was only one problem: I nearly didn't come back. I was travelling on my father's passport at the time and, being a rather small child for my age, the US immigration official hadn't spotted me on the way out – and anyway what did he care, we were leaving the country – but his colleague was not quite so accommodating on our return only a few hours later.

He refused to allow me back into the United States on the grounds that I hadn't properly cleared customs formalities when leaving. This was undoubtedly true but a bit of a poser both logically and logistically: first of all, it was perverse to refuse me entry to the United States on the grounds that purely legalistically I had never left and was therefore still there. It was also obviously not the easiest solution to simply abandon a 12-year-old boy in Canada. Common sense – and perhaps the fact that at the time my uncle was a serving colonel in the US Army – won the day, or no doubt I would have a completely different accent today and last night's conversation in the wine bar would never have happened.

This time around, although the chances of anything even remotely resembling a repeat performance were unlikely, I reckoned that in these days of heightened border sensitivity, just in case, I would content myself with doing all my sightseeing from the American side. I have also realised that although we 'did the falls', in that visit more than three decades ago, by staying on the Canadian side, in fact missed some of the best aspects. With unexpected time on my hands due to the hotel receptionist's misinformation, I walked around the State Park which basically constitutes the American side of the falls and is mostly on Goat Island, the small piece of rocky parkland that sits in the middle of the Niagara River and is responsible for splitting the great cataract into the American Falls on its near side and the U-shaped Horseshoe Falls which, as the border lies mid-river, beyond the island, are wholly in Canada.

Goat Island got its name, a sign helpfully tells me, because in the eighteenth century English settler John Steadman kept his goat here to stop the wolves getting at it, though it begs the question of how he got to it himself; this is not the sort of river you want to be paddling across regularly. The view from the bridge is daunting in its own right and affords an aspect of the falls that people who come to look at the cataracts themselves, usually from below, often miss. Behind me, upstream, is a churning torrent as the water rushes over its uneven rocky bed; ahead, downstream, it seems to become faster and more turbulent still, only to disappear all of a sudden in a fine cloud of mist. Only the persistent roaring sound testifies to the fact that this vast flood of water is actually dropping a sheer 100 feet onto the rocks below. From here it appears to be a vast river suddenly evaporating into space.

Time for a closer look. Although the Canadian side offers the possibility of getting close to the bottom of the Horseshoe Falls it does so in a very civilised, safe and secure fashion, via a set of lifts and tunnels. The US side's equivalent is the Cave of the Winds, and it is an altogether less health-and-safety friendly setup. And a lot more exciting as a result. Nowadays there is a lift, which is where I am standing along with two Asian-American women, all three of us clad in see-through yellow capes with hoods, trousers rolled up to the knees, socks and shoes in a carrier bag and feet in a pair of disposable plastic sandals, all provided as part of the entrance fee. At five minutes past opening time, the lift supervisor in his green national park uniform arrives and ushers us in, telling us how originally there was just a wooden tower built against the side of the cliff. If that seems a bit scary it is nothing compared to the structure that still exists.

The term 'Cave of the Winds' is a bit of a misnomer, it turns out; the cave itself – discovered in 1834 and named with the classical flair of those days after Aeolus, Greek god of the winds – was wiped out in a rock fall in 1954 leaving only a dangerous overhang which had to be dynamited to make access even remotely safe. This is a stark reminder that if nature were left to itself, Niagara's falls would eventually be nowhere near the twin towns named after them: natural erosion of the cliff face behind them is slowly causing them to retreat to the extent that in a few thousand years they ought to reach all the way back to Lake Erie itself and drain it. American and Canadian engineers have for decades now been working to delay this by shoring up the cliffs, but as we are not yet 300 years into their recorded history, nobody can be sure how successful their efforts really are. Having been close up, I reckon they're probably wasting their time.

Mark, the ranger who takes over the tour from the bottom of the lift shaft, is telling us this and reams of other mind-boggling statistics as he hops gleefully over wooden decking down across the rocks. The cave may no longer exist but the tourists come anyway, primarily because the access built to get to it is still there and offers one of the most ridiculously hair-raising possibilities of getting up close and personal to a waterfall that at its peak can create conditions akin to a hurricane. When I say the access is still there, I mean it is for the moment: Mark and his mates will be taking it down in about six weeks' time, near the end of November and re-erecting it next spring. This is largely because in mid-winter it gets so cold up here the falls can freeze, crushing anything in their way and forcing themselves over the edge in time-freeze slow motion, like a fast-moving glacier, with maybe no movement for several days, then a few hairline cracks and moments of spectacular violence when huge chunks of ice topple over the precipice. I make a mental note to try to come back and see that some time.

Right now I am more concerned with keeping my footing on soaking wooden decking amidst a whirlwind flurry of spray from the nearest falls, known as the Bridal Veil, which is really a tiny offshoot of the American Falls cut off from the rest by a rock in the river. I now know why I'm wearing plastic sandals with my jeans rolled up to the knees. I may look like DP Gumby in a rain hood but at least most of me is dry. On the other hand, I'm a bit concerned about how long that will last. I've been looking at the wooden supports for the decking and can't see how they're fixed to the rocks. I ask Mark, who gives one of those big American 'Hey guy' laughs, and says, 'They aren't!' He goes on to tell me, beaming broadly all the time, that the decking supports are simply wedged into crevices in the rock, and have been done that way ever since the whole trestle edifice – which must be at least 200 feet long, up and down the rocks and in a series of raised platforms perilously close to the face of the falls – was first set up in the 1860s. The plan of exactly how to do it is passed on from team leader to team leader, relearned and adjusted each time they put it up and take it down. He seems to think this should be totally reassuring, but I'm left staring at the struts of wood wedged into gaps in the rock beneath me in ashen astonishment and wondering just how quickly a British health and safety department would take to condemn the whole structure. The terrible truth is I know deep down that they would do so without even looking at it, which is one more tragic example of how cosseted we've become and how much our lives have been taken over by a nanny state. This is one of those big differences between our two countries: we're brought up to have an instinctive respect for nanny; here they'd probably shoot her.

I'm still glancing at the supports apprehensively as we get ever closer to the falls, the noise grows and the spray from the onrushing torrent is like pointing a showerhead straight into my face. That's when Mark points up at the highest platform, almost within touching distance of the face of the Bridal Veil, its wooden railings dripping with windblown strings of green moss and with a sign proclaiming HURRICANE DECK, and more amusingly next to it, NO SMOKING. This latter has to be a joke. 'Smoking impossible' would be more accurate. Mark is gesturing towards it but making no move in that direction himself. 'It's perfectly safe,' he assures me, roaring at the top of his voice to be heard over the thunder of the falls, 'but I do this trip maybe 20 times a day, and I'd have pneumonia if I went up there every time. Suit yourself.' I look at it apprehensively. The two little Asian-American women have very obviously bottled out, and are taking photographs of one another a couple of decks below. But, I tell myself, I paid money to do this.

The hurricane deck lives up to its name. I have never, ever experienced such raw power up close. Not for one nanosecond did it occur to me to try and stand up there without as firm a grip as possible on the slippery handrails. It was like standing in a rainstorm in the slipstream of a jumbo jet: deafening, drenching and physically challenging. And a hell of a lot of fun. I came back down with a huge grin on my face, dripping Niagara water and adrenaline in equal quantities.

Mark the ranger may only fancy one soaking a day at most, but I'm a sucker for punishment. Back at the top of the cliff I keep the socks and shoes in their plastic bag and canter off, yellow rain cape flapping in the breeze, to catch the Maid of the Mist. The Maid is by far the most famous way of getting up close to the Horseshoe Falls and has been operating since 1846 when it was actually a ferry service from the US to Canada. It was only when they built the first bridge a couple of years later and the ferry traffic began to dry up that they realised they could make more money not actually taking the tourists any-where but as close as they could to the falls. The service collapsed during the American Civil War but a savvy Montreal firm snapped up the company and relaunched it in the 1890s, with new boats running from both the American and Canadian sides. The boats they run today look alarmingly like they might be the same ones.

The main way to get down to the jetty is by another lift, back on the main shore, and when I get to the bottom I find a large number of people in blue capes, looking disconcertingly like a middle-aged Superman fan convention. It's worrying because I only have an hour and a half left before I need to get a cab back to the train station, the boats only leave every half hour and it doesn't look to me as if that lot will all fit on a single boat.

I needn't have worried, though. They do. And with room to spare, chiefly because they pack 'em in, and with most of them pensioners, they are content to cram onto the lower deck rather than face the elements in the open up top. That, however, seems to me to be the only point in doing the thing at all, and so here I am, yellow cape exchanged for blue – I didn't want to spoil the colour scheme – up by the front railing on a rickety glorified tug boat that looks a hundred years old – it was actually built in 1976 – heading out onto the choppy waters aiming for the roiling heart of the Horseshoe Falls.

It's a fairly ridiculous journey, not least because absolutely everybody is taking pictures of everybody else, taking turns to swap spots by the railings. Except that I'm not giving up mine. There's only one of me and I can't take turns and selfish as it might seem I want to be up front when we head into the maelstrom. For that is exactly what we seem intent on doing, as the captain is now confirming with a set of fairly obvious safety instructions – no hanging over the side, keep hold of your camera etc. – repeated in a language which

I am by now already programmed by the new American reality to assume is Spanish, but suddenly realise to my immense surprise is French. Obviously, of course, given that this is a Canadian vessel, even though from a brief survey of the passengers the only language that anyone might understand other than English is possibly Gujurati.

To my left I can see the wooden platforms, decking and staircases of the Cave of the Winds, and have to say that it all looks even more precarious from here, a child's matchstick construction up against an elemental force. But however impressive the American Falls might be, and from the boat I can appreciate the sheer width of the span, there is something still more daunting about the virtually perfect 'U' of the Horseshoe particularly now that we have gone beyond the ends of the two arms, the air around us is a swirling drizzle and the boat is bucking like an Olympic swimmer trying to breast a tsunami. I can only imagine the helmsman down below forcing the craft to keep straight against the force of millions of gallons of water churning towards us from all directions. The Indians believed that there was a 'thunder being' called Heno who lived behind the Horseshoe Falls and right now it's easy to see why. There is a lot of squealing and giggling going on. No theme park water ride I've ever experienced has come anywhere near close. And then all of a sudden the boat tilts ever so slightly to one side, causing a moment of near panic, but it's only the helmsman swinging us away from the vertical and the onrushing water turns us around and we chug out of the maelstrom, with a collective 'Wow!' Anyone who thinks Niagara is a passive spectacle couldn't be further from the mark. The whole experience is pure white water-white knuckle.

And that's just the basics. Further downriver, I learn from a teenage passenger as we plough back towards the jetty, you can take a jet boat up the lower levels of the St Lawrence. It requires wearing a full wetsuit and signing away all rights of redress before fighting up through the appropriately named Devil's Hole Rapids. 'It was awesome,' says this kid, beaming from beneath the hood of his still dripping blue cape. 'Makes this seem kinda tame.' Privately I think it's lucky my train schedule doesn't allow me the time to try it. I've had just about enough awe for one day. Adding 'shock' might not be advisable.

Back at the dock we file off and begin shedding our blue outfits, the Superman convention disassembling into its component parts. I can't help noticing that most of the pensioners are wearing hats that look like baseball caps just slightly more squared off than normal and all of them say 'Hank'. I am aware that this is a fairly common American name but it does seem just a bit improbable that it is shared by all of them. Unless of course this is the national

'Hank' association day out, a sort of annual bus tour for people with the same name, which at least would spare the need for all those silly badges. But when I venture to ask one old boy who doesn't look quite as gaga as some of them, he looks at me with mild surprise and says with a smile that might or might not be ironic, 'You mean you never heard of the USS *Hank*?' Hank, it seems is not a bloke but a battleship, or to be more accurate, a destroyer. Hank the Destroyer, like Conan the Barbarian. Only different.

This should have dawned on me earlier but Hank is just not the sort of name you expect a warship to have, even an American one. It's rather like a British warship being called the HMS *Dave* instead of *Warspite* or *Ark Royal*. It seems *Hank* has long since joined most of his former shipmates in retirement having seen active service in the Second World War and subsequently in Korea, which makes me realise just why these chaps look as grizzled as they do – they are seriously old. They seem none too sure about what happened to old *Hank* though: one couple seems to think it became a training ship in the late 1960s, another certain it was sold to Argentina, while one 'half empty glass' pessimist bravely ventures that it had 'probably been broken up' by now. That with just the hint of a tear in his eye. I can't help but admire them though, these old buffers and their other halves, turning up year after year for a reunion of former shipmates. It's the sort of *esprit de corps* old British county regiments were famous for before the bureaucrats broke them up in the name of 'restructuring'. The sort of thing that keeps Captain Kirk and Spock turning up in successive *Star Trek* films: *Hank, the Next Generation*.

But it's time for me to get my life back on the rails, literally, with a quick cab ride out through the nondescript suburbs of Niagara, past diners and tyre stores and low-rise streets of wooden houses to the same siding we arrived at the night before. In the daylight the freight yard looks even more enormous, more than a dozen lines at least, enormous trains each with 40 or 50 wagons – 'cars' – stretching out behind them, dwarfing the five-coach Amtrak train stood there like a little silver slug beside so many long, dangerous snakes.

With 25 minutes to go before departure, the train is not yet ready for boarding so I join the motley couple of dozen passengers sitting around in the drab little waiting room. There is a map on one wall of the rail network that reveals how much track there still is around here, and how much of it – maybe 90 per cent – is dedicated to freight. The train has come in from Toronto on its way via Buffalo to New York City. But it takes two hours between arriving at Niagara Falls, Ontario, and leaving Niagara Falls, New York. There are two US immigration men in the waiting room but they have questions for only two passengers, who turn out, interestingly enough, to be one Russian and one Mexican. They take their passports and examine them in some detail, though quite why, or how they picked them out, I have no idea. There is not even any obvious indication that the two have crossed the border. But after the better part of 10 minutes they hand their paperwork back. I'm probably the only other 'alien' in the room. But it doesn't occur to them to trouble me. And I'm not complaining.

Then the conductor calls out the already familiar 'All aboard' and I'm on the train again, rattling past freight yards and warehouses and along the banks of the river rushing towards its precipice. All bound for Buffalo. What a mistake that would turn out to be.

NIAGARA FALLS TO BUFFALO

TRAIN: Maple Leaf
FREQUENCY: 1 a day
DEPART NIAGARA FALLS, NY: 12:35 p.m.
ARRIVE BUFFALO EXCHANGE ST, NY: 1:10 p.m.
DURATION: 35 minutes
DISTANCE: 23 miles

5

Buffalo's Bill

IT SAYS ALMOST EVERYTHING you need to know about the city of Buffalo today that the thing it is most famous for is chicken wings in sticky sauce. Taste doesn't come into it.

Once upon a time, arriving in Buffalo by rail was a truly memorable experience: alighting – possibly from the first class splendour of New York Central's 20th Century Limited – in a magnificent art deco terminal that saw 30,000 passengers a day pass through. Buffalo boasted one of the country's most splendid city halls, several of the influential architect Frank Lloyd Wright's groundbreaking buildings, the grandest hotel of one of the world's great chains and the first in the world to offer a bath in every room. Frederick Law Olmsted, the landscape architect who had designed New York's Central Park, laid out its heart and immodestly proclaimed it the 'best planned city as to its streets, public places and grounds in the United States, if not the world'. I was looking forward to it. I'd seen *Bruce Almighty*. Jim Carrey and God both hung out here. It couldn't be that bad, could it? I had no idea. No idea at all!

Arriving in Buffalo by rail today is still a memorable experience: like being thrown off a truck underneath Spaghetti Junction. The great railway terminal is derelict awaiting a slow process of restoration for office use. In the meantime it has been used as a set for low-budget horror films. The present 'downtown' station would be more suited to comedy: a tiny square brick bungalow on a traffic island dwarfed by overhead freeways. The address says I'm on Exchange Street but whatever was once exchanged here has long since been given away for nothing. The only thing that stands out amidst the sprawl of interlaced urban highways is the giant concrete bulk of the Buffalo Bisons baseball stadium.

I'm already developing a bad feeling therefore as I plod past it, backpack weighing heavily, in search of somewhere to drop the damn thing for a few

56

hours while I go in search of Buffalo's beating heart. It may have only been a short hop from Niagara, but the next train out westwards is 12 hours away and doesn't even stop at the downtown station but at a 'depot' in the distant suburbs called Depew. The bus garage – a sprawling, featureless shed populated by sparse groups of people surrounded by possessions packed into plastic bags and canvas hold-alls (which don't!) – offers no more storage facilities than the Amtrak station (which wouldn't be big enough to store more than a couple of 10-year-olds' schoolbags).

'Not since 9/11, sir. I don't think there's anywhere,' says the large black lady falling out of her too-tight flowery blouse behind the information counter. It is an answer that I am to realise has become ubiquitous: 'Blame it on the terrorist' – justified perhaps but also an excuse for withdrawing a service – the same excuse used by George W. Bush for the Patriot Act, the greatest infringement of America's liberties since the revolution. But what do I know: I come from post-Blair Britain. Nonetheless it seems strange to find America has abandoned left luggage. All those movies with keys left in airport lockers will have to be rescripted. Unless you have a hotel you have no alternative but to carry it with you. Which is what I end up doing.

The only trouble is I don't know where I'm going. I've found a map on the side of the bus station, but like all American maps I've seen so far, it seems deliberately designed not to convey any useful information: just thin straight black lines on a grid. So I do the only thing that seems sensible: head for the centre of it. The first street sign I find tells me I'm on Washington Square, which is a windswept paper-strewn pretence of a municipal park with concrete benches and bus shelters housing hobos. On one side sits the Washington Tavern, a neat nineteenth-century two-storey pub, stripped entirely of its urban context.

The buildings on either side have been pulled down – affording a fine view of the neo-Gothic college building beyond – across an achingly empty parking lot. I have never seen a city with so many parking lots – multistorey lots right next to tarmac lots around the corner from stretches of wasteland with wooden huts to identify them too as parking lots. Hardly any of them have any cars. This is a city with streets wider than most British motorways and enough parking lots to provide spaces for the entire output of the Japanese motor industry, and next to no traffic. Maybe the cars are all parked away in yet another series of vast subterranean lots whose existence is cunningly concealed. Maybe there are just no people any more. The pavements are as empty of pedestrians as the roads are of cars.

The occasional grand nineteenth-century building – a school, a college, a church – stands in what might be deliberate isolation were it not so painfully obviously just the absence of anything else, a spot where something has been pulled down and nothing put up to replace it. The splendidly-named Lafayette Tap Room – another grand old Victorian-style city pub building that would not look out of place in Brixton or Birmingham, is isolated from the community it surely exists to serve. Whoever they are. Wherever they live. This, I realise, is what Jane Jacobs was addressing in the book Laurence told me about in the White Horse Tavern back in Manhattan. Her *Death and Life of Great American Cities* was published nearly half a century ago, but nobody in Buffalo has got round to reading it yet.

A large man in a checked shirt with a baseball cap pulled down firmly over his eyes is leaning against the bus stop, though not in any obvious expectation of a bus turning up. He doesn't look the friendliest of types, but he is the only type available. I'm just a little worried that my question, 'Is this the city centre?' will sound inane, but the answer is hardly less so: 'Well, I guess. Sort of.' This is my first indication that I have just asked a question which many Americans, not just here in Buffalo, will find disturbingly hard to answer. But after 20 minutes of following my nose in circles in a vain search for social or architectural signs of the city centre, there is no other conclusion but that I am already in it, in fact have been all along.

That dark, faceless block-length slab that looks like a freezer factory or supersize storage radiator, I now identify as a mall: a sterile – and little used, it would seem – indoor shopping facility. A small sign over one of the few pedestrian entrances – the chief mode of access is via a gaping parking facility – says 'Main Place'. The heart sinks. And then a glimpse of something that offers at least aesthetic consolation: the city hall with its great yellow stone tower and colourful art deco mouldings on its lofty parapets almost glows in the early autumnal sunshine. Until you get up close.

This is Niagara Square. Once upon a time it really was Buffalo's 'beating heart'. Olmsted made it the centre of his city design with leafy avenues radiating out in eight directions – from each corner and each of the four sides – lined with mansions of the well-to-do who would set an example of gracious living to inspire their fellow citizens. In 1901, with Frank Lloyd Wright himself living and working in town, and the city host to the Pan-American Exposition, Buffalo was on a roll. The railroads were steaming ahead and with the completion of the Erie Canal, Buffalo was a transport nexus, a city light in heart as it entered the century it would leave so miserably. Niagara Square was linked by a long avenue of greenery to the exposition fairground which was attended by President William McKinley himself.

The superstitious could be forgiven for seeing that as the pivotal moment in Buffalo's history, the apex of its grandeur and the moment things began to go wrong. As he greeted crowds outside the Temple of Music McKinley was shot twice at point blank range by an anarchist. One of the inventions on display at the fair was the new-fangled X-ray machine. Unfortunately the doctors were too scared of the new technology to use it to locate the bullet which had lodged in his body. As the local hospital didn't have electric light and they couldn't have candles in the operating room because of the ether which was used to keep the president unconscious, aides employed frying pans to reflect sunlight for the surgeons to work. They got the bullet but a week later the apparently convalescing president had his first cup of coffee and promptly expired.

The granite obelisk surrounded by four vigilant lions in the centre of Niagara Square was erected in McKinley's memory and the square enlarged to accommodate it. Around it today are signs boasting of Buffalo's architectural heritage, oblivious to its desecration, and flags of 'sister cities'. One is Lille in northern France, not one of the greatest French cities but a jewel in comparison; another is Siena, whose city councillors really ought to reconsider their twinning list. The third is somewhere I've never heard of in Ukraine. That just might about fit the bill.

The decline which has hit Buffalo over the past half century could not have been imagined when McKinley met his fate, nor the subsequent decades as the city's prosperity, based on steel and industry grew and grew. The splendid city hall in front of me was its crowning moment, finished just as the Roaring Twenties turned into the Great Depression. The revolving doors' faded brass and scuffed skirting are clearly original.

Inside, the lobby positively glows with an amber and ochre radiance from the vast mosaic in native Iroquois Indian motifs that covers walls and ceilings. Above the entrance is an allegory of peace as a goddess reconciling warriors bearing British and American flags, a reminder that even in the 1920s Canada, just 'a spit away' across the Erie River was still considered the frontier to what had for so long been 'the evil empire'. To the side of the main door is an equally powerful symbol of modern Buffalo: a gimcrack kiosk selling fizzy drinks and cigarettes for the municipal workers, a gaggle of whom stand puffing on the steps outside.

When it was opened, the main attraction of Buffalo City Hall was the 28th-floor observation platform, which offered a view of the founding fathers' original symmetrical cityscape. I decide it has to be worth a look. To my surprise there is no security guard or even municipal flunky to point the way or ask for an entrance fee, just an old sign painted on the wall by the empty central lobby desk indicating the lifts to the right are for floors 15–26, 'and observation platform'. Enticed by the idea of piloting one of Mr Otis's original wood-lined vertical escalating machines myself, I step in and press the button for 26, the highest floor available, with only the slightest trepidation as the thing shudders and takes off like a steam rocket, the floor indicator disconcertingly remaining firmly fixed on '1' until it resumes counting again at '15'. This is an 'express' lift.

Emerging on floor 26 my other question is answered by a sign that says OBSERVATION PLATFORM FLOOR 28: STAIRS ONLY. The only remotely welcoming door amidst all those thick with a thousand coats of dark brown paint, unmarked and firmly closed, leads to a stairwell with peeling emulsion in hospital green and an open door in a security cage marked EXIT. I can only assume it is also an entrance.

My assumption turns out to be correct. Three floors up – from floor 26 to 28 – the stairwell opens into a bare brick-lined circular room with eye-level windows on all sides marked TO SAVE ENERGY DON'T OPEN WINDOWS. And there can be no doubt that Buffalo's city fathers are serious about saving their energy: all but one set are locked shut, as indeed, disappointingly are the doors leading to the observation platform running round the outside. Obviously someone has decreed that not even the perspex sheeting, completely enclosing the outdoor deck, is sufficient to deter would-be suicides. I can imagine there might be a lot of them.

The eye-level windows offer enough perspective over the city to see that the original town plan has been brutally overridden by the grid-and-lot tyranny of erection and demolition. There are a couple of faceless modern tower blocks in the middle distance, an incalculable number of parking lots and, near at hand, the great slab of the Statler hotel building, in its heyday one of Buffalo's great treasures yet so obviously a major contributing factor in the destruction of the elegant nineteenth-century street plan. To the north stretches a panorama of magnificent natural beauty: the vast expanse of Lake Erie reflecting the autumn sun in dark blue placid waters. Along the shoreline is a marina, filled with the yachts of the wealthy, yet devoid of waterfront life: cafés, promenades, people. Buffalo sits this side of a six-lane freeway along which cars rush, everyone in a hurry to get somewhere else. Buffalo sits on the edge of one of the world's great lakes, and shows it its arse.

In the vain hope of catching the genuine 360-degree view I had hoped for,

I try the other four doors, one in each corner, even though none obviously offers access to the viewing platform. All turn out to be firmly locked except for one which to my surprise wrenches open, only to reveal bare brickwork, a bucket and some fuse boxes. I close it hurriedly in case my intentions might be misinterpreted, not that there is anyone to see me. Or is there? Footsteps are rapidly ascending the staircase below. Have I been rumbled? It's not as if I've done anything I shouldn't have, as far as I know, except perhaps open that door, maybe just coming up here in the first place. Then a large man with a loud voice emerges from the exit door. I'm hugely relieved to find he is talking to someone behind him and pays me no attention at all. 'Here we are,' he all but shouts to a young woman behind him. They round the corner to the doors leading out to the observation platform. I wonder if they might have a key I unknowingly had failed to request from some appropriate authority, and then I hear a weary sigh. And they sweep past me with dark faces to head downstairs again. 'Fucking typical, just fucking typical,' says the man to no one in particular. It's hard not to agree.

I am lugging a heavy rucksack around Buffalo because there's no facility for leaving luggage, ostensibly for fear that the luggage in question might contain explosives. But here I am, unsupervised, unnoticed at the top of the city hall. Had I been a bomb-toting terrorist there is nothing to stop me blowing up the only building I have so far seen in Buffalo that doesn't actually deserve it.

Back down to earth, it's time to take a closer look at the great triple-towered monolith of the Statler. It is more than half a century now since there have been any hotels called Statler – the group was sold to Hilton Hotels in 1954 – but the name lingers in the subconscious, if only because Statler and Waldorf were the names of the two old hecklers in *The Muppet Show*. Ellsworth Milton Statler was one of those great American businessmen who had the 'vision thing' at least when it came to making money and building an empire. He saw the 1901 Buffalo fair as an opportunity to prove American hospitality could reach levels other countries couldn't, by building the world's first hotel with a private bath or shower in every room. It was cheap: 'A room with a bath for a dollar and a half' the slogan ran. His competitors predicted disaster. But it turned out to be so popular that he revolutionised the hotel industry with a new level of occupancy and would later boast that he never even touched the half a million dollar credit line afforded by his bankers.

Statler went on to found a chain of hotels across the US and in 1923 built a newer, much grander building in Buffalo which is the formidable edifice that still stands today. More or less, mostly less. In its time the Buffalo Statler was the largest luxury hotel between New York and Chicago with 1,100 rooms and prided itself on supplying its guests not only with a bath in every room but free newspapers and ice, still in those days a luxury at home. He imported the marble for his grand rooms from Italy and guests included the transatlantic aviator Charles Lindbergh, Presidents Roosevelt, Eisenhower and Truman and General Chiang Kai Shek in the days when he ruled all of China.

Statler himself died in 1928. It is just as well he never lived to see the fate of his most beloved hotel. Its days as a luxury hotel ended in the early 1980s; sold off and renamed Statler Towers, it has been converted into flats and offices, the sort of offices that have signs advertising WORKERS' COMPENSATION ATTORNEYS or FREE LEGAL CONSULTATIONS, alongside NO SOLICITORS IN THIS BUILDING (one more proof that our 'common language' is a myth). The NO SOLICITORS sign is next to one that says NO PUBLIC RESTROOMS, the sort of signs people put up in buildings routinely plagued by hawkers and people likely to urinate in the corners, especially when the strategically placed reception desk is unmanned. The one in the entrance to Statler Towers looks like it has been unmanned since 1954. The chandeliers still hang overhead, dusty glowing baubles, like a dirty diamond necklace round the neck of some bag lady. In 2006 the building was bought by a British businessman of Asian descent who reportedly plans major renovation. There is a lot to do.

But then there is a lot to do anywhere you look in Buffalo. Any 14-year-old computer gamer could explain it. All it takes is a couple of hours playing Sim City, one of the world's most addictive games, which over four evolutions and two decades has become so accurate that I suspect it is probably even used by city planners nowadays. At least when you see how cities all over the world appear worryingly to be following the American pattern, you have to look for a conspiracy somewhere. The grid system, the delight of city planners since Roman days, is fraught with danger when it produces lots that can be individually owned and developed – or not – with no obvious sensitivity to the lot next door. Play Sim City and watch how in your grid-aligned city, lots rise and fall relatively independently of one another.

Since the latter half of the twentieth century saw the steel and heavy industry which Buffalo's prosperity had come to rely on turn into the rust belt, the response has been knee-jerk as lot owners develop or raze on their own whim. All the municipal authorities can do is pour dollops of money into specific projects – a marina, a new stadium, urban expressways, even a small downtown public transport tram system – but not one of them has paid attention to the idea of a harmonious whole. A city that was once world famous for its architecture, is today an example of how anything that *can* go wrong *will* go wrong.

Meanwhile, I still have half a dozen hours to kill before the overnight Lake Shore Limited will take me onwards to Chicago. On the dubious advice of the Canadian in the bar in Niagara, who claimed to be a regular visitor to Buffalo, I head first for the Elmwood district which he assured me was the liveliest part of central Buffalo. He was not wrong, except in describing it as 'central'. This has a lot to do with perspective. When I ask directions to Elmwood, I am told it's just 'five or 10 minutes down the road', but then nobody is even remotely imagining I might be on foot. By now I've begun to get a grip of the scale of downtown Buffalo's urban wasteland, and decide it's time to investigate public transport. Of course, what passes for public transport in most of America is taxis. Except that you can almost never find one. They don't cruise the streets in the hope of being hailed – except in New York – and the only way of getting one is either finding a rank (which you won't because it's called a 'stand') or knowing the number of a firm and then being able to explain where you are, and probably how to get there. Taxis are for people who have momentarily mislaid their cars (most Americans would take that to mean people who are about to lose their cars: 'momentarily' here doesn't mean something of brief duration but something that's going to happen 'in a moment'. Confusing, isn't it?).

But I have already clapped eyes on the pride of Buffalo's public transport system: a tramway that runs up and down Main Street. For the central stops it is free. The main reason for this is that public transport, in the sense we understand it in Britain, is intended for two groups: the destitute, and tourists. As a result, the trams don't run all that frequently, every 15 minutes at best, and feel more like one of those little rubber-wheeled trains that ferry tourists around seaside resorts than a serious means of urban transportation. Even this far north, in what I would have assumed to be a typical 'Anglo' city close to the Canadian border, the ticket machines show just how rapidly Spanish is becoming America's semi-official second language: '*Pulse por su idoma*,' the LCD display says. I choose *inglés*, feed in a dollar to get beyond the city centre and it spews out a 'permit to ride'.

The tram, however, also only goes halfway towards where the minimalist city map suggests Elmwood might begin. That means getting back on shank's pony despite my sore feet, but that doesn't matter too much because this is Buffalo's best bit, chiefly because nobody has done anything to it for most of the twentieth century. You know you have reached Elmwood when the parking lots start to fade away and little wooden houses dare to creep into view, skulking along the side of the road in the hope they won't be noticed and pulled down. Most of them have got away with it, enough for them to survive until the first 'bohemians' moved in: middle-class kids with enough money to play at being artists, and who didn't depend on heavy industry jobs that were no longer there. They stand knocking back bottles of Corona on the terrace of the Cozumel Mexican bar-restaurant in the weak autumn sunlight.

I know I should be tucking heartily into that famous local speciality, 'Buffalo Wings', but somehow a plate of fattened wings from bloated factory-farmed chickens that have become the staple diet for bloated factory-working humans is the last thing I feel like. Anyhow this isn't the place to have them; I should be in the Anchor Bar in bleak downtown where back in 1964 Teressa Bellissimo, wife of the owner, found her son Dominic and several pals from college arriving unannounced in search of something to eat. In a fit of inspiration she took the leftover chicken wings she normally boiled up for soup stock, deep-fried them and doused them with spicy tomato sauce. Or maybe not. At least two other bars claim the idea originated there – Buffalo has not enough claims to fame to let even that one go undisputed.

Instead, I settle for tacos, a 'free' plate of tortilla chips and a chunky chilli and tomato salsa that almost tastes as if it might be homemade. Washed down with a pint of Yuengling. It could have been the alcohol, it could have been the pretty waitress with the big smile that it doesn't take too much self-delusion to believe might be there for me instead of her tip, but before long some semblance of humanity has crept up on me unawares. I wouldn't say I feel part of the human race again, or as near as I'm likely to get in Buffalo. The upbeat mood comes with me on the long tramp back into town. With the hours before my midnight train still stretching ahead of me like another empty parking lot, I'm going to try the Canadian's tips for early evening Friday night nightlife: the 'Chippewa entertainment district'. The name alone had me hooked. 'Chippewa' is one of those words that has been on my personal radar for more than two decades without me ever really having a clue what it meant. All because it features in the first line of Canadian singer-songwriter Gordon Lightfoot's 'Wreck of the Edmund Fitzgerald'.

Gordon Lightfoot is hardly a particular favourite of mine. But that one song, first heard sung by a Canadian student in a bar filled with nostalgic expats in the basement of a Moscow embassy in the latter days of the Cold War, has always seemed particularly evocative. Part of that comes from the sheer alien 'otherness' of the place names, places that might as well be on the moon, and yet obviously so deeply familiar to the narrator that they need no explanation. This haunting song tells the tragic tale of a shipwreck in which all 29 crew died. And yet if you'd never heard it the lyrics look like gobbledygook, something Homer Simpson would sing in the bath: Chippewa and Gitchi Gumee. But then words don't just have meanings, they have resonance. Take two exotic, apparently meaningless terms that resonate together as if they come from a common language, then throw in a familiar but evocative word like 'legend' and you have a formula that grabs the attention and sung to a haunting melody in a low lit bar can send shivers down the spine.

One of the reasons I have never simply 'googled' Chippewa is that part of me didn't really want to know any more in case the truth diluted the magic. But when the Canadian in the bar in Niagara used the word, the look on my face prompted him to spell it out: 'The Chippewa – you know, the Injuns.' My obvious ignorance astounded him as much as it would have amused me had he said, 'Paris, now tell me again, which country is that in?' People here know the Chippewa as well as the Sioux or Cheyenne. Maybe it's because they took the land from them. Gitchi Gumee, was their word for Lake Superior. Once you have seen the great cascades of Niagara, Lightfoot's lyrics about this great chain of lakes – Superior, Ontario, Erie – come into their own. After looking out from Buffalo's decaying city hall tower over the bleak, beautiful and empty expanse of Erie, with nothing but a few stationary sailboats, the vision of a great old freighter laden with iron ore, heading for Cleveland from 'some mill in Wisconsin', seems more than ever a poignant evocation of what at the time of the disaster was already a fast vanishing world. The wreck of the *Edmund Fitzgerald* only happened in 1975. It was a cruel last gasp.

'But what have the Chippewa got to do with bars in downtown Buffalo?' I had asked the Canadian, vaguely wondering if like the Niagara casino local Indians they had done some sort of sale and leaseback arrangement. He'd shrugged, thought for a moment and said, 'Not a lot. Hell, nothin' at all that I can think of.' He was right. No self-respecting Indian in his right mind would have been seen dead in the 'entertainment district' of Buffalo.

Entertainment is always a relative term – think public hangings and throwing Christians to lions; there'll always be a market for it, but it's not everybody's cup of tea. The 'entertainment' in and around the Chippewa district of downtown Buffalo is spot-on if you like bars that are pitch dark inside, even in the daytime, except for neon alcohol advertisements and where the music is so loud that you actually have to stand at least 10 yards outside to have a conversation, and order drinks in sign language. If that's what rings your bell then Buffalo has a whole carillon on offer in a series of practically identical establishments about 20 yards apart. If not, that's tough.

So it's in a mood of renewed resigned despondency, with more than four hours yet to go before my train, that I tramp off once more – painfully aware of the pack on my back – in search of something a bit more congenial. Within half an hour I find what looks like the best bet. I should have guessed: this is where I came in, the Washington Tavern, the lonely-looking town bar standing amidst the wasteland on the edge of so-called Washington Square. Standing there, peering through the window and hoping not to be taken for one of the hobos from the bus shelter, wondering if this reasonable but dull-looking bar is really the best on offer, I'm suddenly accosted by a bloke who jumps out of a pickup truck. I've started to panic before I realise that he's just trying to be helpful. He is concerned, in a well-meaning way that in most European cities would verge on the suspicious, in case I might be lost. Which, of course, is not far from the truth. I surprise myself by responding in kind, telling him I'm just looking for somewhere convivial to kill a few hours before making my way to a train station I don't really know how to get to.

His recommendation is the other bar I spotted in my first hour in Buffalo, the Lafayette, which he says on a Friday night has music you can actually listen to rather than just survive. What's more, once he has picked up his fried fish supper from the Washington, he'll give me a lift there. I'm completely taken aback, not for the last time in America, by the sudden spontaneity, the way in which a vast monolithic indifference to the fate of others cohabits happily with remarkable outgoing friendliness. Within less than 10 minutes I'm dropped outside the Lafayette by Ivor – I already know his name, family history and taste in music, with the advice to ask the barman about getting out to Depew and a warm – probably genuine – assurance that if I can't get it sorted out I should ring his 'cellphone' (he writes down his number on a piece of torn cigarette packet) and 'if I can still walk after a coupla beers back with the old lady' he'll come out and give me a lift.

Stunned and grateful, I venture into the surprisingly welcoming Lafayette Tap Room. Unlike almost anywhere else I have been – or seen – in Buffalo, the Lafayette has atmosphere: an old dark oak bar all along one wall, with people on stools chatting to one another and small tables with people eating. I'm not that hungry but having wimped out of the 'wings' I can't turn down Buffalo's other speciality, one that hasn't perhaps become 'globally famous' but looks as if it might be at least more interesting: Beef on Weck.

This is another of America's German inheritances (just how much America's

Anglo-Saxon roots are really Saxon – and Bavarian and Rhineland and Prussian – rather than 'Anglo' is something that is going to become more and more apparent to me over the next few weeks, particularly in Milwaukee). *Kümmelweck* is an old German dialect word for a caraway seed roll. It is not something you often come across in Germany and the Buffalo version is a genuine local speciality, even if nowadays they pronounce the 'w' the English way. It is a large soft roll dusted with caraway seeds and salt. It comes – at least in the Lafayette Tavern – packed with mouth-melting rare roast beef and a liberal sprinkling of pickled gherkins, surprisingly simple and surprisingly delicious.

At the bar next to me, Gary, a petite, trim, dapper middle-aged man with a penchant for flat caps and eye-catching houndstooth check blazers, is fuming against a Canadian disc jockey: 'This guy in Toronto, for God's sake, he's like saying nothing happens in Buffalo because nobody lives there.' I almost find myself nodding in agreement here with the unknown but obviously savvy shock jock. 'I mean,' Gary says, 'just look at us, are we nowhere?'

Absolutely nowhere, I'm about to say, and then I realise he means right here, in this bar and I have to admit he has a point. The Lafayette Tap Room is somewhere, in fact it's somewhere pretty nice. By now it has filled up and there is a cool, blues-skat-singing six-foot-seven black Californian guy warming up on stage and promising us he's come straight from New York City and really wants a nap, but only after he's sung his heart out. And that is what he's doing!

Gary is saying: 'People just can't help being nasty to Buffalo.' Unfortunately, present company excepted, these people still have all my sympathy. 'They think we're about nothing but snow and ice and unemployment.' I remember a sign by the bank opposite City Hall advising that hot water pipes are embedded in the pavement and realise I may not be seeing Buffalo in all its wintry glory. However grim it might appear in autumn, it has to be much, much worse in the dark depths of January.

For all his fervent defence of his city Gary admits that Buffalo today is one of the poorest cities in America, its population at 300,000 less than half what it was half a century ago, with an average family income of barely $28,000 (about £14,000) and an astonishing 20 per cent of its inhabitants below the poverty line.

'They say things like, "Buffalo is a dinosaur and since the steel went we've nothing,"' he pauses for just a telltale instant before adding, 'and obviously they're not wholly wrong there.' This sounds like a sad but accurate admission of unavoidable defeat, particularly as neither Gary nor his female friend Anne who has just arrived can remember exactly when it was the steel mills closed: 'The sixties or maybe the fifties, no probably maybe the seventies.'

Anne says her 'sugar daddy' used to be a steel roller and 'goes on all the time about it'. So how old is he? 'He says he doesn't know, doesn't have a whaddayacallit, birth certificate, but like maybe 83 or something.' Which, I want to reply, is probably how old you have to be if you can remember having a good time in Buffalo. But then it occurs to me that she probably reckons she shows her 'sugar daddy' a good time, and out of sympathy for both of them I keep my mouth shut. Anyhow, as Gary was trying to tell me earlier, I'm not exactly having a bad time at the moment, with a drinkable beer in my hand, moderately entertaining company and a fine performer playing the blues up there on the stage. If only I knew how the hell I was going to get out to the train station I'd be fine really.

At which point, Gary perks up and says, 'Hey, what the hell, you know, I can take you out to Depew if you don't want to leave for another half hour or so.'

Which puts a smile on my face in Buffalo after all, and I buy him a beer which of course he says he shouldn't have because he's driving but what the hell, and then he buys me one and then eventually we stagger out into the night and he fires up his Japanese people carrier in the midst of the vast sprawling parking lot, which now has maybe two dozen cars in it but could take another few hundred without feeling crowded and we drive off into the darkness.

I haven't a clue where we're headed and after a while it emerges that neither has Gary as he's never been to the Amtrak station before, never ever been on a train actually. The only clues we have are his vague idea of where it is located and my note of the address, 55 Dick Street which I still have a horrible lingering feeling might be a joke.

And then we cross under the freeway – which is what I am learning you do a lot in America unless you are actually on one – and spot a sign about the size of a shoebox lid pointing in the opposite direction. It only takes about two miles before we can turn around and miraculously we spot the sign again on the way back, and Gary swings the people carrier off the carriageway and onto an unmade road which leads to what looks like a Portakabin on a piece of waste ground and I know we must be there.

I climb out, throw my rucksack on my back and grab Gary's hand and shake it and he slaps me on the rucksack and looks at the Portakabin – which actually isn't a Portakabin but a medium-sized, nondescript concrete building which manages to look as if it hasn't decided whether or not to hang around for long – and slaps me on the rucksack again.

'Good luck,' he says, meaning it. 'Write nice things about Buffalo.' I give him a smile instead of a lie.

Then in a screech of wheels on gravel Gary is gone and there's just me and Depew depot. But at the end of the day – or even 45 minutes into the next one as the 11:59 p.m. Amtrak departure is put back to 12:30 a.m. and then 12:45 a.m. – I realise I may not have found Buffalo's beating heart, but I did catch a glimpse of its soul.

BUFFALO TO CHICAGO

TRAIN: Lake Shore Limited
FREQUENCY: 1 a day
DEPARTS BUFFALO DEPEW, NEW YORK: 11:59 p.m. (Eastern Time)

via
Erie, Pennsylvania
Toledo, Ohio
Bryan, OH
Elkhart, Indiana
South Bend, IN

ARRIVE CHICAGO, ILLINOIS: 9:45 a.m. (Central Time)
DURATION: approx 8 hours, 45 minutes
DISTANCE: 520 miles

6

Hell of a Town

LIFE IS A BEACH, then you die. It may be a stale old joke, but you can give it a lot of new life by imagining it first spoken by Al Capone on the occasion of the St Valentine's Day massacre. You see, the one thing I had absolutely not expected about Chicago was that it would be a great seaside resort.

As the early morning Amtrak rolled through the golden cornfields of northern Indiana I was ready for my first glimpse of the 'Windy City's' famous skyline, with the spires of the Sears Building – still the world's tallest in terms of actual accessibility to human beings – towering over the rickety tracks of the 'El', the city's famous nineteenth-century elevated urban transport system.

What I was not prepared for was to be sitting barely a few hours later on the upper deck of a restaurant shaped like a steamship sipping a piña colada and watching girls in skimpy bikinis play beach volleyball on golden sand against an ocean of clear blue water.

'Ocean', of course, is something of an exaggeration, but believe me it does not feel like it from the lower shore of Lake Michigan, with the far coast – in a straight line – more than 200 miles away. Lifeguards line the beach at regular intervals and when the trim tanned athletic bodies are not batting volleyballs to one another over nets on the sand they are keeping their shape by cycling or jogging along the shoreline.

There is something almost Australian about the scene which makes me realise why the Americans joined with our antipodean cousins to get beach volleyball included as an Olympic sport. The rest of us may have happily approved if only for the spectator value, but not without a lingering suspicion that it was more about voyeurism than actual sport. I can't help suspecting it won't be quite the same at the 2012 games in London where they intend to cover Horseguards' Parade with sand, so we can huddle together with our brollies up watching shivering girls in tracksuits cavorting in the rain.

71

In any case my own interest is, of course, purely academic. Not least because I am sitting here next to my wife. This is not quite the surprise it might appear to be. She had planned for some time one of her biannual business trips to the US including a visit to contacts in Chicago, partly because it fitted in with my itinerary but also because we could visit her cousin Helen who lives here, 'and you simply must see her kitchen'. I know, I know, but we'll get there. Anyhow I am obviously pleased to see her, not least because it means I get to exchange my usual 'Motel 6' style accommodation for two nights in the opulent 1920s splendour of the Drake Hotel, whose great bulk looms behind us overlooking the beach – even if it did take the bellboys a moment or two to decide to let this rucksack-toting old buffer in frayed denims through the door; but who are they to object if the paying customer likes a bit of rough?

So here we are improbably sipping tropical cocktails just south of the Canadian border on the last day of September, with the temperature a blissful 26 degrees Celsius (or 79 Fahrenheit as the natives would have it), with the edge taken off the heat by a gentle version of the omnipresent inshore breezes that make this the 'Windy City'.

Looking out in one direction, as the cheery Italian-American waiter serves burgers with 'spicy fries' (chips dusted with chilli powder), I can see white sails of yachts dotted around the bay, a small circular nineteenth-century island fort – like the one in Portsmouth harbour, here no doubt intended to guard against marauding Brits from Canada – and the imposing bulk of a cruise liner rounding the headland. In the other: the stone bulk of the Drake against the striking modernist skyscrapers clustered around the elongated twin-horned pyramid of the John Hancock tower, the Sears Building's rival for the title of Chicago's most iconic structure.

It is, in fact, quite beautiful in an austere sort of way, an almost perfect minimalist modernist prop for the organic activity on the beach in front of it. It also occurs to me that, for all people say about the view from the top of tall buildings, looking up can often be better than looking down (from up there the beach volleyball players would be mere specks). Nonetheless, we are going up. Not the Hancock but the Sears, for one simple reason: my past preference for the Empire State over the late World Trade Center in New York meant I have never been up the world's tallest skyscraper. And as the Sears Building has currently regained that status at this very moment – I don't count the CN Tower in Toronto which is merely an observation platform on a television mast – I'm not going to miss my fleeting chance. Fleeting because by the time this book comes out although the Sears Building will still be the tallest – if you take the rather risible measure of judging by the top of the antennae on the roof (527.3 metres) – the actual top floor (412 metres), where the observation deck is situated, will have been surpassed by the Shanghai World Financial Centre (492 metres) due to open late 2008, which in turn will almost immediately lose out to the Burj Dubai, a veritable Tower of Babel that will top out several hundred metres higher. This is, of course, all just ridiculous male penis-envy hubris as any woman will tell you, while checking the size of the wallet of the men who built them. Anyhow, pathetic or not, I've decided that if I'm in the city with the world's tallest building right now, then I've got to go up it.

What a mistake that is going to turn out to be. Not quite as big a mistake as that made by the two young Japanese tourists who stop us on the street on our way there. Would I take a photograph of them? No problem, and I take the neat little Olympus digital camera and frame the two of them side by side beaming happily. Make sure, he indicates by sign language, to get in the tallish building behind. So I oblige, kneeling down to include as much as possible of the maybe 50-storey high yellow-brick-faced apartment building behind them. Maybe it's where they're staying. I also get in the advert for the Sears Tower's Skydeck Observation Platform. It's only a few minutes later, as they acknowledge me with sheepish smiles in the ticket queue in the lobby of the glass and steel tower round the corner, do I realise they had misconstrued their monolith.

Tall buildings have a hold on us. They draw us to their summits so we can look down and see how insignificant our fellow human beings – and of course ourselves, if we are in that sort of philosophical mood – really are. The best – though it is not particularly tall but still offers a panoramic view of a relatively low-rise city – is the Guinness Visitors' Centre in Dublin. Not only does it offer a 360 degree view over the Dublin skyline, the building itself is shaped internally like a pint glass, has three bars on the way up and a bar at the centre of the circular top-storey observation room, where, what is more, you are rewarded with a free pint for getting that far.

The people who run the Sears Tower nowadays – the original Sears Roebuck department store moved out some 16 years after it was completed back in 1974 – would do well to take a lesson. Not only do they not offer you a drink, they manage to deceptively conceal the length of the queue ahead of you by snaking it through a succession of rooms and corridors which I feel certain the Chicago Fire Department – a highly organised and much called-upon service – would immediately condemn as a potential death trap. This includes – just when you're least expecting it – a wholly superfluous auditorium film presentation on the tower's construction. Maybe they feel they are giving value for money, but frankly, even the genuinely jaw-dropping views to be had from the top barely excuse a wait of nearly an hour – much more in peak periods – crammed into a sweaty basement.

There are, understandably, security checks to be gone through, though these are disconcertingly perfunctory. The only thing I hadn't been expecting and which takes me aback is when a man in an official yellow T-shirt insists on taking my photograph. I know passport officers do this now on entry to the country, but are they really going to match them up with pictures of everyone who goes up the Sears Tower?

'Check it out when you come back down, sir. No obligation to buy,' and he points to a photograph of a perfect American family displaying their perfectly straight cosmetically whitened teeth against a Chicago skyline and an azure sky. Wonderful! There you have it: captured forever on a silicon chip, the perfect memory of the scene you haven't seen yet.

A group of pensioners from Omaha, identifiable by their baseball caps and big round button badges with their names written in huge letters – designed for identification purposes not just in both face-to-face situations but possibly also when looking in the mirror – are keen to take up the offer. I reckon at least a couple of them are aware it might be the only memory that had any chance of being durable. A tall stooped woman called 'Arleen' with glasses so thick she was probably hoping to spot the Eiffel Tower from the top, appears genuinely worried that her 'companion Tom' might not even make it up there. Tom, to be fair, looks as if he was long past caring. I know how he feels. A fussy type called 'Jan' oozing a thin veneer of optimism with all the charm of water leeching from supermarket bacon keeps insisting it'll 'be really worthwhile when we get there'.

It isn't, of course. Things that make you wait in sweaty queues for anything more than half an hour rarely are. The view is remarkable enough – on one side the clear blue waters of a lake that even from up here seems to have no opposite shore, and on the other, straight lines of freeways running uninterrupted across vast flat plains for what looks to be half the way to Tokyo. But that's it really. And you can't see the beach volleyball players at all. The trouble is that skyline panoramas seldom look quite as good as the postcards or the wide-angle photographs you've been staring at in the queue for the last 40 minutes to the extent you no longer need to consult the tableau of landmarks because you've already memorised the ones you care about. In real life it never looks that good anyhow, not least because the windows are dirty.

Now I can see why if it's your job to clean the windows on the Sears Tower you might be tempted to throw a sickie now and then, especially when the rota says today's the day for the 103rd floor. Frankly I would rather eat ground glass with chilli fries than hang outside a tapering building some 1,440 feet above the ground. But if somebody's got to do it, then surely somebody's got to do it, particularly if you're charging the punters a healthy chunk of cash to get up there; believe me they're not doing it for the fun of the lift ride, no matter how fast it goes. It could be, of course, that these days such jobs are done by some sort of robot, but if so, he had been throwing a sickie lately too.

The other reason it never looks as good as the postcards, of course, is that the weather is never as good. This may be true of most postcards but it's doubly true of skyscrapers. At that height, in fact, weather conditions are always notoriously unpredictable: if there are clouds on the horizon one minute then like as not you're going be in them the next. It's not called the Windy City for nothing. And that sign right next to the ticket office on the ground floor saying NO REFUNDS FOR POOR VISIBILITY is a bit of a dead giveaway, isn't it?

As it happens, we're as lucky as most people get and the view is clear as far as the distant curved lines of the horizon in all directions, except of course that the sky is not as blissfully blue as it might be, and anyway even if it had been, every time I try to get my picture taken against it, a pensioner from Omaha with a baseball cap and button badge wanders into the frame. Still at least the button badges serve a purpose; back home you can say, 'Oh yes, and there's Arleen. From Omaha.'

᠅

Back down to earth – almost – it's time for a rattling ride on Chicago's famous 'El', which to most natives is more of a symbol of the city than even the world's highest building. The Elevated Railway began back in the 1890s as a series of trains coming into the centre of Chicago from the growing suburbs. It was only when the notorious Charles Tyson Yerkes, a Pennsylvania financier, became involved and bribed, blackmailed and bullied his way into getting them all linked up in the middle around the central business district known then and forever after as The Loop that the institution became what it is today.

And what it is, is an ancient rickety, rattling, incredibly noisy urban railway raised to first-floor level making like hell for anyone whose windows open onto it, causing intolerable congestion on the roads below, hemmed in by its supports. Not hard, therefore, to see why almost anyone with any sense in the city centre opposed Yerkes in the first place. In a city that was not to be known for its principled uninfluenced public office, Yerkes got his way, the 'El' got built and nobody in Chicago today can imagine the city without it.

The only thing to be thankful for – from a British point of view – is that when he finally got squeezed out of Chicago by a reforming mayor, and devoted his attentions to London instead, taking control of half the Tube lines between 1900 and 1905, he at least had the decency to keep them underground. What saves Chicago, though, from being dominated at ground level by the rattling 'El' is the river, another aspect of the city I hadn't quite imagined. The Chicago winds gently through the city named after it, providing a mode of transport – primarily for sightseers – but more importantly, a riverbank for cafés and restaurants to spread out along, oases of relaxation in a bustling but surprisingly relaxed city.

But the wife has been to Chicago before and is keen to show me around and I'm off to take in another of the city's towers, thankfully this time not to queue for an elevator to the top. There again, it's hard to imagine catching an elevator to the top of a thing that looks like Ely's eleventh-century cathedral on steroids. The Tribune Tower was always going to be interesting in an oblique sort of way if only because an old journalistic chum once worked for the paper and it has a reputation as an organ of probity. Newspaper buildings these days tend to be dull functional glass and steel office blocks, but I used to work for the *Daily Telegraph* in the days when it still occupied a baronial building on Fleet Street and had a little lawn outside the sixth-floor boardroom where the proprietor Lord Hartwell could be found watering his tulips.

But even that ill prepared me for a cross between a mediaeval French Gothic ecclesiastical masterpiece and a kleptomaniac's castle. Especially in the middle of such an unabashedly twentieth-century city as Chicago. The Tribune Tower has more ornate flying buttresses than Notre Dame de Paris. Quirkily it has most of them where they serve no purpose at all, near the top of its great soaring tower. This American Gothic Gormenghast was actually completed in 1925, its design the result of a competition held by Col Robert McCormick, the *Tribune's* publisher, who clearly wanted to find the loopiest architect in America. He not only succeeded; he added a few more plainly potty elements of his own, notably that the tower should include a rock from each of the 50 states of the union.

A nice idea, a gesture even towards the ambitions of the *Tribune*, amongst many other regional-based papers none of which have yet wholly succeeded in becoming a genuine national institution. You can even think it laudable that the federal government contributed to this idea by including a stone from the White House during one of its many restorations. And a stone from Abraham Lincoln's home in Springfield, Illinois, though perhaps a bit naughty, is still somehow homage to the nation's history. The trouble is, that this tokenism caught on to the extent of becoming something of a craze among the *Tribune's* far-flung correspondents.

So we have a piece of the Berlin Wall included too. Why not? If ever a structure deserved demolishing and spreading to the four winds, it was that one. I have a chunk in my desk drawer which I prised from the wall myself, and in any case these days there have probably been enough 'certified genuine' bits sold globally to rebuild the damn thing a dozen times over. Equally it is hard not to be moved by the touching expression of solidarity in including a six-inch blackened and twisted mesh of steel wire from the ruined framework of the World Trade Center.

But that's not all. The stone from Flodden Field, I grant you, may not be missed, but how about the cannon ball from Pevensey Castle? It is possible that the fire-blackened piece of mediaeval pinnacle from Cologne Cathedral was discarded during the restoration process after the British-American fire-bombing and therefore has a legitimate place as a 'scalp'. But does the same go for the carved 'fleur de lys' from Notre Dame in Paris, donated perhaps in recognition of the architectural homage? And what's with this stone from Edinburgh Castle? Or the bit of Westminster Abbey? Surplus to requirements in restoration work? Maybe, but if they're good enough to include here, why weren't they good enough to be reused?

And what about the stone from Dublin Post Office? A token of Irish-American solidarity no doubt in sympathy for that building's bombardment by the British during the 1916 rebellion? And does that make the chunk of balustrade from the Wawel Castle in Krakow, seat of Poland's ancient kings, a celebration of Chicago's huge Polish community? Maybe. And the stone from the Powder Tower in Riga? And what about the one from the Tainitzkaya Tower of the Kremlin? And the one from the Danish fortress of Helsingor (Hamlet's Elsinore)? And the bits from Sydney Opera House, the Great Wall of China and the Taj Mahal? And then the piece of marble from the Roman ruins of Leptis Magna in Libya?

I suppose it's just possible that Muammar Gaddafi is such a keen *Tribune* reader that he ordered a minion to hack off a lump of his country's most famed ancient monument to an organ of Yankee imperialism. But my recommendation is: next time you find yourself interviewed at home by a correspondent from the *Chicago Tribune*, frisk him or her on arrival for penknives, picks, jemmies and other easily concealed mason's tools, do a full body search on leaving and check that that garden gnome wandering down the path holding his hand is leaving of his own free will. By the Tribune Tower's front door there are two niches of the type that in European Catholic churches hold statues of saints, and I find it hard to believe there isn't a wager running in the newsroom as to who can fill them first.

I'm just tempted to take my Swiss Army knife to see if I can remove one of the Tribune Tower's trademark lanterns – hey, what's wrong with a bit of reciprocity and it would look great in my study – when the wife grabs me by the arm and hauls me off. No souvenir-hunting for me, I'm off to see the cousin-in-law's kitchen.

You'll be as disappointed as I was to find that the kitchen is a bit of a letdown. Cousin Helen has driven in to pick us up from a bar that I've just located – and made a mental note to return to later – and take us home for dinner. Home is what most Americans imagine homes to be, which is basically what it looks like on all those TV shows from the *Simpsons* to just about any suburban sitcom you can imagine: a nice house, with a nice double garage, on a chunk of manicured green grass lawn – which they perversely call a 'yard' – in a nice part of town.

The nice part of town in this case is Forest Park which is very nice indeed, to the extent that it calls itself a village, which is what nice parts of suburban London do too, if they can get away with it. And Helen is a nice woman with a nice husband – who produces some very nice and very welcome cold beer on our arrival – and a couple of nice kids. In fact she is that phenomenon, largely unknown to us: the 'soccer mom', which means a housewife who takes her daughters to play football. In Britain, of course – *Bend it Like Beckham* notwithstanding – this would be exceptional but over here it is normal. 'Soccer' is a girls' game. Never mind, they'll catch on one day. But don't hold your breath.

The trouble is that the nice kitchen – which I had had described to me in intricate detail as an absolute design classic – wasn't quite nice enough. It's gone. What had astonished her cousin so much was that Helen had been the not-so-proud possessor of an American kitchen circa 1950. Whereas any British housewife would of course be rightly horrified to have a British kitchen circa 1950, an American one was something else altogether. Not only had it had a refrigerator large enough to stand in – at a time when most people in Britain kept things cool by leaving them on the outside windowsill – but it had a built-in oven, something that has only made a serious impact on the British domestic scene in the past decade or so. Certainly not more than half a century ago. And it was pink! Bright puce pink. To die for.

Unfortunately the British, and wider European, craze for retro kitchenware that echoes classic American designs of the 1950s – we have just taken proud possession of a maroon 1950s-style American fridge freezer, made in 2007, in Slovenia – hasn't quite caught on in America itself. As far as Helen was concerned, her classic kitchen was an antique eyesore, and just months before we arrived, blissfully unaware of our enthusiasm for her dated household fittings, she had had the whole lot ripped out and replaced. With the smartest modern technology. But we all have that nowadays: chalk up another victim of globalisation. America used to represent a vision of our future; now it's just another flavour of today.

Next morning I have occasion to investigate another of those American icons that used to seem so futuristic and exotic until varieties of them opened next door to us: the drugstore. I first got acquainted with the concept in France, where they took to 'le drugstore' with some enthusiasm early on. I remember sitting in one on the Champs Elysées circa 1977 thinking what a very strange establishment it was that mixed chemist's, tobacconist's, corner shop and ice-cream parlour all in one.

Back then, of course, the French were still blissfully ignorant of what even they now call 'l'allowine'. Here in Chicago, the month-long run-up to Hallowe'en is already in full swing which is why going into a place that supposedly sells cures for ailments I find myself greeted by a death's head and a dangling life-size skeleton the precise putrid pale green colour of the stuff I'm trying to stop dribbling from my nose. It is one of the drawbacks about long train journeys that the carriages take on some of the characteristics of aircraft: they become a great social rendezvous point for germs, and over the previous 24 hours I reckon I've picked up at least one or two joyriders. In other words I had come to a drugstore to pick up some drugs, in the purely pharmaceutical sense.

Even more annoying than my runny nose, however, is an incipient sore throat that in my personal experience can presage something worse. What I want is Strepsils, or Tyrozets. But those brands appear to be unknown over here and I have no idea what the equivalent might be. As a result I'm standing there scanning the vast array of things vaguely intended to do the necessary job, but all of which seemed excessively medical, not to mention unnecessarily explicit in their discussion of symptoms.

'Do you think you want a "demulcent"?' the wife asks, with a note of humour in her voice which I'm not sure is inspired by the gruesomely technical name or just *Schadenfreude* at my predicament. I have absolutely no idea what a 'demulcent' might be or do, although I reluctantly admit the products advertised as combating 'mucus build-up' might be on my list, though I would rather not have been reminded of it in quite those words. What I really want is something vaguely medicinal-flavoured to suck that would have the same effect as in those old adverts where some bloke with a runny nose sucks a little square sweet and all of a sudden goes around demonstrating his wonderfully clear nasal passages by singing the brand name.

What I really did not want – just at this precise moment – is some of that good old, wholly genuine, completely spontaneous, endlessly irritating American enthusiasm for meeting strangers.

'You from England?' says the jovially smiling gent in blue blazer, red tie and slacks, the raised intonation implying a rhetorical question rather than a statement of the blindingly obvious after hearing me ask for cold remedies from an assistant.

'Yes, indeed. London,' I add, using the line of least resistance. It's not actually true, but most Americans have heard of it. Quite a few have even been there, although this is not always an advantage.

'I've been to London,' says the jolly moon-shaped face beaming beneficence upon me, while preventing me from seeing if there were any nasal decongestant lozenges behind him.

'Really,' I don't say. I have learnt that there is no point in encouraging them. But this bloke needs no encouragement.

'Yes,' he says, in response to the 'really' I hadn't uttered. 'Back in the late fifties,' which confirms my estimate of his age. 'I stayed just in front of Buckingham Palace.'

Now, it's not impossible, but even in the days of post-war belt-tightening I doubt very much if they erected tent hostels in either Green Park or St James's and if they did whether visiting Americans stayed in them.

'That's when I saw the queen,' he says, with the air of a magician producing Kylie Minogue from a beret, as if he somehow expects me to prostrate myself on the floor of a Chicago drugstore facing in the direction of Big Ben at the merest mention of Her Majesty.

'Oh, really,' I venture, in a way intended to suggest that if he wants to indulge his enthusiasm for the British monarchy in public I might not be the best audience.

'Yes indeed,' he continues, undismayed (unlike me). 'She was making an impromptu appearance. We were standing outside the gates, just as her car pulled out,' my genial, well-meaning Anglophile is drifting into happy memory mode, 'and she waved,' he says, displaying the pack of verucca pads clutched in his left hand, reinforcing my belief that other people's personal complaints should be kept on a "need to know" only basis.

'Not at me, well not directly,' he adds modestly. 'She was going,' he informs me sombrely, 'to lay flowers at the tomb of Winston Churchill in Westminster Abbey.'

Were I sadistic enough to scar an old man's crystallised memory – and at this stage I was tempted – I might have pointed out that HM would have been getting it seriously wrong in that case, as old Winnie was in fact buried not in the abbey but in the village churchyard at Bladon in Oxfordshire. But even more particularly because in the late 1950s he was still alive and very much kicking and would have loudly objected to being buried anywhere at all for another half dozen years.

Happily however, fate intervenes at this precise moment as my eyes light on a packet of Halls honey-menthol-eucalyptus lozenges – a familiar brand riding to the rescue like the 7th Cavalry in an 'Injun' ambush. Kemo Sabe, white man, I'm outta here. I head for the till, flashing him a broad smile of my typical rock garden British teeth, that I hope he might just possibly interpret as meaning my life had been enriched by our meeting. He waved back, looking genuinely as if his had. I felt like a shit, but sometimes you just can't take too much niceness.

And in any case, today's the day we've chosen to look up Chicago's legendary bad boys. Oddly Chicago city tourism officials make absolutely nothing of them, and yet they form much of the backdrop of what most tourists know of their city: the crime scenes. Yes, I know twenty-first-century Chicago may have one of the world's premier orchestras and some amazing ballerinas and operas and whatever. But if you're a tourist the image of a man in Chicago carrying a violin case doesn't suggest he's on his way to a Vivaldi recital. At least not in that Jimmy Cagney suit. Let's face it, the musical that's put Chicago back on every culture vulture's lips, isn't about the city's flourishing gay scene, or the annual Grant Park music festival, it's yet another hackneyed exploitation of the phoney glamour of the gangster age which it milks for every red – blood-soaked – nickel. And why the heck not?

Can it really be that the twenty-first-century city fathers are so afraid of a resurgence of their vibrant modern metropolis's violent past that there is absolutely nothing to commemorate one of its most famous events: the St Valentine's Day massacre? Mobster Al Capone's 1929 ruse to lure seven men from rival 'Bugsy' Moran's gang to a garage where his own hoods, dressed as police officers, tied them up and then riddled them with bullets, has not only been immortalised in the movies but become a minor part of modern mythology. People may try to make myths, but they make themselves, and it's a mug's game trying to ignore them. But that's what Chicago does. It took us hours wandering around North Side to locate two of the sights I absolutely wasn't going to leave Chicago without seeing. The first was – marginally – easier to locate than the second, but only with a map reference.

Between July 1933 and June 1934, John 'Jackrabbit' Dillinger robbed no fewer than 10 banks in Indiana and Illinois, escaped from an 'escape-proof' jail with a fake gun carved from soap, and earned himself a reputation – almost certainly unjustified – as a latter-day Robin Hood. On 22 July 1934, he decided to take in a gangster movie, *Manhattan Melodramas*, with his girlfriend Polly Hamilton and Anna Sage, a Romanian brothel keeper, in the Lincoln Park area of Chicago. But Sage had tipped off the FBI, an organisation whose growth was hugely abetted by the largely Chicago-based crime wave of the Prohibition years, and Dillinger was ambushed and shot dead outside the cinema. The Biograph, at 2433 Lincoln Avenue, with its curved light bulb-lined canopy, still exists, but having been shuttered up for years has only recently been restored, although as a theatre rather than a cinema.

At least the conservationists got there before it might have been pulled down, which was the fate of the site of another of Chicago's most celebrated gangland incidents, the S-M-C Cartage warehouse at 2122 North Clark Street, where on 14 February 1929 Al Capone orchestrated the gang killing that entered history as the St Valentine's Day massacre. Capone represented the South Side Outfit who for five years had been engaged in bloody warfare with Bugsy Moran's North Side Mob for control of the illegal trade in alcohol.

The day before, Capone arranged for a false tip to Moran that there was to be a consignment of whisky delivered to the warehouse the next morning. Moran himself was late but seven of his men were already there when what appeared to be two police officers appeared. The mobsters thought it was a phoney bust by police on their payroll, but when the 'police' opened the garage doors and let in two others in plain clothes they realised differently. Especially when the two newcomers produced Thompson sub-machine guns and cut down the seven in a hail of bullets against the warehouse wall. They then disappeared, leaving a local landlady to call the real police because of the noise of one of the dead men's dog howling. The officers who eventually did arrive found a scene of carnage that left them traumatised. Moran who had stopped for a coffee and dallied when he saw the phoney police arrive, immediately put the blame on Capone but the 'Napoleon of Crime' had the perfect alibi: he was in Florida at the time.

The building became a place of ghoulish pilgrimage – a bit like mine – for years afterwards, even when it was turned into a furniture warehouse in 1949. But in the 1960s, that decade of 'cultural revolution' even in the west, it was needlessly pulled down. Today it is merely a patch of grass which belongs to the next-door nursing home. There are trees planted, allegedly for each of those killed, but not so as you would notice. There are rumours that the site is haunted and that people have heard screams and the staccato rattle of machine-gun fire. But try as hard as I can all I hear on this warm afternoon is the traffic passing by and muzak from the Chicago Pizza bar opposite.

Today North Side Chicago is quiet, leafy, residential, with three- and four-storey houses in brick dating back to those violent times and before. In fact it is more like a sedate inner suburb of any British city than anything else I have encountered or am to encounter in America. It is also, I am glad to say, especially after a wearisome few hours street-tramping in search of what turned out inevitably to be less than riveting sights, perhaps the busiest area for bars in the whole of Chicago. Without knowing it, we have wandered into the heart of Wrigleyville.

That's the nickname for the whole heaving pub and restaurant district around North Clark Street in the immediate vicinity of Wrigley Field, the baseball park that is home to the Chicago Cubs, named in turn after William Wrigley Junior, the chewing gum magnate who owned the team in the 1920s. The baseball season, as I know, having just ended, however, everybody here is watching the football (American, that is), which is mostly college teams; the girl at the bar in the John Barleycorn explains, 'because the play isn't so perfect and that makes it more exciting'.

The beer is pretty perfect though, as even the wife agrees, as we tuck into a couple of frothy wheat beers and discuss when we might bump into one another again, which probably won't be for several weeks. She has meetings to go to, and I have a continent and more to cross. The John Barleycorn is a fine pub – and I use that word in the fullest, British sense of the word – an old Victorian palace of a place with high columns and a long dark mahogany bar, and a collection of odd artefacts brought back from around the globe by its former Dutch owner.

It was, fittingly enough, the favourite local of John Dillinger, who was famed for 'buying the house a round', which may well have gone some way towards building up his 'Robin Hood' reputation. During Prohibition or the previous decade the old saloon, like so many others, had been forced to close down. But like so many others, it only appeared to do so, becoming a Chinese laundry in appearance, while actually the basement was used to store barrels of booze which were served to customers in the apparently closed old saloon rooms upstairs. Nipping out to get the laundry done soon became a frequent habit for the people of Wrigleyville.

Even with endless college football on big screens in every direction, it's a fine place to while away a few hours as the afternoon slips into a gentle autumnal dusk. An early night is on the cards.

The wife has a dawn flight. And I have a date with Hiawatha.

CHICAGO TO MILWAUKEE

TRAIN: Hiawatha
FREQUENCY: 7 a day
DEPART CHICAGO, ILLINOIS: 10:20 a.m.

via
Glenview, IL
Sturtevant, Wisconsin
Milwaukee Airport, WI

ARRIVE MILWAUKEE, WISCONSIN: 11:49 a.m.
DURATION: 1 hour, 29 minutes
DISTANCE: 86 miles

7

Willkommen

THE TRADITIONAL SOUTH GERMAN *dirndl* dresses worn by the waitresses would have given it away but the big sign over the door, cut into the stone in elaborate Gothic lettering that says '*Willkommen*' was clear enough. As was the one over the mock half-timbered exit from the car park that said '*Auf Wiedersehen*'. If the majority of Milwaukee's original inhabitants had had their way, then Wisconsin's first city – founded two years before the state itself was incorporated into the union – would have been called something like *Mitschi-ganerhafen* or maybe *Neustettin*.

In fact Milwaukee was founded by a French Canadian called Solomon Juneau who set up a trading post on the edge of Lake Michigan at a place the local Indians called '*milioki*' – 'where the waters join'. By the 1830s the little settlement had become a mecca for immigrants from central and eastern Europe, fleeing the repression and unsettled aftermath of the Napoleonic wars. A substantial number came from Prussian Pomerania, today Poland's Baltic coast, but also from the rest of the then still fragmented German-speaking princedoms of central and eastern Europe along with Polish and Ukrainian neighbours.

I had pulled into Milwaukee a few hours earlier on board the long-distance commuter train from Chicago romantically named The Hiawatha, after the most famous of those local 'Indians', the second shortest trip – after the shunt from Niagara to Buffalo – that I would undertake on my 10,000 mile rail odyssey. But then I could hardly not stop off in a city renowned as one of America's prime brewing capitals. What made Milwaukee famous isn't going to get by without a chance of making a boozer out of me.

The first opportunity of the day is a late lunch at Mader's restaurant – which despite its obviously German heritage is pronounced English-style as 'made-err' rather than 'madder'. Mader's sits in the middle of the schizophrenically named 3rd Street Old World which is what Milwaukee folks call one of the few streets of pre-twentieth-century architecture they haven't pulled down yet. Already on my walk up here from the station I've noticed a disturbingly Buffalo-like tendency to knock things down and not replace them. I can't help wondering what it is you need to escape the bulldozers round here.

Whatever it takes, Mader's obviously has it. The place is almost a historic monument, a testimony to the one-time pulling power of the local German vote, as witnessed by visits from Presidents Truman, Kennedy and Reagan. The politicians competed with the stars of stage and screen to visit Mader's and pour a few 'steins' of lager down their necks to accompany a *Sauerbraten* or a *Schweineshaxe*. 'I have never enjoyed food as much as I have yours. Thanks for the fourth pork shank,' wrote Oliver Hardy, who had certainly dealt with a few in his time, on a menu card on display. Other memorabilia testify that Cary Grant was a fan, as was Boris Karloff.

The original bar, founded by 'Charles' – presumably Karl – Mader in 1902 was called, with less than a native's feel for the cadences of the English language, 'The Comfort'. But the old black-and-white photographs that line the walls next to those of movie stars, show that the original was a regular contemporary American bar, rather than the kitsch temple to faux nostalgic Teutonism that Mader's has since become. With its marquetry mosaics of Frederick the Great, a mediaeval knight and duellists lifted straight from *The Student Prince* musical, Mader's sums up America's 1950s need to re-sentimentalise its view of Germany.

Down the road there is a school named after one of Milwaukee's most famous daughters: the future Israeli prime minister Golda Meir, whose Yiddish-speaking family fled her native Kiev and the Russian Empire, for the new world and chose the Germanic community in Milwaukee as the place they would most fit in. Her father became a carpenter and her mother ran a grocery store while little Golda attended the Fourth Street School now named after her. It is a pertinent reminder of how integrated Jews were in most German communities before the rise of Hitler's crazed anti-Semitism. There were more than a few who had traumatically mixed feelings about what happened in the years 1933 to 1945, particularly the last four when many of them were called up to fight for their new country against the old one. The stigma of the First World War had no sooner been eradicated than here was Germany, the mother country – Fatherland, if you will – once again America's deadly enemy.

Boys named Schmidt, Gruber and Hagenbauer joined up willingly in the

US forces, even to the extent of deliberately mispronouncing their family names if they were called something like Wagner, to fight other boys with similar names, to whom they might even be distantly related. We can safely assume most of Milwaukee unquestionably wanted an American victory, certainly the Jewish population which lived still as integrated with the rest of the German community here as they had done before the rise of Hitler created a stigma and a segregation in the 'old country' that turned it into something they no longer recognised.

By the mid-1950s there was a need – obvious in the dated stereotypical decor of this place – to give Milwaukee's Americans of German descent something to cling to of their recently discredited culture. There is nothing phoney about the menu, though – the beef for the *Sauerbraten*, it explains, has been marinated for 10 days, while the pork shank that Hardy so loved and I order up as much in his honour as to assuage my own hunger is indeed a perfectly done example of the classic Bavarian *Haxe*.

Even my waitress seems more in the cynical European mould than the bright-eyed, bushy-tailed, tip-hungry American model, although I can't help wondering if that's perhaps because a middle-aged American woman doesn't take naturally to the puffed-up bosom and constricted waist of a *dirndl*. She does, however, do the traditional American 'server' thing of telling me her name – Maria – and I detect a distinct if faint hint of an accent. Genuine or put on for the tourists, I wonder, and as German is a language I speak, having been a correspondent in Berlin and Munich, I enquire, as politely as possible, '*Ob sie deutsch sprechen?*' Indeed she does. Almost like a native.

Almost. The odd fact is, she seems more disconcerted than delighted to be speaking her native tongue. She comes originally from Vienna, she tells me, but without the slightest trace of a sing-song Austrian drawl. It is as if her native language, which probably helped her get the job, has atrophied with lack of use. It might be a metaphor for the whole Mader's experience: the service is excellent, the food good, the Spaten beer imported from Munich one of my favourites, and served as well here as it is there, but there is something just ever so slightly sad about the place, something lost or gone missing. Like someone who claims to be a devotee of classical music having only Vivaldi's 'Four Seasons' on his hi-fi. Which just happens to be the background muzak in Maders.

The German heritage lingers here but modern America has mutated so much that today it is little more than skin deep. Sausage-skin deep. A few doors down from Mader's, the Old German Beer House displays signs for Munich's famous Hofbräu lager while across the road Ursinger's Famous Sausage Emporium is painted in the unmistakable white and baby-blue colours of Bavaria's state flag. Inside, shop assistants of fairly obviously non-Germanic origins – black and Hispanic – purvey *Bratwurst* and *Knacker* from spotless marble counters above which mosaic murals proclaim worthy American hygiene mottos such as *'Gibt Fleisch und Wurst dem Verderben nicht Preis, Kühlt ein sie in Nordpols Berge von Eis'** next to pictures of little Germanic gnomes doing just that: hauling their sausages and so on into caves of polar ice.

But the firm that sold 'Northpole' ice to the burghers of America's most German city has since gone the way of most of the big brewers who built the beer industry here – Miller, Schlitz, Pabst – have, save for Miller, died away or moved elsewhere. Way down the far north end of 3rd Street, where it no longer claims to be 'Old World' the great nineteenth-century Gothic castle that was once Josef Schlitz's Brewery, built in the pale yellow brick that gave Milwaukee its nickname of 'The Cream City', is either empty or in the process of conversion into loft apartments, or artisan workshops.

The departure of the big brewers ought to have left Milwaukee an empty husk of the place it used to be, as if the song were turned on its head. What made Milwaukee famous nearly made a loser out of the city when the big brewers moved away. There are parts of town where that impression is hard to avoid: great swathes of dereliction where hunks of what, had it remained, would no doubt be termed 'historic' downtown have been razed to the ground. Walking along Old World's streets grim vistas suddenly open out of vast empty areas – tomorrow's parking lots? – which would once have been vital inner city streetscape. At one point the sole structure surviving in a razed concrete expanse of maybe four acres is a four-storey building of little obvious exceptional architectural importance raised on jacks and then just left there, as if somebody forgot where they were meant to take it.

But things are not as bad as they might be – at least not yet. For one thing, Milwaukee has not wholly lost its heritage. Even with the decline of big brewing, beer remains an essential part of the city's culture, thanks to a new breed of microbrewers. I'm on my way now, footsore, slogging along the waterfront to find one of them, a typical example of the new wave of American beer makers, reassuringly – in this city – called Jim Klisch.

Lakefront Brewery was started in 1987 in the building of a former electric power plant on the banks of the Milwaukee River by Jim and his brother

---

*Don't let your meat and sausages go bad, keep them cold with Northpole ice blocks.

Russel, enthusiastic home-brewers, who had seen the microbrewing phenomenon take off in Oregon and Washington states on the west coast and saw no reason why they shouldn't emulate that success to bring craft beer-brewing back to Milwaukee.

'It's not as if brewing wasn't in the family,' Jim laughs over a glass of his frothing Cattail ale after a brief tour round their premises: 'Our grandfather used to drive a truck for Schlitz.' Cattail is designed to echo an English summer ale, though it is a little too carbonated to be exactly right. But from early tentative trials in the brewer's art, the brothers produce five regular beers plus another five seasonals, including a 'pumpkin' ale for Hallowe'en, which is now just going into brew: a classically American fusion of traditions, in this case from Germany and Ireland.

'Every one of our beers is produced according to the sixteenth-century German *Reinheitsgebot*,' he says proudly, pronouncing the "purity law" correctly. 'In other words, just water, hops and barley malt,' unlike most of the big US brewers, including those in Milwaukee, and notably their one remaining big boy – Miller – who long ago found it was cheaper to add rice.

Despite their German-sounding name the Klisch family were originally from the western Ukraine, he tells me. The authentic spelling should be Kliscze, but Milwaukee germanised it. 'Some of the cousins still spell it "Kliscz", with a "zee",' he explains. It is a reminder of just how young a country America still is, how relatively recently – in European terms – whole families reinvented themselves in a new world.

Disconcerted by my initial downbeat reaction to the bits of central Milaukee I've plodded through to reach his brewery, Jim gives me a few tips on bars to try out to 'get a feel for the real place'. Most of them are located within walking distance – though that wouldn't have occurred to him, on the other side of the river, scattered amid a neatly kept little neighbourhood of clapboard houses painted in shades from pale grey to dark green. Wolski's Bar on Pulaski Street, just in case I needed any reminding that there is a healthy dose of Slav in amongst Milwaukee's racial mix. With its green-painted weatherboards and red-painted shutters, Wolski's could be just another gingerbread house in a district full of them: this is the sort of homespun district that inspired Disneyland's Main Street USA; wooden family homes along leafy avenues with telephone lines strung between them. I sink a pint of Jim's Cream City Ale amid friendly local folk come in for a drink after work, one of whom, a large bloke called Herb, about my age, in a checked shirt and jeans supping a pint of Jim's ale at the bar, thinks I need to know a story about arguably Milwaukee's most famous resident, whose name, he says with a twinkle in his eye, is Gertie, suitably delaying his punchline: 'She's a duck.'

Or rather was. Gertie shuffled off her mortal coil more than 60 years ago, but he's right about me needing to know her story: it's one of those little tales of bathos, poignancy and sentimentality that make you simultaneously feel proud – and embarrassed – for humanity. It's what the *Daily Mail* would call – and probably did – a human interest story, which means it's mostly about an animal. The most significant thing about Gertie's story, however, is the date: April 1945, when the good burghers of Milwaukee were anticipating the day when they would be able to celebrate the return of their Hanses, Axels and Friedrichs from killing other Hanses, Axels and Friedrichs.

'There was this duck, see,' says Herb, leaning forward over his beer, 'and it had made a nest on one of the rotting wooden pilings next to Wisconsin Avenue Bridge. Downtown. And it had laid eggs. Now some people tried to throw stones at her to get her to move on, and that got folks angry. So they set up a guard to protect her. Then just as the ducklings were hatched, the war ended, and there was a big victory parade planned down Wisconsin Avenue. But when they got to the bridge, they stopped all the bands playing and everybody marched as quiet as they could – on tippy-toe like – so as not to disturb those little ducks. Thing is, see, in times like that, that little mother duck bringing up her family in peace was like a symbol of the way people wanted the world to be again.'

At one stage, it appears, they even pumped in several million gallons of water from the lake to push back an oil slick approaching Gertie and her brood, while a local fireman became a celebrity when he set out in a rowing boat with a net to rescue one of the ducklings that had fallen into the water from the nest before it could swim properly. Personally I had always thought ducklings could swim automatically, but I am not going to argue with Herb's story.

Eventually, he tells me, a safer solution for the proud mother and her young nestlings was found by Mr Gimbel, the owner of the town's biggest department store, who opened up one of his show windows that faced the riverside and moved Gertie and brood in until they were all old enough to be released in the city park. It's one of those stories that, as Herb says, needs its context to be understood. He's also surprised that I haven't heard of Mr Gimbel: 'He was the owner of Gimbels, started right here in Milwaukee, went on to be the biggest department store chain in the USA, bigger than Macy's. Gimbels was where they set that movie *Miracle on 34th Street*, and that recent load of rubbish that was supposed to be a remake or something, *Elf.* I leave him wondering at this European visitor's ignorance, but that's the thing about America, you learn something new here every day.*

The next thing I am about to learn is, surprisingly, that some of these small neighbourhood bars impose their own dress codes on customers. A bar on nearby Brady Street sports a notice over the door that strikes me as odd, but is my first indication of the subtle sartorial signals sent out in a society that pioneered 'dress down Friday' for office workers, and in general prides itself – outside the world of high fashion and big money – on an overwhelmingly casual attitude to clothing: 'Caps to be worn straight or back. No excessively baggy clothing!'

Now, the bit about baggy clothing, I get. It has to do with 'attitude', with built-in inverted commas. In Britain we're already familiar with the teen fashion that dictates young men should wear trousers that would fit a medium-sized and particularly well-hung hippopotamus, broad in the beam, enormously wide-legged and with a crotch hanging substantially below the normal human male's knee level. Despite being no paragon of sartorial style myself, I am, I'm afraid, in sympathy with the view that says if someone dresses like an ape, there's a fair chance they might act like one.

But the cap business throws me. The baseball cap may have become, after blue jeans, America's most successful sartorial export but more than a few foreigners who have tried eventually realise that often it simply makes them look silly. The most famous case is former British Conservative Party leader William Hague who wore one throughout the 2001 general election campaign, and possibly as a direct result came a cropper among an electorate who thought that being bald did not excuse a broad-vowelled Yorkshire man wearing American teen headgear.

In America, however, it's a different thing even for older men, especially when many of them are passionate baseball fans. People wearing it back to front is another matter, apart from the immediate impression that they've got their heads screwed on the wrong way round. Perhaps in the southern states, the reversed peak functions as a sunshade for the neck, like the flap dangling from a French Foreign Legionary's *képi*. A sort of 'baseball beau geste'. Whatever I may think, as the sign outside this particular pub makes clear, wearing your baseball cap backwards is now so common as to be almost orthodox.

---

*Gimbels, I have since learned, was closed down in the mid-1980s, but lives on in spirit in the chain it partly owned: Saks Fifth Avenue.

The only remaining sign of rebellion, therefore, it would appear, is to wear it sideways. Partly an evolution from the original northwest Seattle-specific 'grunge' fashion – which as I was to discover is as inspired as much by the weather as anything else – and partly an independent development among young east coast black kids, the sideways cap, in combination with the low-slung baggy trousers, and often matched with ski-jacket style top inflated to Michelin man proportions, mark the wearer out as the sort of person bar-keepers in Brady Street, Milwaukee – and elsewhere, I was to learn – do not want in their bar.

That is not to say they aren't broad-minded folk around here though. Sitting over a pale ale at the bar, I open a copy of a magazine I have come across before and not really paid any attention to: the *Onion*. A free weekly, the *Onion* purports to be over 150 years old and says it acquired its name because it was the only word its German immigrant founder Hermann Ulysses Zwiebel knew in English ('Zwiebel' is German for 'onion'). Happily this is not the average standard of its wit or it would only confirm that British stereotype of 'the German sense of humour'.

The *Onion*'s Milwaukee-German roots are genuine enough, though it goes back to just 1988 when it was founded by two students at the University of Madison-Wisconsin. Surprised by its own success, it has since gone national and has its HQ in Manhattan. But if surnames are anything to go by, the editorial team retains a fairly strong Germanic genetic element, including 'Schneider, Guterman, Dickkers, Reiss, Loew, Kornfeld, Klein, Stern and Ganz.'

With all due acknowledgement to the *Onion*, therefore, I offer a small sample from a much longer piece by Bonnie Nordstrum entitled 'I'm in an Open Relationship with The Lord', a scrumptious fusion of religious infatuation and the adolescent crush.

It all started when I was 16 and asked Jesus to enter my heart. It was incredible. He filled me up with His love. I'd never been redeemed before but with Jesus it felt so right ... For a while we were communing via the sacraments several times a week! And every night we spent what seemed like hours in long mutually satisfying sessions of prayer.

Soon the honeymoon period ended, however. Whenever I spoke to Him, He seemed distracted and distant ... Daily devotionals felt like we were just going through the motions. A few months later I made a potentially disastrous discovery: I found out I wasn't the only one He was sanctifying! ... The next Sunday I followed [Sally] to an unfamiliar church on the edge of town and just sat in my car for a while in disbelief. I finally walked up to the front door but before I could open it, I heard the unmistakable sounds of ecstatic praise coming from inside ... I'd caught Sally red-handed making a joyful noise unto my own special Lord.

I decided there and then to start experimenting outside the boundaries of traditional monotheistic worship... The Lord my God is a jealous God, and He didn't like the idea at first. He made it very clear that I should take no other God before Him, but he never mentioned anything about taking one after Him.

Not just funny, but clever. That's the thing about America, every time you start to get stuck on a stereotype, along comes its opposite. For every *Lion King* or *Bambi* there is a *Simpsons*, for every TV evangelist an episode of *South Park*. In a country where for a political candidate to say he or she was an atheist would be the kiss of death, and 'church' is still perceived as the pillar of most communities, the *Onion's* Bonnie Nordstrum had made me cry: Halleluja! Pennies from heaven.

It was early next morning that I was due to make my own pilgrimage to a place many Americans – and more than a few Britons – regard as a holy site. Especially if they are Hell's Angels. The Harley Davidson factory at Wauwatosa, The problem turns out to be that although Wauwatosa is billed as a 'suburb' of Milwaukee, they mean suburb in the American sense: the plant is 14 miles out of the centre of town. I'm not even a motorbike fan, but I have a friend who is – and keeps a Harley Davidson in his living room to the less than avid delight of his long-suffering wife – and I'd promised him that I'd at least get 'the lousy T-shirt'.

The tours are free before 1:00 p.m. each day which suits me fine as my train leaves mid-afternoon. All I have to do is work out how to get there and back on schedule and at a semi-reasonable price. That turns out to be just about manageable thanks to a taxi-driver called Khalid who's willing to cut a deal – another example of how immigration makes its way in waves through the taxi ranks: 10 years ago he'd have been a Russian called Boris. Americans are not good at seeing themselves from the point of view of the 'enemy', and even if they did, they might find it hard to accept that the best analogy is not the Klingon, but the Borg: their greatest weapon is not martial prowess but the power of assimilation.

The Harley Davidson tour isn't quite what I'd been expecting: big machinery and lots of noise and roaring engines, and maybe there is that somewhere else, but at Wauwatosa these days they make the Powertrain engines, and that is basically a job for semi-skilled production-line workers, sitting at little desks doing their bit as the next item of machinery is trundled in front of them hanging from a mechanical arm. I'm sure my motorbike mate Steve would have found it fascinating – he's the sort of bloke who finds making modifications to a computer motherboard fascinating – but I don't even know where to start asking questions. Instead I just stand there along with a group of about half a dozen American Harley fans, mostly middle-aged blokes with the sort of figure that suggests they're even more fond of the occasional beer than I am, with not dissimilar wives in tow, all kitted out in studded leathers emblazoned with trademark Harley motifs.

Not that even they have any more questions than I have for our guide, whose name is Karl. He tells us he came over from Mannheim, Germany, in the 1960s but he still speaks with an accent out of old British war movies. The Viennese waitress in Mader's notwithstanding, Karl's accent suggests 'Milvokee' even today might not be the place for German immigrants set on instant assimilation. He seems perfectly satisfied that he is giving the answers and that we are not asking the questions.

Khalid dumps me back downtown, still slightly mind-numbed from the engineering experience, only to realise that I've forgotten to buy the 'lousy T-shirt'. Sorry, Steve. But I've other things on my mind: food, for the first seriously long-distance leg of my journey, a 21-hour, nearly 1,200 mile overnight marathon into the heart of cowboy country where I have a rendezvous with some prehistoric Americans.

Down by the river there's an attractive beer bar, offering microbrews and a menu that could come from a Lederhosen theme park – 'chicken schnitzel, bratwurst soaked in beer, sauerkraut with sweet potatoes, pretzel pudding.' But even if experience suggests that Amtrak have a way to go before they make the trains run on time, I don't have time for the indulgence of a long lunch. Instead, I need to make closer acquaintance with another of the great German-Jewish-American traditions, the deli.

The deli may reach its apogee in New York City but it is Jimmy John's in Milwaukee where they tell novices how to order, literally, in a big poster on the wall before the counter, usefully entitled, with just a hint of, dare I say, Germanic efficiency: 'How to Order a Sandwich'.

1. Decide what you want.
2. Get your money ready, i.e. out of your pocket and unwadded.

3. Pick your bread and toppings.
4. Want onions and sauce? Say you want it 'loaded'.
5. Want hot chilli peppers? Say 'with pep'.
6. Say it loud and clear. We are not responsible for mumbled orders

That's telling 'em. But properly followed, I have to say, it works. Without the instructions I would have stood there mumbling and pointing at stuff for hours and still not have got the sandwich I wanted. Instead, I'm out again in two minutes flat with a salt beef, pickle, mustard and onion on rye sandwich that is the most impressive thing between two slices of bread that I've tasted until I hit – or get hit by – the New Orleans *muffuletta*. But that's another story. Equipped for the next stage of the journey, it's back to the station. There's half a continent to cross yet.

And then just as I cross the bridge, which I notice for the first time is on Wisconsin Avenue, I see something small and brown standing on a pillar, not just one but several of them, at intervals. And then it comes to me, and I can't help smiling: it's a statue, or rather a little series of bronzes: of a duck and ducklings. Herb wasn't kidding. I tug a respectful forelock to Gertie and her brood: *Auf Wiedersehen, Pet.*

MILWAUKEE TO MONTANA

TRAIN: Empire Builder
FREQUENCY: 1 a day
DEP. MILWAUKEE, WISCONSIN 3:55 p.m. (Central Time)

via
Columbus, WI
Portage, WI
Wisconsin Dells, WI
Tomah, WI
La Crosse, WI
Winona, Minnesota
Red Wing, MN
St. Paul-Minneapolis, MN
St. Cloud, MN
Staples, MN
Detroit Lakes, MN
Fargo, North Dakota
Grand Forks, ND
Devils Lake, ND
Rugby, ND
Minot, ND
Stanley, ND
Williston, ND
Wolf Point, Montana
Glasgow, MT

ARRIVE MALTA, MONTANA: 1:25 p.m. (Mountain Time)
DURATION: 21 hours, 30 minutes
DISTANCE: 1,191 miles

8

Big Sky

IT'S NEARLY 4:00 p.m. on a blustery, squally afternoon at the beginning of October when the Empire Builder bound for the west coast pulls into Milwaukee station and I catch my first glimpse of the Superliner rolling stock that is to be the new version of my home on wheels once we cross the Mississippi.

It's hard not to be impressed, at first glance. The main difference between American and European stations is that I am at ground level here. Instead of standing on a platform next to the train doors with the undercarriage on sunken tracks I am at ground level with the whole massive machinery of the locomotive rolling towards me. In consequence, and given that the trains out west are all double-decker, the vast piece of engineering shunting towards me appears intimidatingly massive. The great silver and blue stunted snout, splattered with the gory wreckage of a million flying insects, rears above my head as the engine rumbles past.

The lowest-level carriage doors open a foot or more off the ground to reveal steep steps up to the two-storey interior. This division between single and double-deckers is itself the result of American railroad history: the east coast lines had to fit into an existing infrastructure of eighteenth- and early nineteenth-century roads and bridges, none of which were built to accommodate a two-storey train passing underneath them. The land west of the Mississippi, in contrast, was conquered by the train, and the tarmac that followed had to fit in with the railroad, rather than vice versa. The tarmac may have won in the end but the railway carriages have been allowed to keep their stature.

Downstairs is primarily reserved for luggage, with special compartments for crew, the disabled and, underneath the viewing car, a bar that advertises cold beers and cocktails! I have the feeling I could be nipping downstairs quite often. Up above has attractions of a different sort: the same wide, comfortable reclining seats with a small pillow and blanket in Amtrak livery blue laid out on each one. The whole passenger area being at first-floor level means there is a surreal floating feel to the experience as we roll out of the urban landscape towards the prairies. Floating that is, until we hit the first stretch of seriously wonky track and get thrown physically from side to side and it becomes painfully obvious why Amtrak trains never go faster than 79 mph, even when they have a continent to cross. Hard to credit that in the 1930s the Hiawatha service between Chicago and Milwaukee was the fastest in the world with trains running regularly at over 100 mph. But keeping the right speed for track conditions is another of those vital jobs that is the priority of the conductor, in constant liaison with the engineer upfront in the cab. He also has another job: deciding where and when we're far enough ahead of schedule, he can declare the next stop to be a cigarette break, to the relief of both those crew and passengers starved of nicotine.

In a landscape like this driving a train must be as monotonous as ploughing a straight furrow down an endless empty motorway. The further west we go the more there is of nothing. Whole great achingly empty expanses of nothing but flat fields as we head across Wisconsin and into Minnesota as darkness falls and I decide it is time to explore the delights of the restaurant car. On first inspection it looks good news, with proper tablecloths, silverware and napkins, a far cry from the naff eat-at-your-seat airline-style, that most European trains, even the prestigious cross-channel Eurostar, have come to prefer. This is what I had hoped for: if you're going to cross a continent at the leisurely speed of 79 mph, then you might as well take the time to dine in style. Even the menu looks promising: seared catfish (with the option of 'blackened Cajun-style'), braised lamb shanks, roast chicken or an 'Angus' burger, not exactly Michelin-star but sound hearty old-fashioned railroad food. About an hour before the dining car opens the attendant comes through the coaches asking for reservations at time slots 15 minutes apart, telling us the dining car operates a strict 'social seating' policy, which means you get seated next to a fellow passenger. A stranger. In Britain trains are so overcrowded we each do everything we can to exclude our fellow passengers from our own little bubble. But then we are rarely cooped up with them for days at a time: it just feels like that.

My 'social seat' is opposite a middle–aged married couple called Ray and Chantal going home to Portland, Oregon from a visit to their daughter in Chicago. They'll be on this train for a full two days. They have four other kids, 'all over the place – Massachusetts, Idaho, Virginia'. Ray rolls back the sleeves on his red-and-black checked shirt and tells me they're planning to retire soon and buy a Dodge Durango and/or maybe a motor home (which might be what we call a caravan or possibly used to call a dormobile – we probably call it a motor home too these days) and go stay with them all in turn. I'm about to ask why they don't just stick to the train, when the spare seat next to me is taken by a man the size of two John Waynes, only skinny. He shakes hands all round with one of those wiry grips that you just know can bend branding irons and introduces himself as a rancher called Mike from somewhere in the midst of Dakota which we'll be getting to in the early hours of the morning.

Mike's arrival turns the conversation from kids and motor homes to more manly topics such as elk-skinning – he's cut up a few in his time – and the price of hay: he's just been down to Kansas to buy some. I ask him how big his ranch is and he reckons, 'I dunno for sure, 'bout 12,000 acres, I guess. You need at least 10,000 out here to scratch a living with a cattle herd.' These are figures beyond my imagination. I'd been thinking of maybe 1,000 or so at most. Twelve thousand seems about the size of Wales. (This of course is a British cliché, or rather an English one: when we want to suggest something is huge – but not really the size of a proper country. I have since found a website – www. sizeofwales.co.uk – which actually works it out, and 12,000 acres is just 0.002 per cent of the area of Wales which means Wales is really quite big after all; then again, the same website incidentally told me Montana in total is more than 18 times the size of Wales)

What I am really comparing with, of course, is the size of the average English farm which in my experience is something under 200 acres. This, however, is the cue for Mike to tell me a joke: 'There's these three ranchers sittin' in a bar in LA braggin' to each other and one says: "I got me a piece of land back in Texas, she's about 25,000 acres. And I call her Big Sky." The second rancher pushes back his hat and says, "I got me a piece of land back in Texas too. She's about 120,000 acres. I call her Enormous Sky." This third rancher, he's lookin' kind of smug. The other two look at him an' he says, "Well I got me a little piece o' land that I reckons better'n both o' them. She's about 40 acres." The first rancher looks at him and says with a look on his face, and what do you call that. The guy smiles back and says, "Downtown Houston".'

Actually the joke's as old as the hills – even I've heard it before – but we all three of us laugh as we're expected to, which makes Mike happy. Which is probably a good thing. Just then the waiter comes to take our order. Mike orders the catfish – unblackened. I opt for the lamb shank on the simple grounds that it is a dish that can easily be prepared in advance, prepackaged and quickly microwaved, which bitter experience has taught me is probably a safe option given the limited resources of a railway galley. The couple opposite both go for the chicken. When it comes to drinks I'm pleased to see there's a decentish selection of half-bottles of both red and white wine, even if I am mildly surprised to find they come from Chile rather than California (or even upstate New York), but a half-bottle of Cabernet Sauvignon should see off my lamb quite nicely. My choice gets a nod and a smile from the attendant, and from the couple opposite, and even a bit of a look from Mike, and then they order theirs:

'I'd like a glass of cold milk please,' says the woman opposite with a look on her face as if she'd just been awarded the best girl in Sunday school prize. Her husband nods and says, 'That'll do it for me too.' And then Mike puts his menu down on the table with a definitive thunk and says, 'Cold milk sounds real good to me too', and I'm left there feeling like I've just brought a half-gallon of whisky into a toddlers' birthday party. Milk? Milk! These are adults, for goodness sake, at dinnertime. And they're ordering up chilled bovine mammary fluid? With food!

When my little screw-top bottle arrives, for a nanosecond I feel a wave of semi-disapproving mock sympathy for the incorrigible alcoholic from my fellow diners, and then I pour a glass and take a sip and feel only deep satisfaction as I watch them wipe the smear of cold cow juice off their upper lips.

Only the arrival of the food mars my minor buzz of self-satisfaction: far from having been heated up in a microwave, my lamb shank looks as if it's been cooked in a proper oven – for about two and half weeks. Dry, hard, the meat leathern and stuck to the bone rather than succulent and falling from it. The chicken looks dull and dry, and the catfish alone – a long golden fillet – has the appearance of being approximately edible. Mike by now has been telling us all about cattle-keeping and deer-hunting and is just detailing the last time he skinned a stag – I have this vision of him ripping its belly open with his Bowie knife and then reaching back for a quick slug of semi-skimmed – when he suddenly looks at my plate and says:

'Say, just what part of the animal is that?'

'Uh, the lower leg,' I find it odd to be explaining to someone in the animal husbandry business.

'That right?' he says, still looking at it uncertainly enough to make me have second thoughts myself. It only gradually dawns on me that to Mike, the piece of meat on my plate is far too small to be part of a leg. He's a big animal man. Lamb in America is not exactly rare, but it's not real men's food. At least obviously not in the Dakotas. Right now, looking at the hard dry piece of carcass on my plate, I'm tempted to agree with him. But it's hot – or at least warm – and the baked potato with sour cream is good, and the wine is fine – or at any rate better than milk!

And some time in the last hour we've passed into the badlands of Dakota and somewhere out there, there are coyotes howling at the moon. And I order up a second small bottle of wine and head back to my seat, pull the blanket over my head and dream about joining them.

Morning brings breakfast downstairs in the bar, rather than the formality of the dining car. A bagel with cream cheese – for homesick New Yorkers – and damn near a pint of half-decent coffee which I take upstairs to the observation car to watch the early morning pink glow spreading across the ochre-tufted emptiness of western Dakota. This is not, however, quite as easy as it sounds, especially first thing in the morning after a night spent sleeping in even a relatively ample reclining armchair. The state of tracks maintained by companies who use them only to transport cargo is dire enough to cause sudden wobbles and even the occasional out and out lurch. You have to put this together with the fact that a substantial number of Amtrak's passengers are that proportion of the population everywhere in America euphemistically referred to as 'seniors'. This is almost certainly because they are the only ones who can afford the time it takes to get anywhere by train. But given that most Americans aren't exactly masters of the art of bipedal locomotion at the best of times, the result is that moving around the train can be a slow process of following people in check trousers or jogging pants with their names written on their baseball caps – this applies to both sexes – going 'Whoopsie' or 'Steady on, girl' and then flirting dangerously with suicide when it comes to negotiating the interconnection between carriages. The conductor – or one of his understudies – takes pains to issue frequent reminders to his charges to 'wear shoes at all times when moving about the train'; 'these carriages can go up and down a bit and we've had people lose toes between those steel plates'. He's not kidding, either.

The observation car is busy. Despite badly scuffed perspex windows that make photography difficult our height off the ground makes for splendid viewing, if you can call viewing nothing splendid, which – when there's enough of it – surprisingly you can. Gentle low hills of barren scrubland stretch as far as a horizon that seems impossibly distant and without the advent of the railroad might have remained all but uninhabited for another century. It's not exactly overpopulated now. My fellow travellers' attitudes towards the spectacularly empty landscape they are hurtling through varies between the obsessive – the few determined to have every second on their two-day voyage captured on video – and the dismissive. One group of Midwest matrons occupying a line of window seats all but ignores the dramatic landscape passing before them and sits there gossiping over their knitting: 'I only just learned to purl.' 'Really, I find it such a useful stitch. But plain knit's neat too.'

It is not as if all these people knew each other before they boarded the train. It's just that way middle-class Americans of a certain age have of meeting one another and within minutes sharing their life stories. In her book *The White Masai* (which I translated from the German) Swiss writer Corinne Hofmann described something similar among the Samburu people of Kenya: a genuine and sincere fascination with the lives, experiences and families of strangers from the same background, even though they have not the slightest interest in the 'world at large' which is beyond their grasp or experience. These women chatting and knitting would be shocked by the comparison even as they exchange endlessly detailed interrogations about family life, the whereabouts of sons, daughters and grandchildren they will never meet. It's a communality of lifestyle, mutual reassurance. A big village attitude that is surprisingly prevalent outside America's metropolises. You could hear a dozen life stories in a morning in the Empire Builder observation car; you just have to ask yourself if you want to.

The knitters glance up for little more than a second or two even when the broad sweep of the majestic Missouri comes into view. When Lewis and Clark first explored this area in 1805 in the attempt to find a passable route across the continent, it is easy to see how the river was not just the closest thing to a highway but virtually the only means of orientation. If they followed the river they had to be heading towards the continental divide that they hoped against hope lay ahead, despite having just sketchy information from friendly Indian tribes who themselves knew nothing beyond their raiding parties' farthest foray into the territory of other tribes.

This was Sioux country, and they were one of the tribes who early on had an idea these white people coming through might eventually prove not just a trading opportunity, but a serious nuisance. Happy enough at first to barter furs for guns like the other tribes, they also managed to demonstrate that they quickly learned how to use them, and were deadly shots with their traditional bow and arrow too. Both on the outward and return journey, Lewis and Clark's little group learned that if other tribes were friendly and at times indispensable, the Sioux on the whole were best avoided. This has naturally tended to give them a bad press down the years – although it has also served to make their name well remembered while those of their other more accommodating neighbours faded – but only because they were first to suspect that one day the strangers would no longer be just 'passing through'.

Those of us passing through now stretch to catch a glimpse of the little white picket fence that surrounds Fort Buford, just south of the tracks. Just beyond the confluence of the Missouri and Yellowstone rivers where Lewis and Clark were forced to make a brief diversion to find out which body of water to follow, Fort Buford was by the 1870s the army's frontline outpost in the Sioux wars and later provided protection for the railway builders. Seen from the passing train it seems tiny, far too insubstantial to have been important in the conquest of a continent. Yet it was here in 1881 that Sitting Bull handed over his Winchester .44 calibre rifle to Major D.H. Brotherton, and effectively ended the last major Native American resistance to the European invaders.

Half an hour down the line we cross Muddy Creek to pass the Fort Peck Indian Reservation just outside the nondescript little town of Culbertson. This is where Sitting Bull came to live out the rest of his life. He wasn't forced to leave his homelands, but he must have felt them visibly shrink around him.

When the train crosses the state line between North Dakota and Montana – invisible though it means adjusting watches back one hour as we move into Mountain Time – we are officially in 'Big Sky' country. This is no exaggeration. Rocky bluffs rear up on one side, then yield again to endless plains of wheat, and eventually back into scrubland and prairie. We pass the occasional homestead that looks just like you imagine a 'homestead' – as opposed to a home or even a house – ought to look: a rickety shack with peeling paint, a pickup and a couple of rusted indeterminate vehicle chassis outside, a few broken fences and a skinny horse nibbling at the stubble. Sort of the place Jed Clampett left before they discovered oil on his land – okay so that was down south and the land was a swamp – but you get the idea. You just know that if you got stranded there in the middle of the night, the folks would either welcome you with hominy grits and fiddle-playing until the small hours, or shoot you on sight and bury you in a shallow grave by the horse trough.

The reality, of course, is that these are descendants of nineteenth-century homesteaders who fled Europe in poverty, risked violent death and starvation to drag their families and few belongings out west because the government promised them ownership of any land they could work for long enough. The government may have kept its initial promise, but the land by and large did not. Little enough this far north is arable and most cattle ranchers today barely scrape a living. 'These towns up here are just dyin',' says Sue, a south Montana resident I would meet later that evening. 'Did you see some of those homesteads out there in the middle of the prairie? I mean who the hell ever said: Martha, stop the wagon here!'

And then all of a sudden, my wagon stops, as the scrubland gives way to a few low-level wooden houses, a couple of trailers and then a giant grain elevator towering over a couple of rusting freight trains, and a little grey-and-yellow painted clapboard station that announces my destination: Malta, Montana. Only two other people seem to share my enthusiasm.

I have decided to get off the train in Malta partly because this is pretty close to the geographical centre of the entire North American continent, partly because it seems about time to stretch my legs after 22 hours non-stop travel, partly because I am intrigued by the idea of naming a tiny town in the middle of an enormous land mass after a Mediterranean island. But primarily because even though Montana may not have many people nowadays – less than a million in an area more than one and a half times the size of the entire United Kingdom – it does have one of the world's biggest populations of dinosaurs. It seems to me that I ought at least to make an effort to get acquainted with the absolutely original native Americans.

Although almost nobody is getting on or off the train there are a few people hanging around the station. This doesn't immediately strike me as too unusual – I had already observed that in some of the smaller towns Amtrak goes through, even without stopping, sitting out to watch the train go by is considered a valid form of amusement. There is also of course the possibility that the two rather prim middle-aged ladies standing around indecisively really are about to board the Empire Builder themselves though neither has any luggage, and they look to me definitely the sort of ladies who travel with luggage.

It's only after a minute or so standing there by the side of dusty track looking up at the impressive steel grain elevators that are by far the most dominant element in an otherwise almost empty landscape that I seriously hesitate to call remotely urban, and wondering how far the motel I had booked for the night might be, that I hear one of them say, 'Mr MillAR?'

There's a tone of doubt in her voice probably because she's been expecting someone younger, or possibly someone older, but almost certainly someone more impressive, or at least vaguely respectable looking, rather than a dishevelled middle-aged bloke with a Guinness rucksack. But they're gracious enough to look modestly pleased when I confirm that that is indeed me.

I don't pronounce my name like that, and have never come across anyone who did – it being the common Northern Irish and Scottish form of 'Miller', and is there pronounced accordingly – except for my first boss as foreign editor at the *Daily Telegraph* who started out by stressing the last syllable disproportionately as if it were some unusual Anglo-French name that required a suitably aristocratic pronunciation. Actually I suspect my ancestors just ground flour.

As it happens, however, they have a concrete reason for mispronouncing my name: and after whooshing me off in an air-conditioned saloon all of 200 metres down the road to the Philips County Museum they introduce me to him. A large rangy beanpole of a man in his early sixties wearing jeans, a lumberjack's checked shirt and the inevitable baseball cap comes bounding up and greets me with a grip that would make a grizzly bear wince. His name is Jack MillAR, and he and his family have clearly pronounced it like that since they came out here with the original homesteading movement in the mid-nineteenth century. Yes, a fellow Millar's ancestors were among those who told Martha to stop the wagon.

The welcoming party is all thanks to the wonders of modern technology that has done miracles to bring places like Malta, Montana, into unexpectedly close contact with the rest of the planet. Only 15 years ago I would have found it almost impossible to find the telephone number of Philips County Museum – in fact I probably wouldn't even have been aware of its existence – but by now, thanks to the internet and email, I'm already on first-name terms with Sharon the curator. And Sharon in turn had got hold of the people I really wanted to see, inside the Judith River Dinosaur Field Station.

I had made a point of emailing in advance because I had noticed from their website that the field station usually closed up for the winter in early October. I had scarcely expected a trackside welcoming party as a result, but they are friendly folk out in Montana. Also they don't get many visitors. Which isn't too surprising when you consider the population is just 2,120, which makes it one of the biggest cities around. The next nearest settlements are more than 20 miles in either direction and have a population of 224 and 122 respectively. The nearest place of any size at all is Havre and that's more than 100 miles west and still has a population of just over 9,000. By any objective terminology Montana is virtually empty. And that's despite containing, on the face of it, some of the most famous place names in the world. Quite apart from Malta and what was originally Le Havre, you can also find Belgrade, Moscow, Zürich and Glasgow, not to mention the state capital, with a whopping 3,926 inhabitants, Helena, which was named after St Helena, Minnesota, which in turn had been named after the British south Atlantic island where Napoleon ended his days.

I've been waiting to ask somebody why Montana seemed so singularly blessed with the names of great cities or exotic places and Jack seems as good a choice as any. His answer is disappointingly mundane: 'This place was originally Siding 54. The trains had to stop somewhere to take on coal and water. When the rail company decided they wanted to give them proper names, they just spun an old globe of the world and poked it with a finger to make it stop, and that's the name you got.' I suppose I should have guessed.

They have enough civic pride though in Malta to have mustered together a collection of exotica to make their little museum actually worth a visit. It includes local Wild West memorabilia such as 'wanted' posters issued by Pinkerton's Detective Agency offering a $4,000 reward for the capture of 'George Parker alias Ingerfield and Harry Longbaugh alias Alonzo also known as Butch Cassidy and the Sundance Kid'. The photographs on display of this shady pair, with the kid in a pork-pie hat, make them look older and a lot less glamorous than Robert Redford and Paul Newman who would come to immortalise and romanticise them nearly 80 years later. Alongside is Harvey Logan, better known as 'Kid Curry', the other leading member of the Wild Bunch, aka the Hole-in-the-Wall Gang, named after a mountain pass hideout in Wyoming.

The train robbery in the film was based on the infamous heist the gang carried out at Exeter Creek just a dozen miles west of Malta on 3 July 1901. According to the legend Cassidy had been on the train since St Paul, Minnesota, his hat pulled low over his eyes to avoid being recognised from the wanted posters. Sundance boarded the train right here in Malta, also posing as a passenger, while 'Kid' Curry dropped silently onto the train from the water tower. As the train pulled away he produced a pair of six-guns and ordered the driver to stop where he told him. This was at an isolated spot near a bridge over the creek, where the rest of the gang materialised with getaway horses. Butch and Sundance kept the other passengers under control while Curry dynamited the safe. Just how much loot they escaped with remains a matter of legend ranging from $40,000 in unmarked dollar bills to as high as $65,000 though at least one rumour says the safe held nothing but government paperwork (which, of course, could be another way to describe dollar bills). Not least among the Malta museum's mementos of the occasion is a pistol said to have been used by Curry.

There are also two of the last authentic Indian headdresses or to give them the name the Indians used, 'war bonnets', even though they were never worn to war. These were made in the 1920s by 'Fish Guts' of the Assiniboine or Nakopa tribe living on the nearby Fort Belknap reservation. 'It then went to Herb Fish, son of Fish Guts, then to Jake Meyes (who probably paid for it) who then gave it to Walter Phillips in the 1930s'.

'Phillips' recollection was that the feathers of two eagles were required in making the war bonnet, and that in the Indian way of valuing things at the time: one eagle = one stallion = 25–30 mares.' There is also a note to say that the use of eagle feathers was banned in 1940 and that Herb Fish became a well-thought-of ranch hand. The end of a whole world reduced to a one-paragraph note in a provincial museum.

Next door to the museum is its biggest exhibit: a whole house. They insisted on taking me there. It was a wooden house, superficially not unlike a million other clapboard houses you see all over America. The thing about this one, they said with almost awe in their voices, is that it dated from 1900: 'Yessir,' said Jack, 'this here house is over one hundred years old.' This is the thing about much of America for us 'Yurpeans' – it all just came about yesterday. I didn't know how to tell them that I'd never owned any property younger. To have told them that most streets in much of London have no houses that modern would have seemed not only bad manners but possibly stretching their imagination. Then it would have been equally difficult to explain that what amazed me most about this house was not its antiquity, but its modernity.

H.G. Robinson, a New York schoolteacher who had fallen in love with the idea of the Wild West, brought it out here in 1900. Yes, brought it here, or rather the men from Sears, Roebuck did. Jack thought that was probably 'pretty normal'. I was standing there open-mouthed: just the fact that in America more than a century ago you could whistle up a whole house by mail order and have it delivered by the modern miracle of the railroad to the middle of nowhere. That's the difference: in Europe we're used to a lot of stuff having been in the same place for a long time – we call it roots and tradition – in America they're used to getting up and moving on, if that's what makes economic sense – nowadays they call it a flexible labour market.

Back in the main body of the museum, I'm meandering politely around the various cabinets of curios when I stumble across poignant evidence of Malta's own unearthed roots. Two glass cabinets held uniforms and family photographs of young men from Malta who had fought in America's – and often the world's – wars, from Flanders 1917 to Arnhem 1944, Korea and Vietnam. They, I assume, came back. In the front row is the dress uniform of Larry Schwarz who went to Vietnam in 1968 and was killed in action in 1969.

Next to it stands a large framed board containing dozens of photographs, each draped with a yellow ribbon. All of them are local lads who had served – or were still serving – in Iraq. I count 12 currently on duty there, including two brothers. A smattering of their surnames reflects the diversity of America's ethnic European mix: Simanton, Pekovitch, LaFond, Retan, Salsbery, Ereaux, Wilkes. A dozen at one time seems a disproportionately large number of sons in peril for a community of little over 2,000 souls, barely the size of my own village in Oxfordshire.

I mention this to the two ladies who had picked me up at the station, and they just smile wanly, smiles that express pride and pain in equal intensity. The war was something they didn't want to discuss. It was the first sign I had seen since leaving Ground Zero of the impact on America of its current global politics on the empire back home. It was not to be the last.

As it happened, however, there was another matter my two lady hosts were reluctant to discuss: the main reason for my getting off the train in Malta in the first place – the dinosaurs. They had one, downstairs, they were keen to tell me, although he turned out to be quite a small one as dinosaurs go, a mere 33 feet long, a brachylophosaurus, of which there were probably more hanging around here 65 million years ago than there are people now. He is famed for his 'pristine pelvis', Jack told me, indicating the bone in question, then added that that was why they called him 'Elvis'. At least no one was suggesting this one wasn't dead.

But interesting as old Elvis was, what I wanted to see was how they went about discovering dinosaur bones and unearthing them, the sort of stuff the experts did across the road, at the field station. This, however, seemed to produce a momentary embarrassment for the two ladies who had formed my welcoming committee. Normally, they said, there would be no problem whatsoever popping into the field station even when the actual dinosaur-digging season was over. Right now, however, in fact at this very moment, unexpectedly, today, there were people working in there.

Great, I say. All the better. I'd love to see palaeontologists doing their stuff, and in my experience enthusiasts of this nature are only too keen to strut said stuff before an audience. 'Uh, right, yes, of course,' says one, smiling nervously to her friend. 'Yes, indeed, well we'll have to see, won't we,' she replies, resolutely making no move to instigate that procedure, which I imagined might be done by a simple telephone call, or just walking across the road and tapping on the door. 'I know,' she suddenly says, 'why don't we get Jack to take you on a drive round to get your bearings and we'll see how they're getting on when you get back?'

I say, fine, if that's what we have to do and follow Jack out back to a monster Dodge pickup with a National Rifle Association sticker on the windscreen. I guess it's probably not a good idea to tease Jack about Barack Obama's attitudes to gun control, let alone Michael Moore's. I do ask him if he is in fact carrying a gun. He looks at me kind of surprised, as if thinking I mean does he have a Colt 45 strapped to his waist, and then says: 'Sure, I got me a shotgun and a couple of rifles back in there.' My look, I guess, suggests 'Why?' 'Hey, this is Montana,' he says. 'You never know.'

Jack's pickup is big and white and has seen better years. Only one in 10 cars on the streets of Malta isn't a pickup, and not one of them is the world's best-selling make, the Toyota. There are Dodges, Fords and GMC pickups but not one that wasn't made in America. People out here notice that sort of thing. He has a twinkle in his eye and as he clambers up into the truck and drives off past the field centre I can't help noticing that of the half dozen cars parked outside it, most were in fact police cars.

'Yeah, them gals didn't want you to know,' Jack chuckles. 'Think they thought it might have given ya the wrong impression. They've even got the feds involved.' Federal agents at a remote dinosaur research station in rural Montana? My curiosity was whetted. Surely it had to be Mulder and Scully. But Jack didn't know or wasn't telling. 'I'm not sure what the hell it's all about, but you hang about. We'll get it sorted and get you in there.' In the meantime I would have to struggle with my anticipation.

It doesn't take much to find a distraction, as we pass the ranch-style bunga-low – or perhaps out here that should be bungalow-style ranch – owned by one of the two well-to-do ladies, with endless acres of grassland prairies stretching to the horizon beyond it. 'That's where she keeps her buffalo herd,' says Jack in passing. 'Buffalo,' I catch him up short, 'you mean actual buffalo?' Those big hairy woolly mammoth-type things that once upon a time in the west roamed these here prairies in their millions until the advent of men with long-range rifles hunted them to the edge of extinction.

Yep, says Jack, the very same. Am I interested in seeing them? The thought had clearly never occurred to him. Was I ever? As far as I'm concerned, buffalo in the flesh, up close and personal, are better than any amount of dead dino-saurs. Mentally, I had already consigned the buffalo to the same department of the animal kingdom, i.e. ones that I had missed by having been born in the wrong century.

'Well, that's easy,' says Jack. 'Let's go,' and throws his huge 4x4 pickup with remarkable ease off the side of the road and onto a dirt track that led to what looked to me like a barbed wire fence with heavy-duty electrodes on top for good measure.

'Just need to open the gate,' he says, hopping out, much to my mystification because I can't see a gate.

Then I realised that that was because I had been expecting a version of the traditional English five-bar affair, with a latch at one end or at least a rope loop to throw over a fence post. I had briefly forgotten this was the Wild West. Within seconds Jack has lifted what looked to me like a fixed fence post out of the ground and moved it and the three attached by barbed wire, but not it turns out fixed in the ground, to one side. We drive through. I close the make-shift gate which is not as easy as Jack made it look because the loose fence posts pull the barbed wire down so it catches in my trousers, and head on up into the prairie.

And all of a sudden there they are: like something I've only ever seen in a Wild West painting, a herd – admittedly small, no more than a dozen or so beasts – of native American buffalo. The bulls are immediately recognis-able, their great shaggy heads seemingly way too large for even their powerful bodies. And yes, I know they should really be called bison, but that's not what the cowboys called them and cowboy country is where they come from in my mythology, and that's where we are right now. A bison is a creature in a zoo. A buffalo is an animal from the storybooks, found in its element on the great plains of America, and here I am right now staring at a herd of them.

'Hard to imagine, isn't it,' says Jack, 'the sight of millions of them things, as far as the eye can see, spread out across the plains?'

Jack is a hunter himself, like most folks around here – even the motels have signs that proclaim 'We welcome hunters' – but he shakes his head in rueful amazement at the wanton slaughter: 'They did it for the hides, of course. They'd come out first for the otter and when there wasn't much of that left, they took out the buffalo – also for their meat of course, it's rich and low-fat, probably healthier than beef,' he adds, just so I understand that even out here in Montana they are aware of the advantages of sensible eating. Then he adds: 'And of course, they really did it to drive out the Indians. When the buffalo were gone, the Indians went too.'

I do not know how extensive the process of politically correct re-education has been in the United States over the past few decades, but it strikes me here – as it did in Niagara – that there is a genuine feeling of melancholy regret amongst even the most hard-headed American men about the fate of the 'red-skins' they now refer to wholly naturally as 'Native Americans'. No suggestion of course that what's done could – or should – ever be undone, but a genuine feeling of sympathy for a group who got a 'rough deal' from history.

Maybe it comes from a love of the land that the settlers who pushed the natives to the brink of extinction nonetheless inherited from them. And passed on to their descendants. Men like Jack. 'I never knew what people used to mean when they talked about Montana as "big sky country",' says Jack, staring up at a bright blue canopy that extends in all directions to the scrubland of an infinitely distant horizon, 'but then I went east, and all of a sudden I found myself thinking: hey, what happened to the sky?

'You get people who've never been out on a ranch and they come out here and just love it, and then you get kids who've been raised on the ranch, and they can't wait to leave.' And I automatically think of the row of pictures of young men in uniform upstairs in the museum.

'There's not a whole heap for kids to do around here, I guess,' says Jack a little later as we share a beer and a pizza at a Formica table in a noisy little bar-cum-diner lit by fluorescent strips and with a jukebox in the corner. 'They have a racetrack out there,' he points to an area west of town, 'for hot rods. They do 'em up, take 'em out there and race 'em. You can hear 'em miles away when they do.'

I'm listening for the roar of motors above the jukebox when a dark-haired young woman comes up to our table. Jack introduces me to Sue, who is one of the palaeontologists who comes up to work in the field centre in the summer season. She too is cagey about our chances of getting in there today. 'It's kind of complicated,' she says, 'but Professor Bakker is in there working with them, and he says it'll all be finished today, so you can get in there for sure first thing tomorrow morning.'

Which seems as good a promise as I am going to get, as I part company with Jack and Sue with an arrangement to meet over breakfast. That leaves me, as it gets dark and the temperature drops alarmingly, to sample the uncertain delights of Malta's nightlife. Already at five o'clock with the light gone it feels as if the emptiness all around has closed in. There's a shift from the laid-back rural feel of the day to a more sporadic febrile night world. Pickups race around in the dark, kids in lit lock-ups play with welding tools, and outside the main garage sits a row of vintage 1940s Ford saloons, big and bulbous, the sort of thing you expect to see Humphrey Bogart climb out of. Most are rusted through. A signs says AUTOS FOR SALE. It's hard to know if it's a joke or just left there to decay alongside the merchandise.

This is the bedrock of America that George W. Bush has spent nearly a decade mining. For the kids who don't want to stay on the ranch, the army is the best ticket out of mid-Montana, an expenses-paid way to see the world, only to find that the world they see these days looks like the burnt-out barrios of Baghdad.

There is a yellow ribbon in the barred window of the Veterans of Foreign Wars Club, and a huge one in the side window of the Great Northern Hotel. The liquor store – next to the drug and alcohol dependency centre – has a sign by the door proclaiming 'God Bless Our Troops.' I have no idea how many of the good folks of Malta – and they seem to the casual visitor remarkably good folks indeed – support George Bush and his campaign in Iraq rather than the less complicated concept of 'our boys wherever they are'. It is a dilemma not unknown in Britain, but it's not a question I feel, as a foreigner – and make no mistake, even we Brits are very definitely foreigners out here – is overly wise to raise. You certainly wouldn't want to show disrespect to anyone wearing a yellow ribbon, even if nobody seems 100 per cent certain about its origin as a symbol.

I had – perhaps rather rashly – associated it with the rather naff 1973 pop hit for Tony Orlando and Dawn, 'Tie a Yellow Ribbon Round the Ole Oak Tree', about a convict looking for a sign his ex-girlfriend still wants him back. Hardly the most flattering of origins for a military symbol. It turns out, however, that the pop song in itself was derived from an earlier, oral, military tradition, though one popularly believed to relate to a much earlier 'pop' song, 'She Wears a Yeller Ribbon (For her Lover who is Fur [sic] Fur Away)', a US Army marching song from the First World War. The ribbon itself in popular tradition goes back to US cavalry uniform in the nineteenth century, though there is no evidence beyond its widespread adoption in Hollywood westerns. It may even have its origin in the yellow sash worn by Cromwell's Puritan troops in the English Civil War, translated to America by Protestant emigrants. What is for certain is that its symbolism became ingrained in the 1979 US Embassy Hostage Crisis in Teheran when the wife of the most senior diplomat being held tied one around the tree in her Maryland garden. Since then it has been ingrained into the American psyche as reflecting solidarity with its nationals in danger.

There's also a yellow ribbon behind the counter in The Stockman, which has a sign above it proclaiming this to be Montana's largest bar. The other sign puzzles me, however: the one that proclaims, 'Where the pavement ends and the West begins', until I realise that by 'pavement' they mean 'tarmac' – paved road, further emphasising the need for the missing dictionary. The Stockman has a large central floor space permanently cleared for the live country music played at weekends. Right now, on what I would still term an early Wednesday evening but seems already to be night in Montana it is deserted save for half a dozen men in baseball or cowboy hats. A sign above the bar says: 'Even a fish stays out of trouble if he keeps his mouth shut.' This seems good advice.

Despite the ludicrous pictures of fat John Prescott posing in an outfit given to him by a rich American businessman, there's something about cowboy hats worn *in situ* by men whose heads seem to fit them that makes me believe they might just possibly be packing a fully-functioning six-gun as well. I have to remember: this is America. Even back in relatively suburban Niagara Falls the casino asked customers not to bring firearms into the gaming rooms, reflecting the fact that they might actually be carrying them.

The local motel bar closes at 9:30 p.m. banishing even the men in cowboy hats to their rooms. I wander out into the street and try my luck in The Mint Bar and Casino – casino here meaning simply the presence of dollar-swallowing poker machines. Inside is a long bar with a long line of men in baseball caps drinking Bud Light from bottles while the seemingly never-ending ball game plays on a flat screen behind the bar.

I ask for a draught beer and get an insipid, pale and tasteless Bud Light. Seeing nobody looking much like conversation among the line of individuals necking bottles along the bar, I let the poker machine – is this becoming a dangerous addiction? – swallow three dollar bills in succession, and then decide to call it a night, wandering back out into temperatures that have now dropped to a decidedly chilly minus 2 C.

On the way back I notice only one of the local police cars is still outside the field station. Mulder and Scully have packed up for the night. The truth is out there. All I have to do is wake up and smell the coffee. I had no idea it would be in the company of an evangelist Texan in a Stetson.

9

Cretaceous Park

THE MAN WAITING for me over breakfast in the diner of the Great Northern Motel the next morning looks like Indiana Jones's eccentric grandfather. There are people whose larger-than-life reputations precede them, but often in the flesh fail to live up to expectations. Professor Robert 'Bob' Bakker is unquestionably not one of them.

He sets the tone of the day straight away by making a joke about my unkempt frizzy hairstyle. This is a bit forthright, but I'm sort of used to it. It's just a bit bizarre coming from a man with round John Lennon glasses, an unruly long white beard and a mane of greying hair swept back into a disorderly ponytail protruding from underneath a giant white cowboy hat. And then I spot the twinkle in his eyes. Bakker is sending out a challenge. I can tell we're going to get on like a house on fire. It's a question of who can take the heat longest.

Renowned as a polymath, eccentric and one of the great eminences of American palaeontology, Bob Bakker is one of the most quirky, inspiring, intelligent and eloquent companions anyone could have for an excursion into the wilderness of Montana.

He asks what I want for breakfast and while I study the menu trying to make out what the locals would have, he orders for me: coffee and bacon in an English muffin. It's a bit of a cliché, but grand, really. He probably has no idea how hard it is to get English muffins in England: the word nowadays routinely summons up what my mother would have called a fruit bun i.e. an American muffin. Bakker meanwhile reinforces his eccentricity by ordering his own particular start to the day: French toast and cold water.

Straight off, despite the prim embarrassment of my lady hosts at the museum yesterday, Bakker wastes no time in enlightening me to the real story behind the mysterious goings-on in the lab the day before. He had been in there with them, and obviously enjoying himself. Unfortunately not Mulder and

Scully as such but nonetheless a substantial detachment of local county, state and federal police finding their way around among bones that were considerably older than those they might normally have come across in detective work.

The criminal they were on the track of had been employed at the field station several months earlier. He was a felon okay, but not quite run of the mill: a rogue palaeontologist who had turned 'to the dark side' transforming his scientific calling into a nice little earner by pilfering bone specimens. It seems 'bad form' to me but hardly on a scale with grand larceny or art forgery. Which only goes to show how little I know; Bakker wastes no time in telling me. In fact, it seems, corruption in the arcane world of palaeontology has a lot in common with both. For example, a really good, rare bone specimen, could on the black market – I'd not until now really thought of there being a black market in dinosaur bones – be worth between $200,000 and $300,000.

Worse, the suspect was also believed to have been tinkering with classification to make a random piece of bone seem more interesting than it really was. In other words, by falsifying the background of where it was found – almost exactly like an artist forging a more famous signature on a painting – and then leaving it in place for several years, he could effectively authenticate its phoney provenance, thus boosting its value when it mysteriously disappeared to resurface on the black market. I was impressed. If the truth really was out there, it didn't stop someone tampering with it to make a quick buck.

For most of yesterday Bakker was going over boxes full of old bones, some still pending classification, trying to spot things that were obviously out of place. And, more importantly, things that might have gone missing. But now the 'feds' and their lesser accomplices have bagged their evidence – he's understandably not going to tell me what he fingered – and moved on. 'We'll see,' he murmurs with that same twinkle in his eye, now directed towards Sue, his fellow palaeontologist who has joined us. 'We'll see.'

Meanwhile I'm going to see inside my first ever dinosaur field station. And I can't hide a certain frisson. I've been up close to dinosaur bones before, of course. Who hasn't? I still remember my first childhood visit to London's Natural History Museum with its giant reconstructed diplodocus. But this is not just another plaster-cast dinosaur skeleton; this is the real thing. This is where they lived. These are the guys who dig them up. If they ever do get round to cloning them one day, it'll be somewhere like here they come to get the raw material. And you can't have watched *Jurassic Park* and tell me that's not cool.

But who – or possibly what – I want to know is/was Judith River. 'Eh?' goes Bakker. 'Oh. It's a river.' I look around, at the endless empty vista of rolling scrubland extending in every direction beyond the rusty grain elevator and the low-rise buildings of Malta. 'No, not here,' says Bakker, almost with irritation. 'Miles away, to the south.'

I look even more perplexed and Bakker heaves a sigh, realising at last that he is dealing with some sort of paleontological moron. Which I could have told him, if he'd asked.

'This – not this,' he waves a hand at the surrounding sparse scenery, 'but where the bones are found, is the Judith River Formation.'

'It's strata of land exposed down to the level of the Judith,' Sue steps in gently to explain, 'rock from the Cretaceous Period.' And then adds helpfully, although not in any real geological sense but because she has a better grasp of her audience, 'Just after the Jurassic?'

I nod at last. Just before asking, 'And Judith?'

'Ah,' says Bakker, beaming as he turns round to but in. 'Judith was the girl-friend of Meriwether Lewis. You have heard of Lewis and Clark?'

I smile sweetly.

'Well, she was the gal Lewis left behind, back in Virginia. Of course, after he got back she deserted him, which may have been one of the reasons he killed himself, but there you go!'

There we go indeed. For the next 10 minutes Bakker is suddenly rapt, like so many westerners by choice (he was born in New Jersey, but these days mostly lives in Texas), in that great story of adventure. It was Lewis and Clark, he tells me, who on Jefferson's orders collected the first large number of fossil specimens, even though they had no idea what they were, given that even the concept of prehistoric lizards was alien to men in an age when few suspected the world was more than a few thousand years old and all the work of an omnipotent God. This could lead us onto the recent revival of creationism and the concept of 'intelligent design' refuting evolution. Interestingly, for the moment Bakker chooses to skirt it.

'It was mostly clams and squid. In fact most palaeontology still is mostly clams and squid. And turtles. The history of life on earth is written in clams and turtles and squid,' he explains.

'Take Stonesfield slate for example, from Oxfordshire.' I turn to look him in the eye in astonishment. This is one of those coincidences you don't quite expect. Here I am in the middle of Montana and a venerable palaeontologist dressed in cowboy kit has just brought up the scarce traditional Cotswold roofing material that back home I am having immense difficulty sourcing for a small extension to my house.

'Well,' he booms, 'if you get 'em, take a good look at 'em. Just full of clams and squid. It was the Rev. Buckland back in 1822 who first identified them.'

'Take a look at this,' he says, opening the door to the field station and leading us in to a wide open-plan room – still reminiscent of its past as a tyre warehouse – filled with giant bones and what appear to be freshly dissected dinosaur body parts dominated by a hulking, apparently life-size reconstruction of a creature that looks disconcertingly like the unfortunate offspring of a match between a triceratops and George Lucas's gormless Jar Jar Binks.

For the moment, however, it is not the duck-billed dinosaur that Bakker is drawing my attention to, but a set of ancient black-and-white photographs on the wall: pictures of men with whiskers and dusty black suits and cowboy hats standing with horse-drawn carts next to dinosaur skeletons. His favourite is the improbably named Quaker minister Edward Drinker Cope: 'He came out in 1876, at the height of the Indian wars but just after the Battle of the Little Big Horn, because he reckoned the Indians would have other stuff to bother about.'

According to Bakker, whom I am beginning to suspect sneakingly sees himself in the tradition of these ancient pioneer palaeontologists – in every sense of both words – Cope was largely right. But he did have at least one potentially dangerous spot of Indian trouble. It happened in a quiet moment when Cope was sitting in a clearing and had chosen the moment to take out his top dental plate which had been troubling him to give it a polish. It was then that he spotted a fully-armed Nez Percé brave staring at him from the trees. Cope sat there transfixed for a moment until he realised that the Indian was trying to tell him something; after a moment he realised he wanted him to put his teeth back in and take them out again. This he duly did, reducing the Indian brave to hysterical laughter, only to be joined imminently by up to a dozen other braves who all started hilariously trying to see if they could take their own teeth in and out like the white man.

When Cope died he thoughtfully donated his body to the University of Philadelphia, a gift so appreciated by his successor fellow palaeontologists that, according to Bakker, 'A couple of years ago we took his skull on a posthumous sabbatical visiting every major dig site in the country.' At least nobody could say they weren't experienced in looking after old bones.

By now however, I can no longer keep my attention away from the remarkable reconstruction hanging from the roof, nor indeed the fossilised remains beneath him.

'Meet Leonardo,' says Sue, with all the enthusiastic pride of a western schoolma'am introducing her prize pupil. It's not so much the reconstruction she's proud of, though, as the original. Leonardo, she explains, is a 77-million-year-old brachylophosaurus, who just happens to be the most intact and well-preserved mummified dinosaur fossil in the world.

You don't often see a woman get quite as excited as Sue Frary about the contents of a 77-million-year-old dinosaur's lower intestine. But that may be simply because you don't often come across anybody, including most palaeontologists, who's ever seen them.

Back in 2002 a team of field researchers from the field station uncovered a find that remains one of the most remarkable prehistoric discoveries ever: the fossilised, mummified remains of a young adult brachylophosaurus.

Before you turn to your Palaeontology for Dummies handbook or point out that a brachylophosaurus is a bit obscure compared to those family favourites, the Tyrannosaurus Rex, brontosaurus (the long-necked ones) or even triceratops (the spiky-backed jobs whose rubber effigies are particularly beloved as a prodding weapon by toddlers), Sue is the first to admit that a 'brachy', despite being 22 feet (seven metres) long and weighing up to two tonnes, would be a bit dull in movie-makers' terms.

They weren't voracious man-eaters – not least because there were never any human beings contemporary with dinosaurs despite the most contorted creationist theories or Hollywood wishful thinking. Nor, as my description above implies, were they particularly cuddly, not even when rendered in rubber and reduced to manageable dimensions.

'Nope,' says Sue, 'in fact they were rather gangly, with long arms in relation to the rest of their body.' They were also strict vegetarians, living off the plants that grew along the shores of the huge inland ocean that once covered the central United States.

She points to a map on the wall, one of those maps that just draw you in: a map of North America that shows the continent divided into three great chunks: one an isolated chunk of north central Canada, the second a great slab of land from the east coast to the Midwest and then, separated by a great seaway stretching all the way from the Arctic Circle to what is now the Gulf of Mexico, the vast, land-fringed spine of the Rockies reaching down towards the Andes. 'This is what America looked like in the Cretaceous,' says Sue, matter-of-factly.

'With vegetarian dinosaurs foraging up the coast, and the meat-eaters following along after them, you could say this whole area was like a dinosaur highway.' In other words, a lot busier than it is today.

What is so special about the one particular brachylophosaurus that Sue and Bob Bakker are obsessed with is the condition he was found in: fossil-ised whole rather than just a set of bones. This means that eventually not just the contents of his stomach and intestines will be analysed but also whole organs, the first time human beings will have had any real first-hand knowl-edge – rather than just guesswork – about non-skeletal dinosaur physiology. The discovery of Leonardo in 2002 was a milestone in palaeontology because he is the first, mummified dinosaur to be discovered since the early twentieth century when techniques for investigating or preserving them were far more primitive.

In fact, Leonardo is the most important dinosaur find in the last hundred years. Since then, another mummy – of a hadrosaur – has been unearthed in Dakota. But Leonardo remains special. His name, though, Sue admits, has nothing to do with Da Vinci but with two young lovers who scrawled their names on nearby rocks in the middle of the First World War: 'Leonard Webb and Geneva Jordan 1917'. The 'o' – 'just sort of got added'.

Already Leonardo has been subjected to high intensity X-ray – which required the whole building to be evacuated 'and probably left every man in north Montana infertile' quips Bakker – by a team of Kodak specialists who flew in specially. Once the scientists have worked out the complicated logistics of moving him without vibration – 'he's mostly just sandstone, for heaven's sake,' explains Sue – the plans are to take him to Utah for a maximum CAT scan carried out at an Air Force utility more accustomed to analysing the innards of missile systems.*

What is most remarkable about his state of preservation is that indentations in the outer layer of sandstone clearly represent actual scales – about the size of an adult's little fingernail – covering his skin in the tail region. If the CAT scan works out as imagined, they might – just might – be able to discover what colour he was. Our conventional representation of most dinosaurs as green comes simply from the fact that we tend to think of most modern reptiles as green; the latter isn't actually true, so the former certainly isn't either:

'He might have been muddy brown. Or even yellow.'

Bob, she tells me quietly, to spare his blushes, was one of the first to oppose the old, once commonly-held perception of dinosaurs as sluggish, cold-blooded creatures, and suggest they might have been fast-moving bird-like animals. Where would Steven Spielberg have been without him? In fact, I later

---

*CAT scans carried out on site were used in July 2008 by the Ford motor company's parts protoyping system to make life-size models of Leonardo intended to tour the world.

learn, Bob was a key adviser in the making of *Jurassic Park*. Spielberg was so taken with Dr Robert T. Bakker that the bearded palaeontologist Dr Robert Burke was deliberately intended as an affectionate reference. Even if he did get eaten by a Tyrannosaurus. Come to think of it, Bakker might think that one hell of a way to go!

'Old Leonardo here was probably got by a meat-eater who then got distracted. What we're doing is reconstructing the circumstances of his death.'

'Sort of like CSI Montana, 70,000,000 BC,' I suggest.

'Yep, he's a vic!'

She points out thin lines and dots made as if with a fine chisel in the sandstone of the fossilised mummy: 'We've identified at least 20 types of fossilised pollens, in the upper stomach and intestines alone. A lot of conifers and magnolia. It's like having a diary of his last few days. We've also been able to find out more about his beak; it was made of keratin, pretty much like human fingernails.'

But what I want to know is how exactly they identify and then excavate a potential fossil site. Sue makes it sound remarkably simple, if perhaps a slightly more violent procedure than I had anticipated:

'First somebody finds a significant bone: part of a hip or something sticking out of the rock maybe part way down an escarpment. Then we try to identify it, dig a bit more round it, and then when we're convinced there's something there, they use dynamite – controlled – to blow off the top of the rock, then bulldozers to lower what's left. Then we map out roughly where we think the main bones are and start digging.'

At first they use pickaxes and shovels to break up and remove the rock and soil but then as the find begins to emerge, revert to tiny, woodworking-style awls, poking into the surrounding material and brushing away the debris, a long, slow, painstaking process, often augmented by enthusiastic amateurs in scheduled summer digs. Eventually, if a substantial skeleton emerges, they start to coat it in protective cloth and then cover that with plaster. After the top is covered, they begin to dig below until the skeleton rests on a sort of pedestal of the rock from which it has emerged, while the dig team starts the same protective process of applying cloths and plaster from below.

'You actually have to get in there and hold the plaster until it dries.' And finally when almost all of the skeleton has been excavated and covered, they 'flip it over, hoping that no bones get displaced', before hoisting it up with a crane onto a flat-bed truck for removal to the lab, in this case the field station.

'Hey,' says Bob Bakker, as if the idea just occurred to him. 'Maybe you'd like to ride on out to take a look at some of the sites.' My jaw drops – like that of a detached brachylophosaurus – and Bakker smiles, and disappears into an office to make a phone call. 'Just calling the Hammonds to clear it with them. It's their land,' he explains and then ushers us out with a, 'Let's all hop into Jack's rig.' And there he is standing outside with his big red truck and his guns in the back: good ol' Jack Millar is ready to take us dino-hunting.

It's about 10 miles out of town before we roll up off the tarmac onto the rough gravel ranch road, the big Dodge 4x4 rasping stones in a spray behind us as we bump along and then head off abruptly towards the edge of an abyss. Just before we reach it, Jack hits the brake and we come to a halt, breathless on the shore of a primeval sea. It takes Bob Bakker to make me see it. At first glance it looks like a brown and ochre moonscape, an endless canyon-like rocky plain to which rough scrub grass clings like stubble on a pockmarked face. Totally silent, with low cloud drifting in wisps below us. Surreal and savagely, primordially beautiful. To think this was once the tropical, lushly-foliaged shore of an ocean. In the distance there are tiny dark brown dots. Moving. I lift my camera and zoom in to find they are cattle, a dozen maybe at most, wandering separately from each other, picking their way across the mostly barren landscape, nibbling at whatever they can find. If they made a sound we are too far away to hear it. Now I realise why Mike, the rancher on the train, said you need at least 10,000 acres to scrape a living out here.

And then Bob is reaching out his arm pointing out the stratifications in the layers of rock that fall away beneath us. 'Come on,' he says, beckoning me to follow him as he bounds down the tufted rocky slope. 'You shouldn't just imagine it filled up with water,' says Bob as I scrabble after him. 'There's been all sorts of erosion, glaciers levelling off, smoothing down, landslips.' But by and large where the flat plains drop away Bob points out the easily distinguishable bands in the rock: 'That's bear paw,' he says, pointing out the thick dark, lower layers, named for the geology of the Bear Paw Mountains further west, Sue would later explain. 'All of that would have been near the bottom of the sea, and there, where it gets lighter, that's Judith River.' I know enough now to understand he doesn't mean the river itself, but a stratum of rock from the specific geological formation.

He takes me further, down steep slopes of soft clay-like soil and sand covered with tiny prickly cacti and clumps of the aromatic pale green sage that grows like a weed everywhere and makes up much of the scrub. 'Take a handful of that and stick it up your nose. Wonderful.' And it is. Before long, Bakker is scrabbling in the soil: 'Here, look at this, that's a bone,' and he hands me a tiny shard of red-yellow striated material that on inspection I have to agree does indeed look like an ancient bone. A few minutes later, he's found another one, larger this time. 'Here,' he says, pulling out something about the size of a big toe and rubbing the yellow-grey soil off it. 'That's another bone. You can have that one.' I look at him doubtfully for a moment, with memories of the black-and-white police cars and the feds going through the field stations's specimen boxes. And he shakes his head, and kicks at the soil and unearths a couple of small fossils which he bends down to examine: 'Squid, what did I tell you. Turtles and squid.' I realise that this is a man who knows – and would never jeopardise – anything remotely resembling a major find, who also knows that the land we are walking over is rich in the biological debris of a lost world, that is nowhere near as lost as most people imagine.

All of a sudden he surprises me by coming out with an unexpectedly cul-tured English accent, and then I burst into laughter as I realise Bob Bakker is doing an uncannily accurate impersonation of David Attenborough. He enjoys the BBC. Bakker the polymath is something of a fan of certain aspects of British culture – as indeed he is for aspects of Russian and Mongolian culture. He's excavated dinosaur specimens out there too. 'Ulaan Bataar's a great place, but it stinks,' he says in a sudden moment of heartfelt humanity. 'They're storing up a legacy of lung cancer and heart disease in all those coal-fired power stations they use. They can't even think 10 years into the future.'

His enthusiasms extend to the Michael Caine film *Zulu* about the siege of Rorke's Drift in South Africa, and the history of the event itself: 'Imagine 29 Welsh engineers singing "Men of Harlech" in the face of 6,000 Zulu warriors, as well as such quintessentially British institutions as Spike Milligan and *The Goon Show*.' Here I am on a crisp, cool sunny day staring out over thousands of square miles of vanished prehistoric ocean awash with dinosaur fossils next to a long-haired bearded man in a cowboy hat singing 'I'm walking backwards for Christmas across the Irish Sea.' Milligan would have loved it.

But Bob Bakker is not a fan of all things British. He has no time, for example, for Oxford University's celebrated Richard Dawkins, the biology professor tasked with popularising science and undoubtedly the country's most famous atheist: 'He's a loudmouth and an idiot. They use him to hammer God.'

Bakker is no atheist, in perhaps the same way that Einstein would never refute God. He collects religious concepts like he collects evidence of prehis-toric life, claiming a mixed history of 'Presbyterianism, the Church of England and Orthodox Judaism'. Which is quite a brew. But then Bakker belongs to that relatively widely represented school of science that disagrees with creationism chiefly because of the insistence on taking holy books literally rather than as offering metaphorical explanations.

'St Augustine collected fossils,' he says, picking one up from the earth and tracing the lines of some long-dead invertebrate in the sandstone. 'He was working on a way of explaining the stages of the creation, not in actual days but in eras. St Augustine was a very clever man,' he adds, in a way you know he means Richard Dawkins is not.

Bakker is working on a book dealing with a synthesis of Biblical Christian and Jewish theology, Darwinism and palaeontology. He does not see those concepts as contradicting one another in even the remotest terms. In his world view, intelligent people can see correlations between religion and science rather than the stark opposition he believes exists primarily in the limited imagination of fundamentalists on both sides. He would like to think his book will help rebuff the 'ridiculous' claims of creationists who purport to believe the earth is only 4,237 years old: 'Y'know that's a modern idea, not been around that long at all: the churches were amongst the earliest supporters of science.'

'What about Galileo?' I venture timidly, thinking of the Catholic Church's persecution of the great Renaissance Italian scientist. I might have expected Bakker's response:

'Yeah, Galileo was a jerk. He was right, but he was a jerk. What got him into trouble was he was a show-off. He annoyed people. A bit like Dawkins.' That, at least, is one analogy I know Dawkins could live with. I respect Dawkins but I can see where Bakker is coming from. If I were a TV producer with a brief to turn out more intellectual programmes for Channel 4, I would love to put these two head-to-head. There might not be a winner but it wouldn't half be colourful.

Set against the vast calendar of the ages spread out all around us, human life spans seem suddenly incredibly short, our time terribly constrained. Especially if you've got a train to catch. And I have. Amtrak waits for no man, even if it does frequently expect men and women to wait for it. We climb into the rig and head back for Malta halt.

We take a different route only to be jerked brutally back into twenty-first-century Montana as we pass by an outcrop of rock with even more spectacular views across the Cretaceous ocean – the reason we came this way – spoiled by dozens of tin cans littered across the slopes.

'Damn kids,' says Jack as he halts the rig and we climb down to briefly survey the marred landscape. The cans, I notice, have all got holes in them. 'Like I said, there's not much to do around here. They just drive out, have a few beers and shoot 'em up.' Malta's young men, maybe some of them back from Iraq, maybe some of them thinking about signing up, sitting out here, under the stars, in the face of a treasure trove of the earth's primordial history that to them must just look like an endless emptiness, hurling empty beer cans into the sky and firing holes in them with six-shooters.

'Guns,' says Bakker with what I think – but can't be sure – sounds like disapproval, and not just of the despoilation of the landscape.

'I always carry three rifles and a pistol in the rig,' says Jack, just a mite defensively, as we climb back in.

'Is that 'cause you're paranoid?' asks Sue, apparently genuinely.

'Hell no. You might get kidnapped,' he adds with a grin.

'Like by those wild men in Idaho?' says Sue. The neighbouring state has a reputation as a haven for white supremacist woodsmen militias.

'Oh no,' says Jack with a gesture that suggests anything Idaho can do, Montana can do better. 'We got some of our own.'

'How long did it take you last time you bought a gun, Jack?' asks Sue. And he laughs. 'Well, last time they did a full background check, so it took nearly 20 minutes. But if you have a criminal record or something, heck it can take – I dunno – maybe at least half an hour.'

Jack puts his foot down. My train is due, in theory at least, in just 20 minutes. The chances of it being on time are slight, but you can never tell. If I miss it, the next one is the same time tomorrow. And that would throw my whole itinerary for this section of the trip out at least by 24 hours. Outside the short distance commuter lines in New England and between Washington and New York there aren't many Amtrak trains more than once a day.

Given just how empty the roads are, though, I'm willing Jack on to go just a little bit faster than 55 mph.

'These roads can be a death trap,' he says.

'Why?' I wonder, staring out into the emptiness in both directions.

'Ice, elks, speed, people driving too fast just to see how fast they can go and then they find out – too fast, and drunks of course.' He nods towards a ditch beyond a curve in the road. 'There was a young girl got stuck in there. Lost half her butt. Imagine that. Entertaining as hell, sitting there with your butt burning. The grease'd only add to the flames. Mind you, she survived.'

'When I die,' says Sue genuinely, almost cheerfully, if a trifle obliquely, 'I'd like my ashes spread out here,' and she waves an arm back towards the vast fossil fields.

'Well,' says Bob, 'I guess we could do that, including your butt and all.'

'Right,' says Sue.

Back at Malta halt in the shadow of the great grain silo the track stretches forever into emptiness in the direction of Glasgow, and onwards towards the still invisible continental barrier of the Rockies.

The two ladies who greeted me are there to see me off. Like I said, not a lot happens in Malta. These days.

One looks at her watch and then at the other.

'Could have been a derailment,' she says.

The other smiles at me reassuringly and says:

'No. We haven't had a derailment in ages.'

I'm not as reassured as I might be, even when they explain they mean freight, not passenger.

Then the big blue-and-silver snub-nosed snake appears in the distance glinting in the afternoon sun and grows until it is bearing down on us, snorting and panting. I climb aboard and wave goodbye to Montana.

Ashes to ashes. Dust to dust. True grit.

MONTANA TO SPOKANE

TRAIN: Empire Builder
FREQUENCY: 1 a day
DEP. MALTA, MONTANA: 1:25 p.m. (Mountain Time)

via
Havre, MT
Shelby, MT
Cut Bank, MT
Browning, MT
East Glacier Park, MT
Essex, MT
West Glacier, MT
Whitefish, MT
Libby, MT
Sandpoint, Idaho

ARRIVE SPOKANE, WASHINGTON: 1:40 a.m. (Pacific Time)
DURATION: approx 13 hours, 15 minutes
DISTANCE: 600 miles

10

Bingo

YOU WILL HAVE GATHERED by now that taking the northerly land route across the vastness of continental America means travelling if not quite literally in the footsteps of the great Lewis and Clark then very much in their wake. Their exploration is one of the great American legends.

In this there are two breeds of modern American: those who are in awe of that epic pioneering journey and consider its hardships and sense of wondrous discovery at almost every moment. And those who never think of it at all.

Bob Bakker for example – and my cousin Barry, whom you will meet later – definitely belong to the first camp. And right now I was with them, as the Empire Builder rattled across western Montana, admiring the purple silhouette of what the train guide tells me is those same Bear Paw Mountains rising on the far horizon. If I were Bob Bakker would I be interested in the romance or the geology? Probably both.

The land belongs to the Fort Belknap Indian Reservation and somewhere out there Chief Joseph, last great leader of the Nez Percé Indians, finally took off his war bonnet in the face of the relentless advance of the homesteaders and surrendered to the US Army with the words: 'From where the sun now stands I will fight no more forever.'

A few miles further along I spotted a sign on the parallel highway that says simply 'Chinook 20'. Prior to my introduction to Lewis and Clark I might have suspected it was a road sign to a military helicopter plant, but I know now the Chinooks were the last tribal group of Indians the explorers encountered.

Ironically – given that their name is remembered primarily on fearsome weapons of war – the original Chinooks were peaceful river dwellers. In contrast to the many so-called 'primitive peoples' who bared their breasts, it was the Chinooks's custom to go naked from the waist down, literally without a stitch, in order to make it easier to hop in and out of canoes to catch fish. It was a habit that, you can imagine, caught the attention of Lewis and Clark's male-dominated party of explorers. The Chinooks, as it happened, were more than happy to share both their fish and their women with the white men. Unfortunately they knew nothing of syphilis.

I'm only just alert enough to catch a glimpse of the too easily missable small obelisk atop a low hill on the left, commemorating the point where Lewis and Clark were first forced to contemplate with grim foreboding the intimidating barrier of the snow-capped Rockies rising ahead of them.

Over the next hour we climb rapidly – far more rapidly than they could ever have contemplated marching on foot and dragging their canoes – up through ashes into conifers with a barbed wire fence on either side to keep grizzly bears off the tracks, as the distant mountains with their dirty snowy peaks grow closer in the darkening sky, and then finally rise dramatically all around us.

I wonder when we will pass the state line for our brief traverse of northern Idaho (and whether I should be watching out for white supremacist militia in jeeps planning to hijack the train). But by now the dusk has descended fully and the places we travel through, with exotic names such as Glacier Park and Whitefish – camping, fishing and hunting resorts – can be glimpsed only in the low glow of lights at wooden lodges.

There is at least one consolation: I can finally tear myself away from the observation car and escape the clutch of my fellow passengers who fall categorically into that other breed of Americans: the ones who probably don't know Lewis and Clark ever existed and couldn't care less because neither of them probably knew how to purl. Yes, dear reader, for much of the past six hours I had been forced to watch the majesty of the great American Northwest unfold in the company of the knitting ladies.

'Are you crocheting? Oh, I see, no, well you need to use two strands.'

'I've tried that. But now I usually use three.'

'I like crocheting too.'

'This isn't the same as crochet though.'

'Well, obviously not, But you know what I mean.'

From the moment I entered the observation car and cracked open a can of beer to watch the world go by, I had an acute sense of déjà vu, except that this time it was multiple: instead of a single pair of keen knitters, I was all but surrounded by half a dozen of them, a gaggle of grandmothers on God-only-knows-what-motivated transcontinental expedition, apparently intent not only on spending the next thousand miles or so knitting booties/scarves/woolly vests or whatever women of a certain age with more manual dexterity than brainpower do.

And what was worse, most of them were determined to discuss the intricacies of their craft incessantly all the way: 'You've dropped two stitches, if you go back on the left needle you can recatch them.'

The advent of night, therefore, is at least a blissful excuse to escape the world of knitwear and its fabrication and descend a flight of stairs to the altogether less scenic but much more intellectually stimulating world of the refreshment cabin, presided over by a man with a brain. And one to spare.

Rodney Pascoe, I found the rest of the train crew universally agreed, was wasted on Amtrak. One of these days he was going to make it big time as a stand-up comic. What Rodney wanted, however, I discover as he pours me a glass of Chilean Merlot, was to make it in the movies: at the very least as a scriptwriter.

He had already co-directed a couple of amateur shorts and was working on a whole raft of ideas. All he needed was a fairy godmother to pluck him out of the downstairs club car on the Empire Builder and take him to Hollywood. He was aware that at 40 time was not on his side.

The difference is that in Britain he would almost certainly be dismissed as a 'Walter Mitty' figure – a stereotype for a daydreamer that has improbably entered the language from a sentimental Danny Kaye movie – while here in the US his colleagues not only take him seriously but expect him to succeed. And I sincerely hope he does.

It's very easy to feel in modern Britain that the transatlantic cultural traffic has for decades been overwhelmingly one-way – witness 'Walter Mitty' – but there are exceptions, like Bob Bakker with David Attenborough.

Rod Pascoe's interests lay elsewhere but still had a surprisingly British dimension. On discovering I was from 'across the pond' he immediately declared his passion for perhaps the only serious British rival to the *Star Trek/ Star Wars*-dominated constellation of sci-fi cults: *Doctor Who*. He had latched onto the series via the doctor's least known incarnation – his comic book life after death (when the original long-running BBC series was finally cancelled) – and then, with the true devotion of a fan, seeking out videos of the most iconic of the original doctors, Tom Baker.

'Y'know, you look a bit like him,' he added, making an observation which had been made before, to the point where I admit that at university when the Baker doctor was a virtual student cult my wife-to-be crocheted (yes, she actually crocheted – but at least she spared me the technical details) a 13-foot multi-coloured scarf.

'Wow, man, that's awesome,' says Rod.

I feel obliged to point out that at five-foot-six, I am a good head – possibly even a foot – shorter than the real-life Baker, though also even with middle-aged spread, of rather less circumference than the once-and-future Time Lord has attained today.

But by then Rod is already enthusing about the doctor's latter-day reincarnation. I find it slightly weird that here we are on a train somewhere deep in the heart of the Rocky Mountains discussing whether Christopher Ecclestone or David Tennant made the better Doctor Who.

'I still miss Rose,' declares my wannabe Steven Spielberg, revealing an undreamt-of (by me) global audience for Billie Piper.

From there it's on to yet another British invention: Warhammer 5000. Rod is also a fan of the novelised versions of the futuristic tabletop war game played with little metal soldiers, which my sons and I at one stage would spend hours on Sunday afternoons painting. Look, I know this is sad, and the crocheting sorority among you will be laughing their heads off, but I only got into them because of the kids. I can almost see a broody look in Rod's eyes.

Over a second Merlot and in fairness now to the transatlantic spirit, I feel obliged to reveal a childhood and early teens brought up on a diet of Marvel Comics: *Spiderman*, *The Avengers*, and *Thor*, w-a-a-a-y before we thought Hollywood would ever get around to putting them on the big screen. This is Rod's opportunity to pass on a few tips on finding the off-the-wall reimagined versions of those classic superheroes: spin-offs even beyond the Dark Knight graphic novels that took Batman and company so far beyond the children's comic vision of their initial creators.

I try to offer something in return, appealing to both his fantasy world interest and offbeat sense of humour by encouraging him to seek out the lesser-known creations of *Hitchiker's Guide to the Galaxy* creator, Douglas Adams: Detective Dirk Gently and *The Long Dark Teatime of the Soul*, in which Nordic gods lurk among the exotic Victorian Gothic chimney stacks of London's St Pancras, which fortuitously leads us to the topic of the grand old station's magnificent restoration as the Eurostar terminal. Because, after all, Rod's obviously interested in the railways too. (Yes, yes, yes, I know. Get back to your crocheting!)

And then all too early it is the witching hour of 11:00 p.m. when, like British pubs in the bad old days (and an unfortunate number still), all Amtrak's onboard bar services close, and I take the remainder of my little bottle of Merlot and retreat to the half-world above where my fellow passengers grunt and snore like trolls hiding from the daylight, and sadly without the ability to travel instantly in time and space, I have another two and a half hours to go before Spokane.

By the time we clatter into the terminal, I am wishing I really did have super powers as I 'detrain' into a well-lit Amtrak station which for once happens to be in the city centre, only to find it faces an all-too-familiar landscape of empty parking lots and no taxis. And of course, my budget hotel is nowhere near. It turns out, inevitably, to be literally on the wrong side of the tracks, with no way of getting there other than to venture through a darkened underpass along a road with no footpath, past an encampment of hobos beneath an elevated highway. Happily the hobos are all asleep, huddled within their wagon train of shopping trolleys filled with black bags.

This is hardly the lap of luxury – the Quality Inn chain is about on a par with Econolodge (already booked up). But by the time I get there, anywhere well lit, warm and with a soft bed looks more than welcoming. Outside the metropolises budget price American hotel/motels offer a very considerable basic level of comfort indeed to the weary traveller. Sleep. And dreams of Spiderman knitting baby booties out of his web.

Next morning, the world, and Spokane in particular looks very different, at least to start with. The sun is out and even the hobos under the flyover look happy, up and animated, chatting to one another in a sunny patch out of the shadow of the elevated highway. One of them is on point duty with the begging cup and cardboard sign: 'Times are hard; anythin'll do', and if he doesn't seem overly grateful, he at least doesn't overtly sneer at the three quarters I hand him.

But then from a local perspective I soon realise he may be not so much ragged as almost stylish: check out that fleece cap with peak turned backwards, contrasting layers of fleece and checked shirt, baggy jeans – crotch almost down to the knee – and unkempt beard.

In early October it is easy to see how the fashion the rest of the world adopted as 'grunge' had its origins in the US Pacific Northwest. It's not hard to imagine it really began right here in Spokane rather than more sophisticated Seattle. Maybe the name of the better-known city just got attached, the way we say Dresden china for porcelain from Meissen, or Venetian glass for the delicate products of the nearby island of Murano.

With the wind turning a trifle nasty and the occasional spit of rain now falling from a deceptively blue sky, youngsters with baggy trousers, fleecy overshirts and hoods pulled up seem more sensible than silly. And here if you're under 21 the skateboard is less a performance device for pulling acrobatic stunts, as a means of locomotion along the pavements between parking lots.

Spokane's big moment – the 15 minutes of fame Andy Warhol would have recognised – came 35 years ago, in 1974, when it somehow or other managed to land one of those nebulous events that used to be known as World Expositions. A sort of mix of trade fair and national showing-off, the '74 event – as witnessed by the little hexagonal concrete markers in today's Riverfront Park – was dedicated to 'Tomorrow's Fresh New Environment', which in today's ecologically threatened world might sound either poignant, ironic or just another example of the way we keep deluding ourselves we're doing something.

Personally, I opt for the last interpretation, particularly here in a town where, depressingly like Buffalo, you could walk everywhere but nobody does. Forty per cent of vehicles, even in this most urban area of inland Washington State, are huge suvs with the carbon footprint of a giant Jeremy Clarkson. Run on coal

Of the World Expo '74 only the US pavilion – inevitably – remains, and that, I fear, is rather a mistake, sitting there with only the skeletal framework of its roof remaining, like an inverted steel basketball net, while the body is a ruin in the making of slowly crumbling concrete. But then Spokane's construction record has not always been everything the city fathers expected.

The highlight of the city is – or rather ought to be – the great gorge of the Spokane Falls, a natural cataract that once roared and tumbled its way through the great grey rocks that struggled to contain it. A first bridge built in the late nineteenth century – I automatically think of the improbable structure erected each year at Niagara – was allegedly a rickety wooden affair which records from the time say felt a bit like a see-saw. It was replaced with a metal bridge which proved little better and public clamour at the dawn of the twentieth century forced the authorities to knock heads together and get a modern concrete one erected.

Completed in 1911, this massive structure with its bison-skull ornamentation was a major source of civic pride, the sort of thing Spokane, which claimed the grandiose title 'Monarch of the Inland Empire' and was celebrating its heyday as a major railway hub, desperately needed to boost civic pride. The Monroe Street Bridge's river-spanning central arch was, at 281 feet, the widest in the United States – one foot wider than the one in Cleveland. The architects insisted that they had not extended it an extra 12 inches deliberately. The city fathers beamed: 'Of course not'.

Mayor W.J. Hindley declared, 'This bridge should stand as long as some of those bridges built by the Romans which are still as good as the day they were built.' Within less than a single century – rather less than his millennial aspirations – the bridge had been so shaken by the elements and traffic growth that it needed almost total rebuilding *in situ* at a cost of some $18 million. Meanwhile a damn and controls on the water flow to maximise electricity generation have reduced the torrent to a trickle. Maybe some days it's better than this but standing looking over the edge of the overblown bridge at the regulated water passing over the weir by the big redbrick Washington Water Power building, it all seems a bit vainglorious.

For the 1974 fair they built a 'unique attraction', a cable car that ran downhill across the face of the falls. It has been replaced by a relatively modern (1992) ski resort-style gondola system, but there are few takers for the ride that is less than breathtaking when the water flow is so reduced to the extent that the thin stream of water disconsolately trailing down the rocks opposite looks more like an embarrassing leak than a force of nature. Niagara will not be panicking any time soon.

But there's more to Spokane than diminished railways, depleted cataracts and crumbling concrete: the home of its most famous son, one Harry Lillis Crosby Jr, who would come to be known to his friends and virtually the entire planet as 'Bing'.

Spokane gets leafier and less grimy as I stroll along the riverbanks towards what is undoubtedly the city's most splendid institution, the improbably named Gonzaga University. The name's origin lies not, as I initially suspected – as in the case of so many of the odder names across America – in some Native American tribe, but for Aloysius Gonzaga, a first-century Italian martyr and saint.

Gonzaga was founded in 1887 as a school for pioneer children by the Rev. Joseph Cataldo, a Jesuit priest who had come to undo the mischief perpetrated by Protestant missionaries among the fur trappers and Spokane 'children of the sun' Indians ever since the trading post was established just 16 years earlier. It was still in its academic infancy when its most famous son was born only 16 years later.

Young Harry Lillis Crosby, named after his father, was born into a prosperous middle-class family who had bought a spacious four-bedroom home on land set aside by the Jesuits from their original 350-acre land grant. The specification was that property should be sold only to good Catholic families, thereby creating an area of Spokane that came to be known as 'Little Vatican'. It is still the most exclusive part of town.

The university sprawls, in the nicest possible way, along the banks of the river, all red brick and low-rise with respectable-looking kids in jeans and sneakers hurrying along carrying books. The building I'm looking for isn't hard to find – it's now the student union. But not many of the kids piling through the doors to check on gig dates, sports events and upcoming Hallowe'en parties seem to notice any correlation between the word C-R-O-S-B-Y spelt out in big letters on the terracotta marble entrance and the bronze statue nearby of a genial-looking cove in a soft hat with one hand in his pocket and a bag of golf clubs by his feet. I'm willing to bet their university's most famous son doesn't feature on many of the iPods plugged into every other set of ears.

Despite being a full generation older than most of them, I sort of know how they feel. Crosby was an absolute American icon in his day, but his day wasn't mine either; it was my mother's. She used to love him. To me he was just the rather laid-back pipe-puffing straight guy in those old black-and-white 'road' movies with Bob Hope, the funny man, who sounded all-American but we were all told really came from England.

The worst thing about Crosby in those movies was that every now and then he would burst into song, in that strange warbling style that I came to learn was called crooning. If he didn't invent it, he was certainly its master. Crosby inspired the young Frank Sinatra, even if he did lack the same important Italian connections. For Britons in the immediate post-Second World War days, Crosby, with his golf clubs and pipe attended by girls whose hair never fell out of place even when rolling along in an open-top car (largely because the car was stationary and the landscape on a screen rolling along behind them), summed up the seductive 'American way of life': Anglo-Saxon, easy-going, open-hearted, and above all affluent.

Only two of his songs stuck with me: the cheesy 'White Christmas', repeated every year in the seasonal medley of high street stores, and, slightly more bizarrely, a 1950s advert: 'I'm goin' well, I'm goin' swell, I'm goin' well on Shell, Shell, Shell.' The open top, the open road. The soft-sell American dream that seduced the world, and Britain in particular.

Just inside the door of the Crosby Building is Bing's own personal shrine. He was never actually a 'college student' in the modern sense, but attended the High School element of what was then only developing into a university. But he never forgot his formative years. In 1957, by which time he had been a popular idol and movie star for nearly a quarter of a century, he and his brother Larry, who was also his manager, decided to donate a few knick-knacks to the old 'alma mater'.

I'm just coming to grips with the collection of trophies, awards and memorabilia on display in the little room off the foyer, when two female students come in. One of them, with a sapphire stud in her nose, is showing round a visiting friend. I'm rather touched at this passed-on pride in the famous old boy, until she turns to her mate and says: 'It's kinda weird. I've never really seen anyone in here. I mean, like, Bing Crosby?! Whatever!'

The exhibits, however, are a source of amusement as well as mystification. The pair burst into giggles at one showcase. As they move on to the next one I can see why. It contains an extraordinary piece of apparatus which the board beside it says is a 1955 'Delta Stereo 3D Camera', complete with 10 spare flashbulbs, each about as big as my thumb, and a box emblazoned with a photo of Bing and the endorsement of the 'Crosby Research Institute'. Bing, it would appear, liked to be known as an advocate of scientific advance.

Amidst the collection of Crosby recordings in different formats – his oeuvre spans the gap from 78 rpm to DVD – the two girls' eyes hit on the Christmas single 'Peace on Earth/ Little Drummer Boy' by the unlikely pairing of Bing and Bowie, which the plaque says was recorded in 1977 for Bing Crosby's *Merrie Olde Christmas*. I'd forgotten about that one, despite being a Bowie fan. It always seemed a bit too weird, Bowie's high-pitched 'Peace on Earth, can it be' soaring up and down while the old guy next to him hummed 'Ba-rum-pa-pum-pum'. Bowie later said he appeared on the show 'because my mother liked him'. It proved to be one of the last things Crosby ever did: it was recorded in September and he dropped dead on a golf course a month later.

'Wow!' the girls chorus. 'That might be cool.' At least they have heard of Bowie (that freaky English bloke their parents used to like). And then, whether on a timer or triggered by some hidden sensor that registers the presence of three or more people in the room, a quiet crooning of vintage Bing oozes softly from concealed loudspeakers. It's bizarrely at this point that another young woman dashes in for about two seconds, says, 'Hey, there's no music, I'm like totally depressed,' and leaves.

An older passer-by – parent, grandparent? it is the beginning of term – stops outside for a moment to peer in the window, but finds it hard to see through the paint calling for 'team applications for *College Bowl*' (the US version and original of *University Challenge*), and wanders in, his eyes suddenly beaming with appreciation.

Yet for any true Crosby fan the contents of this little room represent a serious cornucopia. And it's just the tip of the iceberg. The few bits and pieces donated by Bing and his brother, the founding stones of what Stefanie Plowman, curator of the Crosby Collection, later tells me could be considered 'Bing's Presidential Library'. Only the most visually interesting objects are on display here. There are thousands of artefacts, mostly papers and fragile vinyl recordings stored in vaults upstairs.

What anyone would want to see, however, is here. Encased behind glass are two of Bing's favourite pipes and, slowly yielding to time, the silver-sleeved feather that was the favourite of the decorations he wore in his trilby hats. There are photographs of Bing in 1944 in France with General Patton, just days before he began his attack on Metz; Bing in more peaceable times playing golf at Gleneagles in Scotland, with Sean Connery and racing driver Jackie Stewart. There is a winner's 'genuine replica' of the Oscar he was awarded for 'best actor' in 1944 portraying Father O'Malley in *Going My Way* (the original remains with his widow Kathryn), a role he reprised in 1946 for *The Bells of St Mary's*, both awarded blue ribbons as suitable for the whole family.

Not only are there most of Bing's Decca gold discs for those timeless classics my own parents adored – although when I look a bit more closely I wonder if I ever did hear 'The Whiffenpoof Song' or the highly unCrosbyeseque-sounding 'Pistol Packin' Mama'. And I have to cringe at the well-buried memories suddenly conjured up by his Irish phase: McNamara's Band or Too-Ra-Loo-Ra-Loo-Ra. Dreadful stage-Irish jollity and weepy-eyed sentimentality put enthusiastically on the gramophone at family parties even into the early 1960s.

Then there is, of course, the 'platinum' disc for the one Bing record none of us I fear will ever be able to ignore – unborn generations beware: 'White Christmas'. It is dedicated by the Hollywood Chamber of Commerce in 1960 to 'the first citizen of the recording industry whose unparalleled sales of more than 200 million records is greatly responsible for the recording business becoming one of America's great industries.' God alone knows what its inclusion on every Christmas collection ever since has added, but just a decade later it looked to have been swamped by over 300 million sales which won Bing a platinum for his version of 'Silent Night'. Those mark the zenith of the Bing Crosby phenomenon that had already gone global a quarter century earlier when at least 15 million American radio listeners voted him, according to the award shield, the 'World's Most Popular Living Person'.

It is hard to estimate how that compares with the trophy next to it, the Donnyflakes Donuts Award 1949 for the 'Radio Star Whose Face Is Most

Conducive to Dunking'. I can only suppose it meant listening to him encouraged one to sit back and enjoy a doughnut dipped in coffee, rather than looking at him made you want to plunge his smiling countenance into a hot latte. All the same, that reference to 'face' in an audio medium is puzzling.

But then Bing obviously enjoyed a cup of coffee himself. To prove it there is another branded product, 'Rancher Crosby's Coffee Tap' 'tested and approved by the Crosby Research Institute for dispensing coffee from a can'. And marketed by a picture on the packet of 'Rancher Crosby' himself in Western mode with cowboy hat and bandana,

So just what was this Crosby Institute? According to the official blurb, what began as the Crosby Research Foundation was Bing's prescient 1940 attempt to do his bit for the coming conflict by subsidising resources to help the military develop the products they required. The museum provides no more information, perhaps for reasons of national security, so whether or not the Crosby Foundation was part of the Manhattan Project – the Bing Bang? – we may never know.

Back in peacetime their efforts extended to almost everything, or at least everything that might sell better if Bing-branded, including the better mousetrap, or at least the 'better built mousetrap', a sturdy stainless-steel construction from the Gerrity-Michigan corporation that looked like it might survive decapitation of more unwanted rodents than most.

For those of us who thought celebrity marketing was a relatively modern phenomenon, it turns out the Beckhams have nothing on Bing when it comes to pushing the brand. Perhaps I should have known, given the way that the 'Shell, Shell, Shell' song stuck, but I had not anticipated Valley Farm Bing Crosby Ice Cream (empty packet on display), a Bing-badged record cleaner, Bing Crosby Pepsodent toothpaste complete with the man's glinting smile on the packet (full five-ounce tube) – Bing's King Values 10 cents off!

Then there's the Crosby quoit game and a gambling horse-racing game that features Seabiscuit, the champion racehorse of the 1930s that became an American icon in the years of the Great Depression. And here's a life-size cardboard cut-out of Bing in later years in full golf fig advertising the latest in air conditioning.

And what about the younger Bing clad in – shockingly revealing for a man who usually appeared in slacks, hat and woolly jumper – just singlet and shorts, to advertise a tummy-toning stirrup and rubber pull-up device called the Stretch to Health, also endorsed by Cary Grant, Dorothy Lamour and Cecil B. DeMille. Now there's a gym club to die for!

Even the music wasn't above prostitution to capitalism. One collaboration on display feature songs by Bing alongside Louis Armstrong and Rosemary Clooney and the Hi-Los, entitled *Music to Shave By*. It won its own mounted disc presented to Bing on behalf of the Adjustable Remington Automatic Shaver for the 'biggest recording of 1959: six million copies pressed'.

Despite this avalanche of Bing Bling, I have to take a look at the place where the legend was born. Over the years as Gonzaga University expanded it swallowed up many of the homes once sold from the 'Little Vatican' estate. Some were built on, but the old Crosby home, a grey-painted clapboard two-storey bungalow with dormer windows, was preserved. Today it is the 'Alumni House', responsible for organising events for former students. When I knock on the door, I'm greeted enthusiastically by a member of the post-grad staff with, 'Hey, come on in, sir', in that endearing, reverential way young Americans of a certain class have of referring – at least face to face – to their elders.

Back in Britain I might expect to be ignored at best; here I'm invited to look around and even try a glass of the hot cider (non-alcoholic) set up for a pre-Hallowe'en party, even though the day itself is still a few weeks away. The house is a classic design of the early twentieth century, remarkably open-plan by British standards. You walk into a wide hallway with stairs ahead, a living room to one side and dining room to the other, the entrance to each framed by an elegant hardwood surround. They have kept it furnished in 'period' 1940s style, with a pink clamshell sofa and a couple of comfy armchairs. There is a poster for the Oscar-winning *Going My Way*, and a blown-up black-and-white photograph of the old crooner in his heyday. All remarkably safe and middle class. But then so was Bing.

⁂

Heading back along the riverside towards the less leafy and a lot more tarmaccy town centre, it's not only painfully obvious that the students have very much the best of Spokane, but that yet again here is a US city centre decimated almost to the point of ruination by a lack of planning regulation and the obsession with the automobile.

I hate to go on about what might seem an old hat observation, a well-documented truism about urban America, but you have no idea until you experience it on the ground, and I mean on the ground. Outside an indoor, air-conditioned (or heated) shopping mall, to be a pedestrian in most US cities is to lead a lonely existence wandering amid half-empty parking lots like the gaps between rotting teeth in an urban infrastructure palpably going to pot.

As I am becoming ever more acutely aware, pedestrians inhabit the same world as drifters and hobos, a world middle-class Americans try to ignore, oblivious to any concept of interdependency. Nineteenth-century buildings – the sort that are being restored in Manchester or London's Docklands – sit, separated by patches of tarmac half-populated by gigantic empty suvs, slowly going to seed. A few, dotted here and there, have been turned into flourishing bars or shops, but too few, and too far between.

For a country with so relatively little historic fabric, and which purports to care so much for what it has, this is the tyranny of the 'empty lot', market capitalism taken to an extreme where it becomes synonymous with apathetic cynical vandalism. It is deemed more economical to raze a building than restore it, or even build in its place. Cheaper to hire an unskilled employee for a pittance and charge what you can to park on it.

These are the rather gloomy thoughts going through my mind as I realise I have still nearly seven hours to spend in glorious downtown Spokane. The thing about endless empty parking lots, you see, is that they're empty. This can only make logical sense – even in the world of dog-eat-dog, live-and-let-die capitalism – for so long. But how long can it be before the parking lots – already half empty in working hours – become unviable because there is simply not enough activity in the remaining buildings for anyone to drive to visit? The doughnut effect reaches its maximum: a ring of gated suburbs surrounding an empty, eviscerated, lifeless city centre, given over to office blocks and parking lots.

Jeff, barman at the Onion, a bustling burger restaurant selling the northwest's excellent microbrewery beers along a magnificent 1900 oak bar brought west in 1978 by train, says he has seen at least three popular downtown venues demolished and replaced by parking lots. That's one reason why the Onion is bustling, he admits. There's nowhere else much to go.

So Jeff and I sit and chew the fat endlessly, putting the rotten world to rights. And the long slow hours tick by until midnight when he apologetically throws me out and I stumble across the empty tarmac to the echoing Amtrak station which is gradually filling up with my few fellow westbound travellers, hoping like I am that today's Empire Builder will come trundling into town as close as possible to 1:15 a.m., 24 hours after its predecessor, the last train to pass this way. In the end it's only 20 minutes later which is something of a cause for celebration, though there's still another hour and a half to kill as it splits into two in the station before, in the wee small hours of the morning: one half heads to Portland, Oregon, while the other, mine, slides down the remaining slopes of the Rockies into Seattle, the 'most happening city on the seaboard', home to Bill Gates and Starbucks. I'm not sure whether to laugh or cry.

SPOKANE TO SEATTLE

TRAIN: Empire Builder
FREQUENCY: 1 a day
DEPART SPOKANE, WASHINGTON: 2:15 a.m. (Pacific Time)

via
Ephrata, WA
Wenatchee, WA
Everett, WA
Edmonds, WA

ARRIVE SEATTLE, WASHINGTON: 10:20 a.m. (Pacific Time)
DURATION: Approx 8 hours
DISTANCE: 329 miles

11

Gates of America

THE LITTLE COFFEE SHOP at 1912 Western just by Pike Place Market in Seattle's West Edge district ought to be one of the least conspicuous in a city where a thousand temples to the cult of the brown bean clamour for attention. Except for the gaggle of gawping tourists outside.

It is less heavily branded than most, the name written in an unfamiliar font on the glass panels above the door, one letter per pane. It takes me a moment to recognise it, which is a full 59.9 seconds longer than it takes to recognise any other of its 15,010 franchises across the world. But that doesn't stop backpackers from as far afield as Melbourne and Tokyo grinning insanely as they photograph one another outside what was once the only branch of Starbucks on the face of the planet. An era that seems as far distant as when Rome was just a few mud huts on the banks of the Tiber.

Starbucks No. 1, as it is wholly unofficially known, has acquired almost international monument status – on a par with the first McDonald's. Americans might like to think their gift to the world has been the dream of 'life, liberty and the pursuit of happiness', but not one of those have the same international recognition as the Starbucks logo or the golden arches. This, of course, is probably a sadder comment on the rest of us. After the Boeing Aircraft Corporation and Microsoft – and I'm coming to that – Starbucks is what put Seattle on the map of the globe and helped give this damp, mostly grey city a reputation as America's hippest city and turned its climate-conditioned anti-fashion grunge streetwear into an iconic style statement. Weird!

To call Seattle grey and damp however is to do it a serious disservice – although it is indeed frequently both. It may only get 56 days of sunshine a year but its actual rainfall total is less than Atlanta, Georgia, or even New York City, if only because it is not prone to heavy tropical downpours. Its climate in fact is remarkably similar to British cities but its setting is spectacular:

143

surrounded by mountains and squeezed between the beautiful waterscapes of Lake Washington and Puget Sound. Seattle is a city of surprising elegance. I had been aware of that ever since stepping off the overnighter from Spokane and making my way out of the dingy station concourse to find myself standing in front of a larger than life-size replica of the Campanile from St Mark's Square in Venice. It's one of those moments when you have to pinch yourself, walk back into the building you've just left, and then come out again to take a second look.

Seattle's King Street station is a splendid railway-era folly on a grand scale, built in 1905, and now – thankfully – in the middle of a long and expensive restoration process. The grimy tiles above my head as I emerged from the train were a false ceiling put in place while the original gleaming white moulded 45-foot-high vaulted canopy above is brought back to life. Unlike Buffalo, where the original building is all but doomed to decay, King Street will once again be not just a functional building but a landmark to be proud of.

Meanwhile, back at that other landmark, Starbucks No. 1, I'm trying to decide whether I should pay homage by indulging in a cup of coffee. The trouble is, middle-aged child that I am of a British generation that couldn't tell a mocha from a mud pie – my biggest achievement in the coffee world was explaining to my mother that cappuccino was not a Venetian painter – I have still never really been able to get my head around a tall latte or a frosted frappuccino. Under the circumstances then, and given the fact that inside the hallowed portal, the corporate clones have been unable to resist transforming even this, the mother ship, into an identical replica of every branch from Belfast to Bogotá (and no, I haven't been to either but how much do you want to bet?) that even the chance to try Pike Place Blend ('uniquely on sale here') fails to tempt me (though I suppose it gives them something to offer the pilgrims as a souvenir).

It is one of those supreme accidental ironies that a brand that has come to symbolise the triumph of monocultural marketing over local individualism has its origins so firmly rooted in what miraculously remains one of the most exciting, individual, anti-corporate street markets in the whole of the United States. In a country that teems with plenty, but mostly displayed on the sterile shelves of supermarket giants, it is a rare delight to come across such a vibrant, natural, popular and flourishing urban market as Pike Place. The downstairs levels, on the underfloors descending to the waterfront, are full of quirky privately-owned shops that offer anything from Pacific seashell necklaces to useful bits of domestic hardware, but it is where the market meets the bustling street on the uppermost level with its fishmongers, florists and fruit and veg merchants that makes Pike an outstanding experience.

It is immediately obvious that this is Pacific Rim America: the Asian racial influence stronger than anywhere I have been outside a Chinatown. And the mix has more in it of Japan than China. The first Japanese passenger steamer ever to reach the United States docked here in Seattle in 1896 with 259 immigrants on board. Racial tensions that emerged during the Second World War, when born-and-bred Japanese-Americans were interned and often stripped of their property (something that never happened to the vastly more numerous but more racially homogeneous German-Americans), left a bad taste that lingered for many years. Poignantly addressed in the bestselling novel and movie *Snow Falling on Cedars*, the injustice has been forgiven, if not wholly forgotten. There are now some 56,000 Japanese-Americans living in Washington State, more than anywhere else except Hawaii and California, where they form a much smaller proportion of the population.

The market's showcase is the Pike Place Fish Co., with its jaw-dropping display of the great – remaining – wealth of the Pacific Ocean: whole albacore tuna, salmon from the coast and rivers of Alaska, Dungeness crabs of monstrous proportion, great legs – up to two feet long – from snow crabs caught in the Russian arctic.

'Okay, watch yo' heads. Flying fish,' calls a portly grinning Japanese-American fishmonger, as an assistant in front of the glistening fish racks passes him an order.

'Yo, got that boy!' the assistant comes back as a huge salmon – at least 20 pounds of pink and silver glistening fish flies over the heads of customers into his hands.

'Too big? Yo' want another?' and a second, then a third comes soaring over our heads to be caught in a gentle cradle of swooping arms until the perfect fish is selected and the others are sent spinning back through the air to be recouched in their cosy beds of crushed ice.

The whole thing is as much choreographed theatre as sales pitch and the tourists cluster round, digital cameras extended as they try to follow the flying fish, and capture the busy banter between the grinning fishmongers hamming it up for their captive crowds.

It's hard to avoid the impression that 80 per cent of visitors spend more time taking photographs than making purchases; for many visiting Americans the fish, crabs, squid and octopus on sale here are just too far away from the food processing chain for them to be entirely comfortable. But Pike Place is one of the world's great advertisements for commerce on a human, rather than pre-packed, supermarket scale. And yet it is a miracle that it is still here at all. Founded just over 100 years ago – which makes it a genuine antique by American standards – Pike Place began as a market for fishermen and farmers from the surrounding countryside, set up in answer to complaints by local housewives in what was still a relatively poor pioneer city that middlemen were hiking the prices.

But by the late 1960s – with the recent success of a World's Fair filling their tills – the narrow-minded commercially motivated businessmen and politicians – the parking lot tycoons of middle America – were casting their eyes lustfully over Pike Place. It was too old-fashioned, they argued, for a city on the cusp of the future – they were right, of course, just not remotely in the way they imagined – and the interests of the city and its citizens would be best served if it were simply pulled down. In its place they wanted to erect that joyless eye-catching waste-space of urban planners everywhere, a convention centre, which would also incorporate a hockey arena, thrown in to appeal to the plebs. Oh, and perhaps just as an afterthought: a 4,000-car parking lot.

It took one man in particular, lifelong Seattle resident and, of all things – bless him – professor of architecture at Washington State University, Victor Steinbrueck, to see the crime that was about to be committed and rally public opposition. Against the odds, he succeeded not only in making it an issue rather than a rubber-stamp job, and forced a citywide referendum which in 1971 voted definitively to retain the city's much-loved market. It is hard to imagine what single move – alongside founding Microsoft and maintaining Boeing – could have done more to boost and preserve Seattle's character and reputation. Without the market, for example, would there ever have been such a groovy, laid-back, urban sophisticated place to hang out, and think, 'Man, this would be a cool place to start a real chilled coffee shop?' Maybe it wasn't such a good thing after all.

But if saving the fertile earth for the germination of a coffee shop crop that has wiped out little family businesses across most of the inhabited planet, could be regarded as a dubious achievement, at least the benign radiance generated by Pike Place ensured the growth and survival of other excellent enterprises, not least among them the Pacific Northwest's home-grown renaissance of microbrewing. The microbrewery revolution which took off in Washington and neighbouring Oregon finally gave Americans – and grateful visitors – beers that have flavour and taste and eroded the monopolistic dominance of the corporate gnat's piss producers: the men that ate Milwaukee.

One of the Northwest's finest micros is just on the edge of the market, though it's not that easy to find, being as you have to go down an indoor staircase at 1415 1st Avenue to find it. But I have done my homework in advance and within minutes I am seated blissfully at the horseshoe-shaped bar of Pike's Brewery waiting for Nancy, the bright-eyed effervescent barmaid, to pour me a second velvety glass of Seattle stout, pulled from an English-style hand pump and deliciously free of the otherwise omnipresent carbon dioxide.

Coca-Cola and Pepsi may be two of the best-known brand names on earth and the planet's bestselling soft drinks, but I have to blame them for the near-universal American insistence on pumping all drinks full of so much CO_2 that it is a wonder the population isn't permanently belching. I don't want to sound trivial on a major issue here but in a country perpetually dosed on bargain refills of fizzy drinks, it's easy to imagine flatulence might be America's biggest contribution to global warming.

Yet bizarrely, the one thing it is all but impossible to find easily in America is carbonated mineral water. Posh places stock Perrier – and charge accordingly – as they should, given the air miles it has clocked up, being flown in from France. Ditto the mountains of Evian on display in every supermarket – a real testimony to the enduring reputation for 'chic' still exuded by the French. But where oh where, particularly in these northwestern states of gushing crystal clear mountain streams, are the domestic bottled waters? Surely a city like Seattle would soak up the 'designer waters' that do so well in Europe. When every French or Italian – or even nowadays Scottish or Welsh – hill region boasts its own varieties of 'pure mineral waters' – when you get the likes of ridiculous failed wine snobs holding 'water tastings' – I would be sorely tempted to say the Americans have held on to their sanity.

Except of course that they haven't. America has bottled water, and enough people drink it, but it is almost exclusively 'purified' drinking water from the local mains similar to the Dasani brand which Coca-Cola had to withdraw from sale in Britain when it was laughed off the shelves after the revelation that it was 'treated' tap water bottled in the London suburb of Sidcup. But will they be back? You bet!

I digress. Here I am sitting on a bar stool with a pint of delicious stout, perusing another miraculous find picked up from the ubiquitous displays of tourist tat. It is, wait for it: a 'Downtown Walking Map' of Seattle! Okay Europeans, you need to think in context here. This is a 'walking map', geddit? A map to be used – while walking! Moving around on two feet, by putting one in front of the other. A map! An actual map, suggesting that bipedal locomotion is a concept that can be employed for greater distances than that between mall and car. The parking lot planners of Buffalo or Spokane wouldn't even understand the concept. I can't wait to experiment!

Meanwhile, however, there is lunch. It remains true that you can – and many people do – eat very, very well in America: the French Laundry in the hills north of San Francisco is regularly listed as among the top 10 restaurants in the world (and has several times been top). There are first-class establishments in almost every big city. But by and large they are precisely that: first class. As in first class opposed to economy. First class in terms of table linen, genteel atmosphere, a respectful hush. Even silver salvers. And definitely price. You can also – and sadly most people do – eat very badly indeed in America. Albeit for very little. The Americans may not have invented fast food – Japanese sushi and German sausages in a roll are just two of the many competing claimants – but they sure as hell industrialised it. Add the salt-and-saturates to the supersize sugar-and-Co2 'soda' and it is not hard to identify one obvious endemic cause for what is beginning to look like a national physical characteristic in a nation made up of so many others: the outsize rear end. Oh, all right, if I'm going to risk offending the entire American nation, I may as well do it in their own language: the fat ass!

It's not that we Europeans are immune. Far from it. Anyone who has been to the Munich beer festival will have seen some stupendous lederhosen rumps, while the amply endowed Italian 'pasta mama' is no more a spurious national stereotype than an archetypal English 'lardy-arse' overfed on fish'n'chips. Britain in particular these days is dangerously hooked on a love-hate affair with obesity. How else do you account for the fact that one of our most slender and internationally celebrated beauties, Princess Diana, and one of our most grotesque, fat-bottomed politicians, former Deputy Prime Minister John Prescott, were both confessed bulimics. If we're not chugging it down, we're choking it up. But the growing trend towards fatter kids in particular has undeniably gone hand in pudgy hand with our growing enthusiasm for the cheap, cheerful, instant gratification of mass-produced fast food. Where America leads, we blindly follow. I'm just amazed you guys are so far in front, given the weight you're carrying.

But – and it is a big but – there are places in America, and more than the casual tourist might think, where you can also eat astonishingly well for relatively little. Unsurprisingly they tend to be the places where you can drink reasonably well too. Like Pike's Brewery. So spare me for a minute, if I offer up a sample. As a starter for $3.75 (under £2 at October 2008 exchange rates) Nancy has brought me a little bowl of chopped radishes with a Seattle speciality: a little dipping saucer of salt liberally flavoured with specks of black truffle. Now I am familiar with radishes as an accompaniment to beer – it is an old Bavarian speciality, the sharp tang of the radish piquing the thirst and contrasting with the sweetness of the beer – but add the salt and the hint of truffle! Inspired. Nothing less.

For my main course I've ordered a starter-sized portion – always a safe option at lunch, American main course dishes can be humongous – Dungeness crab with Chilean bay shrimp, globe peppers and Japanese 'puko-style' breadcrumbs with a Thai sweet chilli sauce. I don't often let the menu speak for itself but this is every bit as good as that sounds, even if I still haven't a clue what 'puko-style' means. Pure heaven. As I bite into it, my faith in the small god of incidental music, breaking free from the confines of my iPod now to the restaurant's sound system, contributes an old song by Bryan Ferry: 'More than this, there is nothing!' A bit of an exaggeration perhaps, but right now it would seem churlish to disagree.

Odd circumstances, then, in which to think of the challenge of industrial espionage. That, however, is the thought that automatically comes into my mind as I involuntarily catch snatches of conversation wafting over me from the two other men eating at the bar. It's easy enough to ignore the bit about property prices, a global staple though high-employment Seattle has remained relatively sheltered from the sub-prime collapse. But after a few minutes I can't help hitting on a whole series of archetypal Seattle buzzwords: 'system backup', 'soft viruses', 'overly proprietorial hookups' and similar. Computer geek-speak obviously, but then Seattle is home to Microsoft, the world's biggest corporation. This is the city that prides itself on having made 'geeks' chic.

Such is the pulling power of the United States most northerly and most westerly metropolis – despite its famously dreary weather – that a recent issue of *Seattle Metropolitan* magazine boasted of '50 ways in which Seattle will change the world'. And what makes otherwise dodgy bar-room eavesdropping so tempting is that they just might be right. Amid such questionable boons to humanity as the enhancement of the world bestselling Halo 3 'shoot me up' computer game, the magazine's list included dozens of serious scientific projects under development in the greater Seattle area from a potential cure for cot death, to a handheld machine for diagnosing tropical diseases to a hyper-effective wave energy generator (Washington State gets the biggest waves of any stretch of US coastline outside Alaska). In other words if you're worried about child health care, Third World development or alternative energy, Seattle

149

is a good place to start looking for answers. Greater Seattle is taking over from California as the place where America designs tomorrow for the rest of us.

That doesn't mean we have to like it. Amongst the other plans being drawn up locally are a few that sound like escapees from science-fiction plots: spaceships that can take off from airport runways (including an intercontinental bomber capable of 10 times the speed of sound, ref: Dr Strangelove, *Starship Troopers*), a Pentagon-commissioned ultrasound instant blood coagulator that could stop bleeding straight away (ref: *Star Trek's* Dr McCoy), micro-implants in the human body to grant keyless access to your home, office or car (*I, Robot, The Fifth Element*), 'brain-fingerprinting' that could prove innocence or guilt by automatically detecting reactions to a crime scene (*Minority Report*). Just to prove this last one isn't necessarily negative, the magazine cites an early version used in Iowa in 2003 to help clear a man who had served 25 years for a murder he didn't commit.

Then there's the sky elevator made of nano-strips of super-tough carbon that will extend 62,000 miles to a geo-stationary satellite, be held taut by the earth's rotation and be ascended with minimal energy by a robot the size of a Boeing 747 to transfer cargo to spacecraft (Arthur C. Clarke *passim*) That one might sound the most fantastic, but they actually have a delivery date, albeit not exactly imminent: October 2031.

Time therefore to get a satellite's eye view of the man who not so much inspired the white heat of the technological revolution as the white rage of fury most of his customers feel when faced with the blue screen of death on a computer running Microsoft Windows: Bill Gates himself. Actually, it's easy enough to get a satellite view of the Gates' estate – just go to Google Earth – but it's a good excuse for trying what I had been tipped was the best way to fully appreciate Seattle's extraordinary geographical location: from above.

As it happens in Seattle, nothing could be easier. What is still called Lake Union is actually now a bay on the Lake Washington Ship Canal that cuts across the north of the peninsula on which Seattle sits, separating the commercial heart of the city from the student-dominated university district. It not only hosts a marina of pleasure craft – Seattle has enough berths to provide two spaces for every three citizens – and some expensive little waterfront homes, virtually built out onto the lake, but also a couple of small seaplane companies.

An aerial sightseeing tour might seem an extravagant indulgence but here it is nothing of the sort and rates as one of the best value, most exhilarating treats you can give yourself. There is a seaplane taxi service out to the islands, and that probably is an indulgence, but at the time of writing the 20-minute air tour of Seattle cost an affordable and highly worthwhile $67.50 a head (£35). And believe me, the ride is worth it. I mean, how many times do most of us actually get to take off from and land on water?

To book my ride I had called in advance the nice young woman who runs the front desk for Seattle Seaplanes. The aerial side of operations is actually a one-man show run by a genial white-haired pilot in his fifties called Jim Chrysler. He used to call it Chrysler Air, but motor manufacturers can be a bit touchy about their trademarks. It could have led to problems if anyone had assumed Jim's little business was Mercedes-Benz's attempt to emulate Rolls-Royce with a leap into the aerospace sector.

In fact, Seattle Seaplanes has just one seaplane, a little, single-engined Cessna that sits at the end of a wooden jetty, along from the neat little shack that serves as an office. It looks more like it should be selling bait and fishing tackle than serving as a check-in for an airline.

I stumble in through the door, somewhat out of breath from the longer-than-expected yomp up from the city – taxis as ever in America proving remarkably thin on the ground – to find Jim talking to three other customers, guys from Chicago in their mid-twenties who're holidaying in Seattle and taking the flight as a birthday treat for one of them. Jim is a genial but gruff bloke with a big droopy white moustache that just vaguely suggests a minor character in a *Bugs Bunny* cartoon. He also has a very droll sense of humour.

'Have you been doing this long, sir?' asks one of my three slightly nervous about-to-be fellow travellers in the six-seater seaplane. Jim turned, eyed the young man up and down and said coolly:

'What's today's date?'

'Uh? The sixth, sir.'

'Hmmm, not that long then,' comes the deadpan reply, neatly rounded off with: 'The regular guy's not on today.'

I watch the nervous doubt on my fellow passenger's face turn to scepticism and finally, as Jim grins broadly, the suspicion he's being teased. Nonetheless, they're more than happy to let me sit up front, alongside the pilot, with the propeller just inches in front of my nose and a parallel set of controls in front of me. Jim gives flying lessons as well. Then he turns the key in the ignition, with a sound disconcertingly reminiscent of cranking up a Morris Minor and starts the little seaplane taxiing out at the legal limit of seven knots an hour across Lake Union.

Then there's a shuddering under the floats as we accelerate to what seems breathtaking speed but is, Jim shouts over the roar of the engines, just over

45 mph. And we lift off smoothly from the wake of white waves left on the lake surface and see the city falling away beneath us. There's a giddy feeling of euphoric freedom in a small plane flying above a big city, exaggerated by the surreal sight of the controls in front of me moving to and fro, echoing Jim's.

Up and away we soar on a par with, then above the skyscrapers of the downtown area, out over the sound and the lakes, and immediately it is apparent what a blessed situation Seattle has, straddling the peninsula at the heart of a vast oceanic lakeland. How fragile and improbable the two floating bridges look, the longest in the world, a silver-grey filament a mile and a half long strung across the northern half of Lake Washington, and the world's second longest linking the city to Mercer Island further south. Then we turn, banking steeply enough to draw sharp intakes of breath from all of us but smiling Jim, out over rugged Bellevue peninsula.

'That's the Gates' place, down there,' says Jim, nodding with his head to indicate a line of waterfront mansions far below. 'His is the one with the silver roof.'

Gates is America's richest man and the story of his rise to head of a globe-spanning software empire from origins as a lad tinkering with electronics in his dad's garage is legendary. What is less known is that although far from a multi-millionaire he wasn't exactly a poor boy either. The rags to riches story actually belongs to another of Seattle's most famous sons – Jimi Hendrix (whose body was brought back here to be buried). The Gateses are an old Seattle family and amongst those who always preferred to live out on the islands rather than in the city. So by building his mansion out here he was not so much opting into an exclusive community as continuing a family tradition. In fact, the most striking thing is how densely packed they are, these billionaire's mansions along the shoreline, each with their private jetty. I suppose I had imagined Bill's billions would have bought him not just luxury but seclusion. But then the mega-rich are not exactly exceptions to the rule out here. And maybe he just likes to be sociable with the neighbours: for the first (and last) time in my American odyssey the music that springs to mind unbidden hails not from these shores but from Lancashire, an ancient George Formby song: 'If you could see, what I can see, when I'm cleaning Windows!'

For the next 20 minutes or so, we bank and climb and all but hover just beneath the blanket of cloud that even Seattle's greatest admirers admit is their city's habitual cover. Then we wheel down audaciously to loop round the 'Space Needle', concrete proof that even in the city where they invent tomorrow today, they still had a pretty daft idea of it yesterday: yet another silly sixties 'observation tower'. The city fathers who authorised its building for the 1962 Century 21 Exposition no doubt imagined that towards the end of the first decade of that century the Jetsons would be flying round it in their cartoon space bubble cars. Instead it's still being buzzed by vintage seaplanes.

Then we are coasting down once again onto the surface of the lake, skimming the waves to come to a halt smoother than on many wheeled aircraft I've flown on. It occurs to me that maybe 'landing' isn't the right word on a seaplane. The French use 'amerissage' for landing on la mer as opposed to 'aterrissage' for coming back to terra firma but they also used 'alunissage' for the lunar landing, which is either very clever or just plain silly.

Back to earth, as it were, I decide I really must go and take a close-up look at the 'big spike' we just flew around. Not because I found it particularly impressive – even though it is Seattle's most famous landmark – but because I have a sneaking suspicion that it might be as tacky a remnant of the World Fair craze as the crumbling concrete in Spokane. The recommended way to get there, according to Big Jim's assistant, is by monorail. Involuntarily I cringe: 'monorail', like the Jetsons' bubble hovercars, was one of those concepts of the future that figured heavily back in the sixties. I had an Understanding Science book for boys that depicted twenty-first century people queuing up at platforms in the sky to board monorails. But then they were all wearing what appeared to be Superman suits, something that seemed not just improbable but impossible until the advent of Lycra, and given the evolution of the human shape it will hopefully still be some time before we are all wearing it.

For a long time, however, monorails maintained a strangely magical grip on the human imagination: witness the episode of the Simpsons in which the people of Springfield, encouraged to build this extravagantly expensive piece of technology to get one up on neighbouring Shelbyville, go into a crazed song and dance routine chanting, 'monorail! monorail!' In fact, monorails do exist all over the world nowadays but rarely as anything more than short-distance transits; airport terminal shuttle transfers spring to mind. Seattle's monorail starts on the third floor of a modern downtown shopping mall, which must have replaced one – or at least something of the same height – that was here back in 1962.

The monorail itself is, inevitably, a bit of an embarrassment. It is obviously painfully old, and despite the fact that its total length is not more than a couple of hundred yards at most it still requires a driver, unlike London's computerised Docklands Light Railway, itself already more than a quarter century old. And the monorail can't even leave the single rail it straddles.

Unfortunately, because up until now I've been impressed with this low-key user-friendly city, the Seattle Center at the other end is not much better: the usual sad, sorry collection of run-down amusement: a rickety roller-coaster, roundabout with flaking paint, tacky ice-cream parlour and cafeteria serving greasy food. I'm dismally reminded of a run-down British seaside pier stubbornly harking back to its Victorian glory while resolutely running to seed. Perhaps there is simply nothing more ephemeral than a purpose-built tourist attraction. And then I think of the Eiffel Tower and even the giant wheel of the London Eye, both of which – the former in particular – have gone on to outlast their creators' expectations.

Seattle's 'Space Needle' must indeed offer fine views of the city, I concede, though having just experienced an overview vastly more impressive – and exciting – than anything it can offer, I'm far from tempted to join the queue. I have the recent memory of my Sears Building experience in Chicago engrained in my brain like an acid scar. But looking up at this extraordinary and essentially useless concrete spire I realise that if there is any merit in these curious mid-twentieth-century failed visions of the future, it is as grandiose follies, a more modern version of Victorian mock-Gothic turreted towers. To me it looks faintly embarrassing, like a 1970s hairstyle. But then I know people who say I've still got one of those. In any case Seattle is not quickly going to be rid of it: what else would they put on the T-shirts?

Unless of course, it's The Japanese Gourmet, or probably any one of several dozen other excellent eating houses. I make no excuses for describing another meal in Seattle, if only because it was probably the best sushi I have ever had. The Japanese Gourmet is a relatively small, mid-priced eating house back down near Pike Place, but, I reason, anything that serves raw fish next to one of the world's outstanding fish markets can't be all bad. And it's not. In fact, it's wonderful.

Never have I tasted better, fresher, more melt-in-your mouth tuna – *tonbo*, fresh albacore, not easy to get at all in most places. Then hunks of juicy cooked snow crab leg meat, bound on to the sushi rice by strips of seaweed. A succulent piece of *tai* snapper is marred – for me – only slightly by a more than usually nostril-searing dose of wasabi.

But then 'heating up' sushi is the chef's speciality here, as he demonstrates by offering me his latest creation, a maki roll he nicknames 'Ring of Fire'. I'm not at all sure I really see Johnny Cash as having been a big sushi fan, but hey, if it was meant to challenge the Man in Black, I can take a stab at it.

'Hot hot hot,' he warns, describing it, less helpfully than I'm sure he intended, as 'Nagi Hama topped with red tuna served around siracha pit'.

This turns out to be a variation on what is loosely known in the sushi world as an 'inside out' roll. The core is, the chef explains, *hamachi* – yellowtail – with chilli seeds and sliced spring onion, wrapped in *nori* seaweed, with the sushi rice outside and the whole wrapped with a slice of red tuna held in place with a little wasabi. Then just to add that extra bit of spice: a heap of fiery red chilli sauce, delicately served on the side on top of a half lemon so you could use as much – or as little – as you wished.

Little turns out to be the right choice; to have used none at all would have been to turn down the challenge. The Man in Black would have considered me little better than a Bee Gees fan. So adding just the merest drop of the bright red condiment, I pop the whole thing – as best Japanese tradition dictates – into my mouth. And explode as quietly as possible. The Ring of Fire has to go down as one of the most extraordinary sado-masochistic sensual pleasures of the culinary world: an eye-wateringly spectacular blend of textures, flavours and tongue-tingling titillation. A gastronomic wipe-out in one bite.

It is also the most classic demonstration in my experience that the mastery of a sushi chef's job lies not just in ensuring the freshness of the fish and the precise firmness of the rice, but in conjuring up combinations that both appeal to the eye in terms of composition and colour while at the same time challenging and expanding the repertoire of the taste buds. I am sure there are simpler and more refined treats on offer in Japan, but as an example of a red-blooded Japanese-American take on tradition, this was a masterpiece.

A masterpiece like that, however, gives you a taste for a cold beer or two. Thankfully Seattle is one of those places where that is not a problem. It is time to check out the nightlife on Pioneer Square, the oldest part of town, down by the railway station as it happens. This is where I came in. It was also, when the railroad was the main means of getting here from California, where most people arriving in Seattle for the first time came in. Hence the name. And it was, when things went wrong, as they often did for gold prospectors, where people often ended up. The usual grid-like street pattern of central Seattle skews as it tilts towards the oldest part of town. It also tips downhill so that the incongruous Venetian clock tower on top of King Street station becomes a useful orientational landmark. In the nineteenth century a lumber merchant called Henry Yesler used to keep his depot down here, and the street today is still called Yesler Street. It didn't have that name in his day, or any other name. It was the rough and ready road down which labourers rolled their felled timber to the sawmill. If your gold mine had failed to deliver, your ship failed to come in or if for any reason you just couldn't get another job, your best chance was to hang out on the road where they skidded the lumber down. They called it Skid Road.

Early in the twentieth century a fiery local nonconformist pastor would preach about the loose morals and evils of the district that the area round Yesler's Yard soon became. Instead of a skid road for lumber it had become a 'Skid Road down which souls skidded into hell.' A twist of the tongue later and the English language had a new colourful metaphor: Skid Row. And people across the planet have been landing on it ever since.

The past half century has seen various attempts to drag this original Skid Row back uphill. Metaphorically at least. It is only now that they are seriously beginning to show signs of potential success. The Central, opened in 1892, is Seattle's oldest pub, and still going strong. But it, like so many of its neighbours, has fallen into the modern trap of age exclusivity. Anyone is welcome but if you're much over 30, you'll soon start to feel your age.

Once upon a time the American Cowgirl must have had a different name. Whatever it was, that incarnation has long been forgotten in the metamorphosis into a raucous bar that anywhere in Europe you would describe as for teenagers, were it not for the fact that in the US – incredibly – the minimum drinking age is 21 (a piece of Puritan lawmaking that has made almost every teenager in America a criminal, possessed of some form of fake ID – another major own goal in the 'war against terror').

The American Cowgirl is what old farts like myself call a 'meat market'. And the meat is queuing up at the door: a group of six girls, just piled out of their car – who I can't help wonder is the 'designated driver'? – all shedding their thick outer jackets in the process to reveal virtually identical black sleeveless, bare-shouldered spangly tops. In a flash their naked flesh erupts in a pimply ocean of goose pimples. This is still Seattle. They didn't invent grunge here for nothing, girls!

On the advice of a taxi driver – yes, in a district given over to late night bars, you can actually find them on the street – I head for somewhere more convivial for someone not shopping for rare veal. The driver deposits me outside The Hop Vine in a university and residential district. This is a man who knows his mark: inside I find a reassuringly heterogeneous crowd of local regulars, couples popped in for a pint and maybe a bite to eat, students merrily arguing away the troubles of the world over jugs of flavoursome ales.

When I finally stagger out into the night I find additional reassurance in the fact that my own innate fashion sense owes more to Seattle grunge than sparkly tops: typical Northwest weather – drizzly, cold and blustery.

But walking into the night through the streets of an American city on a more human scale – or was it just with a more humane face? – than any I have yet encountered, I head happily for bed. Sleepless in Seattle? Not me.

SEATTLE TO SACRAMENTO

TRAIN: Coast Starlight
FREQUENCY: 1 a day
DEPART SEATTLE, WASHINGTON: 9:45 a.m. (Pacific Time)

via
Tacoma, WA
Olympia-Lacey, WA
Centralia, WA
Kelso-Longview, WA
Vancouver, WA
Portland, Oregon
Salem, OR
Albany, OR
Eugene-Springfield, OR
Chemult, OR
Klamath Falls, OR
Dunsmuir, California
Redding, CA
Chico, CA

ARRIVE SACRAMENTO, CALIFORNIA: 6:35 a.m. (Pacific Time)
DURATION: approx 20 hours, 50 minutes
DISTANCE: 824 miles

12

Terminates Here!

OF ALL THE EXOTIC NAMES Amtrak gives to the routes plied by its otherwise identical trains, the Coast Starlight has to be one of the most deliberately romantic. Rattling down almost the entire length of the western American seaboard, if you board it mid-morning in Seattle you can, if you choose, still be on board 35 hours later as it pulls into Los Angeles.

I had a somewhat different route in mind. But as we rolled out of the mock-Venetian folly on King Street, along the rugged Pacific coastline until veering inland, into the depths of the great forests of Oregon it came home to me that I was at last California-bound.

For a start the dining-car attendant was called José and was the first Amtrak employee I'd come across who very definitely preferred speaking Spanish to English. And then there was the sign at the end of each coach: 'Smoke-free zone: including the restrooms and the spaces between cars. Anyone who is caught smoking will be removed by law enforcement at the next station stop.'

Britain is just as bad – or good, depending on your viewpoint – these days, but the first stone in the war against smokers was definitely thrown in California, which is a bit of an irony given the attitude of its governor, as I am to discover. But then this is the state that gave the world hippies and health farms, as well as not just 'nuclear-free zones' but also – in Sausalito, north of San Francisco – a 'cholesterol-free zone'.

The California clichés slowly start to multiply after I 'detrain' in bright sunshine early the following morning at Sacramento's lovingly restored old station. The rubbish bins are labelled 'Recycling Facility: Please separate trash accordingly'. Then I walk out of the station and catch sight of the tall palm trees swaying gently in the balmy breeze, so implausible given that it's not a week since I was shivering in below freezing temperatures in Montana. Shades of the Mamas and the Papas roll out California Dreamin' on a Winter's Day.

And then I spot a flotilla of traffic wardens rolling along silently in three-wheeled electric cars. Wearing plastic cycle helmets. Yep, this has to be Sacramento! The capital city, no less, of the Golden State.

Sacramento may get sniffed at – and it does – by the metropolitan, metrosexual elites down in the much more famous cities of San Francisco and Los Angeles, as a northern provincial town where out-of-touch state legislators meet to further loosen their grip on reality. Which is perhaps why in 2003 they turned out a relatively sensible if conventional politician as governor and instead sent them an Austrian body-builder turned movie star best known for playing a killer robot. And this is the seat of his government. Arnold Schwarzenegger, nicknamed 'The Governator' on black T-shirts they try to sell to the tourists (successfully in my case) has his HQ in Sacramento. How fitting then, that the world's first transcontinental railroad terminated here!

You could, of course, also say it began here. It was from the spot where I am standing, just a few yards from the existing Amtrak station, in front of a line of buildings now restored to their mid nineteenth-century appearance at the junction of Front and 'K' streets that the Chinese coolies broke the ground on 8 January 1863, to begin the western section of what would be the world's first transcontinental railroad. Not the line I came in on, but the line I intend to leave by, up and over the spine of the Rocky Mountains, a route that cost a fortune to build, claimed thousands of lives, and created a superpower.

It is to Sacramento that California owes its statehood, and therefore arguably that the United States as we know it owes its existence. This is where the gold rush started, back in 1849, a year after the first flakes were found at the sawmill owned by a Swiss emigré called Johann, later John, Sutter, a short, tubby businessman of dubious character from Burgdorf in Switzerland, whose route to California had been anything but straightforward.

After doing a runner from his native Switzerland to escape debt in 1834, Sutter made his way via New York to St Louis, still very much a frontier settlement, to deal in trade from Santa Fe, but when that didn't work he once again fled his creditors, this time out along the Oregon Trail to the Pacific coast. In case that wasn't far enough he then took ship for Hawaii where he made such an impression on King Kamehameha of the Kanaka tribe that he gave him eight of his men. Sutter then headed back to the North American mainland ending up in the town of Sitka, in the still Russian territory of Alaska, before drifting down the coast to the warmer climes of Mexican-owned California.

Intent on establishing himself as a merchant he persuaded Governor Alvorado to give him a generous land grant. Hoping to rely on cheap native labour he took out a loan and built himself a baronial estate at the confluence of two rivers, the American and the Sacramento, which had been named by Spanish explorers after the Holy Sacrament. Sutter called his estate New Helvetia in honour of his homeland. He set to work building up a farm, fort and various trading companies, but his incompetence was such that the local Indians he had hoped to exploit ended up stealing from him. His agricultural skills were nil and his crops failed. Then to cap it all his fur trading business fell apart when he discovered his own employees had been selling off valuable beaver pelts to the rival, British-owned Hudson Bay Company.

When the territory was ceded to the United States he briefly considered flying the French flag, but was persuaded otherwise by the arrival of a battalion of US troops. To keep his head afloat Sutter went into partnership to build a sawmill in the lowest foothills of the Sierra Nevada Mountains. It turned out to be the most significant thing he ever did, albeit purely by accident, because one morning in January 1848 his partner James Marshall discovered some sparkly flecks in the mill water which turned out to be gold. It says much of Sutter's naivety that he initially hoped their discovery could be kept a secret. Within months the gold rush had begun and Sutter found his land overrun by squatters, miners and would-be settlers who considered his property as much up for grabs as anything they might find in the streams or mountains.

Under pressure, Sutter did what he always did: tried to pretend it wasn't happening and shift the problem elsewhere, in this case onto the shoulders of his son, and retreated to a modest farmhouse. His son, meanwhile, had seen that despite the fact that the land around the Sacramento and American riverbanks was a muddy quagmire in winter and a dusty plain in summer, and the fact that the water was undrinkable, that was where the influx of fortune hunters continued to arrive.

He teamed up with a couple of builders, apportioned a chunk of land facing the Sacramento River into 10 lots and auctioned them off for more than enough money to settle his father's remaining debts. On the banks of a river named for the Holy Sacrament, Sutter Jr gave the influx of miners everything they desired; buckets and spades, beer and bordellos. His motto was to drive an expansion without precedent: 'Build it and they will come.' And come they did! Almost without noticing it, Sutter Jr had founded the city that was to become the capital of California.

Sutter's town was laid out on a perfect grid pattern, which the oldest parts of the modern city still adhere to. Before long it had become a riotous river port of miners, traders and whores. But it was also by far the most important place in California and in 1854 was designated the new state's capital, which to the bemusement of San Franciscans and Los Angelinos it remains today. It is also the reason I shan't be getting to San Francisco itself on this journey: the trains don't go there. The closest you can get, on the magnificently-entitled California Zephyr which runs along much of this historic route each day from Chicago, is the less-magnificently named Emeryville, a rather dull industrial city town on the eastern side of San Francisco Bay.

I might, however, have been able to get that far, had my accommodation for tonight still been fulfilling its original role. The *Delta King* riverboat, a beautifully restored old paddle steamer now permanently moored by the riverside in 'Old Sacramento', in its heyday back in the 1930s used to ply the river from here down to San Francisco every evening, a 10-hour trip which cost $3.50 – or just a buck if you brought your own blanket and opted to sleep on deck. Its popularity was unsurprising: in the days of Prohibition it was one of the few places where you could not only gamble but get a drink! Out of service since the Second World War, during which it served as a floating hospital in San Francisco Bay, the thing actually sank in 1981 and lay on the bottom before being salvaged and undergoing a five-year restoration. I went out onto the aft deck and drank a late morning beer in the old girl's honour as I surveyed the picture-postcard 'Olde West' townscape laid out in front of me: Old Sacramento in all its glory.

Unfortunately 'Old Sacramento' is probably the newest part of town. At least the most perfectly polished. The shops and stores have signs painted on them that say things like 'Saddlery and Ironmongery', or 'Mining Supplies, Dynamite,' when actually what they sell is scented candles and designer humbugs. They all sparkle pristinely with fresh bright paint, as they might have done on some mythical day back in the 1840s in the midst of the gold rush when they had all just been newly erected. Except, of course, that the gold rush was a rush and the river shores would have been heaving with people and dirt and horses and carts and oil and grease and sweat. And some buildings would have been going up while others would have been falling down.

A good proportion of them indeed did subsequently fall down or get torn down, and although some of those that make up Old Sacramento today have indeed been lovingly preserved – or more accurately heavily restored – a fair proportion have also been completely reconstructed 'true to the original'. Old Sacramento is pretty, but it's picture-postcard pretty and about as authentic as Disney's Magic Kingdom. There is an 'authentic replica' – completely reconstructed – of the 1876 Central Pacific Depot and on weekends in summer you can catch a steam train from it for a six-mile jaunt along Feather River Canyon.

The real city of Sacramento is separated from the Disneyfied waterfront by the inevitable freeway, which has to be crossed by the inevitable concrete pedestrian underpass. Even here, in sedate Sacramento, I'm prepared for the worst: the usual gaggle of drunks and beggars. But no. Hey, maybe California is different. The underpass certainly is. For one thing it's painted in bright – if this were still the sixties I'd call them 'psychedelic' – colours. For another there was piped music playing. Not supermarket muzak, but syncopated jazz. Only in California?

I'm headed for the governor's mansion, helpfully marked on a tourist map picked up on the paddle steamer. It's a bit of a tramp away towards the edge of the grid that marks the older bit of the real, as opposed to the waterfront, city. But with the tall palms swaying and the sunshine beaming down with Mediterranean warmth, for once a 'bit of a hike', as I'm learning Americans refer to anything more than a stroll round the garden, is a not unappealing prospect.

A few streets in from the tourist trap, however, and Sacramento is beginning to look depressingly less unique: a concrete 'Downtown Plaza' area filled with the usual fast-food joints and chain stores. Then, a couple of blocks further I come across a delightful open green area that proclaims itself Cesar Chavez Park. This is where I embarrass myself. Okay, American readers laugh now: this is your chance to get one back on all that supposedly sophisticated Worldly knowledge Europeans have tried to patronise you with over the years. The name of the park has got me wondering what sort of political revolution is going on in northern California. How can it be that the nicest park in the state capital is named after George W. Bush's bitterest enemy, the crypto-communist anti-American president of Venezuela?! Yes, I can hear you chortling already. It gets worse. In my blissful naivety I actually go up and ask the question – as delicately as I can – of one of the nice girls in bright yellow suits wearing badges that proclaim them willing to offer information to visitors.

They smile, look at each other, look at me – they may be checking here to see if I am mad or just a leg-puller – and then one of them says, calmly, politely, as if talking to a small child: 'It's *Cesar* Chavez. Right?' And they walk away, not exactly quickly but quite clearly not wanting to hang around someone so obviously off his trolley. For a second I'm left standing there, wondering what's up and then it dawns on me that the president of Venezuela – much as he might like to have been named after Julius Caesar – actually labours under the first name of Hugo. It's only later – quite some time later and thanks to Wikipedia – that I learn who Cesar Chavez was: one of the most widely revered

Mexican-Americans who founded a farm workers' union and whose birthday is a holiday in eight American states. For British readers, just in case there are any out there as ignorant as I am, a comparison might be if I had gone up to Tony Blair's adviser Jonathan Powell and asked if he wasn't still a bit embarrassed about that 'rivers of blood' speech.

I'm still unaware of the extent of my gaffe, however, as I plod onwards in search of Arnie's pad. It's only by the time I get there – or where the map says it ought to be – that I really notice how the streets en route have got just that little bit dingier and neglected – this is California dingy, mind, not Buffalo dingy, dingy with sunshine and palm trees – but no longer quite the chocolate-box Sacramento of the riverside.

When finally I do turn a corner and find myself right next to the governor's mansion it's something of a shock. For a start it's wrapped in what looks like grey cloth. For half a second it crosses my mind that I've come upon an unheralded installation by Christo (the celebrity artist who has a thing about wrapping up famous buildings like brown paper parcels). The explanation was far more mundane: a sign that said 'Under Restoration', which had to explain why on closer examination – poking my head under the sheeting – I could see that the elegant external carved woodwork was in the process of being substantially dismantled. Arnie is obviously not at home. In fact it doesn't look as if there's been anyone at home for quite some time. Is this the right place, I ask myself once again rather stupidly and naively as it turns out, is this the residence, even notionally, of former indestructible twenty-third-century robotic terminator and now California governor, Arnold Schwarzenegger?

It isn't of course. Never had been. That indicator on the map, like the sign outside, proclaiming 'Governor's Mansion' was 'historic'. What it meant was that this *used* to be the governor's mansion and as it was old*ish* (probably about the same age as my London semi), someone had declared that it ought to be proclaimed a monument and preserved. But then I spot the guy sitting placidly in the shade provided by the wrapping, at a little table next to the doorway. He gets up, holds out a hand and introduces himself as John. John seems inordinately pleased to see me. This is because, as I was about to discover, John is a mine of information that almost nobody ever cares to excavate. And he was just bursting to dig up his treasures.

The building I've come to see, John explains, handing over an entrance ticket and waiting for me to proffer a couple of dollars, is the 'Old Governor's Mansion,' so called, he explains, because it's very old, and also because it's no longer the governor's mansion. It dates, he goes on enthusiastically, hustling me inside the door, all the way back to 1877. He's looking at me expectantly here so I do my best to smile encouragingly while not exactly letting my jaw drop; 1877 of course doesn't seem particularly old to me, but we have been here before: it's only when dealing with dinosaurs that Americans and Europeans agree on degrees of antiquity (and that's assuming you're not dealing with the types who believe the dinosaurs are actually just 4,000 years old like the rest of the planet and put on the earth as a clever trick by God to test our faith).

The house, most of which I couldn't see from the outside because of the giant dishcloth draped over it, in fact looked splendidly like something the Addams family would have inhabited: a turreted, Franco-Italianate monster of a place, all made out of wood. If it were made of brick it would look at home in posher Parisian suburbs. I can tell this because there are photographs of it on the walls. John, meanwhile, is pouring out its history like one of those computers on a science-fiction spaceship that has been waiting two hundred years for the humans to emerge from hibernation and press the 'on' button. 'The mansion was originally build in 1877 for Albert Gallatin who was a well-known Sacramento businessman. It was purchased by the State of California in 1903 for $32,500 and includes furnishings left behind by many previous governors. Altogether the mansion has been the home of 13 governors, from George Pardee who was the first to live here to Ronald Reagan, who was the last.' For a moment he slips into an aside, pointing out the sanitary facilities: 'Nancy Reagan would have used that toilet.'

Thankfully by now he is pointing out the 1902 Steinway piano that belonged to Governor Pardee and the Persian rugs that once belonged to Governor Pat Brown. Brown, it seems, remains the house's guiding spirit and John has an obvious fondness for him, taking pains to direct my attention to a photograph of Brown with JFK in the mansion. Most of the mansion's downstairs decor is heavy Victorian in appearance, all chintz and brocade, though the furniture, John reveals, is actually mostly replica stuff bought by Governor Warren's wife in the 1940s. The upstairs, he says, mostly dates from the 'Brown period', including the outdoor swimming pool. Hey, it's California, the governor had to have a swimming pool.

'The mansion is unusual among museums in that it is not a replica or a restoration,' John is saying, but I'm not quite sure what that means until I think of 'Old Sacramento'. 'It stands much as it did when vacated by the Reagans in 1967,' he adds helpfully.

'So why,' I have to ask, 'did the Reagans do a runner?'

'Well, it's kinda like this,' John starts, and I gather I'm in for a bit of a story.

What it boils down to in the end, is that Nancy just didn't like the location. Or the house, come to that. Back in 1967 when Ron and Nancy moved in, the street outside was still part of US40, the main highway connecting New York to San Francisco. US40 was one of those legendary US highways that had gradually taken the place of the railroad as the nation's favourite means of transportation. If you wanted to get from coast to coast, the grand transcontinental railroad that had united the nation and cost so many lives and so many millions of dollars had been replaced by the strip of tarmac that ran right past the parlour windows of the governor's mansion. 'There was a gas station right across the road,' adds John, shrugging his shoulders as if that was something you could obviously not expect future First Lady Nancy Reagan to have put up with.

The wooden house, John tells me, was also considered a fire hazard, although why it should be deemed more of a fire hazard than any of the tens of thousands of other wooden homes across America and indeed down the California coastline, was a mystery to me. Maybe governors were deemed more inflammable.

There was another problem for the Reagans too as the first Hollywood-anointed occupants of the governorship: celebrity dinner parties. 'They had just one big table that filled the dining room, but wasn't big enough to cope with all their guests. Some had to sit on a folding table they put next to it in a kind of T shape. But that poses a question: when you've got John Wayne, Dean Martin and Frank Sinatra round for dinner, which of those guys do you make sit at the little table? Obviously not Frankie!' Obviously! Even the Krays wouldn't have dared 'diss' Frankie.

The Reagans moved out, into upscale rented accommodation. And then of course they were given government accommodation, at 1600 Pennsylvania Avenue, Washington DC. None of the following governors ever moved back in, least of all the present incumbent. But that doesn't stop the curator of the mansion being the big man's number one fan. He's less interested in whether Barack Obama or John McCain makes it to the White House, than the change in the law that means only US-born citizens can become president.

'Unstoppable! Absolutely unstoppable!' gushes John, with a twinkle of genuine enthusiasm in his eye. 'That was my first thought when I heard that Arnold Schwarzenegger was going to run for governor. If they changed that law, he'd be president! And I'll tell you why: people like a cartoon hero, a guy who puts the bad guys in their place and always comes out on top.'

We can even imagine his re-election slogan: I'll be back!

So where does big Arnie live in Sacramento when he's up here running the state that would on its own be the world's tenth largest economy? It appears the governor may share some of his fellow southern California residents' ideas about their state capital. He's only here when he has to be. As befits a movie star – even one who's moved into politics, Arnie still lives in LA, rents a top floor apartment of the Hyatt Regency Hotel next to the Capitol, home to the governor's office and state legislature, and flies back and forth at his own expense (he can afford it), even to the extent of occasionally taking a helicopter which lands on the pad on the Hyatt roof. He can then descend via a private elevator to a basement level passageway that crosses the road into the Capitol, where another lift takes him up to his office. Or so the popular legend has it, and I see no reason to contradict it.

It's not, after all, as unlikely as another politically incorrect piece of Arnie legend which the great man himself has confirmed, and even boasted about: the 'stogie tent' in the governor's courtyard. The courtyard in question is a closed-off quadrangle in the middle of the Capitol building with access directly from the governor's office. Shortly after his arrival in November 2003 Schwarzenegger had it 'grassed over' with AstroTurf and erected a 12 by 16 foot tent on it. The purpose: specifically to get round California's anti-smoking laws, which ban smoking not just inside but within 20 feet of a government building. The man who had twice graced the cover of *Cigar Aficionado* magazine was not about to give up the habit of a lifetime. Whether or not Schwarzenegger's smoking – given the mild California climate, the tent effectively became his office – was breaking the law remained a moot point, hotly disputed by anti-smoking campaigners. As was the time in 2007 when he was seen lighting up a Havana Partagas, even though it is illegal for US citizens to buy them: Schwarzenegger picked one up in a hotel shop, but had an aide pay for it. Unsurprising, therefore, that the Governator was not lectured to by the anti-smoking lobby, and was as proud of his tent as Libyan leader Colonel Gaddafi is of the Bedouin tents he regularly uses to receive world leaders. Arnie too regularly invited guests from state politicians to visiting celebrities out to the tent to 'join me in a stogie'. It's a 'stogie-smoking, deal-making meeting tent,' he described it.

Right now it is gone – not a victim of political correctness – but at a request from the maintenance people who needed to take it down to perform essential repairs to the building. As a result, for the first time in four years, California's August budget debate – a matter of tense negotiations between legislators and the governor – was carried out in the open air rather than behind a veil of smoke in a tent. Whether or not the outcome was any clearer remains to be seen. Will the tent stage a return? It would be a brave man who bet against it.

Heading towards the Capitol itself, I can't help thinking that it looks remarkably like a rival to the one in Washington, except that here its glistening white dome is picked out against a perma-blue sky and framed by a long avenue of towering palm trees. It is an impressive building. I am discovering that when it comes to state capitols, they pretty much all come out of the same box – a standard variation on the Washington-shape but a little smaller depending on the pretensions of the state – but somehow California's looks that little bit special. Ah, yes – the avenue of 40-foot palm trees! And the sprinklers embedded in the lawns.

The guards on the door of the Capitol are California State Troopers, but to my inexperienced eye they look like Canadian Mounties in mufti, with their wide-brimmed hats and beige short-sleeved uniforms. The one at the door smiles broadly and says 'Welcome to the Capitol, sir.' Compared to entering most British government offices the security seems rather lax – as if even under George W. Bush Americans are encouraged to believe that government is something that supposedly belongs to them as opposed to the established attitude of British officialdom that we belong to the government and had jolly well better not speak until we're spoken to.

On the other hand we have nothing quite to compare with a US state legislature – except perhaps for the devolved assemblies in Scotland, Northern Ireland or Wales. There's always a bit of a wrangle in America over just how important state laws and the men who make them actually are. For example California has legalised the medicinal use of cannabis, which unsurprisingly led to the establishment of a wide number of 'alternative therapy doctors' who have successfully applied for a licence to distribute it. In fact over a relatively short period of time it is quite remarkable how many illnesses, physical and psychological, it apparently helps. It is also remarkable how many of these 'alternative therapy doctors' have been raided by the federal Alcohol, Tobacco and Firearms bureau. In response they have argued that they are operating legally under California law. The result has yet to be decided. I can't help thinking that what is needed is a variation on the pragmatism of the Dutch: the Netherlands banned smoking tobacco in public premises from 1 July 2008, but has continued to tolerate the widespread, though technically illegal, sale and use of cannabis in 'coffee shops', strictly providing that a 'joint' no longer contains tobacco. Put that in your pipe and smoke it, California!

It says much about the relative powers of state and federal legislatures these days that much of the California Capitol – almost the whole ground floor – is a museum, given over to how these rooms of state would have looked a century ago. America may have begun life as a federation – and the states still jealously cling to their limited autonomy – but the tendency of recent years has been for centralization, at least to the extent of making abundantly clear that federal, i.e. national, law takes priority.

But there is nothing modest about the sign above the door of one office, guarded by two armed 'mounties'. The name of the occupant is emblazoned above it in huge gold letters that given the length of the name stretch almost the width of the double doors: ARNOLD SCHWARZENEGGER, and on the line below: GOVERNOR

'Is the governor in?' I ask as politely as possible.

'Can't say, sir,' one of the state troopers (I've tried to stop even thinking 'mountie' in case he can read my mind) replies equally politely.

'Is that because you're not allowed to or because you haven't seen him?'

'He has his own elevator,' he replies, not quite answering my question, but confirming the answer to one I hadn't quite dared ask. I wanted to see where the tent had been, but apparently the inner courtyard is only visible from the offices above, and none of them are open to the public.

So there you go, I'm not going to meet the Terminator after all. Well, not here. Maybe in LA? On the way back to the riverboat I come through the psychedelic underpass again. The syncopated jazz is still playing, and all of a sudden I realise its true purpose. There's nobody here. Nobody stinking of urine and sleeping in a heap against the wall. Nobody hanging around drinking from bottles. They just can't stand the goddamn music.

Actually, I know how they feel. On an impulse I plug in my iPod and treat myself to a large dose of nostalgia with Neil Young's 'After the Gold Rush'. Most of the time I believe travellers should keep both their eyes and ears open to where they are: to miss out on one sensory input is to get the whole picture wrong. But there are moments, just now and then, when it can be a little luxury to be able to use modern technology to treat yourself to your own, on-demand soundtrack. I didn't just choose old Neil because of Sacramento's connection to the original gold rush, but just because listening to that west coast voice whining nasally on about 'mother nature on the run in the 1970s' is pure personal self-indulgence.

Ahead of me the *Delta King* sits lazily on the calm blue waters of the Sacramento River – they really are blue, I'm not sure I've ever seen another river that was blue, and certainly not the Danube – while over on the deck outside Joe's

Crab Shack waitresses are serving up cold beers. This may be toytown America but right now it's too good to turn away from.

And then, just as I'm about to unplug again and return to the world of pre-production values, the small god of the iPod makes his mischievous presence felt. This may take some believing, but I swear that just as I was about to extract the tight little plugs of my Sennheiser headphones I caught the unmistakable opening chords of REM's 'All The Way to Reno'. My next destination.

I kid you not: this is the way religions are born. I've only been in California for 24 hours and already I'm going native.

SACRAMENTO TO RENO

TRAIN: California Zephyr
FREQUENCY: 1 a day
DEPART SACRAMENTO, CALIFORNIA: 10:54 a.m.

via
Roseville, CA
Colfax, CA
Truckee, CA

ARRIVE RENO, NEVADA: 3:51 p.m.
DURATION: 4 hours, 57 minutes
DISTANCE: 131 miles

13

After the Gold Rush

GIVEN THAT THE WESTERN END of the great railroad project which created America began in Sacramento it is scarcely surprising that this is home to one of the finest monuments to a mode of transport it has all but abandoned: The California State Railroad Museum. And it says something for the romance and nostalgia which the railroads still evoke that it draws 600,000 visitors a year.

But just walking through the door it is easy to see why. Standing in front of you – on a par with any reconstructed dinosaur (even Leonardo) – are some of the world's great locomotives, beautifully restored and most of them available to be explored and in some cases even climbed over. For a start – almost literally – there is the magnificent Gov. Stanford, a great black brute of an engine with a funnel like a popcorn machine, a cow-catcher that could carve its way through a *corrida* and a vast, front-mounted lantern the size of a World War II searchlight. It is, even to modern eyes, a stupendous thing: somehow antique, futuristic, impressive and ridiculous all at once. In an electronic age of ever-diminishing moving parts, it is outrageously – almost frighteningly – mechanical. When we want to praise something we say it has 'all the bells and whistles'; take one look at a train like this and you see why.

The Gov. Stanford, named after a California governor and one of the men who made the railroad possible (and himself rich), was built by the Norris Locomotive Works in Philadelphia, Pennsylvania, and transported by sailing ship all the way around South America via Cape Horn to Sacramento, where it arrived in late 1863. It would become the first locomotive on the Central Pacific Railroad, the western branch of the transcontinental track.

What makes the Sacramento Railroad Museum special is not just the trains but the staff: this is a railway anorak's dream job. You can see it in the faces of the mostly male, retired volunteers who beam as they welcome you aboard their own particular charge: one of the hulking behemoths of the early steam age, or maybe The Gold Coast, a restored, ridiculously opulent nineteenth-century dining car with heavy draped curtains, mahogany panelling and tables set with linen, fine china and candlesticks. Or a Streamliner from the 1930s, glistening with polished stainless steel and aluminium (and even air-conditioning), one of the few luxuries that survived even in the Great Depression.

Railway enthusiasm surpasses political correctness. A jovial African-American man was proud to show me around the St Hyacinthe, one of the plush sleeping cars built by the Pullman Company (founded by George Pullman) which became a global concept. But what surprised me most was the openly genial way he sported the uniform that he explained would have been worn by 'Negroes, who were only allowed on board these cars as porters'. It was, he said, one of the most prestigious jobs open to African-Americans right up until the civil rights movement of the 1960s. With an African-American standing for president, he found no problem accepting that the injustice of the past was what it is: something belonging to the past. The railroad helped change American in more ways than one.

Just how the transcontinental railroad came to be built is a story worth a book of its own* and requires at least a brief diversion here. The discovery of gold had changed California forever: by 1850 it was declared a state of the union, even though the rest of the union was half a continent away. Lewis and Clark had blazed a trail across the hostile wilderness but it was not a route that invited the average citizen to follow on horse and cart, though, as we shall see, some did. Since its capture from Mexico, California was the United States' newest, and with the discovery of gold possibly richest, colony. But it was still that: a colony of a country on the far eastern seaboard. It was far from obvious that the huge expanse of land in between, populated by suspicious and increasingly hostile natives, would ever join it.

The 3,000-mile overland route from coast to coast was risky in the extreme and with no roads or clear tracks a long and incredibly arduous traverse. The safer way was not exactly quick either – or particularly safe. It meant rounding Cape Horn, a hazardous business at the best of times, and was in total a journey of 18,000 miles that took over six months. It wasn't cheap either. Clearly, if California was ever really to belong to the United States, something had to be done. Thus was the concept born that would grandly be known as

---

*There are several but the most comprehensive has to be *Nothing Like It In The World* by Stephen E. Ambrose.

America's 'Manifest Destiny', a phrase that managed to imply that creating a single country to span a continent had somehow been decreed by God.

The very first railway engines to be seen in the United States had been four British coalmine engines imported in 1829. Christmas Day 1830 marked the opening of the first passenger line at Charleston, North Carolina. What followed was an explosion into empty space. Within 10 years the lines of track had multiplied from 23 to 2,800. By 1857 the eastern United States had half the entire world total of railway lines. The man who would make a serious start on the project of a railway line that would cross a continent was a civil engineer called Theodore D. Judah who was brought to California – via the fearful Panama route – by the promoters of the new state's first rail project: the 22-mile-long Sacramento Valley Railroad which linked the city to the western terminus of the Pony Express. But by the time he had finished their task in 1856 Judah was convinced he could build something a lot longer than 22 miles: a railroad that could cross a continent.

Judah had managed to catch the eye and ear of a young Kentucky-born congressman called Abraham Lincoln, who friends in the Republican Party said was going to do well. Judah lobbied in Washington and in Sacramento and by 1860 managed to put together the business interests of four California businessmen (all originally from upstate New York), who were also supporters of Lincoln's campaign for the presidency. Collis Huntington and Mark Hopkins were partners in a Sacramento hardware store, Leland Stanford operated a grocery business and Charles Crocker ran a dry goods company. Modest businesses but they had all done extremely well out of the gold rush and had money to spare. Allowing Judah to persuade them to put it into his 'madcap' scheme was the best business decision any of them would ever make. They were to become known as The Big Four, eventually controlling a transportation and property empire that stretched halfway across America, and would be admired and detested in almost equal measure.

All of them knew in detail the problems of getting from California to the nation's financial capital, New York, and its political capital, Washington. Huntington had first made the journey at the age of 27 in the early flush of the gold rush. Rather than the epic round-the-Horn ocean trip, he was one of the first to try the Panama 'short cut': boarding a steamer from New York down past Florida and the tip of Cuba – an eight-day journey in itself – to a fly-blown port at the mouth of the Chagres River (which then belonged to Greater Colombia). There they had to disembark via native canoes and hire Indians to help them downriver, sleeping on the muddy shores, then trekking over the mountains for five days to reach so-called Panama City which turned out to be nothing more than a sea of tents in an ocean of mud plagued by frequent epidemics of malaria and cholera. From there they trekked on through 24 miles of jungle to the coast to wait for a northbound ship to call. Judah himself had been seriously ill on the same route. In 1863 on his way back to New York to try to raise more funds, he contracted yellow fever in Panama and subsequently died of it that November, only a few weeks after the Gov. Stanford arrived in Sacramento.

What created the political will needed for such a vast undertaking was the outbreak of the civil war between North and South. California sided with the North – providing crucial supplies of gold – though the fighting was half a continent away. But the conflict highlighted the potential of secession in a disconnected nation spread over such vast distances. The North declared it a political necessity for the survival of the union. The groundbreaking for the great project took place at the intersection of Front and K Streets in Sacramento, right outside Huntington's and Hopkins' store, in January, 1863, a full two years before the war ended. The completion of one of the wonders of the nineteenth-century world was not to be achieved without greased palms, dodgy dealing, and the labour – and death – of thousands of Chinese workers who more than any other group forced the route over the seemingly impassable barrier of the central Rocky Mountains.

Boarding the train just after 11 in the morning for what is one of the most scenically beautiful railway journeys in the world, it's hard to imagine how they even started, let alone breached the summit of the peaks ahead. And I'm not hanging off a cliff in a basket loaded with gunpowder! But in case my imagination fails, there are two volunteers from the Railroad Museum on board for the mountain crossing section to give passengers a running commentary on one of Amtrak's most spectacular routes. The American word for these guys is 'docent', which is not a term I've ever heard before, but is widely employed to describe these keen, usually elderly, well-informed volunteers. It has the huge advantage of sounding more scholarly than 'anorak'.

But I am being unfair. The term 'trainspotter' is used so widely and pejoratively in Britain that we automatically conjure up a vision of some bloke with thick specs standing under grey drizzly skies in the aforementioned anorak, cowl pulled up over his head, myopically recording locomotive serial numbers in a notebook. Maybe it's the weather – sunshine does wonders for the soul – but the California equivalents tend to be bright-eyed 'seniors' – retirees with a spring in their step – conveying a genuine enthusiasm for not just the technicalities of the railroad but the history and circumstances of its construction.

'Ladies and gentlemen, you may think the land around here is pretty flat,' drawls the laid-back voice over the intercom as we pull out of Sacramento past a vista of suburban houses, brown scorched fields, roads and trailers with not a molehill in sight, never mind the mountains we know lie ahead. 'The elevation above sea level here is just 80 feet,' and it is so palpably flat that the next thing we pass is an airfield: 'This here's McClellan Field, an important military base for more than 60 years, only relatively recently turned over to the local county for development as an industrial site.' A little further on we pass through a drab landscape of industrial development, but the onboard guide manages even to squeeze an iota of interest out of this: 'Right now you're lookin' at the works of the Blue Diamond Company.' Ooh, we stare, wondering where they dig up brilliant stones in this unlikely landscape. 'It has nothing to do with diamonds,' the docent lets us down gently, 'but is the largest almond-processing facility on earth, dealing with most of the one million pounds (450 tonnes) of almonds produced in California each year.' See: anoraky for sure, but interesting too.

We've barely left the outskirts of the city and there's still no perceptible increase in gradient when the docent comes in with what is obviously one of his most practised lines: 'Okay now, you've heard tell of people trying to move a mountain, well right here's where four men moved an entire mountain range.' He's not kidding either. 'You see folks, when they passed the Pacific Railroad Act of 1862, which laid down the financial support for building the railroad, they agreed there would be more government money made available for sections over the mountains. ''Cept those congressmen back in Washington DC had no idea where the mountains began, had they? So they decided the mountains would begin where President Lincoln said they began. Thing is, old Lincoln, he didn't much know either. So he asked the state geologist Josiah D. Witney, man they named the highest mountain in the USA outside Alaska after. Crocker, one of the Big Four, took Whitney out here in his buggy and got him to say the Arcade Creek, which we've just gone over' – we crane our necks to look out the window – 'was where the Sierra Nevada started. Lincoln said that was good enough for him. So there you go, folks, who said faith couldn't move mountains?'

It's a good story – and true! – and gets the laugh it deserves. This is a regular scheduled daily train, not a tourist excursion, but the docents have managed to create a jokey school day-out atmosphere. On the other hand, most of my fellow travellers do seem to be here at least as much for the spectacle as the means of transport. If they simply had wanted to get from A to B they would have flown.

'Now this here town,' the docent meanwhile starts up again, as we pass through what seems to me like nowheresville suburbia, 'was originally known by the romantic name of Junction – because it was a junction – but in 1864 the people who had moved here, followin' the railroad, were allowed to choose a better name. They called it after the prettiest girl in town: Junction became Roseville. It didn't make the town any prettier though.' Another laugh. 'And more than a century and a half later, if anything, things have got worse,' this as we pass though a vast wilderness of sidings and freight trucks. 'Although the local people probably wouldn't agree: the western freight lines invested $140 million in the 1990s to renovate Roseville as the most important rail yard west of the Rockies.'

Eventually, some miles further on, the land does just noticeably begin to rise and our guide points out we are at a less-than-colossal 100 feet above sea level when we reach the nondescript little town of Auburn: 'The courthouse which you can just see over there, was built in 1894 and' – the usual tone of expectant awe – 'is still in use today.' The 'old building' stuff is gradually beginning to lose its amusement value to the extent of becoming comic.

'It's just two miles south of here that gold was first discovered in California in 1848, at a place called Sutter's Mill. Auburn grew up to be the administrative centre for the area, and long before the present ancient [sic] courthouse was built the grounds in which it stands were known for meting out justice in the form of hanging for the growing number of outlaws who decided there were fatter pickings to be had stealing from the miners than to join their number.'

There's not the slightest doubt now that we're going seriously uphill, and fast, through a couple of tunnels and along tracks that seem increasingly to cling to the side of steeply-wooded gorges. All of a sudden the slowly rising land becomes foothills which in a matter of a few miles become mountains – reinforcing how mad the notion of a railway across them must have seemed 150 years ago. Just looking out the window as we climb rapidly on winding tracks, the idea of cutting a track into this mountainside falling away at an angle of nearly 75 degrees seems virtually impossible today and unimaginable with the engineering equipment of the mid-nineteenth century. It seemed pretty much the same to the men tasked to build it who found it hard to believe the engineers had decreed this to be the only feasible route. Amazingly the solution was genuinely ancient even if it did come from another continent.

In 1865 on a trial basis 50 Chinese who had come to California to seek work were taken on by Central Pacific as casual labourers. They turned out to be more reliable and hardworking than most of the rest of the workers, many of whom were Irish and had been shipped in – at great expense – from New York and the east coast, but were given to fights, drinking and simply running off to work the gold mines. The Chinese took less time off work for sickness, inebriation or injury than any other workers. They also brought their own food – because they preferred it – but that made them cheaper too. It also had the unacknowledged bonus that it made them healthier.

It was the Chinese who had a solution to the seemingly impossibly steep slopes. One of the foremen approached the site boss and explained that they had long experience in this type of work from the days when their ancestors built fortresses along the Yangtze gorges. What he needed, he explained, was a supply of reed to be sent up from San Francisco. The reed was duly ordered and the Chinese began weaving it into round, waist-high baskets with eyelets at the top which could be fixed to a cable and suspended from a pulley mechanism high above. One at a time workers would climb into the basket to be lowered from a bluff above and would use small hand drills to bore a hole into the mountainside into which they would fix a black powder charge – it was after all a Chinese invention. Then they would light the fuse and shout to be hauled out of the way before it exploded.

It was incredibly successful, though not without casualties. Exactly how many died in the operation is not recorded; although the Central Pacific paid its Chinese workers the same as its European workforce, it didn't bother to keep track of their fatalities. But it was a spectacular piece of work, the result of which can still be admired today on the rocky bluff known as Cape Horn where the train crawls along a hairpin bend etched into the side of a pine-clad canyon wall that drops 1,800 feet to the American River below.

'In the olden days,' the docent tells us, 'trains would stop here for passengers to get out, stretch their legs and admire the view, but that was in the days when travel was less hurried.' Given that the 40 miles an hour, which is the most we can manage at this point due to the gradient, hardly seems hurried, it is a pity they gave up the custom.

The Chinese became known as 'Celestials' because they described their homeland as the 'Celestial Kingdom', but I can't help thinking it's because so many of them found themselves ascending to heaven rather earlier than intended. One way or another the railroad builders were so impressed that they began actively recruiting in China and by the time the transcontinental route was finished in 1869 there were more than 10,000 Chinese on the company's employment register.

James Strobridge, who was in charge of construction on this section of the route said of his Chinese workforce: 'They learn quickly. They do not fight, have no strikes that amount to anything, and are very cleanly in their habits. They will gamble and do quarrel among themselves most noisily – but harmlessly.' On the odd occasion when there was any trouble Strobridge settled it himself by picking out the ringleaders and confronting them with an axe handle.

Getting the railway built was big business that went far beyond the labours of construction. Except where the railway passed through cities and over rivers the companies that built it were granted 10 square miles of land on each side of the tracks for every other section of one-mile track built. In total, during the 21 years from 1850 to 1871 the land the railway companies were granted by the federal government – with no reference of course to the Native American peoples who might foolishly have thought their centuries-old occupation of it gave them some rights of ownership – amounted to 175 million acres, or one tenth of the total land mass of today's continental United States. The Big Four became very big indeed.

As we continue relentlessly uphill the docents, taking turns to fill in rather like a pair of news anchors, explain that part of the gradient here was cleared by hydraulic miners, who simply sprayed the rock and gravel with high velocity water until it gave way and crumbled and they could sieve gold from the run-off. The quantities to be obtained in certain areas were hardly commercial and the railroad was actually laid over a gold-bearing gravel surface. But if it was one thing to declare it uneconomic to mine, it was quite another to scare off penniless prospectors who continued to spray the gravel even after the tracks were laid, eroding the bed. In the end the railroad company had to hire armed guards to keep them at bay. Meanwhile the mud and gravel run-off pouring downhill clogged both the American and Sacramento rivers so badly that eventually the state court in 1884 declared it illegal, thereby passing California's first environmental law.

Up here though the main value of the land is its spectacular rugged beauty and the fact that railroad or no railroad – and the modern winding highway also notwithstanding – it remains remote and relatively inaccessible. Particularly in winter. We are now a mile above sea level and several thousand feet above the Bear River that winds its way through the deep canyon below. Even nearly 90 years after the Chinese labourers first blasted their way along these ledges, trains could come close to disaster in the wrong weather conditions.

One of our docents has taken to the microphone again now with a tone of voice that suggests he is reading a ghost story in front of the fire in a log cabin. 'These mountains can also be terrible places,' he says quietly. 'Back in the winter of 1951 the City of San Francisco 'Surfliner' train became trapped after an avalanche blocked the track ahead. The train stopped but got caught in a heavy snowfall – the like of which nobody had ever seen before – which dumped more than 16 feet on top of it. That train was stranded. For nearly four days, the 196 passengers and a crew of 30 were trapped. A major rescue attempt involved not just everything at the railway company's disposal but also army, air force and workers for the power and water companies who maintained high-mountain reservoirs. In the end they only got to them when a footway was dug through the deep snow to reach the end carriage. All the people on board that train escaped to be taken to safety in a fleet of 11 private cars with only a few minor injuries and, remarkably, no fatalities.

'Unfortunately the same could not be said for the rescuers: the engineer of a locomotive trying to plough its way up the tracks towards the trapped train was killed when a sudden avalanche swept him and his locomotive down the precipice below. Another man, an employee of one of the power companies who operated a snowcat for 48 hours continuously during the rescue attempt died of a heart attack a day later.'

It's impressive stuff and makes us understand the need for the avalanche protection sheds that cover the tracks up here even if they do spoil the extravagant views. And then we enter what our docent calls, 'The Big Hole'. 'This is a two-mile-long tunnel, ladies and gentlemen, and when we come out the other side we shall be at the highest point across the Sierra, 7,500 feet up.' With that he lapses into silence and the train whooshes into darkness.

Emerging is almost a shock to the senses. We have sprung from darkness into light, on the top of the world: a great blinding blaze of blue-skied sunshine beams down over an unspoiled vista of forest, green leaves flecked here and there with autumnal golds amid surprisingly gentle mountain tops and in the distance as we begin our gradually curving descent towards it, a wonderful lake of the deepest darkest blue. No sooner have we all got our cameras out than the fatalist in the engineer's cab turns to a sombre story that cuts to the quick of the wagon train legend.

'Now, ladies and gentlemen, below you we have Lake Donner. Back here in 1846 there occurred one of the worst tragedies of the pioneer days. A group of settler families who'd set out from Illinois heading for California camped here by the shores of this beautiful lake you see in front of you for a day or two. But they made the mistake of taking the weather in the mountains for granted to get shut in by a blizzard. This was in October, mind. Well, they were here for more than a day or two. In fact, it took until January for the first handful of them who had put together makeshift snowshoes to struggle on the next 100 miles to reach Sutter's Fort. It took weeks more for a relief party to get back to the others, by which time half of the 87-strong party had starved to death, including five women and 14 children, while many of those who survived had had to resort to cannibalism, eating the bodies of their loved ones. The original family who had begun the trip in Illinois was called Donner, and the lake was named after them.'

All of a sudden Lake Donner's placid dark blue waters look a lot less inviting. This is a tale that obviously has deep resonance with one group of passengers who have come into the observation car specially. For an unkind minute I think we have been invaded by the cast of a live-action Disney remake of *Snow White*. Beaming broadly are two middle-aged balding men with large beards in identical blue shirts, black dungarees and big black boots, and next to them two dumpy middle-aged women also dressed identically in green dresses with white bonnets and thick black stockings. And more remarkably still, a teenage girl dressed exactly the same. Back in Britain, if someone were to describe a family group all dressed in clothing that clearly related to their religion I would visualise chadors or at least headscarves and assume them to be Muslim. Here, I have little doubt I have come across my first Amish. Just to make it clear as they take their seats along the wall of the observation car facing Lake Donner they all burst into a tuneful rendition of 'Amazing Grace'. I'm not sure what it is about the scene of great disasters that inspires the Godly to sing His praises when what they are confronted with appears to be proof of divine indifference.

But by now the little Amish group has taken us by surprise again, this time by pulling out a pack of cards and dealing hands.

'Hey,' says a big bearded ticket inspector passing through at just that moment – though his own hirsute appearance is more reminiscent of a mountain grizzly than one of Snow White's dwarfs – 'I though you guys didn't do that kind of stuff.'

'Sure we do. Get on,' says one of the two women with a twinkly smile. It occurs to me that I would find it remarkably hard to tell the two men or the two women apart. It's not that I couldn't – they're obviously not twins or anything – but it's something to do with the identical clothing, identical glasses, identical hairstyles (at least as far as the men are concerned, the women's hair is modestly concealed beneath their bonnets) and their remarkably similar shapes. Put them on stage and they could be an Amish ABBA tribute act! Except for the girl, of course. She's probably about 15, I guess, though it's hard to tell dressed like that. Pretty in a shy sort of way, behind her glasses and with her bonnet on, and overshadowed by the dumpy ghosts of her probable future, with whom, however, she is politely chatting and playing cards with a far greater good humour than many teenage girls dragged on holiday with their parents and parents' similarly middle-aged friends might display.

And a holiday is indeed what they are on, I discover, getting into a casual conversation with one of the two men, who unfortunately reinforces my ABBA image by telling me his name is Ben (at least it isn't Benny – or Bjørn). 'From Benjamin,' he explains, pronouncing the 'j' like a 'y', German-style.

It's the language in fact, which has given me an opening into the conversation. As a German speaker it's impossible not to be intrigued by a snatch like the following, overheard as they examined the cards in their hands:

'Was bin ish?'

'Troumpf.'

'Hasht du a veildcard?'

'Ach, my pen schreibt nit.'

It's a wacky, unartificial, easy-flowing hybrid dialect of American English and an archaic German. (What suit am I playing? Trumps. Have you got a face card? Blow, my pen isn't working.) Not one thing or the other, but the sort of language that families and close friends who are all bilingual drift into when talking casually among one another.

I don't want to eavesdrop but as a linguist the blend is fascinating. Every now and then, the conversation slips away from me as they drift wholly into an archaic dialect of German that even a modern Berliner would find incomprehensible. And then all of a sudden they switch wholly back into American English. 'Aw, man!' says the teenager suddenly, laying out her obviously useless cards on the table. It's not, I realise, as if they're dropping into their own tongue to share some secrets but have momentarily forgotten that for politeness' sake in mixed company they should speak the lingua franca.

'Yeah, it's a kind of German,' one of the women says, when I dare to ask. 'We call it Pennsylvania Dutch, but that's really "deutsch". Our testament is in German,' she adds with that disarming beaming smile.

Ben explains their holiday route. I know the Amish, who keep mostly to themselves on their farms in and around Pennsylvania, prefer to shun most aspects of modern life, including cars, television and certainly aircraft. It just hadn't occurred to me that they would have embraced the train. I guess it just depends at what stage you put history on hold. They have already crossed the country twice, visiting Chicago and Texas, and are planning on doing it again. The Amish turn out to be the only American travellers I meet who have been on more American trains than I have.

I've been assuming that the card game is something like Snap or Happy Families. I can see it does not use traditional playing cards – the sort my own staunch Presbyterian Northern Irish grandfather routinely referred to as 'the devil's cards'. But the women explain to me that it's actually a form of rummy, with suits and wild cards of its own. Sin, like beauty, it would seem can be wholly in the eye of the beholder.

There was more than enough sin in our next stop; the docent interrupts our conversation over the microphone. Truckee owes its quixotic name not to being a truck stop but to Chief To-Kay of the Paiute tribe. 'It began as a lumber town and had 14 mills working by the time the railroad arrived in 1867. But it soon had more saloons and became known for its lawlessness.' It seems unlikely looking out at the little row of gentrified late nineteenth-century shops and the car parks full of SUVs. 'In fact, in the space of 11 years, between 1871 and 1882, the whole town burned down six times. Today, however, the town is a popular outdoors vacation stop and the Truckee River has some fine fishin'.'

The Amish, clearly happier with God's bounty than the fires of hell, nod happily and one of the women – I'm still not sure which is which – leans over towards me and nodding towards Ben says, 'He's a real good fisherman.' And Ben, who despite my earlier evocation of him as one of Snow White's pint-sized retinue has to be at least six-foot-three, blushes to the roots of his thinning hair. Ahhh, bashful. I was right after all.

But by now our docent has cut in again for 'one last anecdote, folks, before we leave you' (once safely over the Rockies they turn around again and head back to Sacramento to perform the same service for westbound travellers). 'We are comin' up to Verdi,' (up until now I had been inducing Italian origins, but he pronounces it Verd-Eye), 'and it was near here that almost as soon as the railroad went through, it saw its first armed robbery.' But then we have crossed the state line into Nevada now and the state that made the mafia respectable has to be expected to have had a chequered history.

What is it about railway robberies that somehow accrues glamour? I suppose we had it in Britain with the grudging admiration for the thieves who carried out the Great Train Robbery in the 1960s and went on, mostly, to be rehabilitated. In the story of the American West they have acquired a legendary status all of their own. Montana had Butch Cassidy, the Sundance

Kid and the Hole in the Wall Gang but it was here in western Nevada that the precedent was set. Barely 18 months after the first transcontinental railroad had been completed a gang of ex-stagecoach robbers turned their attention to the new Iron Horse, helped by inside information from a mine agent at Virginia City, one of Nevada's oldest mining towns and, as it happens, the site of the fictional Ponderosa Ranch in the classic TV series *Bonanza*. The agent, Jack Davis, was aware of a shipment of gold coins due from San Francisco to pay the miners and informed the gang who struck as the train was leaving Verdi for Reno just after midnight on 5 November 1870. Their ringleader was John Chapman, who just happened to be the local Sunday School superintendent. Three men boarded the train in Verdi, to be joined by five others already on board as passengers. Two of them tackled the 'engineer' urging him to fire the train on, while the others beat off an attack by an axe-wielding conductor, detached the rest of the train which was left behind while they, the locomotive and the 'express car' – which contained the strong room – sped on down the track. Six miles further on, they stopped, tied up the engineer and clerks, broke into the strong boxes and escaped with $41,600 in gold coins.

They were eventually tracked down in a manhunt across the two states, but a substantial proportion of their loot was never found, believed to have been stashed in caves in the desert. Even today there are still strange characters to be seen wandering around isolated desert valleys of western Nevada with metal detectors. But perhaps it's no more foolish than the original gold prospecting. And certainly – as I'm about to find out – a lot more productive than hoping to find a pot of gold in Nevada's casinos.

The casinos loom all around us now as we pull into Reno, self-proclaimed 'biggest little town in the world'. The Amish, wisely, stay on the train.

14

All the Way in Reno

I'M STANDING ON A BALCONY looking up at the inside of a giant silver golf ball on which a simulacrum of the night sky revolves around the pinnacle of a 50-foot creaking, groaning construction of steel and plastic that I've only just realised is a theatrical mock-up of a functioning nineteenth-century silver mine.

Then lightning crashes in the artificial heaven, thunder peels out, a wave of green lasers flashes out into a completely phoney but disconcertingly realistic impression of infinity and amidst the gigadecibel cacophony there explodes a tune of cathartic intensity, a piece of music that is as essential to the soul of America as perhaps nothing save *The Archers* theme tune is to Britain. Sing along now: 'Bump-diddy-ump-diddy-ump-diddy-ump, BONANZA!'

Instantly my inner eye conjures up a black-and-white picture of paternal Ben Cartwright, dim but lovable Hoss, dull old Adam and teenage heart-throb Little Joe, four abreast astride their steeds about to shout 'Yee-hah!' on the threshold of an ever-optimistic future. A few people descending to the lower floor of the Silver Legacy Resort Casino stare up at what appears to be a middle-aged bloke having a fit of hysterical laughter while at the same time consumed by a bout of uncontrollable nostalgia. You have to be grateful for magical moments like that. And hope that they don't happen too often.

The ranch on which the classic 1960s series was based, long before Lorne Green evolved from humble rancher to command *Battlestar Galactica*, is just up the road, in Nevada terms, from Reno. From 1967 until 2004 there was a Ponderosa Ranch theme park on the site but it is now closed down. Nonetheless a bonanza is what every visitor to the 'biggest little town in the world' is hoping for. In its dizziest daydreams Reno would like to grow up to be Las Vegas, even though the best thing about the place is the fact that it isn't. Even still it can be an assault to the senses.

Arriving by train – as most visitors don't – immediately reveals Reno's greatest statement of belief in its future: it has all but buried the tracks. Having grown up literally around the railway, Reno discovered that by the late twentieth century having traffic halted repeatedly during the day for mile-long-plus freight trains to trundle by, was a serious nuisance. As a result, the city – backed by the private finance invested in the casinos and a generous grant from federal government – spent some $284 million on cutting an open trench through the centre of town, allowing road traffic to pass uninterrupted.

Happily the station – a minor detail given that only two passenger-carrying Amtrak trains (one in each direction) call per day – substantially survived, with the addition of a lift down one floor to the new platform level. Entertainingly they left the 'restrooms' at street level, calling for much anxious lift-button-pressing by passengers apparently equally terrified of having to walk up one flight of stairs to the convenience or missing the once-a-day train (an admittedly serious inconvenience).

From the station it's a modest trot to the Silver Legacy where I had booked a room. You could stay somewhere other than in a casino in Reno, but it would be odd, and it wouldn't be easy. The Silver Legacy was identifiable, I'm told by the station attendant, by a silver golf ball the size of a small planet perched on its roof. It was only later that I found out why. Being identifiable from the outside, however, is quite another thing to being readily accessible on the inside, particularly to that little known and less regarded life form: the pedestrian.

It takes me three attempts to work out that all the obvious entrances from the street lead straight into the main, slot-machine throbbing casino floor and that to get into the hotel which towered above it, with the reception and lobby on the first (in American: second) floor, you're expected to drive straight to the underground parking. Or failing that, be chauffeured through a cavernous concrete-pillared approach about as pedestrian-friendly as the docking slot on a Death Star. Despite it being less than a five-minute walk most people coming here from the railroad station catch a cab.

Having finally negotiated the entrance procedure, I find myself suddenly enshrouded in a thin but deceptive veneer of luxury. Casino hotels are designed to look five star, even though they charge only two-to-three-star prices. If you look closely at the fixtures and fittings you'll find it's only rarely you hit the jackpot, but the reckoning is that if you're feeling flush and comfortable enough they'll soon get their money off you.

When I've checked in and been handed my fistful of vouchers for the 'casino resort attractions', I make my way to the 18th floor to find a view that is five star and more: endless limpid azure skies with just the wispiest of clouds floating over distant barren hills, and in the foreground this small but outrageous concrete and neon oasis of Mammon. Looking at Reno today, it is hard to imagine that the city it might have aspired to rival is not Las Vegas but Salt Lake City. This was originally a Mormon settlement, but sold its soul for 20 pieces of silver, although probably more like 20 million pieces nowadays. Annually. At whatever the going rate for silver is.

The discovery of silver in the second half of the nineteenth century finished off Reno's ambitions to becoming a strict Mormon community as the settlers were swamped by an influx of those who'd missed out on the gold rush. Silver was easier to find and easier to mine. It might not be worth as much but you could still end up rich if you got your hands on enough of it. And with the prospectors, as usual, came the saloons, whores and, most importantly for Reno – and all of Nevada – the card tables.

Gambling was legalised in 1931, just in time to take over as the local community's main source of income. With the sun still high in the sky, however, my first plan is to find out what else there is to Reno apart from gambling, by the simple if unorthodox plan of taking a stroll through town in the crisp dry desert air. Unfortunately this turns out to be a lot harder than I had imagined. I don't mean finding what else there was to the city, I mean simply finding fresh air or sunshine again. After 40 minutes wandering through a maze of slot machines and fast-food outlets, I'm despairing of ever seeing the light of day again. When they say 'resort casino' they mean it: the operators' clear intention is to prevent you as far as possible from ever venturing outside. Once your income stream – however small – has trickled into the casino's great well, there's no way it is easily going to trickle out again.

When they say 'complex' they mean downright confusing. Turn the wrong way at lobby level and you find yourself staring at a sushi bar or a Caribbean-themed rum pub. Or a designer shirt shop. Or a handbag emporium. Move a few feet in the other direction and there is a pizza joint next to a 'surf-and-turf' restaurant offering modestly priced steak with lobster tail. Then there are the signs beckoning to the night club, to the ballroom, to the circus acts, to the microbrewery (I was tempted), to the Aura martini lounge which advertises 'sophisticated sexy waitresses' (and for which a two-for-one voucher had been pressed into your hand with your room key – I assumed it related to the martinis, that is, not the waitresses). And so on, and so on, seemingly *ad infinitum*.

What the American 'resort casino' concept really is – and I am sure there are devotees out there who will point out that Reno is a pale shadow of Vegas, but it was enough to blow my novice mind – is Disneyland with an 'over-21s only' label. Not that under-21s are excluded. They're offered ice-cream parlours, cuddly-toy shops, circus rides, games arcades which all seem just perfect for families with 10–14 year olds. It's scarcely enough though – what is? – to improve the mood of the clutches of older teenage boys in huge baggy jeans lurking sullenly on their side of the 'over-21s only' demarcation line. This is nothing more than a yellow line on the floor, but it is a barrier between virtual worlds. For 'their own protection', not just teenagers, but young adults up to the age of 21, including young men who may have fought for their country in Iraq or Afghanistan, are forced to stand on the wrong side of the line and watch those who are older and therefore supposed to know better pour alcohol down their throats and dollars into slot machines.

They can also watch them smoke. Whereas not so long ago American anti-smoking laws seemed draconian to Europeans, now that we have caught up, the US situation seems more chaotic than anything else, not least because each state has its own variation. The Nevada Clean Air act, for example, forbids smoking in enclosed public spaces – other than those which cater mainly for adults and specifically permit it. Such as casinos and bars which don't opt to ban it. The practical upshot of this is that on one side of the yellow line painted on the floor – in the over-21 gaming and drinking area, smoking is allowed, but no more than a foot or two away, on the other side of the line, it is banned. Even though the whole lot is under one roof and if anyone has told the smoke not to cross the yellow line, it seems blissfully unaware of it. The weirdly perverse effect of this is that it feels, within the topsy-turvy logic of this confined ecosystem, as if you can smoke 'indoors' but not 'outdoors'.

When I say the whole thing is under 'one roof' of course, that too, is a deception. I've been gradually discovering this for half an hour now, in my search for an escape. There is what *Doctor Who* fans would immediately call a TARDIS effect here – and that as we all know stands for 'Time And Relative Distance In Space' – the inside appears hugely bigger than the outside. The secret is that it actually is. Because the hotel lobby level is on the upper floor you easily forget that the shape of the building at street level is irrelevant. Ground-floor Reno is in a different dimension to the world one storey up. On the higher plane, as it were, the Silver Legacy is linked to two other equally humongous casino resorts by walkways that don't look or feel like walkways because they're avenues filled with shops or bars. I didn't know it, while I had been wandering in a vague and self-deluding search for the exit from the Silver Legacy, I had in fact been exploring a substantial area of Eldorado and Circus Circus as well.

You not only lose track of space but of time too. Which is of course what the designers intended. There are no windows, no indication of daylight. This is a world in which time is measured by the revolution of digitally generated wheels on electronic slot machines and the dealing of hands at virtual poker tables. It's only after 40 minutes of hopeless wandering that I find myself back in the Silver Legacy hotel lobby which is when it finally dawns on me that to find my way out of this seemingly subterranean labyrinth back into the sunshine, I have to go down, what seems like further underground, but is actually the way out.

Downstairs the world is pretty much the same, an artificially lit environment of smoke and drink and gaming. Girls in slinky thigh-slit skirts deliver drinks to the slot-machine players who are as oblivious to them as they are to the news-ticker style slogans running above the rotating wheels they stare at: 'Welcome to Silver Legacy Resort and Casino, United we stand, God Bless America, We support our troops.' These are of course the same troops, who if they were still under 21 – as many of them are – would not be allowed to have a beer or play the slots, no matter how heroic their exploits on the field of battle.

There is a crowd around one roulette wheel, a rare intrusion of old-fashioned physical gaming in this electronic-dominated world, through there are also poker, blackjack and craps tables, all of which are relatively quiet. And then I remember why. It is still the middle of the afternoon. And the reason I know is that there is a subtle difference down here: in a far corner I can see a light that is neither neon nor fluorescent, a light that reminds me of the time of day and the fact that somewhere out there the sun is shining. I push it and fall out of the singularity into what I dimly remember as reality.

It's pretty quiet out here. The odd pickup truck cruises by, down Virginia Avenue and through the Reno arch, the city's landmark emblazoned with its neon 'little big town' slogan in the neon-trashing bright desert sunlight. Following the faded photocopy map acquired from the Legacy's bemused bellhops who were obviously not familiar with the concept of 'outside', let alone 'on foot', I head towards the edge of the town centre to see if the beautiful babbling clear waters of the Truckee River have, like Amtrak, been sunk in a concrete canal.

It hasn't. Just a few hundred yards from the Silver Legacy, the strip is suddenly brought to an abrupt halt by a bridge across a river that is every bit as brightly bubbling and indomitably fresh and clear as it was a hundred miles or so back in the mountains. There is another Reno 'beyond-the-Truckee', a green civic space with grey granite municipal buildings – post office, town hall

– while the riverfront itself is a peaceful oasis of rippling water, calm and coffee shops.

But in Reno terms this is suburbia. The real town is the strip, so I head back along it, unsurprised to note that Reno is competing with Vegas in another of Nevada's state specialities: quickie weddings and divorces. I'm just not sure they've quite got the hang of it yet. Is the Antique Angel wedding chapel sure they're sending out quite the right message, unless of course it specialises in second marriages. The sign on the door read 'closed', but the window dressing advertises: 'Hispanic ceremonies available.' And matching white 'bride' and 'groom' sun visors. But then maybe Reno has something of a blind spot when it comes to naming its facilities. Mountain View may seem a romantic customer-attracting name for most businesses, but a mortuary?

But Reno looks on the bright side. Traffic bollards on street corners are brightly painted to look like piles of casino chips. On the corner of E Commerce the effect is spoiled by a hobo asleep on the pavement next to them. A passing ambulance truck halts and two paramedics pile out and take a look at him, pulling on plastic gloves before they consider actually touching him. One of them gives him an investigative kick. He sits up, clearly wondering what time of day it is, which if he has just emerged from a casino I can understand, and stares wildly at them. They get him on his feet but rather than help him into the ambulance, tell him to move along. This is a no-loitering zone. He's not keen on loitering anyhow, and hurls a lungful of obscenities at them as he shambles off. Disconcertingly, they respond in kind.

A few minutes later, two tough-looking blokes wearing black helmets, black T-shirts, black Lycra shorts and dark glasses jump off mountain bikes next to him and demand his identity papers. It's only when they turn their backs to me that I recognise the words 'Reno Police'. It's not exactly the 'bobby on a bicycle' of English mythology, but then in my experience that always was just mythology. I assume they're genuine, though the souvenir shops along Virginia Avenue will print just about anything on a T-shirt. One of a group of less than sylph-like young women in their twenties heading for the Eldorado casino is wearing a T-shirt that reads, 'Lord, if I can't be skinny, please let my friends be fat'. The Lord has clearly answered her prayers.

The three casino resorts that dominate central Reno compete for the take with a couple on the outskirts, a city centre branch of the bland national casino chain Hannah's, the Woolworth's of the gambling world. And then there's Fitzgerald's.

The name is a clue, but any doubts I might have had about which particular theme Fitzgerald's hopes will pull in the punters, are blown away by the thick layers of old green paint and, standing near the end of a grubby rainbow near the door, the life-size plastic leprechaun (possibly larger than life-size depending on your personal experience of leprechauns). Yep, Fitzgerald's is playing the Irish card. From the bottom of the deck. And if I were the Irish government's public relations adviser, I'd sue.

The lettering on the sign above the door is done in stick-on letters against a white neon background, like cinemas from the 1960s, except that it isn't retro, it's just left over. While advertising hundreds of five-cent and one-cent slots suggests it is really scraping the barrel to pull in the punters. I wander inside and immediately regret it. The bottom of the barrel is the summit of most of Fitzgerald's punters' ambitions. The green carpets are faded to the colour of putrid moss, the slot machines still have mechanical arms: you know, the ones you have to pull, unknown anywhere else in Reno. The drinks brought to the sad souls doubling a lifetime's exercise limit by pulling them are served by dumpy Chinese blokes or women who no longer care to know that the days when they might have looked good in tights and skimpy leprechaun costumes are long gone. Too little Tai Chi, too much Mah Jong. The only exception, as far as age goes, is one young woman who looks as if she might be in danger of producing a whole litter of little leprechauns any minute. The drinks that aren't free are cheap, as is the food. But I just do not want to know what the 'House Special 99 Cent Prawn Cocktail' even looks like. Ah, the luck of the Irish! A sign opposite proclaims 'Jewellery and Pawn Store'; not exactly an advertisement for big payouts.

I hurry out, back to the comforting mahogany veneer of the Silver Legacy complex, although it is only now that my jaded eye takes in the obvious: that the outside is a crude *trompe l'oeil*. It has been decorated – if it was meant to be a disguise it is signally unsuccessful – to look like the nineteenth-century street front that was presumably pulled down to erect it. There is even the date 1895 inscribed on the pediment of one of the series of pseudo-terraces, one of which is a phoney grocer's, the next a mock-up 'Sierra Pacific' railway office, and another – with almost a nice touch of irony, the Silver Legacy Casino and Saloon – although pushing the fake doors will get you nowhere.

The real doors on the end, however, are always open, 24 hours a day. I wander back in, with the vague intention of cashing in my two-for-one cocktail voucher with the 'sophisticated sexy waitresses' in the Aura bar. The two-for-one deal turns out to apply exclusively to a range of brand new house martinis, *'each designed to reflect the aura made up by your personality and chakras'*, a bit of

New Age mumbo-jumbo obliquely intended to imply you can open spiritual energy channels by getting wasted on sweet spirits. It's what the 'sophisticated sexy waitresses' are supposed to sell. But they're all on a cigarette break, and the male bartenders are having none of it.

'It's either those or well drinks,' says Eric, the one nearest me. Unfortunately this doesn't help. It's another of those linguistic things. 'You mean like fruit juice, or energy drinks?' I ask, assuming – not too stupidly it seems to me at the time – that a 'well drink' is something akin to a 'wellness drink', which doesn't make a lot of sense either but back in Europe I would assume to be some sort of vaguely 'healthy' alternative to alcohol.

Eric gives me one of those 'You from Mars?' looks, and says, 'Nope, I mean a drink out of the well,' indicating the sunken reservoir of bottles set into the lower part of the bar on his side.

'So that would include, say, a vodka martini?' I suggest hesitantly, off the top of my head.

'Sure thing,' he says, taking me at my word, and nonchalantly throwing a half full vodka bottle some four feet into the air, catching it behind his back in between flicking a slice of lime into a cocktail shaker, adding ice, a dash of the vodka followed by a splash of vermouth from another bottle which miraculously appears in a third hand that is obviously his cheating secret, before hurling the vodka bottle back into the air, catching it in the lid of the shaker and putting it back on the shelf, while another previously unsuspected appendage has put the lid on the shaker, shaken it and is now pouring the drink. A vodka martini, shaken, stirred and taken on a day trip to Alton Towers all in less time than it takes to say, 'The name's Bond, James Bond.'

'How do you learn to do stuff like that?' I asked.

'Not having a life for the past two years,' he replied with refreshing honesty.

I sit down next to the bar, mostly it's there, and so am I, and so's the drink. But also because I'm more than a little in awe of what Eric might perform next. His bartending pyrotechnics are far more riveting than anything I expect the two rather bored-looking females to put on display. Of course, when I say 'pyrotechnics' here, I'm speaking figuratively. At least I thought I was. Impressed by having such an impressionable audience, Eric decides to show me one of his specials. This consists of dowsing a chunk of paper towels in something seriously alcoholic, stuffing them into the necks of a couple of bottles, and setting them on fire. Before proceeding to juggle with them, leaving trails of flame in the air, like a kid with a sparkler on Bonfire Night.

I watch this with some amazement, about five steps back from the bar. Up until now it had never occurred to me that a Molotov cocktail was something you could actually order at a bar. It's only a little disappointing therefore when he explains the bottles were in fact empty and made of reinforced plastic, kept specifically for tricks rather than the dispensing of alcohol: 'Even so, you have to be careful, sometimes the plastic can melt.'

Yeah, right. I'm just (in)digesting that little nugget when Eric gets called off to mix a drink for someone at the other end of the bar. A tipple for which only he, it seems, knows the recipe. An Amateur Arsonist perhaps or a Napalm Nightcap.

With that efficiency that sums up the American casino industry, however, his place is immediately taken by Sean, who turns out to be a South Korean called Sung, who changed his name because the Americans had trouble with it, 'and I like Sean Connery'. Sean tells me he's been working in Reno for six years, moving up the casino league to the Silver Legacy which according to him is unquestionably the best. Having seen the Fitzgerald, I'm not about to argue.

At 36, Sean clearly considers himself something of a veteran on the bartending scene, even if he takes his metaphorical hat off to talented 'flair' jugglers like Eric. But in his eyes, Eric's still a kid, a lad in his twenties who may juggle bottles like a genius but hasn't even had to think about the far more difficult business of juggling money. Sean's main concern is to stay on the upward escalator in the casino business, while still earning enough money to service a large mortgage on a 'three-bedroom, two-bathroom house' in the valley.

His home is clearly his pride and joy, his mark of success as an immigrant, but it is also his biggest headache. Bartenders, like most people in the service industry in America, rely heavily on tips, which means they don't have a high guaranteed salary when it comes to applying for things like mortgages. Polishing a glass with a rueful look in his eye, Sean admits to having been enticed into the housing market at its height by a shark broker who secured him a large loan at an affordable introductory rate. But the rate had run out and he was now struggling to pay a whopping eight per cent interest on a property which thanks to the general crisis in the mortgage market, provoked by people less prudent than him defaulting on overpriced loans, was deteriorating in value. This, at last is the mother lode! Here in Reno, I have unearthed the root of all evil: it was guys like the mortgage shark who conned Sean that started the whole global meltdown from which, nursed and fertilised by the greed and stupidity of our own bankers, the world is now suffering.

Supposedly bright-boy traders bought 'securitised financial instruments', that were nothing more than a repackaged share in the debt owed by a blue-collar worker who'd been conned by a shark on a percentage into taking a bigger loan than he could afford which quickly reverted to an interest rate he couldn't repay. All over America in recent years, people who thought they were getting a rung on the ladder to middle-class respectability have had it pulled out from under them and as a result have walked away from the financial system leaving the men who sell the ladders with no customers and barely a leg to stand on.

Sean was by no means an obvious bad debt, with a steady job and a decent credit history, but the mortgage rate he'd been lured into paying was barely sustainable and the costs of rearranging formidable. So far at least he still has his house.

'Do you ever have a flutter here?' I asked, considering the temptation he must be under and almost dreading the answer.

Sean stops polishing the glass he's holding for an instant, looks at me in mystification as if he's not quite sure what I could possible mean, and then when I wave my arm in a general circle indicating the casino, the whole 'get-rich-quick' dream at the heart of Reno, he suddenly laughs, shakes his head and says: 'No. No, no, no. I just work here. I take my money home.'

A man after my own heart, I tell myself, as he moves away to serve another customer. Then again, as a rare visitor to a casino – my brief experience in Niagara notwithstanding – there's no harm in risking a dollar or two on the touch-screen poker machine winking seductively from the glass bar surface underneath my martini. It's blackjack, so why not? Just for a laugh. If you play the odds right, you can hardly lose. The machine even tells you how it – the dealer – plays: it always sticks on 17. It's better still, safer, I've read somewhere, to stick on just 16. That way, over time, and if you don't do anything silly, you're bound to come out ahead. If not, what the hell? It's only a dollar.

Hey, what do you know, actually, it's eight dollars for the price of one, after only a few minutes. Easy as can be. Slide in the note, hit the buttons and out slides a ticket I can cash later. Double or quits? No thanks, sucker! I wish Sean luck and head off to cash my winnings. If only it had been a hundred to start with instead of one, now that might have been something to celebrate.

Nonetheless, with eight nice clean dollars in my pocket – spewed out by another machine with either better security clearance or more important friends – I'm off to the Brew Bros in Eldorado, or wherever it was in the labyrinth, your very own in-casino microbrewery for a swift beery nightcap. Just the one.

Brew Bros have a band on, playing cover versions of old Oasis hits, so I have a couple, like I'd probably planned to all along, and how can I resist taking another stupid machine for a ride. There's one there, of course, lurking as always under the glass, even in a microbrewery. You don't just get the chance to hand your money over the bar, you can feed it into it.

And I'm on a roll. Ten minutes later it feels more like I've been rolled. My eight dollars is down to just two (which means annoyingly that the beer has been paid for out of my own cash and not, as intended, the casino's). Well, there's no point in sitting here with just two dollars, especially when I've already proved I can turn one into eight. Magic. Just like that!

Except of course that I've also just turned eight into two. How did that happen? This is where I – and probably every other sucker – start to suspect the machines of being in the casino's employ. I mean, it may say that each game is played with one pack of cards, but come on, they're virtual cards, aren't they. How do I know the machine hasn't got a whole stack of whatever it fancies concealed up its virtual sleeve? Short of it committing a real howler, like dealing up two identical cards – and these machines aren't that stupid, they'd have holes blown in them if they were – how on earth would I know?

I start to get suspicious when the machine deals itself a lucky run of 'blackjack' – by this time I need another beer – and the way it keeps getting 20 or 21 every time I'm sitting pretty with a promising-looking 19 or 20. The way it keeps winning with a 17 when I've gone bust because I've broken my golden rule of sticking on 16. Not that it would have helped, of course, would it? As if the machine didn't know, smirking there beneath its bulletproof glass, flipping cards at random inviting me to try another hand, as if the night was young and I didn't have a bed to go to. Okay, machine, you asked for it. I slide in another five-dollar bill. Put up or shut up, you inane piece of plastic-shielded electronics. Let's see the colour of your chips, Intel or otherwise.

Three five-dollar bills later, I tell myself it's not about winning or losing, just playing the game. It's not gambling, it's entertainment, something to do while you're having a social beer to stop you having to talk to another human being.

I put my fourth pint glass down on its electronic smiley face and head for my bunk in the stratosphere. I know it didn't really say, 'Y'all have a nice night now!' That was my imagination.

RENO TO SALT LAKE CITY

TRAIN: California Zephyr
FREQUENCY: 1 a day
DEPART RENO, NEVADA: 3.51 p.m.

via
Sparks, NV
Winnemucca, NV
Elko, NV

ARRIVE SALT LAKE CITY, UTAH: 4:05 a.m.
DURATION: 12 hours, 14 minutes
DISTANCE: 394 miles

15

Heavens Above

WE'VE ALL DONE IT. I have. You have. We've hidden from them! Lurked motionless behind the curtain at the first sight of the pair of serious clean-cut young men with scary US marine haircuts and sober dark suits marching up to the front door like a recruiting detail. Which is what they are, of course.

Of all the people you really don't want to open the door to – Jehovah's Witnesses, Conservative Party canvassers, squeegee-sellers, the gas man – the Mormons have to be absolute top of the list. The worst thing about them is that they're so polite – unlike the gas man or Conservative Party canvassers – so instead of shouting 'get the hell out of here you insane alien proselytising god-squadders', you end up wetting your hair and wrapping a towel round you and pretending to be just getting into a bath, and then feeling guilty because the look in their eyes tells you they know you're lying. They are – they want to tell you, and for a moment you wonder if the dark suits and sunglasses are deliberate – 'on a mission from God'.

Of course, out here 'God' puts on rather a better show than he routinely manages in South London or even the English countryside at most times of the year. Just the train journey from Reno to Salt Lake City is one of the better arguments in favour of the wonders of creation. There is just one word for the Nevada desert: awesome. In the most literal sense: it inspires awe. For a start there is such a lot of it, such a lot of nothing: I have never seen so much nothing. And believe me, that's awesome. For mile after mile after mile after mile after mile, just rocky scree and scrubland, brown and grey and occasionally russet, or streaky white where salt has dried on the surface, with distant silhouettes of low mountain ranges on the horizon. At times the mountains come closer, the highest already in early autumn dusted lightly with snow on the summits, but most just furze-covered ochre slopes rising to barren eroded crests.

This is the vast, wild, inhospitable and still largely unconquered wilderness of every Western you've ever imagined. And the one thing you really, really would not want is to be out here alone on a horse. The emptiness – so easily forgotten in the heart of the world's most developed nation – is genuinely astounding. Amtrak's big silver double-decker trains are dwarfed by the immensity of the emptiness around them, their tracks no more than a scratched line across the surface of the desert.

The journey between Reno/Sparks, Nevada, and Salt Lake City, Utah, takes 13 hours by train, and there are just two other stops – Winnemucca (named for a Paiute Indian chief and once the scene of another Butch Cassidy bank robbery) and Elko (which means 'white woman' in the local Native American language). This is not because the train in question is an express; on a network with only one train every 24 hours, as the conductors are keen on reminding us – 'if you step too far away from the train, folks, we may go without you, but don't fret, there'll be another one along tomorrow' – the simple fact is that there is nowhere else to stop!

Nothing lives here and it is easy to see why. Now and again you might spot a buzzard wheeling above in vain search for prey, or a sign of movement when the train line briefly travels the same route as trucks on a distant interstate. It is easy to see how the aircraft of Richard Branson's favourite pilot, the global circumnavigator Steve Fosset, could have gone down unnoticed, unimaginable that anyone ever thought he might easily be found.

It is also almost impossibly beautiful, with sunsets beyond compare. Great swathes of pink, grey and orange-tinted cloud march at oblique angles towards the crimson bands and golden sky beyond the purple mountains. If it sounds almost garish, that's because it is. As if to put the bright neon lights of Reno in their place the evening sky seen travelling east across the Nevada desert puts on a show that is almost heart-stopping. The lights of Vegas must seem second-rate compared with the evening entertainment that the desert has put on for free for millennia.

Somewhere in the night I could tell we were approaching the state line – when it would be time to put watches on an hour, meaning Salt Lake City is an hour closer than I feared – because out of the darkness a great neon explosion occurred. For no more than 15 seconds the uninterrupted black is awash with red and white light and the inevitable flashing gold that reads 'CASINO'. I'm missing my last chance to throw $50 out of the window. I have left the state of legal gambling, legal whores and loadsamoney, and entered that of the Tabernacle, genealogy and the Church of Jesus Christ of Latter-day Saints. I'm not sure whether to cry 'Hallelujah!' or 'Help!'

Either way my prayers are answered when we pull into the station and find there actually are cabs in attendance. I've booked a hotel in the city centre, a two-mile walk away down deserted dark and dodgy streets. Except that they can't be dodgy really, can they? Not here in the hometown of the Latter-day Saints? But I'm glad to see a cab, not least because it's almost 4:00 a.m., never the best time to arrive anywhere. It certainly wouldn't have been my choice but then there are only two times you can arrive at Salt Lake City by train: 11 at night or four in the morning. And you only get the 11:00 p.m. option if you're heading east. That's the thing about only having one train a day in each direction: it spares you complicated decisions.

Except of course, where on earth to lay your head when you arrive at that sort of time. I've pre-booked a hotel that let me have the room from whenever I arrived for just half rate. I would get some sleep rather than plunge into the hedonistic delights of Salt Lake City bleary-eyed. This is sarcasm, in case you hadn't recognised it. The Mormon capital has a reputation for being one of the most staid places in America, where it's hard to get a drink at any time. Happily, it doesn't live up to it.

Emerging into bright sunlight later the same morning, I'm surprised to find myself in one of the prettiest cities in America. The roads are wide – founder Brigham Young decreed they should be spacious enough to turn a horse and wagon in without 'cussing' – and, a whimsical touch this, the pedestrian crossings chirrup birdsong at you when it's safe to cross. The architecture runs from Victorian Gothic – the city hall – to the neo-classical Capitol (yet another replica of Washington's) to modernist mall, but at least there are more buildings than parking lots. And behind them rise the serenely beautiful Utah Mountains.

The first thing I notice is the air: it almost sparkles. There is a clean, crisp, crystalline clarity to the Salt Lake City air that is unmatched anywhere on the planet, even in the Alps. Part of it is the altitude – it's 1,228 metres (4,226 feet) above sea level – but it's also to do with being located in the middle of a high desert plain (the Salt Lake itself is some miles away across mudflats to the north of the city) that strips the air of moisture. Coming from Britain, where we don't just have moisture in the air but in our bones, there's initially something initially incredibly invigorating about this dry clarity. It's only gradually that I start to become aware of an effect that will be at its most obvious after a couple of days in this sort of atmosphere: it is ferociously desiccating of the sinuses. The problem I had begun to experience in Chicago is coming back to haunt me over the next few days, with a vengeance. We low-lying coastal dwellers aren't cut out to survive up here on the high central plains of a continental land mass. I began to sympathise with Leonardo the dinosaur. Maybe eventually people here will evolve into a different species, with larger, self-lubricating nostrils. I wonder what the Book of Mormon would have to say about that.

No better place to find out! After all those years of hiding when the Mormons came to the door, it's my turn to go and ring their bell. Which turns out to be a completely different experience to anything I'd anticipated.

Salt Lake City is not an exclusively Mormon city. The transcontinental railroad, which ensured its incorporation into the rapidly expanding United States, saw to that. Freedom of religion is allowed as it is everywhere else and there are other churches scattered all around town including Roman Catholic, Anglican and Greek Orthodox cathedrals, which is a lot of religion for a city of only 180,000 souls, especially when the Mormons occupy a 35-acre site in the middle of it. In fact, every distance in the city is calculated from the southeast corner of Temple Square, the edge of the walled site of their most sacred buildings.

With its strangely unfamiliar uniform design – soaring vertical white granite with only arrow-slit windows high above head-height and three spires at each end – the Salt Lake City Temple, though not the first of the Mormons' places of worship (there were others built before they began their great trek into the desert), is today pre-eminent. It forms a strange contrast to their second most important building, the great aluminium-roofed tortoiseshell that is the Tabernacle. Dwarfing both, however, is the monolithic skyscraper church headquarters.

Although the Temple Square complex is walled off, it is open to the public – though the Temple itself is out of bounds to non-believers – to wander round, and on any given day there are a series of weddings taking place, though these days to only one woman at a time! Nonetheless, the woman at the gatehouse who was more than happy to fix me up with one of their regular free tours of the publicly accessible buildings, does an impressive job of finding me guides: not, as I anticipated, one of the Blues-Brothers-cum-Secret-Service lookalikes we get in the UK but two extremely personable young women in their mid-twenties, one from the Philippines and one from Peru: Sister Wang and Sister Anna. Just for me! The Mormons may have long since officially abandoned polygamy but there must be something deep-seated that still goes by that old Beach Boys motto: two girls for every boy! And who was I to complain?

So off we go, me and my two 'Saints' – which they inform me is how Mormons prefer to be known – Sister Anna taking me by one arm and Sister Wang by the other, we make our way into the Tabernacle. The strange low domed roof gives the Tabernacle excellent acoustics, making it well fitted for its prime use as a concert venue. It dates back to the early days of Salt Lake City – 1867 – an antiquity my two Saints refer to with awe, though there are Catholic churches in both Lima and Manila (from which they have both converted) that are nearly 300 years older. But then there is context to be taken into account: this dates back to a few years after the birth of their religion.

Right now it is hosting a rehearsal for a concert later in the week: a few hymns that have an interesting jazz feel to them thrown in with a bit of Gershwin. Hey, this is – or was initially – the first all-American religion. It's being played on an absolutely stupendous organ and the Saints tell me how many pipes it has which means nothing to me, other than that Sherlock Holmes used to class mysteries by the number of pipes it took him to solve them. Happily I remember not to mention that. The one Holmes adventure that includes an episode set in Salt Lake City* depicts the Mormons as kidnappers and white slavers, and the city's founding father Brigham Young as an out-and-out villain.

The girls – sorry, Saints – clearly have a different view of old Brigham, telling me the story of his heroic 1,350-mile wagon-train trek out to Utah, how 250 of his followers died en route but 3,000 made it. Of their early travails including a plague of locusts that descended to consume their first crops, and how the fledgling Saints' city was only saved by a flock of seagulls which suddenly appeared to gobble up the locusts. Hence the monument outside: a pillar with a couple of golden gulls on top. Seagulls? Em, excuse me, but aren't we hundreds of miles from the nearest coast, inland, across a desert. Precisely, they beam: a miracle! (I have since discovered that my cynicism was misplaced: California gulls do indeed travel as far inland as Utah.)

We round off my tour in the purpose-built Visitors' Center which features a history of the church with a series of displays, uncannily like wandering around Madame Tussauds: waxwork figures not only of Brigham Young and the church's founder Joseph Smith but even of the angel Moroni who revealed God's word to him. Then it's up to the top floor where, standing proudly before a giant alabaster Jesus against a vaulted dome painted to look like a cross

---

*A Study in Scarlet.

between a planetarium and a sci-fi cover, the saintly sisters give me a brief – obviously well-rehearsed – formal welcome and a wish that I might learn more about the true religion. It's a bit cringe-making and more than slightly embarrassing given that they've an audience of just two – by this stage a Japanese bloke who was being escorted up to the top by another pair of Sisters has joined me – but it's the closest they've come to hard sell all morning. Then they say goodbye and tell me I'm free to wander round the exhibits as long as I like.

And so I spend the next half hour or so doing just that: staring at the waxworks and watching a brief video of the spiritual descendants of the prophet himself: today's church leaders. These are mostly elderly gents in black suits who look spookily like a cross between German bankers and the old Soviet Politburo. It's less than reassuring to find it works a bit like that too: 'Today only the President of the Church receives revelations for the whole Church. He is a prophet of God. Members of the Church should obey the prophet.' The President is chosen from The Twelve Apostles who themselves are chosen from the Seventy. As a former reporter in Soviet Moscow it just sounds uncomfortably like First Secretary, Politburo, Central Committee. I am not saying that the LDS are crypto-commies; I can think of few churches more instinctively drawn to the tenets of capitalism and big business. But there are some interesting structural similarities in the hierarchy.

The theology is another thing entirely. I'm looking at a tableau of Jesus appearing somewhere in Central America around the time of the crucifixion when the Japanese bloke comes up to me and taps his head in that universally recognised signal to suggest our hosts may be just the odd sandwich short of a picnic. Superficially I'm tempted to agree though it does occur to me that most religions are founded by people who appear to be perfectly normal humans at first, until they announce they've had a revelation or been touched by the divine, including Mohammed, Buddha, and er, em, L. Ron Hubbard...

Even Jesus Christ himself can be loosely grouped in this category, though he did go one step further by claiming to actually be divine (but there again so did the Roman emperors). Anyhow, in the interests of fairness, I decide to do something the earnest young men in suits calling at my door while I cowered behind the curtains would have been delighted by: I go down into the vast basement bookstore beneath the church headquarters and buy a copy of the Book of Mormon. And just to make sure I get the gist correct without embarking on a lifetime study of texts which, despite being written in the mid-nineteenth century, are in an English more reminiscent of the King James Bible, I pick up the picture book version for children. From their own sources, therefore, I offer the uninitiated a personally potted history of the Church of Jesus Christ of Latter-day Saints.

Back in 1819 a 14-year-old boy called Joseph Smith growing up in Vermont, is out in the forest one day when he has a vision of God and Jesus who tell him all the contemporary Christian sects in the young America are confused. Three years later an angel called Moroni shows him where to dig up a stone box that contains gold plates with secret writing on them. He also guides Joe to two magic stones that will help him translate it.

The story, which approximates to the Mormon 'Old Testament' goes like this: in about 600 BC a Jerusalem family led by a wise man called Lehi (pronounce to rhyme with Yee-Hi) warns that the city will be destroyed because of the people's wickedness, and prophesies that eventually Jesus Christ will be born to save them. He and his family are driven out and wander in the wilderness guided by a golden compass. Eventually they come to a coast (near the Persian Gulf) where God tells them to build a boat to sail to the Promised Land. One of his sons, Nephi, is keen, but the other, Laman, is not.

Eventually they build the boat, set off, and with a few mishaps sail across the Indian and Pacific Oceans to the west coast of South America. Lehi dies and passes on the leadership to Nephi, but soon the brothers argue again and split into two tribes: the Nephites and the Lamanites. The former are known as 'the righteous' while the latter 'became a dark-skinned people. God cursed them because of their wickedness.' (2 Nephi 5:14, 21)

Over the next few centuries the Nephites and Lamanites fight, there are false prophets and bad kings, a massacre of innocents in a city called Ammonihah and a bruising encounter with a sect called the Zoramites who worship in buildings called 'synagogues' and are described as being inordinately fond of gold, believing they alone are God's chosen people. (Alma 31:12)

At the time of Christ's birth, the sky stays light all night and a new star appears. Thirty-three years later, storms and thunder shake the land, several cities are destroyed and it is dark for three days. Immediately afterwards the resurrected Christ appears among the Nephites and picks a dozen apostles, nine of whom he eventually takes with him to heaven, leaving three immortals to teach on earth. For the next couple of centuries there is virtual heaven on earth in the Americas. Then it all goes wrong again, and they start fighting. At this time a young boy called Mormon is appointed by God to be guardian of their sacred writings, which would come to be known as the Book of Mormon. In the Visitors' Center there's a waxwork of a Mormon writing it on the golden plates.

Mormon eventually passes on the plates to his son Moroni, who spends his own final years writing the words of the sacrament prayers and baptism rituals on the plates before burying them on the hill, where they will be discovered by a young lad called Joseph Smith who will become the first prophet of the resurrected true Church of Jesus Christ.

Mormonism is then the first truly all-American religion. It preaches what a lot of modern Americans believe anyway – that they do indeed inhabit the Promised Land. Literally. Cynics might point out that Jews and dark-skinned people might find a few mid-nineteenth century Anglo-Saxon prejudices mysteriously lurking in these ancient scriptures, but then gays and gentiles in general aren't exactly loved by the more orthodox Christian Old Testament. Although they recognise the Christian New Testament (except for the gospel of Matthew which Joseph Smith – under angelic guidance – rewrote) they effectively also have their own, called the Doctrine and Covenants which tells the story of Joseph and his followers.

Like this: Joseph's new religion didn't go down well with folks in his Puritan home state of Vermont so he set off for Pennsylvania where he met Oliver Cowdery who was to become his fellow prophet. To confirm this, John the Baptist followed by a trio of saints, Peter, James and John, appeared to both of them granting them the two top levels of the new priesthood – the 'Aaronic' and 'Melchidizek' – allowing them to baptise new followers and give them absolution from sins. Oliver was not able to read the gold plates and had to make do with writing down what Joseph translated. Jesus told them to show the gold plates to two other people who would go down in Mormon history as the 'original witnesses' – just in case anybody might get the idea the gold plates didn't exist – then sent Moroni to take them back to heaven, as Joseph didn't need them any more. If you have questions I suggest you invite in the next couple of well-spoken young men with crew cuts who turn up at your front door.

Over the coming months Oliver and Joseph baptised more followers and ordained some of these 'Saints' to the priesthood so they in turn could baptise more. One of the new converts was a young man called Brigham Young. They also developed their own concept of infallibility: 'Jesus said that only one man could receive revelations for the entire church. That man was Joseph Smith.' Joseph banned alcohol, coffee, tea and tobacco, and ordered his followers to give one tenth of their income to the church. It might be seen as compensation – from one point of view – that he also said they could have more than one wife, following Abraham and David who 'received many wives and concubines'. This was going to cause trouble.

Joseph's chapter and verse reads: 'If any man espouse a virgin, and desire to espouse another, and the first give her consent, and if he espouse the second, and they are virgins, and have vowed to no other man, then he is justified; he cannot commit adultery for they are given unto him; for he cannot commit adultery with that that belongeth to him and no one else. And if he have 10 virgins given unto him by this law, he cannot commit adultery, for they belong to him and they are given unto him; therefore is he justified.' The concept of 'belonging' obviously is one that would hardly sit well with modern feminism, but then Joseph didn't really see the law as applying equally to men and women: 'But if one of either of the 10 virgins, after she is espoused, shall be with another man, she has committed adultery and shall be destroyed.'

Given the essentially puritan nature of American society in the mid-nineteenth century it is hardly surprising that the Mormons were forced to keep moving west. They founded a new town called Nauvoo (allegedly from the Hebrew for 'beautiful') in Illinois. The trouble was that with whole populations flooding westwards across what they considered an 'empty' continent, no sooner had a new town been founded than other people flooded in. When a new newspaper criticising Smith was set up in Nauvoo, his followers attacked the building and destroyed its presses. Smith left town only to be arrested 'on trumped-up charges' in a nearby town. But while he and his brother Hyrum were imprisoned there, the jail was stormed by a mob and both killed.

Brigham Young takes over and, getting the message (from the locals if not from heaven), leads the 'Saints' on an almost literally biblical exodus to the west, eventually to the beautiful, clean-aired, mountain-ringed valley where he founded Salt Lake City. It is important to see the Mormon odyssey in context. In the 1840s the United States, though growing fast thanks to the Louisiana Purchase, was still essentially a coastal country with a few inland provinces. Texas had seized independence from Mexico in 1836, but did not join the US until 1845, and then seceded to join the Confederacy in 1861. California was far away, its future still uncertain.

In 1847, when the Saints founded what would become Utah, Young almost certainly imagined he was creating his own Mormon country. He had not anticipated that their trek would be emulated on a mammoth scale, or that the civil war would create the political impetus for a transcontinental railroad. When he realised its inevitability, however, he rapidly espoused the cause. In the magnificent and now sadly disused old Union Pacific station in Salt Lake City there are two hugely significant murals, one at either end. The first depicts the pioneers of 1847 arriving in their virgin wilderness. The second is a scene just 20 years later, in 1867, the arrival of the railroad and Washington's dominance assured. Salt Lake City's brief period of isolation was over when it had hardly just begun.

The Saints had to face the reality that despite the limited autonomy of the states, they would come under federal law. Which meant polygamy was a problem. Next to the church headquarters, hard by the Temple, Brigham Young's pleasant pastel green wooden house still stands, much as he left it, including the quarters for his veritable harem of wives.

Within a generation, however, the practice was to come under such pressure that on 6 October 1890, Wilford Woodruff, named church president just a year earlier, announced that 'inasmuch as laws have been enacted by Congress forbidding plural marriage… I now publicly declare that my advice to the Latter-day Saints is to refrain from contracting any marriage forbidden by the law of the land'.

Fundamentalist Mormons carefully noted however that far from actually banning polygamous marriage – which had after all been recommended by Jesus Christ himself speaking through the prophet Joseph Smith – Woodruff was merely advising Mormons not to break the law of the country. Once upon a time they had tried to flee the USA and its laws, but the country – riding on the railroad – had caught up with and overtaken them; they were now required to submit to federal law. But as stories from distant parts of Utah still regularly report, there remains a hard core out there who think that federal law matters less than God's.

Of course, whether or not we are talking the same 'god' here – or even the same 'Jesus Christ' for that matter – is a subject of some debate, especially given that Mormons believe both Jesus and 'Heavenly Father' possess bodies of flesh and blood. Mormons insist they are Christians; indeed they insist they are the real Christians. For example it did not stop Mitt Romney running for the republican presidential nomination in 2008. At one stage it looked as if it might well have been him rather than John McCain fighting Barack Obama for the presidency. And who knows how that might have turned out? But not all their faith has parallels in the more mainstream branches of the religion. Here for example is the core of Mormon theology as told to me by the two 'saintly sisters':

'Life on earth is part of an eternal existence which began long before we were born, when we lived with God as His spirit children. We came to earth to be tested to show whether we would obey God's commandments. At death our spirits leave our bodies and go to a spirit world where we continue to learn and progress. We retain our individual personalities and our ability to chose. Those who do not hear the Saviour's teachings on earth will have the opportunity to do so after life.'

That last sentence, you might have noticed, is signally different to more established Christian teachings about a 'weeping and wailing and gnashing of teeth', for those who fail to heed the message. If so, you have spotted one of the critical elements of the Mormon creed, and, moreover, one that explains their strangest obsession: genealogy. If you have ever tried researching your family tree online, the odds are you'll have come across FamilySearch.org. This is the digitised entry portal to the Family History Library which has its physical presence next to the Tabernacle in Salt Lake City. Extraordinary as it may seem, over the past century and more the Mormons have built up the biggest genealogical research facility in the world.

And seeing as, after my guided tour and my lightning initiation into the mysteries of Mormonism, it seems a shame not to take the opportunity to track down a few missing members of the Millar clan. Not, I hasten to add, for the same reasons most Mormons do. They do so in order to convert them. Yes, even the dead ones. Those who never had the good fortune to hear the words of Joseph Smith. Mormons believe that it is their duty to give their ancestors the same chance as themselves to enter heaven, even posthumously, by being baptised in their names. 'I've been baptised 12 times,' Sister Anna told me proudly, blissfully uncaring if her Peruvian Catholic ancestors would have appreciated the gesture (although it was probably an easier option than the ones the conquistadors offered those who turned down Catholicism in the first place).

It doesn't have to be ancestors either. Controversially, those whose deceased spirits have been offered a posthumous chance to get to know the Mormons' 'Heavenly Father' are Christopher Columbus, Methodist founder John Wesley, several American presidents, the original signatories of the Declaration of Independence. And Adolf Hitler. Even mass murderers are given a chance to repent. You sort of have to admire the generosity of spirit, if perhaps not the political nous.

The FHL building is outside the walled confines of the Temple Square and if you have taken the trouble to turn up yourself, use of its remarkable facilities is free. No questions asked. And any questions they can possibly answer will be answered. Also free. With enthusiasm and patience. When I explained that my roots – indeed my family – were Northern Irish, I was given into the care of a bright-eyed red-haired woman called Miranda with green horn-rimmed glasses who immediately directed me to a typed index book of the records they held from the Public Records Office in Dublin, which is where all important

Irish documents prior to partition in 1921 were kept. Unfortunately, during the Irish Civil War the archive was blown up and vast numbers of priceless documents destroyed, including many registers of births, deaths and marriages. The tragedy is that we didn't have a genealogy-obsessed religious group around back then to do what the Saints subsequently did in the early 1950s, which is to send someone to sit in the archives day after day for more than three years, photographing every single remaining page to put it all on microfilm. They've done the same job for most of Britain too!

Despite the gaps in the Irish records, guided by Miranda I spent the next several hours winding reels of microfilm onto the spindles of readers – they are in the process of digitising the archive but that may take at least as long as it did to film it for the last generation's bulk storage technology. I'm not a family tree buff, but if the lacuna in the Irish records hadn't blocked my route, I could have spent a week there, poring into the lives of my ancestors. It's one thing knowing roughly when your great-grandfather was born but staring at his birth and wedding certificates, even on film, is still a strange sensation. I discovered that my grandmother had a middle name she never used and found myself musing on the occupations of Victorian Ulstermen with names like Isaac and Jeremiah. My great-great-grandfather Isaac Callan had been a 'water bottler' in Belfast in the 1860s. The only interference – and you could scarcely call it that – was when Miranda asked politely if I planned any baptisms. I smiled and said 'not just yet'. Mormons believe it's best to know as much as possible about your ancestor before you take that step. I believe it's best not to tamper with the religious beliefs of Ulster Presbyterians. Even dead ones.

By now, as you might be able to imagine after such a dose of religion and family history, I was ready for a drink. Or two. I had been warned this would be a problem. Mormon lawmakers had tightened up since Brigham Young's day when, although he claimed not to drink, he distilled his own Valley Tan whisky which was sold to other settlers. In the late nineteenth century Salt Lake City was famous for its saloons. By the mid-twentieth, post-Prohibition, Utah was one of the most anti-alcohol states in America, even if the restrictions were relatively easy to get round, usually by bars requiring a 'membership' which could be bought at the door. When the city hosted the Winter Olympics in 2002, the laws were relaxed and today – unless you are a hardened spirit drinker – Utah is almost like anywhere else.

Almost. Nearly all restaurants serve wine or beer, but only with food. But then, isn't that why you're in a restaurant? And if you want, you can get away with a bowl of chips (fries). Beer is easy to come by provided it is less than 3.2 per cent alcohol by weight, which is a funny way to measure alcohol as most of the rest of the world measures it by volume. In fact, 3.2 by weight works out at around four per cent by volume, which while weaker than premium German beers, is substantially stronger than most American lager, and perfectly on par with an average English ale. Or indeed, the product of most American microbreweries. Which may be why, paradoxically, 'dry' Utah has more microbreweries per capita than any other American state.

One of the best happens to be directly opposite my hotel. It's called Squatters and just to prove that you can live in 'SLC', as I discover most locals call it, and have a light-hearted attitude to your Mormon neighbours, they offer up Polygamy Porter. It is, as you may imagine, a heady brew: delightfully dark, with a bittersweet aftertaste!

On the advice of the barman – motto: always listen to barmen; don't always take their advice – I head down the road to another establishment which also has its tongue if not exactly poked out at the Mormon establishment at least firmly in its cheek: The Tavernacle. Yes, it's a bad pun, and yes, they also do music. Their speciality is Duelling Pianos: two blokes sit at baby grands facing each other and each hypes the audience into paying him to play their song. Whenever someone bids the other guy more for a different song, he takes over. It's fun – for a bit – and clever – it certainly pays the piano players' wages – but primarily it's 'frat boy foul-mouthed', an improbable reminder that this was indeed once not just a religious 'capital' but a yeehaw cowboy town.

I'm used to the version of 'Living next door to Alice,' that adds: 'Alice? Who the fuck is Alice?' But I start feeling old and prim when the piano player rattling out a version of 'You Picked a Fine Time to Leave Me, Lucille', adds: 'You bitch, you slut, you whore, you suck, you swallow, you cunt.' And this in what my rather overly proper friend Philip from north Oxfordshire would call 'mixed company'. The girls don't seem to mind, though, hollering right along with him.

As I wander out into a starry crystalline mountain-air night, I recall there are more than enough volunteers to save their souls out here. Even if it has to be posthumously.

SALT LAKE CITY TO DENVER

TRAIN: California Zephyr
FREQUENCY: 1 a day
DEPART SALT LAKE CITY, UTAH: 4:35 a.m.

via
Provo, UT
Helper, UT
Green River, UT
Grand Junction, UT
Glenwood Springs, Colorado
Granby, CO
Fraser-Winter Park, CO

ARRIVE DENVER COLORADO: 7:43 p.m.
DURATION: 15 hours, 08 minutes
DISTANCE: 570 miles

16

Downhill to Denver

'HEY, SUSAN,' the woman in the tight jeans and blue sweater calls, gazing out of the window as we head towards the highest railroad pass in America. 'There are some bars.'

I shoot her a questioning glance and scan the vast panorama in front of us – it's not as if we're going to stop even if there is a bar – but all I can see across the great brown plateau to the distant snow-capped mountains is a couple of hundred contemplative-looking cows. Nothing that I would call a decent watering hole vaguely in sight. And then I turn to look at Susan, her teenage daughter, beaming away in delight, mobile phone clamped to her ear.

Bars. 'Cellphone speak'. Reception. In fact the first trace of it for several hours, several hundred miles and several thousand feet difference in vertical altitude. 'I'm on the train,' mobile-phone syndrome is still a relatively new phenomenon for most Americans, if only because so few of them have ever used a train, and it is a small mercy that for most of the transcontinental routes reception is patchy at best. When it isn't they have an overwhelming desire to phone their friends and tell them about it. And like everyone else in the world, they talk louder on mobile phones than they do at any other time. And in the case of some of them, that's saying something.

But here we are at 6:30 on a Saturday night, in my case having been on the train since the extremely ungodly hour of 3:00 a.m. – and that only because the Zephyr's arrival into Salt Lake City had once again been mysteriously ahead of time – at long last anticipating the run downhill to Denver.

'Downhill to Denver' is not a phrase people use a lot, not least because Colorado's biggest urban agglomeration is famously known as the 'mile-high city', with a celebrated mean altitude of 5,280 feet, one of the few measurements on which Britons and Americans agree.

Unfortunately Amtrak's timekeeping had lost its edge somewhat. There were urgent works going on in the Moffat Tunnel and that meant we had to wait. The Moffat is not only one of Amtrak's longer tunnels – at six miles – it is also the highest point the railroads reach in America, coming in at a quite remarkable 9,239 feet (2,820 metres). There are not many ski resorts in Austria that will take you up to that level even on their highest lifts.

But you can hardly tell how high you are, trundling across a high-altitude cattle-grazing plain through rocky crags and sparse scrubland. The Moffat was built in 1928 and was a hugely important development in cross-country rail transport. Cutting through the mountain saved 65 miles on the journey between Salt Lake City and Denver. Far more importantly, those miles were along twisting steep gradients around the continental divide, the 13,260 feet (4,040 metres) James Peak. That journey alone used to take five hours. Now, in theory at least, it takes 10 minutes. Not, however, when they're working on it.

So here we are stopped outside Granby, a little town in the middle of a nowhere that just happens to be the Rocky Mountains' – and the world's – highest altitude road, the Middle Park Trail Ridge.

Disconcertingly, for someone fresh out of Salt Lake City and carrying more Mormon baggage than I'd anticipated, according to our train conductor, it is also near a site* where evidence has been found of habitation by people older than any of the known North American tribes. If the archaeologists ever dig up some inscribed gold plates there's going to be an awful lot of smug 'I told you so' stuff coming out of Utah.

The result of the delay, however, is that by the time we are finally getting towards Denver we are more than three hours late and it's pouring with tor-rential rain. The one bright side in all this is that for once, I don't have to face tramping the streets. I'm being picked up in Denver by my cousin Barry. This, dear reader, is where, I have to admit, I'm going to cheat. Despite my best intentions to complete my entire US pilgrimage by train, there is simply no easy way to join the next leg on my itinerary southwest towards the Grand Canyon and Los Angeles without going all the way back to Chicago or making an overland connection. Amtrak recognise this by offering a bus connection south from Denver to Raton in New Mexico. I had been intending to take this when I realised that it in fact passed through Colorado Springs, which is where Barry lives and he has kindly insisted on making the connection for me and is right now waiting in Denver.

---

*The Lindenmeier site in Larimer county, Colorado.

Thanks, however, to the very technology I've been moaning about – mobile telephones – he is not sitting staring at his watch in the train station, but ensconced across the road in the warm and welcoming surroundings of the Wynkoop Brewing Company, Denver's oldest brewpub (est. 1988). He is my cousin, after all.

Dashing out of the dark damp into a steaming fug of beery conviviality it's reassuring to hear a voice drawl, 'Hey, cuz, how ya doin?' and spot a familiar face at the bar, eyes twinkling behind glasses on the other side of a large steak sandwich. I should point out straight away that Barry is not one of those Americans with a weight problem. Given that he is of modest height (we are not a family of giants) and hardly a sportsman even in his less than athletic prime, he remains remarkably trim and active. He has also just passed the milestone age of 60 but you wouldn't know it, primarily because he has the mischievous zest for life of a testosterone-fuelled 14-year-old, just occasionally tempered with a world-weary lassitude. We get on well together.

Not least because Barry is already ordering up for me a pint of Wynkoop's highly recommended Railyard Ale, which he thinks I absolutely have to try. Never one to fight an argument like that, the long day's train journey is soon soothed away in a tide of richly hopped, mildly fruity amber ale. Railyard – so named obviously because they are right across the road from it – is Wynkoop's flagship beer, which they describe as a German Oktoberfest lager made from their house yeast and finished with Tettnang hops. All I can tell you is it went down full steam ahead. Barry watched just a little enviously; he was on Coke, having experienced difficulty with law enforcement driving home from a bar before.

And then it's out into the cold rainy night – Colorado can get very hot but also very cold and when it rains, it rains – into Barry's 'bus', a 20-year-old Ford Econoliner that has seen the 100,000 mile mark roll round more than twice, and head for the hills. Colorado Springs is another thousand feet higher than Denver on the eastern edge of the Rockies and at the base of one of America's most famous mountains, Pikes Peak. It was also rated Best Big City in *Money* magazine's 2006 list of Best Places to Live. Barry would agree, although *Money* magazine is definitely not on his regular reading list.

Barry was born, like myself, in Northern Ireland, just a decade earlier, shortly after his father had returned from serving in the British Army. He was four when his parents emigrated to America, and even though he has an American passport still considers himself an Irishman at heart, although as he actually is one, he doesn't make much of it. What brought him to Colorado is a complicated story: for much of his late teens and early twenties, he was unenthusiastic about being drafted into the army and getting sent to Vietnam. In the course of that he got a lot of education, including a year at Queen's University in Belfast where he wore Aran sweaters, drank Guinness and sang Dylan songs in smoky bars to great effect with the local young ladies. A varied collection of careers, divorce and remarriage later, he did what he had least expected to: joined the army. As a drugs counsellor. 'It was something I felt I knew about.' Fort Carson in Colorado Springs was where they were posted to. He left after his wife died and devoted himself to bringing up a talented son who became a surfer, deep-sea diver and fighter pilot, joined the military and is now based in Hawaii, and serving in Iraq.

Barry, meanwhile, still enjoys female company, smokes his daily weed and soaks up conspiracy theories – including intergalactic ones – like the old hippy he is, while working on a semi-autobiographical novel that one of these days will win a Pulitzer. He is, however, clearly not yet fully attuned to North American ley lines because despite Denver being laid out on a grid pattern it takes us 45 minutes to find our way out of it, and then it's only after asking a second set of strangers for directions. The first attempt had failed when Barry got out of the van next to a little bar lit by red neon to the side of the inevitable freeway overpass to ask if anyone knew where we might get on to it. He came back a few minutes later none the wiser: 'I couldn't even find out where we are never mind where to get on the freeway. Nobody in there speaks English.' There are clearly parts of the state named for the reddish-brown coloured Rio Colorado that are going back to their roots.

Outside Barry's house on the edge of Colorado Springs the next morning I realise just how close he is to Pikes Peak: the great conical mountain that is a focal point in the landscape for leagues around almost sits on his doorstep. Pikes Peak is named after the magnificently monikered Zebulon Pike, an explorer who was the first white American to see it, though because the US Board on Geographic Names back in 1891 ruled against the possessive apostrophe in place names it is officially called Pikes Peak.

Pike tried and failed to climb it, predicting it would never be possible, which was a bit out as the first man made it up there just 14 years later in 1820. By 1893 even a woman had made it. Katherine Lee Bates was the daughter of a congregational pastor from Massachusetts who came out here to teach a summer school and was moved by both the journey and the view from the top of Pikes Peak to write what many Americans, on the left of the political spectrum at least, would prefer as their national anthem: 'America the Beautiful', with its references to 'amber waves of grain, purple mountain majesties above the fruited plain'. An altogether less martial image than that conveyed by the 'Star Spangled Banner'. But we shall get to that in just a minute. Today there's a gift shop on top and you can get there by a partly paved road – the mountain is chiefly famed for the annual Pikes Peak race, and the annual marathon run to the top and back. There is also the Manitou and Pikes Peak cog railway which it had been my intention to take, but as we sat there trying to locate the timetables, thick fog rolled in and over the peak, and announced its intention to settle. A trip to the top in those conditions would be as scenic as a day out in an old-style London pea-souper.

Instead we take what Barry calls a 'hike' – a leisurely stroll – around the romantically named Garden of the Gods which is virtually Barry's back garden; he chooses his property well. The 'garden' is actually a park created around some of the most spectacular sandstone formations on earth: great pinnacles, towers and strange eroded primeval animal shapes of pink and red rock shaped by millennia of Colorado's occasionally awesome climate that varies from beautiful mild Mediterranean-style days to extremes of wind, snow, rain and searing sunshine. It's a favourite spot for climbers and walkers and a cool spot to take a short after-dinner stroll round if you live next door.

It got its name back in 1859 when two of the surveyors laying out the Colorado Springs city plan came across it and one, being a practical man, suggested it would be a super spot for a beer garden. His chum, obviously of a much more prosaic and dull disposition, added: 'Why, it is a fit place for the gods to assemble. We will call it the Garden of the Gods.' I think they should have gone ahead with the beer garden.

Barry, however, has that aspect of the day sorted out, having booked dinner for us, his long-term girlfriend and a couple of other pals at the Phantom Canyon Brewpub. In the meantime, it's a chance for me to wind down into domesticity for 36 hours. I had half hoped we might take in a rodeo. Colorado, being classic cowboy country, is famous for them. Rodeos are an odd obsession. A neighbour of mine in England is a fervent fan, donning his Stetson and dragging his wife and daughter out to the Wild West every couple of years to watch him yippee and yeehaa his way around the rodeo circuit. Strictly from the stands, I stress. But then he is a Chelsea fan, so what do you expect?

Barry took us to my only rodeo the last time I visited him. It was an odd affair. Out on the opposite edge of town. Pickups parked for miles in every direction. Concrete tiered seats around the stadium – for want of a better word: corral? – and every other man in a cowboy hat with a shoelace tie held together by some little Navajo jewellery woggle.

These, I suspect, are not people you'd want to discuss gun control with, or invite to a gay wedding, come to that. These are the sort of down-to-earth Americans who'd tell you their heart is in the right place. And put their hand on it just to check. And stand up and sing the national anthem at the same time. Which is, in fact, as I sat there cringing, exactly what they then did.

Now I don't have a problem with national anthems. In fact, I sort of collect them. Some of them have remarkably good tunes – the British one being a bit of an exception here – and quite a lot of them have entertainingly quaint lyrics. The Marseillaise is a good example: cracking tune and those endearing words about 'letting impure blood slake the thirst of our trenches'. I once embarrassed myself in Germany by singing the now unused first verse of theirs: the one that goes 'Deutschland, Deutschland über alles,' while these days they only pick up at the 'Unity and law and justice' line. When the Soviet Union collapsed we held a party at home where we played their anthem with its cynically hilarious opening line about 'Indestructible union of republics so free'. Corker of a tune too, to the extent that Vladimir Putin restored it. And the way things are going he may be thinking about bringing back the old words.

The American anthem has a fine tune too, one of the best in fact. It also has pretty par for the course embarrassing words: that bit about 'the bombs bursting in air gave proof through the night that our flag was still there' really does lack a little subtlety when you're the only country to have dropped an atomic bomb or two, and has a worrying tendency to go in for the air strike as a weapon of first resort.

Not my problem, of course, I didn't have to sing it. Or did I? Surrounded by the Stetsons, staying sitting was not an option – not that I'd intended to – but even that not to join in full-throatedly might be taken as an act of irreverence, disrespect or even treason, for which the excuse of being a foreigner might not be acceptable. I'm wary about these things since my childhood in Northern Ireland where they used to play the British national anthem when cinemas closed at 10:30 p.m. You had two choices: either make a run for it while the titles were rolling, or stand rigid and sing along in case someone thought your allegiances were to the Irish tricolour rather than Her Majesty. In Colorado therefore I decided to do what any brave Brit would do under the circumstances: I stood up and mimed.

And then they brought on the Rodeo Queen. This is an institution which is to the bucking bronco business what cheerleaders are to American football or page three to readers of the *Sun*: a bit of mostly harmless soft porn for the lads. The girl in question was your typical western American dream with long blonde hair and long tanned legs beneath a white leather cowboy suit with micro-mini skirt. A fetishist's fantasy.

And then we got down to the serious – or depending on your point of view rather silly – business of blokes on broncos: men with leather leggings on their trousers flapping their hat and trying for dear life to cling onto a horse that thinks it's in the Olympic equestrian trampolining final. Impressive, at least for the few seconds most of them manage to hang on, and undoubtedly very skilled, particularly for those who manage it for a bit longer. But – and I would never say this to my neighbour – it's just ever so slightly... samey! Once you've seen one bronco buck...

Anyhow at this stage I decided the evening could only be improved by a couple of beers – which despite a general prudishness about alcohol are grati-fyingly on sale at absolutely every American sports event – so I headed off to the beer tent. Lots of beer, none of it very interesting but all of it chilled. The only trouble was that when I tried to pick up a couple of cans the sweet young cowgirl responsible for taking the money asked if she could see my ID. It took a minute for me to realise what she was on about and then of course I launched into my – soon, no doubt, to be outdated – proud spiel about Britain being a free land which does not require its citizens to carry identity cards, much less have the state register how many beers we consume (although the way Britain has changed I fear it soon will). And then it dawned on me: she was checking to see if I was old enough to buy beer. This was really rather flattering. In fact absurdly so. It may seem insane to us – and it certainly does to me – to ban your citizens from buying a beer for three years after they have attained full legal adulthood, but the idea that a man approaching 50 might be mistaken for being under 21 was unlikely to say the least, even with my baby-faced com-plexion. She was obviously just complimenting me. I beamed and said some-thing like, 'Thanks luv, but I'll just have the beers.' Which is when she went and ruined it all: 'No sir, it's perfectly obvious you're over age, but I need to see your ID. It's state law.' So off I trekked back to find my coat with my passport in the pocket. All for the sake of a few swigs of tasteless Coors Light.

That experience, however, was not to be repeated, Barry tells me: the rodeo season finished in September. At least he can promise better beer though. We're due at the Phantom Canyon Brewpub about 5:30; it seems in the wild west, everybody chows down at teatime. In the meantime, we've got shopping to fetch. I need new ear buds for my iPod and I'm still in search of a remedy for my parched sinuses. The air in Colorado is as pure as the blue skies it boasts in summer; there just isn't enough of it. It's not as bad as Salt Lake City but we're still pretty high and dry here.

More at home on the 'Springs' grid than he was in Denver, Barry's telling me what a small town boy he's become even as we're driving through miles of affluent low-rise suburbia to a Wal-Mart five miles across town. I'm not wholly sure why we're heading to one Wal-Mart in particular given that the landscape we're driving through is littered with things that if they're not Wal-Mart are only marginally smaller and often specialised in slightly smaller product ranges (hardly difficult since Wal-Mart stocks most things known to man, and some known only to Americans). I suggest that 'the Springs' isn't exactly a small town. Barry thinks for a minute or two before conceding that actually it has 400,000 inhabitants.

It seems that each of these inhabitants personally has several miles of urban expressway to themselves and lives at least half a dozen miles from wherever they routinely need to get to. Despite there being a compact 'downtown' area with a not wholly contrived 'old west' feel to it, everybody who lives outside it – which is more or less everybody – spends most of their time driving somewhere else.

Sprawling modern western cities such as Colorado Springs have not just adapted to the motor car, they have been designed around it. There are not only drive-through McDonald's (and other fast-food chains) of the type we have come to know in our own American-cloned out-of-town retail parks, but also drive-through banks, drive-through DVD rental outlets and post boxes that you have to drive up to in order to post a letter. In fact, if you want to do something as quirky as post a letter and happen – even more quirkily – to be on foot, then the only way to do so is to venture out into the road and risk being run over just to get access to the post box. A substantial number of the sprawling retail outlets are tyre suppliers: the good people of Colorado Springs probably keep Goodyear and Firestone in business.

The Phantom Canyon Brewpub is a relief. They do not just an excellent range of beers but a decent menu. Ever more proof what a thriving institution the gastro-brewpub has become in modern America. The real Phantom Canyon, a roadless remnant of pioneering days, is actually way to the north of Denver but the brewery named after it produces excellent beers: from Zebulon's Peated Porter, a rich dark drink, to aromatic Bavarian-style effervescent

Hefeweizen and Coulter's Kölsch, a pale golden beer in the style of Cologne in Germany.

It goes down a treat, though I'm not sure whether it's the beer or the conversation that is making my head swim. Barry is big on alternative explanations, for life, the universe and everything, ranging from the pyramids of Giza in Egypt and Chichen Itza in Mexico, crop circles and the Pleiades, before getting on to Area 51, who shot JFK and whether or not the moon landings were faked – actually Barry is pretty sure they weren't, he remembers them too well – before settling down to 9/11.

Barry has just come back from Oahu, Hawaii, where his son is based. 'Everywhere on that island they have these stickers that say "9/11 was an inside job" – and y'know I dunno, have you heard this guy who says the other buildings that collapsed were obviously taken down with controlled explosions? You know, like they didn't fall over but just sort of folded down into their own footprint? Like there was some command post in one of them, for the spooks, who orchestrated the whole thing so Bush could get his war on terror? Huh? You know, would you put it past him?'

No, I wouldn't. But then you only have to google '9/11 conspiracy' these days to get, on average, 7,740,000 hits. Which is a lot of hits. You can either take the 'eat shit: a hundred million flies can't be wrong' attitude, or you can apply Ockham's Razor and say the real answer is likely to be the simplest. And however far-fetched the idea of a gang of terrorists learning to fly airliners, then hijacking a couple and flying them into the World Trade Center may seem – and it did seem pretty far-fetched even as they did it – the idea of Bush and the CIA planning the whole thing in collusion with Mossad just so they could invade Afghanistan and Iraq and clamp down on personal liberty all over the so-called free world is even crazier. Isn't it?

I'm starting to get the feeling that what people perceive to be reality – other than what they can see, hear and feel immediately around them – has a slightly tenuous hold on existence for some of them. Including my cousin. Everybody watches television almost constantly – even in bars and restaurants – but what they're mostly watching is just whatever's on. First-class drama series like the *Sopranos* or *Sex and the City* draw huge audiences, as do chat shows like *Oprah*, but news is another matter. With no real national daily newspapers – you can hardly count the lightweight *USA Today* – and the sprawling diversification of TV news, most of it heavily opinionated, means any semblance of unbiased reporting on air is rare.

The only constant is the adverts, so frequent and so interlaced with other programming that the two are often hard to separate. Fox News, the Rupert Murdoch-owned, madly jingoistic, out-on-a-limb tabloid television news channel has even signed a product placement agreement with McDonald's for its regional news shows. For that's what the news mostly comes down to: a show. The closest most people get to watching informed current affairs programmes is the chat shows, which is why people like David Letterman, Jay Leno and Jon Stewart wield such influence: the people believe their jokes more than they believe the newscasters. The problem is a collapse in faith in the old 'anchor' system as it has moved towards flashy teeth and shiny smiles rather than any semblance of investigative authority, while there was virtually never any concept of informed neutrality other than in the sober organs of the major newspapers in the big cities which in any case only a tiny, already well-informed section of the population reads.

Barry, to be fair, gets most of his serious news either online or from BBC World or his favourite, the English-language service of Germany's equivalent, *Deutsche Welle*: 'You feel at least they're aware there are other countries out there as well as their own.' Inevitably one beer flowed into another and with the chauffeuring services of Barry's girlfriend, Pat, for us soaks to rely on we ventured out finally as far as Manitou Springs. Virtually a suburb of Colorado Springs these days, Manitou has been surprisingly successful in maintaining the atmosphere of a small western town, without succumbing to too much tourist tat.

Manitou is an old Native American word for 'spirit' and at the low point of Barry's life it had served to maintain his. The bar we have come to find is The Ancient Mariner – I can only suppose with very loose apologies to Samuel Taylor Coleridge, because of his fondness for hallucinogenic substances, Colorado Springs being about as far as you can get from anything imaginably marine. But it has been a favourite place for Barry and his son to hang out for a spot of father-and-son mutual solace while the boy's mother was seriously ill. They had played pool there to escape for an hour or two from the strains of living with daily evidence of mortality – the lad was under age but in the circumstances everyone turned a blind eye.

Subsequently it turned into a lesbian bar, but, as Barry adds with his trademark mischievous wink, 'not aggressively so, if you know what I mean, and is still full of some nice women who didn't mind you looking, up to a point'. He has no idea what it's like now, as it's been a few years since he's been here. As it happens, the lesbians have gone and 'The Mariner' has expanded, taking over the small shop next door to become a music bar, with a fine band playing interesting experimental jazz-flavoured rock, including an outstanding female electric violinist. But most importantly for Barry, it still had the pool table. We shot a few games, then gamely lost to some locals. And then it was time to hit the hay: we had an early start the next morning if I was to make Raton in time to catch the Southwest Chief. And there was a mountain pass to cross on the way.

As Barry's girlfriend said before we turned in: 'Fall's a comin' in. There could be snow, sweeties. Oh yeah. And black ice.'

There wasn't. The only problem was another of Barry's incurable attacks of the munchies. We were by no means certain of the situation on the pass as we drove south. Big heavy-looking clouds were indeed marching in from that direction – 'could be full of moisture if they've blown in off the Gulf' – the only snow we saw was on the tops of a stunning camel-backed double peak mountain group to our right. Barry didn't know what they were called which once again had me lamenting how annoying it is that most American maps show little more than road: spidery thin lines on a blank background.

'Yeah, well, maybe Homeland Security just doesn't want you to know,' says Barry with that smile of his that always leaves me uncertain whether or not he's serious. In this case I reckon he's not too sure himself. Google Maps' hybrid photographs from military satellites offer spectacular resolution in this part of the world. What they lack, however, by and large, is that old-fashioned British ordnance survey-style meticulousness for naming peaks, giving elevations and pointing out the whereabouts of churches and pubs. Particularly the latter.

There is another reason why Barry might well be right. Pikes Peak isn't the only nationally significant mountain in the Colorado Springs area: there's also Mount Cheyenne. This is less of a lofty peak than a great bulk of a mountain looming over the US Air Force base outside the town. I say 'looming' because Mount Cheyenne is one of those mountains that would loom no matter what shape it was. That is because deep inside, and probably very far beneath it, Mount Cheyenne houses a hub of the American strategic nuclear missile control system. As Barry has told me on several occasions before: 'We don't worry about the risks of a nuclear war. If anyone ever launches a first strike against the United States, the war'll be over for us before anyone else even knows it's started.'

But it's not nuclear war that's worrying Barry as we head for the high mountain pass. And it's not the threat of black ice either. It's the rumbling in his stomach. I'm looking at my watch worrying that we're not going to make it over the mountains into Raton, New Mexico, before my train. He's worrying about making sure we have time to stop at McDonald's on the way.

I'm not terribly impressed by this. Not least because having dreaded being forced to live off McMeals and the like for a month or more and ballooning as a result, I've actually managed to totally avoid them: the microbrew pub phenomenon has largely gone along with a good food ethos. It hasn't all been gourmet standard, but it's really only on Amtrak that I can say in best American fashion that 'the food sucks'. And now my cousin, my own cousin, is dragging me to a McDo. And for what: 'This little place in Trinidad do just the greatest sausage biscuit.'

Excuse me? This little place in Trinidad? It's a McDo for Christ's sake, Barry, not some quaint little Caribbean restaurant. And it is, as it turns out, everything I expect. And less: a smaller than usual, but much more crowded little McDonald's roadside stop, tucked in just next to the I25 freeway, with just one obvious blessing: it is also right next to the railway track so if the train comes through I should see it. Barry meanwhile has queued up at the counter and comes back with the object of his lust: a fairly unrecognisable bun thing with an even less recognisable might-once-have-been-related-to-an-egg thing and some meaty goo next to it. I settle for a large coffee and orange juice. The morning after the night before has different effects on different people. I need rehydration. Barry clearly needs starch. And stuff. And that's what he gets. The sausage biscuit with egg (regular size biscuit) and hash browns on the side provides a not necessarily vast 660 calories, but more disconcertingly 65 per cent of your daily recommended intake of fat, 77 per cent saturated fat, 83 per cent of recommended cholesterol and 62 per cent of your salt recommendation. And that's from McDonald's own website.*

I'm not sure Barry could care less: 'Man, I was dreaming about that sausage biscuit and hash browns for the last 70 miles,' he purrs as we roll out of McDo's and back onto the highway only to see the train pulling out ahead of us. This induces a moment of blind panic on my part – the next train is same time tomorrow – and also a sheer Homer Simpson 'D'oh' moment as I pull out my timetable to check how long we've got to get to Raton and find out the train made its previous stop just 10 minutes ago. In Trinidad. The simple fact is I hadn't looked at a map, just thought the only option was to take the same route

---

*http://nutrition.mcdonalds.com/bagamcmeal/nutritionInfo.do

as Amtrak's 'Thruway' coach link. So if we miss the connection now, I can't even blame McDo and Mister Munchie next to me, who's still licking his lips as we coast up the winding road that for the next 20 miles over the mountains and down into Raton is part of the historic Santa Fe Trail that ran from Missouri through the 'disorganised territory' as they then called the Native Americans' lands, down to the genuinely ancient city of Santa Fe which had been a collection of Pueblo Indian villages since at least the end of the first millennium.

There is one consolation: the train, still in view, is obviously having more difficulties than we are with the gradient, huffing and puffing its way up an admittedly steep incline before plunging down the other side: all in all, according to Amtrak's timetable, another hour, while we should need, according to McDonald's man next to me, 30 minutes at most. Even with the rain settling in, and cold grey clouds scudding overhead. My brief foray onto road transport has left me hankering for the comfort zone of the steel rails – yes, all those stories about Lake Donner and the Rockies snowdrifts notwithstanding – our little truck seems suddenly less reliable than the iron horse.

I need not have worried. Weather in the Rockies is like weather in Iceland, where the favourite local saying is: 'You don't like our climate? Hang around an hour or so.' By the time we reached Raton station, it felt like a particularly pleasant British June, the temperature in the upper twenties, warm sunshine on my face and just a few small white clouds drifting by above the mountains.

Raton itself is something else: a one-horse town where the horse packed up and left some years ago in search of excitement. Atop a limestone cliff there's a white giant-lettered sign clearly modelled on the Hollywood sign in Los Angeles, except that this one says 'RATON'. Because it's in Raton. And because it's in Raton, it dominates not Beverly Hills but Marchiondo's 'Golden Rule and New York Stores', which according to the painted signs sells 'Dry Goods' and Levis, or must do when it's open, whenever that is, and certainly not today. In fact there's no sign of much at all open in Raton. Well, actually nothing. Not even the station. I mean, I suppose trains stop here, once every morning as it says on the timetable, but there's nothing much to reassure the uncertain traveller that they really do. Just an old, adobe, pinky-cream painted station with no sign of human habitation, and just a few quietly rusting freight cars on the second track, while occasionally-humming telegraph poles march off like the totems of long-vanished tribes towards a desert horizon beneath a high cirrus-flecked azure sky.

'Like, are you sure this train's gonna come?' asks Barry, gazing up at the sky, then down at his watch, and shuffling his feet, almost certainly wondering how long it'll be before he's due his next McMuffin. But in Amtrak we trust. Especially having seen the train snaking up the mountain behind us and I persuade Barry that his 'cuz' can cope and wave goodbye as he heads the Econoliner back towards the state line.

Within minutes my residual fear that the Southwest Chief might have done a downhill spring and I've missed it subsides as, five minutes after it's due to depart, a van pulls up with a screech of breaks and a bloke the size of a not-very-small grizzly bear in wraparound sunshades jumps out and rolls – he is that sort of shape – up to the track.

'Not here then yet,' he says. When I mutter a few words of well-meant reciprocal doubt-cum-optimism, he decides I need a few instant stranger-in-a-station bonding lessons. I though I was just waiting for a train, but no, I realise with a weary inward sigh: it's time to make friends again.

'So you're from England, heh? What's that country like? Compared to this country round here?'

It's sort of hard to know where to start. That's the trouble with the questions some Americans ask: they can be disconcertingly direct, and not as easy to answer as they expect.

'Well, it's smaller,' I try. 'And more crowded, and wetter.'

'That so. Yeah, it's pretty quiet round here these days. But this town used to be hoppin'', he says, his interest in faraway parts instantly assuaged. As if England were Wyoming. Although he might have found that easier to relate to. 'They used to mine coal and stuff and then they stopped. Dunno why and it went real dead for 10 or 15 years, and then they found natural gas up the road and now they're workin' on that.'

Richard, as he tells me his name is, shaking hands with a paw that could probably tickle salmon out of mountain streams, is none too pleased with the way the economy is going. Or anything else: 'What with the way they keep tellin' us to save fuel and all. And then there's the DUI* laws, they're real strict on that. I could just spill beer on you and they'd pull you in.'

Before we can delve further into the rights and wrongs of the local law officers' enforcement of Driving Under the Influence legislation – widely seen out here to be not only iniquitous but unfair – we're joined by another apparent passenger. It looks like Raton rush hour is hitting its peak.

'Train not in yet,' the new arrival says though it's by no means clear if it's a question or a statement. He's a man of that indeterminate age you seem to

---

*Driving Under the Influence (of drink or drugs).

come across out west, on the blurred upper edge of middle age. He says, just a mite improbably, his name's Paulie.

'Glad I got here on time. Boss got on that there train. But forgot his computer. He called me on his cellphone so I came on up here ahead. He's goin' back to California. He has a trailer park out here, in Trinidad. I kinda look after it for him.'

'That so?' says Richard, with the kind of genuine-sounding interest I couldn't even hope to emulate. Within minutes these guys, who had never met before and might never meet again, have exchanged details of who they work for, how long they've been there, where they come from, what they've been doing today, and just about anything else they can think of.

'My granddaddy used to bootleg hooch over them there mountains,' says Paulie, apropos of nothing I can identify. 'There was a fella in the store in Trinidad a while back buyin' up a whole mess a' rye and sugar at the same time. And I'm tellin' the storeman after he's gone, he oughta watch because there's no way he's buyin' that to feed chickens. And the storeman says, "That so? You intendin' to tell someone?" An' I say, "Hell, no, I mean he's makin' moonshine an' all, he at least oughta buy the stuff separately." An' the storeman says, "Yeah, well he's my cousin." And we had a laugh about that.

'When it came round to Christmas he gave me a bottle, but I was careful because it's moonshine and moonshine can hurt ya, real bad. But I know this fella he got a lab and he checked it out and said, man that's good stuff. And it sure was.'

'That illegal nowadays?' says Richard.

'What's that?'

'Brewin' up hooch. Whaddaya call it, spirits?'

'Man, it ain't ever been legal. No, sir.'

'That so? There's way too many regulations in this country nowadays. This so-called land of the free.'

Paulie thought that was true too, and started telling a story about a time he was 'torn a strip off' for getting into an argument with one of his boss's trailer tenants: 'This here guy, he done pay no rent and he has the nerve to say I'm discriminatin'. Hell, I ain't never discriminated. Most o' the folk I know round here have some Spanish blood.'

'Me too,' says Richard. 'I don't discriminate 'gainst no one less they discriminate 'gainst me. Me, I got Spanish blood.'

Paulie, not to be outdone here, says: 'Well, my kids is half Mexican. I done speak no English till I was 'bout five, just Spanish.'

Richard clearly sees this as a challenge: 'Lot o' folks round here part Injun too. Me too, I'm part Injun. Don't see no reason to deny my heritage.'

All of a sudden I have the surreal impression I've drifted into a politically correct American West version of the Monty Python Yorkshiremen sketch, that any minute one of them's going to claim he was brought up 'in teepee with nowt to eat but buffalo droppings and refried beans', and the other'll say, 'Luxury!'

In fact, we're pretty damn close when Richard – whom I'm already reclassifying as Ricardo – says: 'Back in the day all we had to live on was beans and potatoes.'

'Nothin' wrong with beans and potatoes.'

'Hell no, you can live on that okay.'

'In fact I'd prefer it!'

And then, mercifully, its long low horn-blast drowning any further conversation, the train arrives (I travelled with my laptop and got it out as soon as I got on the train!!!).

RATON TO GRAND CANYON

TRAIN: Southwest Chief
FREQUENCY: 1 a day
DEPART RATON, NEW MEXICO: 10:56 a.m.

via
Lamy, NM
Albuquerque, NM
Gallup, NM
Winslow, Arizona
Flagstaff, AZ

ARRIVE WILLIAMS JUNCTION, ARIZONA: 9:33 p.m. (Mountain Standard Time)
DURATION: 11 hours, 37 minutes
DISTANCE: 632 miles

WILLIAMS TO GRAND CANYON

TRAIN: Grand Canyon Railway
DEPART WILLIAMS DEPOT: 10:00 a.m.
ARRIVE GRAND CANYON DEPOT: 12:15 p.m.
DURATION: 2 hours, 15 minutes

return
DEPART GRAND CANYON DEPOT: 3:30 p.m.
ARRIVE WILLIAMS DEPOT: 5:45 p.m.

17

A Mountain Lying Down

WHEN PEOPLE TALK of the romance of train travel there is always an element of the sinister involved. For every brief encounter with strangers on a train, there is a scene of swirling mist on an empty platform at night.

Believe me it is worse when there is no platform at all, the train is running late and you are the only person getting off a once-a-day train at 10 o'clock on a dark October night in a clearing in the middle of the woods surrounded by mountains.

You may gather that I was not altogether full of confidence when the Southwest Chief lurched to a 'request halt' in the pitch darkness and the conductor comes up to where I was sitting comfortably doodling in my little notebook and suggests I get off. I give him an aggrieved look wondering what cardinal sin I have committed that gives him the right to make me walk the railroad equivalent of the plank. He points at the little piece of cardboard he had scrawled on earlier and wedged in the rim of the luggage rack above my head. It said WJ.

'This is your stop. Williams Junction. That's why we've stopped.'

It is? I thought bleakly, hauling my rucksack down and making my way downstairs, peering without much hope into the blackness of the night as he opens the door and I clamber down the steps to the platform. Except there isn't a platform: just cold hard earth, with trees growing all around. Lots of them.

'You have a nice night, now,' says the conductor, leaning out the window with what seems to me like a sadistic smile on his face as the door closes on the world of warmth and light. My sense of deep misgiving only grows as the long silver cocoon of safety and civilisation slides off with a screech of steel wheels on steel rails into the night. I peer apprehensively around me for a station building or sign of some sort to indicate that I am indeed where I'm supposed to be. If this really is Williams Junction then whatever it once was a junction with has long since vanished.

I'm not sure whether to be reassured or more worried still when, as my eyes gradually adjust to a world lit only by a few stars peeking out from behind the clouds, I make out what looks like two human figures and a large looming bulk on the edge of the clearing. It occurs to me I've been reading too many Stephen King novels. Then headlights flare, blinding me for a brief instant of near panic, until with a palpable jolt of relief I see the white van facing me has a logo on the side: Grand Canyon Railway. This isn't an ambush after all, it's a welcoming party. Not just for me, though tonight I am their only passenger. Transport from the little railway turns up to meet the big one every time a train passes through – there is only one a day, remember.

The Grand Canyon Railway is just about the only show in town these days in Williams. With a population of 2,842 at the 2000 census, Williams, Arizona – named after an old trapper called Bill Williams, is little more than a 'village'. I hesitate to use that word about small American communities almost as much as they hesitate to use it themselves. This is not a country used to thinking of 'small' as good, and virtually any settlement of any size calls itself a town if not a city. Any ambition Williams might have had to grow into either ended in 1984 when it became the last community to have its section of the famous Route 66 bypassed as Interstate 40 was built a few miles north.

It was the train that put Williams on the map in the first place when the Atchison, Topeka and Santa Fe Railway built a branch spur in 1901 to link the main line with the little settlement that had begun doing a brisk trade in tourists on the south rim of the Grand Canyon. Incredible as it seems today, it had taken time for the tourist potential of the canyon to be recognised. Its speedy success, and the fact that even today 90 per cent of the four and a half million visitors each year see it from the south rim, was originally down to the railway and an entrepreneurial runaway from the East End of London called Fred Harvey.

Fred ran away to America at the age of 15, became a waiter in St Louis, then a mail clerk on the railroad. Nothing in Victorian Britain had prepared him for the terrible conditions of the American West: dirty fly-blown accommodation where travellers were fleeced by hoteliers who never expected to see them again. Harvey thought he could make money offering them good food and civilised service. He opened a railway restaurant in Kansas that did unexpectedly well, helped not least by his policy of hiring neatly dressed, intelligent young women from the east coast and paying them a good wage.

Over the next two decades he set the model for American hotel chains, opening one after another, approximately 100 miles apart, along the Santa Fe

Railway. 'Harvey Houses' became famed throughout the country, as did the 'Harvey Girls'. In a region more accustomed to horse thieving, train robberies, bar-room brawls and attacks by Indians, the Harvey girls in their starched white aprons, tailored black shirts and dresses, were a reminder of another world.

Their moral well-being was catered for by mature 'housemothers'. Their good reputation was vital. Mr Harvey had no desire to be seen as a whoremonger: gentlemen callers were permitted at certain hours only in the well-chaperoned parlour. Before long ribald westerners were escorting Harvey girls to church. One contemporary newspaper article remarked in wonder that Fred Harvey had made 'the desert blossom with beefsteak and pretty girls'. By the end of the century two of the most common boys' names in the west were 'Fred' and 'Harvey'.

He also ended the railroad cheat where diners at station stops paid in advance for meals which were only brought when the train was about to leave. As soon as it was put on the table the crew shouted 'All Aboard'. The same meals were recycled for successive trains – and the train crews received a 10 per cent tip. Harvey offered the crews a similar tip for doing it his way: passengers placed orders in advance which were telegraphed ahead. A mile out of town the train blew its hooter and by the time the passengers arrived at the station starters were already on the tables. A five-minute signal was blown to warn those still dallying over their meals.

He was quick to see the potential of the Grand Canyon and in 1901 built hotels in Williams and at the canyon rim. But by the 1960s America's love for the car – and cheap petrol – nearly finished off this railway for good too. On 30 June 1968, the Santa Fe and Topeka Railway ran their last service, with the locomotive hauling just one passenger carriage with four passengers and one baggage car. For lovers of the railroads it was a heart-rending blow, but for the people of Williams, it was far worse; it was the beginning of a long period of economic decline that could have spelled the end of their settlement altogether.

Williams had been two-timing the railroad for quite some time. It also lay on the main 'paved' route between Chicago and Los Angeles, a road that had by then, thanks to Woody Guthrie, Jack Kerouac, Bob Dylan and others entered the nation's consciousness as a modern myth: Route 66. Every year, particularly in the sixties as the cross country trek west to join the California cult of sunshine, cannabis and free love accelerated, the number of kids flooding through to 'get their kicks on route 66' provided an improbable but much appreciated economic lifeline for small towns like Williams.

And then the inexorable logic of the automobile revolution came full circle and closed the loophole. The romance of the old roads winding through small town America was rapidly being overtaken by the freeway, the new transcontinental 'interstates', successors to the railroads, dedicated to the internal combustion engine and the victory of cheap 'gas'. Petroleum was plentiful. America had its own stocks, the world was full of it, and American oil companies dominated the world.

Williams may have been the last town on 66 to be bypassed by the Interstate, but being the last didn't ease the pain. When the final segment of tarmac was laid in 1984, the silence in the little town was deafening. Over the next few years it went into steady decline, haemorrhaging population, the young men in particular drifting away into that time-honoured route out of Nowheresville, USA, the military.

One man and his wife broke the cycle of decline. In 1989 Max Biegert, from Phoenix, who had made a sizeable fortune out of crop-dusting decided he and his wife Thelma would do the impossible: reinvent the railroad. They raised $15 million, bought up the land, track and decaying depot from the Santa Fe Railway which had been content to let it rot, and put together some vintage rolling stock. Their purchase included 65 miles of track held together with 30,000 ties (sleepers), a run-down crumbling property in Williams that had once been Harvey's hotel, and a fabulous if neglected log depot up at the southern rim of the canyon. They caught the mood and have been hugely successful, building a new trackside hotel in Williams, and taking up to a quarter of a million passengers a year on the most ecologically friendly way to visit the canyon. The Biegerts since sold off to a large company called Xanterra, but the railway is definitely there to stay.

Thanks to the lads who'd turned up at the 'junction', within half an hour I'm checked in and heading out to sample the Williams nightlife. Except that there isn't any, it seems, for the first 20 minutes, as I trudge past one closed establishment after another – even the hotel bar had closed at 10:00 p.m. The only sign of (bleak) hope in the town is a cavernous so-called 'cocktail bar' with pool tables, incredibly loud music and no customers. I'm just beginning to think it's time to cut my losses and settle for an early bed when I follow my nose round one last windswept corner. There, like a siren emerging from the waves, out of the darkness off the main street – and Williams is very much a one-street town – is a sign in blue and red neon that reads Grand Canyon Brewing Company.

It turns out to be even more of a miracle than I knew. The brewery has only been open a matter of weeks, after 18 months hard slog by three brothers: John,

231

Josh and Jeremy Peasley. I know this because Jeremy himself is serving me a foaming pint of Williams Wheat beer, and before long giving me a tour round the stainless-steel vats of the brewing equipment:

'We worked 100-hour weeks, 18 hours some days, me and my brothers, putting this place together,' he says. 'It was John's idea originally, right after he got out of the navy, but we all sweated on it.' They bought up and tore down an old barn 'on the edge of 66', and re-used the wood. John chainsawed ponderosa pine logs to make rustic bar seats, and they installed that essential for any American small-town bar: a pool table. Then their most important acquisition: a head brewer, Tom Netolicky, a 20-year veteran of the American microbrewery revolution. And as I switch from my Williams Wheat to a rich velvety Oatmeal Stout, I can testify to the man's talent.

John, the 'big' brother, has just arrived, and two things are immediately obvious: 1) that he's the man in charge, and 2) that he's the man who's served in the armed forces, even though he was lucky enough not to be sent to Iraq. His destination was rather different. In fact, that's where he met his first 'Brits': on a tropical island half a world away that is one of Britain's most far-flung remaining colonial possessions: Diego Garcia in the Indian Ocean, leased to the US as a military base. I didn't know there were any British forces there at all, but according to John there are 'a few dozen', alongside more than 3,000 Americans, who are split between official military and civilian 'contractors'. He was in the navy. The few British servicemen who maintain a token presence on a coral atoll that is effectively an American aircraft carrier are Royal Marines. Given that the nearest sizable land mass is a thousand miles away, these guys are pretty much thrown together for their tours of duty. He remembers one in particular: 'Man, that guy was tough. He could lift an icebox and throw it around. They were all good guys, they just didn't have any money.' I make a mental note to pass on his comments on the state of British servicemen's pay to Her Majesty's Secretary of State for Defence.

It doesn't look like money is going to be a problem for John and his brothers. The Peasleys are, in fact, probably number two after the Xanterra corporation and the railroad in keeping Williams alive. In addition to the brewery they also own Cruiser's, a bar-café in a former 'gas station', complete with a Texaco pump converted to a neon sign, dedicated to the memory and mythology of the 'good old days' on Route 66. And I stress the word 'mythology' here, not least because neither John, Josh nor Jeremy can have any memories of it. John, the oldest, has still several years to go before his thirtieth birthday. It's hard not to be impressed at the get-up-and-go.

Right now it's time for me to get up and go 'grab some shut-eye', as John puts it, if I'm going to make the next day's appointment with America's second natural wonder of the world.

It might seem insulting to call the Grand Canyon 'second', even to Niagara Falls, but I use the word only in the historical sense. Niagara was a much-visited 'wonder' long before there was even the slightest prospect of Arizona joining the union; it didn't become a fully-fledged state until 1912 making it the last to join before Alaska and Hawaii. It says a lot for the vastness and physical inhospitality of much of America which we Europeans frequently find it hard to come to terms with that it was only late in the nineteenth century that anybody in the United States of America really noticed the canyon much at all.

Native Americans had lived near – and even in – the canyon for thousands of years. The oldest culture that has been positively identified is that of the Anasazi, frequently referred to as 'Pueblo Indians' because the Spaniards who first encountered them thought their intricate system of cave dwellings were like towns. Later archaeologists have preferred to call them 'basket-makers' because that is what they did, as well as hunting deer, rabbits and 'bighorn' sheep. There are 2,000 sites associated with the Anasazi within what is today Grand Canyon National Park, although most are extremely small and the most impressive – called Tusayan Pueblo – is reckoned to have been home to just 30 people, albeit around the end of the twelfth century.

The first European to set eyes upon one of the world's most spectacular natural phenomena was a soldier come north from Spain's new central American colonies in 1540. His name was Garcia López de Cárdenas and as far as he was concerned the vast chasm he'd come across was simply annoying. He had been sent by his commander to get as far north as possible. The canyon put a definite – if dramatic – stop to that ambition and he returned to Mexico only to be court-martialled for failing to get any further.

More than two hundred years later a couple of Franciscan friars – Francisco Atanasio Domínguez and Sylvestre Vélez de Escalante – left the by now well-established Spanish settlement of Santa Fe in search of an overland route to Monterey (which translates as Royal Hill) in California. They succeeded, travelling over the Rockies, through northern Arizona and Utah, crossing the Colorado River in Glen Canyon just a few miles away, but almost unbelievably missing out on the 277-mile-long Grand Canyon itself. They failed to spot it on the way back either. Like I said, sometimes it's easy to forget just how vast and empty this part of the American West was. And still is.

It was only in 1848 after the Mexican-American War that anyone set out to explore the area in detail. Even then, it was not exactly appreciated to the full; US Army Lieutenant Joseph Ives, who reached the canyon in 1857, reported back: 'Ours has been the first and will doubtless be the last party of whites to visit this profitless locality.' Lieutenant Ives's depressing report put other explorers off for a dozen years and it was not until 1869 that another soldier, Major John Wesley Powell, one of those adrenalin-driven souls whose thirst for danger had not been slaked by the blood-letting of the American Civil War – in which he had lost an arm – decided to make a 1,000-mile navigation of the Colorado River.

He took with him four stout wooden boats and few rations – on the grounds that they would be bound to lose most of them when the boats inevitably capsized – and just nine men. The conditions they faced were awesome: searing heat, ferocious rapids – in which as predicted the boats repeatedly capsized – and no idea of what lay round the next corner, least of all that they were about to enter the greatest natural cauldron on the planet. Three of the nine died, but Powell survived and being the kind of man he was – barking mad – he did it again in 1871–72, taking copious notes which finally filled in the map on one of the least known regions of the emerging continental nation.

Powell was not only brave, possibly to the point of idiocy, he was intelligent, educated and humane, and went on to found the US Geological Survey, the Bureau of American Ethnology championing Native American rights and negotiating several crucial peace treaties. He also happened to be one of the first to understand the importance of ecology and advocated strict measures to control the use of water in the region, which are only gradually being rediscovered – and, as we shall see, still widely ignored – today. It was Powell who routinely used and publicised the term 'Grand Canyon'.

But inevitably what really made America sit up and pay attention to this big hole in the ground somewhere out west was the discovery in the late 1870s and early 1880s that it contained valuable deposits of zinc, copper, lead and that wonder material of the age, asbestos. While no one was looking, as it were, the miners moved in, and in remote areas of the canyon small-scale mining still continues. Amongst the metals it contains is uranium. The main campaigner for a railway was William Owen 'Buckey' O'Neill, who was mayor of the town of Prescott, Arizona, and had staked substantial mineral mining claims at the canyon and built himself a log cabin on the south rim. He wanted a railway to get his copper and iron ore out. It took years for O'Neill to persuade investment companies in Chicago and New York to put up the money until one bank finally took the risk in 1895.

O'Neill meanwhile had made his own name in other ways, becoming sheriff, jumping from a moving train to capture a prisoner and surviving a treacherous river crossing in which even his horse drowned. By the 1890s he had signed up with future president Theodore Roosevelt's Rough Riders, fighting in Cuba during the Spanish-American War. He organised a makeshift band of miners, cowboys and loggers into the Troop A, 1st US Volunteer Cavalry whose success was remarkable given that their horses been left behind in the United States. It was while serving as infantry therefore that O'Neill met his end, taken out by a Spanish sniper at dawn on 1 July 1898.

It was to be another three years before his dream was realised when the Atchison, Santa Fe and Topeka Railway finally finished its line to the canyon. By the time it got there it was discovered that money could be made not just by providing transport for the miners but for another valuable commodity which the railroads themselves had effectively created: tourists.

And here I am with a gaggle of them, lined up next to the tracks at 8:00 a.m., ready to board our train to the rim. First though, there is the inevitable bit of tourist hokum: a Wild West show, with various baddies and goodies shooting at each other outside a saloon bar prop frontage. It's primarily for the kids, of course, and as we're now outside the school holidays there are more adults, which is reflected in the jokes: 'Are you staring at my weapon, ma'am?'

And then finally it's onto the comfortable restored coaches from an earlier age of rail. I'm in the Pullman car, literally: 1923 Harriman coaches built by the Pullman Company (it even says so on the door). Unfortunately the steam locomotive only runs in summer so we are being hauled by a 1950s vintage diesel. (I know someone out there will be wishing I had got its number.) As far as I'm concerned though it's more important that the Pullman car has hot coffee and 'muffins' for breakfast and a bar for later.

Or not much later as our hostess Katie, an effervescent post-punk-platinum blonde would have it: 'You're on VAC-ATION folks, which means it's all right to have a real drink at 9:00 a.m.' And also, of course, because it means Katie gets more tips. But she deserves them, with a routine of slapstick jokes and keen commentary as we wind uphill through a landscape of tall pines and gorse scrub. 'Now, you see those trees, those are aspens. And they may look like a whole lot of separate trees to you, but they're all interconnected through their root systems. Basically the whole forest is just one big organism.' Wooh, spooky. Katie shares our sentiment: 'Isn't that kinda weird or what?'

'Keep your eyes open for big black birds,' she says a few minutes later. 'If you see a real daddy, it just might be a California condor, one of the rarest birds in the world. They were nearly extinct until a breeding programme back in the nineties. Even today there are only a couple of hundred pairs in the wild, most of them right here around the Grand Canyon.'

'How will we know if it's a condor?' asks one middle-aged woman with large gold earrings, looking extremely worried.

'He'll have your daughter in his mouth,' says Katie, with a laugh. 'No seriously, you'll know: they're big big black birds with a wingspan of maybe nine feet across. The Indians call them Thunderbirds, 'cause they follow the storm. And we've had a good monsoon this year.'

I look at her sceptically. Monsoon? Arizona? I mean, doesn't the very name come from the Spanish for arid zone? Looking out the window it's hard to imagine much rainfall around here, though there are those aspen pines...

'Yessiree, we get some real storms out here. The whole works: thunder and lightning and everything. You need to see one over the canyon. That's something. A lot of the year we don't get no rain at all, but when we do, we do.'

I start eyeing the sky in a whole new way, but even if the temperatures are a little nippy it still looks faultless blue. And there's – regrettably – no sign of any big black birds.

So far at least there are also no signs of any of the other natives Katie's been telling us about: the 'rattlers'. The Grand Canyon is not just home to the common or garden Western rattlesnake, but also the Mojave rattlesnake – 'strictly speaking a Californian interloper but don't try telling one that' – the Diamondback rattlesnake (after whom the locals endearingly named their baseball team) and the Sidewinder (after whom the Pentagon endearingly named a surface-to-air missile delivered in large quantities to the Mujahideen in 1980s Afghanistan to use against Soviet helicopters, and latterly used with equal success by their rebranded successors the Taliban against American ones). The Grand Canyon also has its own Pink rattlesnake, an evolutionary variant colour-coded to blend in with the oxidised iron exposed over millennia by the rock striations. Now there's a marketing exercise for you.

There are also the lesser-known Gila monster, one of the world's only two poisonous lizards and the Thistledown ant: a nasty blue furry flying thing which delivers a venomous sting. Despite its name, it is actually a member of the wasp family; there is just something about being blue and hairy that makes it that extra special bit scarier still.

By now Katie's also coaxed a few of us at least into her special cocktails and we've hardly noticed it's two hours gone by – the uphill route means the train barely goes over 30 miles an hour, even less within the boundaries of the national park – and we're pulling into Grand Canyon halt. This is a mildly depressing start to my visit to the canyon proper, a tourist 'village' which is the headquarters of the 'canyon industry': the unsightly but inevitable and in some cases necessary panoply of national park management, rescue services and provision of food, drink and accommodation for the tourists.

With only limited time available and a reservation back on the evening train into Williams I've booked a seat on the motor tour of the rim which boasts of giving the most different perspectives of the canyon in a one-day visit. The bad bit about this is immediately apparent: we're given tickets for lunch! Lunch? I can grab a bite later. But no, if I want to be on the tour lunch is part of the deal. Reluctant to get involved with this packaging of the experience, I have to admit I am hungry. Much as it seems perverse that the first thing to do on arrival at the scene of one of the earth's great wonders should be to go to a self-service canteen and stuff one's face, that is what I – and two busloads of other sheep – end up doing. To my regret, the food is the usual pre-prepared canteen fodder – chicken, pasta and soggy vegetables – there's no wine or beer, but what strikes me most is the complete casual disregard for even the lip service most Europeans now pay to 'green' measures.

Katie had already stressed on the train that despite the fact that the canyon had been carved by the fast-flowing abundant fresh waters of the Colorado River, the river is in fact a mile away – vertically! – and that there was an ecological price to be paid in ensuring supplies of fresh water at such a relatively remote location (without piped water) and then freezing it. She was wasting her breath. The soft drinks dispenser also has a sign asking users please to conserve ice, but without exception every single American using the drinks dispenser filled their glass with the stuff.

I opt for lemonade – when needs must! – prepared to pop in an ice cube or two if necessary, in that British way we have inherited from the days when refrigerators were a luxury, and perhaps because even today few of us have what we call an 'American' fridge, which is the size of a wardrobe and dispenses ice. But the lemonade straight from the machine is already so cold I can hardly drink it.

I decide to point this out in an environmentally friendly sort of way to one elderly, rangy-looking man in a baseball cap (what else?). In response he stares at me as if I'm challenging his right to bear arms and ostentatiously fills his glass with ice before topping it up with iced tea. 'The tea isn't so cold,' he adds gruffly, with a sort of 'so there' look before stomping off to wash down his mountain of stodgy food. I want to point out he hasn't even tasted it yet. Just to give him the benefit of the doubt, I try some myself: the iced tea, straight from the dispenser, is so cold that it's hard to believe adding ice won't turn the entire drink into a solid lump of the stuff.

The moral lesson to this is rather depressing, and a parallel to what I had experienced in Montana: whenever green campaigners tell us to switch off the standby on our television or computer, or to replace a light bulb with an economy one, do it because you want to, but do not do it with even the remotest delusion that you are helping the fight against global warming, because on the evidence of my own eyes, one single rig-riding, ice-swilling American invalidates almost an entire European city's attempts at energy conservation.

I'm more tempted than ever now to just wander off rather than join the horde of icemen on the bus but I'm only too aware that I really have no idea where I'm going, can't even see the canyon from here and could head off in the wrong direction and spend a couple of hours wandering aimlessly in the woods (think of the Franciscan friars). Also the bus is revving up now and will surely take me to a better view than I'm likely to discover independently.

There was also the sobering factor of a book I'd noticed at the inevitable gift shop entitled *Death at the Grand Canyon*. Here's a resumé: the earliest recorded tourist death was that of Lewis Thompson who on 22 March 1925, while attempting to take his own photograph with an early push-button-wired remote, took a step sideways, stepped on a crack, lost his footing and toppled over backwards into the abyss.

In September 1946 fashion model and media celebrity Dee Dee Johnson was persuaded that a 'canyon shot' was just what she needed to give her that extra push towards stardom. She duly obliged, posing near one of the south rim's best known scenic vantage points in nothing more than pedal pusher pants and a then highly risqué halter top.

It took two admiring rangers to realise all of a sudden that her outfit wasn't the most 'daring' aspect of the shoot. They had just time to shout 'Get her away from the edge' before the photographers, fearing that their one chance to get a truly memorable shot was about to disappear, flashed their big bulbs and Dee Dee duly disappeared – backwards to attain a celebrity she hadn't quite envisaged.

Less than a year later, on 17 July 1947 Herbert Kolb and his girlfriend in a romantic mood crawled under one of the few barriers with their legs dangling into eternity. They stayed like that for about half an hour, Herb's arm slung round his sweetheart, until the moment when they decided to get up and old Herb did a whoops-a-daisy and disappeared from his true love's sight.

He disappeared so completely that even when the rescue party arrived to recover what they knew could only be a corpse, they were unable to find him until they tied together a straw bale, took it to the precise point where Herbert and his bereaved had been sitting and eased it over the edge. They then watched its brutal bounce down the cliff face and deduced where it had most likely ended up. Sure enough, when they got down to the spot they had estimated, 930 feet below the lip, they found not only a large quantity of shredded straw but also the broken bodily remains of Herbert Kolb.

The list goes on and on and it is to the great credit of the American way of life, that the entire perimeter of the canyon at the most visited sites is not cordoned off behind barbed wire, iron railings and Plexiglas screens. In Britain it would be.

Scarcely a week before my visit, a little girl of barely four years of age, who had been walking the rim with her parents, suddenly – as small children do – spotted something interesting and ran off. Before they knew it she was a dwindling scream heading for a rock face below. Rescuers and her distraught father reached the scene of the tragedy within little more than 20 minutes. The child had fallen no distance at all in relative terms: barely 130 feet. It did not make much difference.

I've just digested all this when the bus makes its first stop at the canyon rim, and I realise all of a sudden the blindingly obvious: why it was so easy for early explorers to miss such a colossal phenomenon. It goes down, not up. Obvious, you might say, but all photographs you have ever seen of the Grand Canyon focus on the opposite: the buttes, mesas, whatever you want to call them, the whole 3D-ness of the canyon, the vast ups and downs of it. But of course, if you are approaching it from any direction – other than on a boat down in the Colorado River as Powell did – especially on foot, it simply isn't there until you walk up to the rim and it takes your breath away.

The Grand Canyon is one of those wonders of the world that you worry won't live up to expectation, simply because you have seen it so many times before you even get there. Like the Pyramids at Giza – or on a lesser scale the Eiffel Tower or Sydney Opera House – it is an image so pre-imprinted on the retina of the average twenty-first-century human's eye that it almost seems unwise to visit the real thing for fear of disappointment. Particularly when approaching it from a tour bus with a gaggle of baseball-hatted camera-toting middle-aged American tourists. But the canyon can cope. The canyon can cope with anything. It is more a question of whether you can cope with it. And right now, there on the edge of it – careful, step back a bit – face to face with the sheer, jaw-dropping, physical immensity of it, I'm not sure I can. Really not sure at all. The first thing it inspires, even in a group of noisy, trivia-minded tourists, is silence, a great, timeless, noise-swallowing silence. The silence of the abyss.

The Paiute Indians who inhabit the area of Arizona-Utah closest to the north rim call the Grand Canyon 'a mountain lying down'. It is hard to think of anything better, as long as you imagine that as not just one mountain but an entire mountain range lying down. Inverted, hollowed out. I once knew a professor of topographical mathematics at Oxford who was reputed not only to be able to use equations to turn the visible world inside out but to be able to visualise it in his head. Seeing the Grand Canyon for the first time is like a glimpse inside his universe.

There is no more three-dimensional view on earth and certainly not one that at the same time can suddenly project a more *trompe l'oeil* illusion of two dimensionality. It is the scale of the thing, in part, the fact that the opposite rim here is more than 10 miles away, half the width of the English Channel, and yet you can see it clearly. But there is not simply a gulf in between; it would be easier to cope with if there were. There is an entire landscape, inverted, a world of scooped-out pyramids. I had always imagined that what would strike you about the canyon was how the great buttes of uneroded rock jut up from the depths; it is not, it is the great mountains that climb downwards to the all but invisible inverted summit. You sense, you almost physically feel the process of millennial erosion, of 17 million years of slow continuous irresistible wearing away.

The silence of course doesn't last and by now there's the usual roundabout of people taking photographs and being photographed and asking other people to take photographs of them with their camera – and I even join in for God's sake – because I have to have a picture of me here, a snapshot in the mouth of infinity. But then I'm back chasing the silence, moving out and away from the mob who are, awfully but all-too-humanly, already coming to terms with it and chalking it up there with the Eiffel Tower after all. The tour guide is telling us details, dimensions, widths and breadths and so on, but none of it really seems to matter compared with just looking at the damn thing. Looking across it. At the other side, at the sides all round. You can play tricks with your own eyes: just look out ahead – don't look down – and it's flat. The other side is flat, perfectly flat. You are standing on a plain, a very flat plain, one of the flattest plains in North America, that just happens to have a hole the size of an entire mountain range gouged out of the middle of it.

Just for the sake of comparison here, let's put those other world sights in perspective: you could pick up St Paul's Cathedral and pop it down anywhere you liked in the Grand Canyon and if you could still see it, it would look like a tiny toy. Not something you lift up with both hands: something you position between thumb and forefinger in a giant landscape. The same for the Eiffel Tower: it would look like a carpet tack. Same goes for the Empire State Building even – not quite a carpet tack perhaps but a child's toy nonetheless, one that would barely reach a quarter of the way towards the summit and even then could get lost in the great immense meandering maze of rock formations four times its height. Even, I fear, the Great Pyramid of Giza, 4,500 years old, would be like a modern pimple next to this 17-million-year old chasm that would have looked pretty much as it does today when the pyramids were being built.

I haven't even mentioned the colours: the red-end spectrograph of pinks, ochres, vermilions, crimsons, that uncannily merge with the blues, the purply greys and in the distance, the far far distance, the dark green of the Colorado River itself, flowing through its handiwork. I use my camera, with an impressive enough 15-times optical zoom, to focus in on a tiny puddle of it far away. At seven-times magnification it increases to a wide river in between high cliffs, with a few odd coloured specks in it. At full stretch, fifteen times, those specks are only just identifiably multicoloured rafts with people on them, whitewatering on the greatest ride on earth. I make a mental note to do that one day. Once it was chic to take helicopter rides down the canyon: it must have been an awesome experience, but horribly defiling of this almost spiritual experience for everyone else. There were also a lot of accidents! Now only overflights are allowed, and over distant parts of the canyon. Most tourists barely graze the rim. You can walk down, but numbers are limited and without an overnight pass you have to walk straight back up and as it's three hours down and six back up, that's maybe not the best plan. Burros descend too, though no faster.

On the rough red face of an escarpment jutting out to my right I focus in on a small party, ant-like in perspective, with one burro, making their way down a line scraped across the face of the precipitous rock. This, the guide has told us, is Bright Angel Trail. Almost all the tracks used today are those used for millennia by the Native Americans. The eastern edge of the canyon is a Navajo reservation, to our west are reservations of the Havasupai and Hualapai tribes, while the Paiute are to the north on the border with Utah. It is over there that I glimpse the looming, building bulkhead of a storm brewing. I scan the skies and just in the distance, out above the emptiness, there's a dark shape wheeling that might, just might be a California condor, a Thunderbird. What is certain is the darkening grey brooding as it spreads and settles beyond the utterly flat line that separates the sky from the bowels of the earth: the plain is so flat that you simply cannot see beyond the canyon, the rim is the horizon in every direction. Just as it is invisible until you reach it, standing on the edge it consumes the world in every direction. Except behind, which is back to the bus. And the train. And civilisation.

The thunder claps in the distance as we board the train but rain fails to overtake us on the two-hour journey back. Katie tries to get a party atmosphere going, more hindered than helped by the horseback 'Great Train Robbery' and the pistol-toting bandits: 'We'll take anything except husbands and children.' But with a couple of her cocktails inside – I recommend she stock up on Grand Canyon beer next time – by the time we grind back into Williams we're even laughing out loud at her jokes: 'What do you call a two-legged cow? Lean beef. What do you call a cow sitting down? Ground beef.'

Which reminds me I have just time for a last meal: an almost perfect steak fajita from a little Mexican restaurant near the tracks, rare chargrilled beef served with an eye-wateringly lime and chilli spiced salsa that is the most delicious I have ever eaten. With just the slightest suspicion I may come to regret it.

It's raining now as I pick up my rucksack from the hotel. And dark, which means it must be time for me to go. There's a white van out front and two men standing beside it, waiting to take me to an abandoned clearing in the middle of the forest.

GRAND CANYON TO LOS ANGELES

TRAIN: Southwest Chief
FREQUENCY: 1 a day
DEPART WILLIAMS JUNCTION, ARIZONA: 9:33 p.m.

via
Kingman, AZ
Needles, California
Barstow, CA
Victorville, CA
San Bernardino, CA
Riverside, CA
Fullerton, CA

ARRIVE LOS ANGELES, CALIFORNIA: 8:15 a.m.
DURATION: 11 hours, 42 minutes
DISTANCE: 1,167 miles

18

Angels and Demons

I HAD BEEN WARNED off Los Angeles. By just about everybody who had ever been there. Including myself. That may seem odd for a city variously dubbed Tinseltown, the Dream Factory, the Street of Stars. But all those refer of course to one particular part of Los Angeles: Hollywood. And even then they mean the product, not the place. That was one of the worst bits, friends had told me.

I got warnings that were little short of horror stories: 'Don't stay in a motel in Hollywood or the door'll get broken in and you'll get robbed or raped or both'; 'Don't go out at night on foot or you'll get mugged'; 'And stay clear of downtown, people get shot.' And anyhow there was unanimous agreement that actually Los Angeles didn't have a downtown. Not as such.

What it had instead, glimpsed vaguely through the smog when landing at the airport, was a motley cluster of skyscrapers grouped together for dubious effect, towering out of a neglected urban wasteland amid a vast sprawling jungle of single-storey clapboard houses inhabited by gun-toting poor people. What you did on arrival in LA, I was told, was grab a car and head for the hills: Beverley that is, if you had an invitation, otherwise out beyond to sedate suburban Simi Valley or up the coast to Malibu and other millionaires' playgrounds. I could hardly argue otherwise. My own single previous experience had been on a journalistic job a dozen years ago, covering the aftermath of riots, and when I took a wrong turning in my hire car the cityscape metamorphosed without warning from shacks to dark streets of old department stores transformed into seedy bargain warehouses, crowded by resentful-looking people.

Los Angeles didn't even have a name, not properly. Just LA: the first city to be known by its initials, like PJ Proby or PJ O'Rourke or JFK, who of course also became an airport. Angelinos are probably the only people outside New York who also refer to their airport almost exclusively by its international call sign: LAX. Even though it has no reference to anyone famous and to the uninitiated looks like an abbreviation for a bowel purge or a Jewish form of smoked salmon.

Coming in by train, from the clean air of the desert and the natural splendours of the Grand Canyon, does not give much more grounds for optimism: I pull my head from under a colourful Indian blanket – or sort of Indian blanket: 'made of acrylic, sir, top quality' – picked up from a Navajo woman selling stuff on Albuquerque platform when we stopped for a cigarette break the evening before – and all I can see is the same nondescript clutch of skyscrapers loitering with intent in an unruly group under a smoggy sky. In the foreground, beyond the tracks and sidings, stand cold storage warehouses and loft conversion companies.

And then we pull into Union Station – they do lack originality with the names, but I suppose the railroad built the union – and everything changed. All of a sudden I was no longer dreading a world in monochrome shades of smog inhabited by rejects from the cast of *Blade Runner*. Instead, I had stepped straight off the train and onto the set for *The Long Goodbye*. In colour. Technicolor, come to that. Los Angeles station is on a par with any of the great termini of the world, yet completely unlike any other. It feels as if I have just stepped into the baronial dining hall of some Mexican-inspired plutocrat's mansion: great red-brown wooden beams soar to make a ceiling, from which art deco chandeliers hang over a patterned floor in ochre and white marble. Sets of squared-off art deco leather armchairs sit in formal groups where passengers lounge with newspapers if they're not leaning at the smart little bar where a great arch links through into the next chamber of the mansion. I half expect to see Humphrey Bogart buying Lauren Bacall a drink, while Peter Lorre lurks behind an LA *Times*. I haven't my iPod plugged in but if I had it'd be playing Al Stewart, singing about a morning from a Bogart movie in a country where they turn back time. LA?

Then I walk out into the sunshine, with those trademark soaring California palms reaching on their spindly-looking mile-high trunks for a sky that is all of a sudden improbably blue. I turn to look back, across a sea of pink and orange azaleas at a station that, with its gabled frontage, ribbed red tiles and tall clock tower, resembles nothing so much as an over-scale replica of a whitewashed church in some Mexican pueblo. Maybe that defended by the Magnificent Seven. All of a sudden I'm suffused with a sense of deep, tranquil well-being, and then I realise why: I can breathe again. Back down to sea level, the warm air with just a hint of the coast in it – and, God knows, maybe the traffic fumes my system recognises – has worked an irrigational miracle with my nasal membranes. I haul out my trusty pocket handkerchief and for the first time in what seems like months successfully blow my nose. Never had I thought I'd be so glad to see snot.

With air finally circulating through my sinuses, I feel more than up to finding my motel in Hollywood. Yes, I know, there's the robbery and rape and mad axe men to put up with, but I'm in LA for heaven's sake, how can I not stay in Hollywood? Happily also, there is public transport – an underground even – that gets there. And what's more it's clean and works, which is not something I had been relying on. I still remember Dionne Warwick singing about LA being a great big freeway where you had to put a hundred down to buy a car, before you could hope they'd make you a star. These days maybe they do it if you travel by metro. Get off at Hollywood and Vine and the station's as good as anything at Universal Studios (really!), with mock palm trees supporting a domed roof of thousands of reels of film and ancient movie cameras on pedestals at the top of every escalator. Lights, camera, all that's missing is the action.

That's upstairs, above Hollywood and Highlands. At Mann's Chinese Theatre. I haven't even dumped my bag yet – I didn't take the advice and am staying in a cheap hotel in Hollywood, I mean, really, where else? – and already on the pavement I'm swamped by stars of stage and screen. There's Batman, right there: the Dark Knight himself next to that fat bloke in shorts, the great cape flowing to the ground and the harsh rigid bat silhouette of the mask. Except, I'm sure last time I saw the caped crusader he wasn't wearing four-inch platform soles. It would make some of those athletic stunts a bit tricky. It does make him tower over the girls though. And the fat bloke in shorts.

And then there's Spiderman too, good ol' Spidey, crouched low in that trademark arachnid pose. Except that he must be wearing his second suit today – the one made of rayon instead of Lycra – which is a pity because that saggy arse with the clearly visible lines of his Y-fronts underneath really does dent the image a bit. Still never mind at least he'll deal with that nasty-looking bloke with the skull-face and red hands who just might be Darth Maul, but then you shouldn't really ask me, old Darth and I haven't hung out together for years. And then there's the bloke with the tri-cornered hat, the sash round his waist and the dodgy line in earrings. I wonder if he's looking for Johnny Depp. He certainly doesn't look like him.

But then the real celebrities outside Mann's are the ones beneath your feet: the hand and footprints of movie stars down the years, persuaded to dip their appendages in wet cement by Sid Gruman who founded this preposterous mock-Chinese pagoda cinema in 1927. Look down and there's Bogey's shoe prints with the hands next to them – remarkably long spindly fingers – and the scrawl: Sid, may you never die, till I kill you. The tough man even bent over with his hands in cement. There's Gregory Peck's, John Wayne's, Maurice Chevalier's, a tiny set belonging to Shirley Temple and Mae West's – though no sign that he tried to get her to lie down to leave a more tangible impression. One star was more obliging. Not only did Roy Rogers leave both hand and footprints but he dropped his gun there too. And even Trigger planted a couple of hoofs.

But will these marks in the concrete be the only way anyone will remember Freddie Bartholomew? Or Constance Talmadse? Or Norman Shearer? I apologise to their fan clubs but I've never heard of any of them. Nor, I have to admit, of a vast number of the more than 2,000 'stars' commemorated with physical stars set into the pavement along Hollywood Boulevard. I can't help feeling maybe Hollywood lost its way when it first allowed celebrities from other walks of life to intrude. Jim Morrison and the Doors have their place in music, but a star on the Hollywood pavement? And what about the Harlem Globetrotters? All of them? Or was it just one season? And who were Frank Morgan, Eugene Palette and Norris Stoloff. The Ozymandias syndrome of the twentieth century. In multiple.

It's only clear just how much effort has been put into reviving the fortunes of the Hollywood area – as opposed to the movie industry, most of which is located miles away today – as I walk further down Hollywood Boulevard itself. By now I've dumped my bag at the motel on North Highland Avenue, checking the doors carefully for axe marks or other signs of breaking and entering (there weren't any!), and negotiated the honking, parping traffic and the inevitable hustling bums by the roadside, back down to the main drag.

There is a moving borderline somewhere along Hollywood Boulevard where tacky turns into tatty. Hollywood and Highlands is the hub of the restoration project, with a new smart semi-open-air shopping-centre development and a view of the Hollywood sign – it's forbidden to get anywhere within reach of the great absurd piece of sentimentally-hyped hubris, and has been ever since unemployed actress Peggy Entwistle earned her own little claim to dubious immortality by fatally leaping off the top of the H. The metal letters are 50 feet high, and have a claim to fame other than what most people imagine: the world's most famous and protected estate agent's hoarding, which is what they were built as back in 1923.

But Hollywood glamour seems a long way away already by the time my footsteps carry me beyond the Hollywood and Vine metro. Long gone are such tourist traps as the ubiquitous Ripley's Believe It or Not, the Waxwork Museum, even Frederick's of Hollywood Lingerie Museum, famed in particular for displaying bustiers worn by Madonna and a few of Cher's old bras. In their place are cut-price electronics stores, Levi retailers, fancy-dress sellers and a few tawdry porn shops. Anything vaguely reminiscent of the glitter has long faded by the time I reach Pantages, the 'grande dame' of Tinseltown, an extravagant completely over-the-top early art deco palace, opened in 1929 as Hollywood's superlative cinema. Its fame soared until its glory days from 1949 to 1959 when it was the home of the Oscar ceremony. Following that, like so much of the city, it suffered gradual, later serious neglect to become shabby and embarrassing. Only now, after a major job of root-and-branch restoration has it come back to its former glory as a theatre for Broadway musicals. But you only have to stand in the entrance lobby and stare up at its gilt cornices, elaborate star-shaped ceiling centrepiece, emblazoned with gold, silver and pink like the palace of the Emperor Ming in some Flash Gordon fantasy to get a feel for the escapist magic that summed up the original Hollywood dream. But by now even the stars on the pavement are getting few and far between and it's been at least 100 yards since I recognised a name.

Time to take the metro back towards whatever can loosely be termed the centre of a metropolis that is actually a sprawl of unplanned development covering much of two counties (there are 10 million people here and the urban territory is larger than that of the US's smallest state, Rhode Island). I want to see if there really is such a thing as downtown LA. There is of course historically an area where the city first began, not far from Union Station, although even that wasn't here in the eighteenth century when a couple of dozen Spanish settlers first founded *El Pueblo de nuestra Señora, la Reina de Los Angeles* (The city of our Lady, Queen of the Angels). Surprisingly, the city has managed not only to maintain, but in recent years also to refurbish a little area which is still known as 'the pueblo' and, spanning maybe half a dozen streets or so, includes most of LA's oldest buildings from the nineteenth and early twentieth centuries.

Inevitably there is a bit of a touristy feel to it with Mexican sombreros and carved donkeys on sale, but they are alongside genuinely good restaurants and food stalls. Olivera Street has been a market for all things Hispanic since the 1930s. Settling in for some tacos and a margarita at the Casa Golondrina with Spanish spoken all around feels more like the Yucatán than downtown LA, even if it does awaken a rumbling remembrance in my intestines of last night's chilli salsa. But it is after lunch when I hit the Grand Central Market a few blocks away that I really come to understand how much the Hispanic presence in Los Angeles has come of age. For all the size of the city this is hardly Seattle's Pike Place but it is a bustling marketplace full of fresh farmers' produce – mostly fruit and veg – but the remarkable thing is how little of it is labelled in English. Walk in and the first thing that hits the eye is a giant sign proclaiming *Especialidad en Chiles Secos* (Dried Chiles Our Speciality – the translation is mine, there wasn't a word of English in sight). Next to it a neon sign is touting somebody else's *'chiles secos'* along with *'moles'*. There are stalls called *La Huerta* (garden) and *La Casa Verde* (the green house) and at least a few offer help: alongside *'antojitos mexicanos'* the sign offers 'Roast to go'. It's apparently a famous downtown LA institution. The other elements in cosmopolitan LA are also on show: a Japanese restaurant and someone offering Chinese massage, translated into the vernacular: *Masaje Chino*.

LA also has its bustling restaurant-filled Chinatown, just north of Cesar Chavez (I won't make that mistake again) Boulevard as well as Little Tokyo, which was the hub of the Japanese community that first began to settle here in the 1880s. Unfortunately the ill treatment of the Japanese-American community during the Second World War and a thoughtless redevelopment programme during the 1960s which replaced most of the original architecture with bland buildings, has left little to see. Even the designation of the buildings along East First Street as a protected National Historic Landmark has been more of a sop to the errors of the past. The most poignant structure is a monument to Ellison Onizuka, the Hawaiian-born Japanese-American who died in the Challenger space shuttle disaster. Unfortunately it is also the most kitsch memorial I have ever seen outside a Soviet cemetery (the Russians used to put scaled-down tanks or rocket launchers on the graves of military men): a 10-foot-high full-colour model of the Challenger on lift-off, still strapped to the massive fuel tanks whose explosion would cause the deaths of the astronauts inside.

Bizarrely it echoes the similar-shaped structure in the background, LA's iconic city hall, a great rocket-shaped tower, built in 1928 and for four decades the city's tallest structure. It is also incredibly familiar, and then I realise why: it's been used in so many movies, from the original 1954 movie version of the *War of the Worlds* when it was attacked by the invaders to the modern *Superman* series where, with a bit of computer-generated assistance, it has served as the offices of the *Daily Planet*.

The rest of the rocket ships are just a short stroll away. This is the clump of skyscrapers that looked so unfriendly from a distance. They don't look much more welcoming close up. The five glass cylinders of the Westin Bonaventure Hotel look just like five glass cylinders while the US Bank Tower which proudly boasts of being the tallest building between Chicago and Hong Kong (though as from here on out that means basically the Pacific Ocean I'm not sure how much of a boast it is) is imposing only because of its height. Bizarrely, to be allowed to reach that height it had to purchase 'air rights' from the neighbouring Central Library. Reinforces my belief that Americans and Russians aren't so different after all: an old Russian saying is 'the law is like a telegraph pole, very difficult to get over, very easy to get round'; the only difference here is that you have to buy your way round. Come to think of it, maybe that isn't a difference at all.

On my last visit, when I didn't spend a night in the city, and only ventured downtown by accident, I drove through this area as quickly as legally possible feeling intimidated by a surly population. Today, I'm surprised to find myself wandering in relaxed mood into Pershing Square, which extensive remodelling has rescued from a dubious inner-city empty space to become a remarkably pleasant oasis, which is what it literally resembles with its forest of small palms and bubbling fountain. Along one side stretches another of those former American architectural archetypes: the great triple-pronged bulk of the Millennium Biltmore. For a moment I'm struck by a sinister sense of déjà vu and then it hits me: the Buffalo Statler. The difference is stark: whereas the former Buffalo palace for presidents and industry moguls is a crumbling neglected heap, the Millennium Biltmore still oozes the money it had when it was built in the 1920s – palatial public rooms, a smart cocktail bar and a Roman-style marble-floored indoor pool. What a difference a few thousand millionaires make!

Not just millionaires though: looking up at this example of preserved 1920s opulence I'm accosted by a grubby, foul-smelling beggar demanding 'change' rather forcefully. He's caught me by surprise, still trying to work out what would make someone name a city square after a nuclear missile. It takes a bit for me to get my head round the idea that the missiles – so notorious for years amongst the peaceniks who fought their deployment in Britain and Germany – were themselves named after a general. How come they never named any after Custer?*

---

*I subsequently discovered that despite having achieved fame in the First World War and being promoted to the rank of General of the Armies, only held by one other person, George Washington – and that was a posthumous promotion – Pershing belonged to almost the same era as Custer, having started out in the US cavalry, and taken part in the controversial Massacre at Wounded Knee.

But, apart from this little intellectual digression, the main reason I've not managed to avoid the attentions of the bum is that my mind has suddenly become fully engaged by another semantic interpretation of that word. For the past 20 minutes or so, encouraged by my cathartic consumption of tequila and tacos, the rumbling in my lower intestines has become increasingly intense. My Grand Canyon chilli salsa is threatening to produce an earth movement all of its own. So here I am standing in the middle of a square named, as far as I'm concerned, after a nuclear missile, eyes watering and buttocks firmly clenched, trying to ignore a smelly man persistently saying, 'Well, you gonna give me a few bucks or what?'

This would be annoying enough at the best of times but right now it is positively excruciating. If you can imagine sitting on top of a volcano that has suddenly decided a few centuries of dormancy are enough and it's time to let the old lava flow again, then you are close. Except that I'm not sitting on the volcano, it's inside me. One way or another, perhaps misinterpreting my clenched fists – actually nails digging into palms to aid concentration – the tramp (the word 'bum' is one I daren't even call to mind at the moment) ambles off, allowing me to close my eyes for a few seconds, channelling every last ounce of energy to my sphincter's efforts to control its inner Etna. And eventually, like the sound of war drums slowly retreating into the jungle, the crisis subsides and it occurs to me that, rather than face up to the challenge of finding a public toilet downtown, it might be time to head back to Hollywood and see if the axe man's been yet.

❊

He hadn't. Suitably relieved, in every possible way, it's time to head out west, for another view of Hollywood culture: Sunset Strip. It's not really called that, of course, the road: it's called Sunset Boulevard and runs out to Beverly Hills and beyond to Laurel Canyon and below the Hollywood Hills, which is where the real celebrities live these days. Leonardo di Caprio, Kylie Minogue, Cameron Diaz, all have their pads up there.

But I can't help my fascination with the 'Strip' itself, which is basically the mile and a half that runs from west Hollywood to Beverly Hills. The reason is not the night clubs or the bars that increasingly attract celeb-spotters rather than the celebs themselves, but an ancient, black-and-white television series called 77 Sunset Strip.

It was the predecessor of all the cop shows you've ever seen and ran from the late 1950s through to the mid-sixties, which is the reason I remember it so well: I was still a child and wasn't allowed to watch it. With its catchy jazzy theme tune, 'Seventy-Sev-en, Sun-Set-Strip' represented a glamorous exotic world that was totally alien to families in provincial Northern Ireland. My father lapped it up – the gangs, the guns, the girls and strange slang – while I was sent to bed with that theme tune and an image of men in dark suits and women adjusting stockings that stirred vague sensations I didn't really understand.

I should have hired a limo and cruised it. Instead I took the bus. I had thought I might start at 'Sunset and Vine' just because of the Bowie song 'Cracked Actor', about a Hollywood star down on his luck trying to squeeze one more blow-job on the price of his fame, but – perhaps unsurprisingly – that's the wrong direction: one of those things we Europeans have a problem with in America, and LA in particular, is streets that go on forever. Almost literally: miles and miles and miles. Sunset Boulevard stretches nearly 16 miles in total, from the wiggly bit on the far side of downtown LA, along the dead straight bit that runs through Hollywood to the wiggly bit again that is the start of the 'Strip' and runs beyond it for miles of twists and turns right down to the Pacific Coast Highway that is the extreme edge of the vast Los Angeles conurbation. So when I catch my bus – a 217 heading west – my main concern is where to get out. I opt for Fairfax and Sunset, which turns out to be at least a stop too early. But already I realise that any chance of actually locating a number 77 on the 'Strip' – where the detectives supposedly worked out of – or in fact any number remotely similar is ridiculous, given that the first number I actually find is 8225. But then it's not in black and white either.

In fact, it's hard to find anywhere less black and white than the 'Strip' with its gaudy, garish riot of neon, big hotels, bustling bars with kids hanging out on the streets, beer bottles or cocktails in hand. This is theoretically one of the world's greatest rock'n'roll meccas, home to the Whisky a Go-Go club where the Doors and Guns'n Roses got their big breaks, not to mention being the home of the original Go-Go girl back in the sixties when their female DJ started dancing to the records she was spinning. There's also the Roxy, The Troubadour, The Rainbow Room – all of them legendary venues, if you happen to be there at the right time. On most other nights, though, they're just familiar noisy nightclubs, especially if you're a middle-aged bloke not dressed in the height of fashion. Superficially, I have to say, it feels more like Magaluf on Majorca with an 18–30 Club tour group in town.

Even the famed Viper Room, owned by Johnny Depp himself, is just another old rock'n'roll club on an ordinary night. You wouldn't know that this was where megastar-in-the-making River Phoenix was found dead by the doorway in October 1993, overdosed on drugs, aged just 23 and only a few days before he was due to start filming *Interview With a Vampire* alongside Tom Cruise. If he had snorted less up his nose we might never have heard of Brad Pitt. There are people who make pilgrimages to scenes of famous Hollywood deaths, though as far as I can make out, cyberspace father William Gibson's virtual reality art recreation of his corpse *in situ* (in the novel *Spook Country*) hasn't materialised yet. Or maybe I was just missing my VR helmet; there are times on Sunset when it's easy enough to lose your grip on what's real and what's made up on the spot.

The only bit of true upmarket chic on Sunset is the quaint little collection of shops and cafés called Sunset Plaza, a low-rise throwback to the 1930s, stuffed with expensive designer stores. Bruce Willis and the Governator himself are said to favour Billy Martin's Western attire store, while Tom Cruise and Nicole Kidman pop in at Oliver Peoples. Richard Gere took Cindy Crawford here to buy her wedding ring, though the shop where they bought it has gone. Even Sunset Plaza is not immune to fickle fashion trends and the credit crunch.

But I've seen enough to get the flavour and a stroll down into Beverly Hills suddenly seems irresistible, the change in the noise and traffic immediately palpable. Wandering along just a few of the verdant, almost subtropical avenues, listening to the sound of the cicadas and taking in the aroma of orchids, it's easy to imagine myself back in Bogartland. The celebrities have changed though – even if the one name the address Beverly Hills still conjures up for me is Jed Clampett – today's superstars cosseted in their mansions up in the hills around me include not just movie stars but pop singers and British footballers. Well, one footballer in particular. But I've got a date with David Beckham tomorrow, so there's no need to rush.

I had ordered up my ticket for the LA Galaxy's match against the New York Red Bulls several months before leaving Britain. Not because I'm a particularly big Beckham fan – though few England supporters could fail to owe him a debt of gratitude for that miracle free kick that saw us through to the 2002 World Cup. And I certainly was never a fan of Manchester United who have long since been not so much a club as a brand: it would be like being a fan of Starbucks. Yes, yes, I know some people are. I have seen them paying homage at the site of the holy latte grail.

But 'Posh and Becks' have made themselves into such remarkable – and despite the extravagantly immodest displays of excessive wealth – remarkably likeable symbols of modern Britain, that I can't resist the temptation of seeing how the great man goes down in his new homeland. Especially as he's come with the express aim of infecting the planet's only nation immune to proper football (okay then, Yanks, soccer) with the germs of passion for 'the beautiful game'. Also, it's been almost a month since I was last at a game; I'm suffering withdrawal symptoms.

But kick-off is not until 7:00 p.m. according to my ticket so there's most of a day to kill. Under the circumstances I do what any British football fan in LA for the day would probably do: Universal Studios. I'd like to tell you it was an extraordinary, culturally captivating insight into the secrets of Hollywood moviemaking. Unfortunately it wasn't. Apart from a couple of modestly interesting short shows about special effects, Universal is basically a theme park like any other. True, there is the 'studio tour' but it's basically a bus ride around the back lots of sealed-off sound stages where the real action goes on. There are a couple of outdoor sets, most notably the pond that doubled for the oceanfront in *Jaws*, complete with the hilariously unrealistic-looking but allegedly original rubber shark (somehow not the same when you're expecting its appearance any moment, rather than a blinding flash out of the dark on a cinema screen). Other than that – and the fact that the rides are named after Universal blockbusters: *Jurassic Park*, *The Mummy* etc. – its main concern is that of any other theme park: churning the punters and selling hot dogs and souvenirs.

By early afternoon I'm ready for something different. Like the part of LA where most of my British friends said I should have been staying: Santa Monica beach. As the name implies, it's not really Los Angeles, but then nor is most of what is generally called Los Angeles, any more than most of what is called London is actually the original Roman square mile city. Santa Monica is merely the bit by the beach, at the end of – logically enough – the Santa Monica Boulevard. And as a Sheryl Crow fan from way back I know I ought to hang out there until the sun goes down. But I have to be gone a bit earlier or I'll miss the start of the game.

The most fascinating thing about the Santa Monica Boulevard – apart from its musical fame and, as I'm about to discover, its length – is that it more or less passes directly over the La Brea tar pits. This may sound less than interesting until you know, as I had just learned, that America could make a significant dent in its reliance on imported oil if they only drilled there. It is the supreme irony of a great city whose prime problem in growing to the size it is today was initially the shortage of water wells – see Jack Nicholson in *Chinatown* – they ended up unwittingly building it over one of the country's largest onshore oil deposits. The only reason La Brea hasn't been turned into an oilfield is that it lies underneath some of the most expensive real estate in America. And the inhabitants of Beverly Hills are amongst the few Americans who wouldn't think it was worth drilling into a guaranteed oil well in their back garden. Whatever would Jed Clampett have thunk?

A rare Angelino public transport fan later that night, would tell me: 'Effectively, the whole of Los Angeles is sitting on an oil well. A federal bill was enacted to ban pushing the line west in case it exploded a giant methane bubble more or less underneath Beverley Hills. Since then the ban has been rescinded – in theory, and with obvious conditions – but no one has found a way of extending the line that would cost less than billions.

The bus ride down to Santa Monica takes longer than I imagine, quite a bit longer in fact, so that it's nearly 4:00 p.m. by the time I'm strolling along the Pacific seafront and down the pier with seagulls wheeling in the salty air above me and a bottle blonde in a bikini doing an interview on the sand to a guy with a sound boom and a very long lens. I do a double take for a moment, in case it's Pamela Anderson. But it isn't. At least I don't think so. But then I once stood next to Noel Gallagher at the bar of a London club for an hour without recognising him. Celebrity status isn't absolute. And nor is my eyesight these days.

Santa Monica is nice, as nice as my friends had said it was: a bit like Brighton, but with a better beach. And sunshine. I could have stayed there longer – though if I'd booked in there I doubt if I'd ever have seen anything more of LA – but football beckoned and the admittedly uninspiring Home Depot Stadium, home to LA's own 'galacticos' was in the southern part of the city, and starting to look a lot further away as I came to work out the scale on the map I was looking at. I had no idea. Simply no idea.

The only obvious route by public transport – and I'm beginning to realise that a taxi ride might be a lot longer and a lot more expensive that I had considered – seemed to be to take the express bus back to the 'light rail' network which would whisk me across downtown to the 'South Central' area and the stop I had worked out to be closest to the stadium. When a bus reassuringly rolls up within a minute or two, this plan seems to be working fine. Until it stops again about five minutes later, still – as far as I can tell, there being no break in the urban continuum – well within Santa Monica.

The reason it has stopped is traffic, which is a good reason, because there is a lot of it. In fact, it is not a good reason at all because there is a hell of a lot of it. And none of it moving, other than – very occasionally – between one red light and another. And there are a lot of red lights too. Before I know it the sun is indeed going down on the Santa Monica Boulevard. And unless I do something, and quick, it'll also be going down on my chances of getting to the game for kick-off.

With the bus sitting there stationary, I decide to take a little advice and edge up front to ask the driver how long it'll take us to get to the junction with the rail line. 'Oh, I dunno,' he says with that air bus drivers seem to be born with, 'at this time of day… could be 40 minutes, could be an hour and 40 minutes.' Which sends me into a blind panic as that means they'll be booting the ball downfield before I'm even on the right tracks. Clearly touched by this odd foreigner's predicament – or deciding I'm a bit touched and better off his bus – the driver does something wonderful and almost unimaginable in health-and-safety-obsessed London: he opens the door for me between stops and says, 'You can get off if you think you can get there faster.'

All I know is that I can hardly get there much more slowly. I take him up on it, and indeed before long am a good hundred yards in front of the bus, not that this is much good because the rail line is maybe four or five miles away – I told you it was long, that old boulevard. The only answer is a cab, and to hell with the cost: a driver who knows his way and can cut the corner across town, taking the backbearings, the 'rat runs' as we'd say in London. The only trouble is: there isn't one. And even if there was it wouldn't be any good, not on a grid system. A London cabbie would be ducking and diving down. Showing off the secrets of 'the Knowledge' and making the route up as he went along, playing a great maze game to beat the jam just for the hell of it. But not here. I examine the cross-streets hopefully but in vain. The cross-streets only funnel more cars out of them into the main road; it's like watching arteriosclerosis in real time.

There is a James Joyce short story in *Dubliners* which is one of the best things he ever wrote, certainly one of the most comprehensible. It is called 'Araby' and is the brief story of a boy determined all day to get down to a bazaar to buy something and when he gets there it is too late, and the moment that he realises that fact, in a closing market, with the stalls shut and dusk falling all around him, is a life-defining bittersweet realisation of the poignancy of the human condition.

Well, that's what I feel like right now, with the sunset faded into an eerie purple neon- and traffic-lit dusk, and here I am stranded on the endless Santa Monica Boulevard of life, with the street numbers somewhere in the low thousands with an infinite number ahead and behind, having hopped back on the bus when it catches up with me, then off again in fresh despair, with no escape down side streets leading nowhere, and the creeping insurmountable certainty that the game I had arguably travelled 6,000 miles to see would be started – and at the current rate possibly even finished – before I got there.

It's not that in the great scheme of things it matters all that much. But what hurts is the conspiracy of the universe to trample mindlessly on even our most modest aspirations and remind us of our own essential insignificance. Nothing hurts more than being told simply, 'You don't matter'. And absolutely nothing hurts more than being told it by a series of traffic lights.

In the end it was past a quarter to seven when the 720 pulled up at a stop near a junction where a building opposite displayed the world 'Wiltern' and something made me ask the driver if we were near the Metro Rail.

'Sure, just over there,' he indicated, and I realised with a feeling of almost nausea that 'Wiltern' was another of those 'cool' contractions – Wilshire and Western – that Americans seem to love so much in the absence of proper place names. I jumped out, only to realise that I then had to stand while my bus and another wave of unthinking traffic ploughed past – one day American transport planners will realise it makes sense to put underground rail entrances on both sides of the road, won't they?

Wilshire/Western is the end of the line. It would have improved Los Angeles's public transportation no end – not to mention made my journey that evening almost tolerable – to have pushed the line out west, ideally as far as Santa Monica. But that would have brought us back to those La Brea tarpits.

At least the train is ready to depart within seconds of my boarding it. I look at my watch. The trouble is that I have no real idea how long the trip will take. At least being on the metro line frees me from the tyranny of the traffic but there's no way I'm going to catch the start of the match.

By the time I'm changing at 7th Street/Transit Center just four stops later I realise they're probably already kicking off. The Blue Line south is right there in front of me, irresistibly tempting even though I know that on the overlaid map, the striped beige 'transitway' route comes closer to the stadium. The trouble is I don't really know what the transitway is or how to get on it. I do the obvious thing: I ask a man in Metro Rail uniform. He seems amused by my question, or at least the accent in which I ask it and replies in heavily Spanish-accented American: 'Is not here.'

'The transitway?'

Quizzical look. 'The bus.'

'No, this,' I said, pointing to a map with the stripy beige line, 'transitway. Is it a tram,' then remembering my vocabulary, 'a light rail.' ,

'*Si*, this,' he indicated the train at the platform. 'Train. Metro Rail. Blue Line. Very quick.'

'But to Artesia Transit Center, the other tram. Does it go from near here?' I had noticed that the beige line said that from 37th Street it was at street level, before, I assumed, descending underground.

'Is on the other side of the square. A long walk. I think they should put it here, but is on the other side. The bus.'

But I'm not talking about the bus, I want to scream, or am I, I start to wonder? The truth is I haven't really got a clue what I'm talking about here, in any language. Then the horn sounds to close the door on the Blue Line and I jump on board, just in case. 'Very quick,' the metro man tells me, so I sit down and seal my fate. Opposite me a Hispanic-looking girl sitting reading a book looks friendly and intelligent.

'Excuse me,' I start to explain, 'do you know the Home Depot Soccer Stadium?' She smiles encouragingly, but not optimistically. 'Near Artesia,' I add, hopefully helpfully.

'This train goes to Artesia,' she says in perfectly comprehensible American English.

'To the Home Depot Soccer Stadium?'

'I don't know where that is.'

'I think it's nearer to here,' I say, pointing to the end of the beige 'transitway' line.

'Oh,' she says, 'then you need to get out here,' – points to Imperial/Wilmington – 'take the Green Line and then the bus.'

'Right,' I smile dubiously and sit back to wait, as the train suddenly surfaces and turns out to be a tram, trundling along the streets next to the cars and, like them, stopping at red lights. I grit my teeth, not quite audibly: my companions in the compartment by now include four pudgy but tough-looking white guys in their early thirties who are discussing whether the tattoos they just had on their forearms in order to get a free T-shirt might be some sort of advertising gimmick. Yeah right. Apart from them there are two middle-aged women telling a not terribly bright-looking 20-something bloke, 'And he financed the Nazis.'

'Who, the president?' says the young guy, unwilling to believe this, even of George W. Bush.

'Naw, not him. Nor his daddy. His granddaddy, they bankrolled them Nazis in the Second World War.'

This is news to me too, and I wonder if they are possibly confusing the Bush dynasty with the Kennedy dynasty, but right now I am more concerned with the ticking clock which shows I've already missed the first quarter hour of play. The list of stations shows eight more to go, and the view from the window is increasingly of unlit streets, broken-down trucks, and low-rise dwellings with broken windows and beat-up cars outside. The one thing signally lacking is pedestrians of any kind. Or taxis. This is not the sort of area I'm keen to jump out in.

Eventually, almost 25 minutes into the first half by my reckoning – but to give up now would make a mockery of the whole day – we pull into Imperial/Wilmington, and the friendly girl opposite says: 'You want to get that bus,' (meaning 'if'), 'you need to get out here.'

So I do. Uncertainly. Particularly as when I reach the platform above there is another blockade of metro ticket inspectors, backed up by armed police already detaining serious numbers of my fellow passengers, though happily not the friendly girl, who waves as she points me towards the Green Line and disappears into a night that looks less than welcoming.

My ticket is fine, but I am torn now between jumping on the Green Line for two stops to catch an unspecified bus to Artesia Transit or getting back on the Blue for another stop to where the ground appears to be further but at least in a straight line west. This is a straight-line city, I'm thinking. The Blue Line arrives first deciding the matter for me.

The next two stops to Artesia are not reassuring. There is a fat black woman in the corner surrounded by black bags which I suspect contain all her worldly possessions. She has her hand over her mouth as if trying not to be sick. I move up the carriage and stare through the door into the pitch black of the outer LA suburbs. The guy standing by the door I am staring through is big and black and wearing excessively baggy clothing and I glimpse something in his hand which looks like a curved handle that I realise might easily be that of a flick knife. He snatches a glance at me, and pulls a length of cloth from his pocket with his other hand. The train pulls into Artesia station. It looks like we are both getting off here, except that I am having second thoughts.

Now, I pride myself as being pretty much colour blind when it comes to human beings, but you can't ignore context. The one previous time I had been in Los Angeles, I was writing an article for *The Sunday Times* on racial attitudes between Simi Valley – home to the jurors who had just acquitted four white policemen of beating up black motorist Rodney King, even though there was clear video evidence of them doing so – and South Central LA, where I was now. The verdict had led to rioting which caused $785 million in property damage, and in which 2,300 people were injured and 55 killed. They made the race riots in London's Brixton or Liverpool's Toxteth pale into insignificance in comparison. To put it bluntly, I'm nervous here, even though I'm fully aware that this young black man might be equally worried about some middle-aged white bloke with wild eyes peering over his shoulder in a dark station. After all, who's to say I'm not carrying a gun? People do. Especially around here.

The station is a bleak, empty car park with lots of parking spaces for buses but no actual buses. The guy with the object in his hand that might have been a knife and might not melts into the dark. Central LA is awash with street lighting, so why not here? Maybe the mayor's once-a-month 'green' initiative to get citizens to turn off non-essential lighting is applied permanently in South Central. Maybe it all depends on what you think is essential, and for whom. It certainly doesn't look like level standards apply citywide.

By now it's gone 7:35 and my attempt to reach the Galaxy ground by half-time has obviously drained into the dust and even getting there by the start of the second half is beginning to look bleak. As usual there are no cabs. On the other side of the station is a neon-lit casino, providing the only illumination in the car park, but a sharp fence has been erected to block off access even to its car park. I wander up and down aimlessly, all of a sudden completely at a loss and obviously looking it. Suddenly bright torches shine in my face from across the car park, and I hear: 'Hey, you, come here.'

Terror mingles with the idea that armed muggers don't usually carry torches, not in England at least.

'You okay?' sounds a less than threatening question. Certainly less threatening than they look. There are two of them, bulky, white 30-somethings in uniforms of some sort, not obviously police. Private security according to their shoulder badges, though security for whom is not clear.

'I'm lost,' I admit hopelessly.

'Where you lookin' for?'

'The Home Depot? Do you know it? I mean the soccer stadium?'

'You need to buy something, for your house?'

'No!' I almost scream, even if this is maybe a reasonable thing to assume about someone asking how to get to the 'Home Depot'. Bizarrely, of course, we can all see the Home Depot itself, in big red letters on the side of a warehouse a few hundred yards away that seems to stretch for miles. Unfortunately it, like the casino, is on the other side of a high, sharp fence, and then again, even if it weren't, there is always the possibility out here that it actually does stretch for miles; and even if the stadium was next to it – which is by no means certain – the game would probably be over by the time I've walked its length. But these guys haven't a clue what I'm talking about. I'm not dangerous or in danger – a little loopy maybe but that's not their problem – so instead of giving me a lift, as I vaguely hope, they clamber back into their unmarked cruiser and cruise off, leaving me looking at their vanishing tail lights. And then a voice comes out of the dark, soft, quiet and uncertain: 'Hey, señor.'

I look over and there's a dark-skinned guy – so dark he might have been African but his features are Latino – leaning against a large stone pot containing some sort of semi-tropical tree; he's beckoning me over. What have I got to lose? He's about 70 – or maybe 35 and just had a hard life (which is how I'm feeling right now) – and making an instant value judgement from my appearance, switches to English: 'You want futból?' (the vital word is definitely said in Spanish). I nod, trying not to look too desperate. He smiles: 'You need bus, it comes here,' he points to one of the parking spaces with a sign next to it, 'maybe five minutes. Goes near stadium, you ask driver. Okay?'

Okay? I could almost embrace him. I head for the stop, about 20 yards away, leaving him to smile and mutter something to a woman seated next to him whom I hadn't even noticed, wrapped in a swathe of blankets like a Peruvian Indian. Who knows? Maybe they are. But after five minutes there's still no bus. It's nearly 8:00 p.m. now. At best, if I'm lucky, I'll catch the last few minutes. Then it rolls up, out of nowhere, and the driver stops and opens the doors. And turns off the lights.

'Uhh,' I hardly dare ask him, knowing from south London that displaying the teensiest sign of impatience to a bus driver will encourage him to start reading the paper and open a flask of tea, 'When does this bus leave?' He's black – I mention this because he's clearly looking at me, thinking 'he's white' – and after a pause of about nearly 30 seconds says, 'You want to get on this bus?' I nod, doubtfully: 'It goes to the footb… soccer stadium?' He thinks for a good minute, then nods: 'I guess.' By now a few more passengers have materialised, black or Mexican – Hispanic (funny how I'd never really thought of 'Hispanic' as a racial term before now, certainly not one I'd apply to the Spanish. I wonder if Americans ever do, and decide it's a catch-all euphemism that implies mixed Native American – Inca or Mayan – blood). None of them are white. I've been a racial minority often before – on buses in southeast London, but I've never been looked at as if I shouldn't be there. Until now.

We move off and I'm standing – which gets me more looks – hey, it's what we do in England – up front, near the driver. I suggest it would be kind if he could give me a nod when we reach the nearest stop to the ground, 'I mean, stadium.' And he just shakes his head and says, under his breath but meant for me to hear, 'You people. You should use your cars.' I've no answer to that. At least none that he would understand. And then eventually, after 15 minutes of trundling along mostly dark streets, the Home Depot's red neon comes back into sight, from the other direction, and there's a wash of white floodlights in the sky and the bus stops and the driver yells, not turning to look at me: 'Saaac-cer.' And I get the message. And get off. I can hardly believe it. I've got there at last. Alive and in one piece. There's still everything to play for, except that the game's nearly over.

It still takes me a good five minutes to walk to the stadium – just across the car park, which must hold at least 15,000 vehicles, though it is probably more full during Home Depot shopping hours than for games. I look at my watch and reckon there can't be more than 15 minutes at most left to play, but no one seems surprised to see a fan turn up near the end. There's a complication when the security check – we don't have those usually despite the English game's bad reputation in the old days – uncovers my Swiss Army knife: 'You can't take a weapon in, sir.' A what? Oh hell, never mind, I've had this happen at airports before. I reluctantly hand it over. 'Oh no, it's okay, sir,' he says nodding over my shoulder towards the acres of parking space, 'you can leave it in your car.' I tell him I don't have a car, and he looks hugely relieved to have taken the knife off me. I resign myself to its loss and go into the stadium.

And then there is – after all – the football. Down there on the floodlit pitch, the familiar sight of 22 lads in their team strip engaged in mortal combat. And suddenly it all seems surreal. The stadium is strange, as if the floodlights are directed as much at the people in the stands as on the pitch, which they are because there are people wandering up and down trying to sell stuff – baby blue and pink candy floss – or beers to people sitting in their seats (unheard of in English football grounds for decades). All this is incorrigibly alien, and yet somehow familiar: it reminds me of something I can't quite put my finger on. And then immediately, I can: the baseball game at Shea Stadium.

But this isn't baseball – or cricket – one of those drawn-out all-day rituals, that are more about being there than watching the game. This isn't an occa-sion to share a glass and a chit-chat with chums, grabbing something to eat and occasionally glancing down at the pitch to applaud a particularly good shot or up at the scoreboard to check some statistics. This is football, for God's sake – even soccer if you must – the 'beautiful game', a taut, nerve-straining 90-minute conflation of chess, ballet and gladiatorial combat of which the great Matt Busby once said, it isn't a matter of life or death: 'it's far more important than that'. Except that hardly anyone seems to notice it. True there's a Hispanic-looking bloke sitting near me, not next to – there are far too many empty seats for that – with his son, who both appear to be paying a fair bit of attention to the game, and even to understand the offside rule, as they alone don't boo incredulously when the ref halts the game after some Red Bull clodhopper lobs a pass to a forward who's so close to the Galaxy goalie he can probably share his deodorant. To make matters worse, Becks isn't even playing. I can just make him out kicking his heels on the subs' bench.

What sort of manager is this who doesn't bring his best player on – the one they pay a daily wage enough to run a fleet of Hummers for a year – when the score's 1–1 and there's only a few minutes left to play. Isn't there? And suddenly it dawns on me that the electronic timer which I thought had been counting the halves separately really does mean we're just coming up to the 44th minute. I ask my nearest neighbour and he confirms the incredible, delicious truth – that the time on my ticket wasn't kick-off but the time the stadium doors opened and we are indeed just approaching the end of the first half. I've got a full 45 minutes to go. The referee blows his whistle and I could almost sing for joy. Instead I celebrate by doing something totally unimaginable in England: I nip out to the concourse, negotiate the incredible number of fast-food and drink franchises touting for business – rather than just one overcrowded bar selling bad beer and Balti pies – and fetch myself a huge plastic beaker containing a pint, yes a full – well, full by American standards – pint of frozen margarita. And take it back to my seat.

Okay, so I've sold out already. But I haven't. Not really. Because by instinct I've already swigged it down before the second half starts – can't let anything spoil your focus on the game. To the extent that I'm still more tempted to stuff the candy floss down the vendor's throat than buy one when he waves his noxious wares in front of my face five minutes after Becks has at last come on and is preparing to take his first corner. 'Are you f***ing insane,' I scream at him instead, causing a burst of near panic as he scuttles off. Becks hasn't lost his touch. It's a perfect cross but nobody has a clue what to do with it, on either side. It neither gets knocked decisively into the net, nor deftly cleared upfield; instead they sort of play keepie-uppie with it for a few minutes, before somehow or other it bobbles out of their midst and we're back to the stages where they all look at each other wondering whose turn it is to kick it and to whom.

I'm sorry, but this is the state of American 'soccer': woeful! I can see why nobody watches it. It's no bloody good. Not that we don't get games like this in England too. I'm painfully reminded of watching Charlton, losing to Wycombe Wanderers, a team two divisions lower while the away supporters gleefully chanted in our faces: 'Premiership? You're having a laugh!'

But that is what is missing here. Not only is there no segregation of home and away fans – a move some fans of the English game regret – but there are no away fans at all that I can see. It's a long way from New York after all. There's no feeling of tribal loyalty and camaraderie, emotions that in the cauldron of a British football stadium provide twenty-first century British men – and women – with the closest equivalent, I hope, they'll ever get to the spirit of a Napoleonic army, that sentiment of which the Duke of Wellington said: 'I don't know what effect they have on the enemy but they scare the hell out of me'.

If even an iota of that atmosphere had evolved in this big, over-lit, under-populated stadium then it would have been dispelled in an instant by the message that appears on the big neon scoreboard: 'Keep the game clean,' – welllllllll, yes, maybe, we're used to slogans against racism and about respecting referees, so I can just about take that, except that it's spoken OUT LOUD, while the team are playing, in fact just as Becks is about to take another – well-placed but futile – corner. Talk about putting a man off his stride! And as if that's not bad enough, here comes the punchline: 'And keep your weekly wash clean with Tide!' It's a bloody advert, on screen and in our ears in the middle of a game. Does nobody understand? This isn't just 'not done', it's tantamount to heresy. Sacrilege even.

Maybe the American game's too nice – maybe Americans are too nice – maybe the concept of sports teams as mobile franchises rather than rooted in local communities (which is something I fear could yet happen to our increasingly foreign-owned Premiership stuffed with foreign players) means they just don't care. But until they do, and until their players play with passion because they know their fans live for it, and until they understand the exquisite agony of a 0–0 draw in which both teams had chances, or the untrammelled joy of a fightback from 3–0 down to win 4–3 in a goalfest, then 'soccer' hasn't a golf ball's hope in a bunker.

And then all of a sudden, from a far corner of the pitch, where a solid group of fans, all in LA Galaxy shirts are standing – against modern English rules but according to old football tradition – I make out the strains of a familiar chant that is pure music to my ears. Can it be true? Can those really be Americans? Yes, it is and they are. With almost a tear in my eye, I make my way round towards them – unthinkable in a tight-packed, seating-only European ground, but here there are people wandering all over the place – and watch with genuine warmth in my heart as the stewards gather with consternation and bemusement on their faces this deliriously joyful, increasingly drunk, beer-clutching crowd emulate scenes they can only have witnessed on European television, howling for blood in time-honoured fashion, bellowing at the top of their lungs, in chorus, the hallowed refrain beloved of every English football crowd: 'The referee's a wanker!'

Maybe there's hope yet.

Which leaves me with just the slight matter of getting 'home'. And preferably not by the route I came. There's a bus stop outside the stadium – by which I mean just over half a mile from it, i.e. beyond the car park – but the timetable is less than encouraging: one bus an hour, and the last one left just before the game ended. Am I missing something here? I mean, this isn't baseball; we know what time it'll be over at. And it may not match the Home Depot on sale day, but there's at least 15,000 people here. And nearly, as I look around me at the building jam at the car park exit, 15,000 cars!

I'm reluctant to hang around here for an hour but I don't see much alternative.

Nor do the three other people – just three out of a crowd of 15,000 – who within the next 10 minutes join me. And two of them are Scottish. Out of the fairly large crowd that has made its way to this football ground (soccer stadium) tonight, only one Angelino did so by public transport! His name is Ivan, he comes from Seattle, and he apparently makes a habit of it: 'My friends think it's kinda weird. But like, you know, it's a green thing too.'

It's the first time I've heard anyone in the US apparently take the green/global warming agenda seriously. I know lots of people do, or at least say they do, including both presidential candidates, but I've never come across anyone who actually lets it affect their way of life. Ivan, however, does. He's – fairly obviously – a Democrat, and also the first person I've met who actively wants to talk politics. He is campaigning enthusiastically for Barack Obama, though he thinks John Edwards would have been a better candidate; he has serious reservations about the willingness of middle America to elect their first black president.

'Aye, ah dinnae know about that either,' says Mark, the rangy tall Scotsman who's over here visiting his sister and just came to the football, 'because I hadne seen a game for a while.' Ivan asks us a genuinely interested question about British politics – this is a first too – as in whether we think 'the new guy' – well, come on, you would hardly expect even him to know Gordon Brown's name – is a good successor to Tony Blair, who remains something of an icon for Americans, even on the left.

'Blair was a right wanker,' says Mark, which seems to me as fair a way of putting it as possible. But we stay clear of discussing Brown. Maybe because we just can't be bothered.

Eventually – though unfortunately not before its timetabled hour – the bus arrives and we join the now thinned throng of northbound traffic. I tell Ivan how impressed I am by the sea of change in downtown Los Angeles. He beams back, 'Yeah, it's been a real revolution. People like me, young professionals, are moving back, converting lofts and stuff, it used to be dangerous but now it's a pretty cool scene. I got lucky too; I bought a condo near the Staples Centre.' Ivan credits the recent multi-million dollar sports venue and concert arena, financed by the eponymous office supplies company, as being a crucial element in restoring respectability to the downtown area.

Ivan wants to know what I'm going to call a book about train travel round America, so I toss out a few options: partly inspired by memories of Colorado: Iron Horse Rodeo, or in reference to my scant funds: Iron Horse Bareback. And he smiles and says, 'Well, that's certainly an arresting title,' and adds that this is his stop. As he leaves I pick up a leaflet lying on the seat opposite advertising LA's Midtowne Spa: a 'place for the gay and bisexual community to play safely: no drugs, no alcohol, condoms provided – no bareback.' Whoops. A bible for unprotected sex wasn't exactly what I had in mind...

LOS ANGELES TO NEW ORLEANS

TRAIN: Sunset Limited
FREQUENCY: 3 a week
DEPART LOS ANGELES, CALIFORNIA: 2:30 p.m. (Pacific Time)

via

Pomona, CA	Alpine, TX
Ontario, CA	Sanderson, TX
Palm Springs, CA	Del Rio, TX
Yuma, AZ	San Antonio, TX
Maricopa, AZ	Houston, TX
Tucson, AZ	Beaumont, TX
Benson, AZ	Lake Charles, LA
Lordsburg, NM	Lafayette, LA
Deming, NM	New Iberia, LA
El Paso, TX	Schriever, LA

ARRIVE NEW ORLEANS, LOUISIANA: 4:00 p.m. (Central Time)
DURATION: approx: 51 hours, 30 minutes
DISTANCE: 1,995 miles

19

N'Awlins

I HAD NO IDEA. Absolutely no idea. Nothing in America prepares you for New Orleans. I'm standing like an overdressed man in a Turkish bath on the rotting wood of the balcony tilted at a precarious angle towards the street below, running my fingers over the thick layers of paint on the wrought iron as I watch the gas lamps flicker in the onset of a tropical dusk. Exotic, romantic, and just slightly forlorn. I could be in Abidjan, Réunion or Martinique. But surely, surely, not in the United States.

Most striking of all is the quiet. No roar of traffic, no parping of horns, just the quiet drip of condensation forming on metal and falling onto wood, and maybe the occasional creak from an opening shutter. There are 'for sale' signs on railings down the street, past the little neighbourhood convenience store that sells fresh watermelon and wine and cold beer. You could sit here, and watch the sun set, maybe forever. And then I remember, this is New Orleans: there's no such thing as forever.

My mind had been convulsed between anticipation and apprehension as we rolled across the vast waterways of the Mississippi Delta, yawning mouth of one of the greatest river systems on earth, and looked out at the docks that stretched for miles upriver, at the heavy freighters moored at them, resting low in the swollen tides, and at the freeway systems improbably suspended above the lake water and the low-lying retail parks defended only by patched-up levees. In LA a cab driver downtown had asked me where I was heading next and when I said New Orleans, he just gave me a rueful smile and shook his head and said, 'Man, they got nuttin' down there. I know folks left there and they ain't never goin' back.'

As we pulled out of LA across the deserts of southern California, past the veritable Golgotha of wind farms on the hills outside dry-as-dust Palm Springs, the flooding that swamped the fabled 'crescent city' on the Gulf of

Mexico during Hurricane Katrina in August 2005, seemed almost unimaginable. I would like to tell you I gloried at the magnificent Texan landscape as the train rushed through it on the longest of my individual routes, but I would be lying: the fact is that Texas is not only vast, it is mostly extremely dull – not so much cowboy country, as cow country. And not very many cows per square acre either. Rancher Mike's old joke about the vast size of Texan farms, told as we rumbled through Montana, now came home as achingly true. Out here 25,000 acres is nothing. Literally nothing. Look out the window once every hour and you'll be lucky if the landscape has changed. I had thought of making a stop or two in Texas, but with a train service that only came by every other day at best, decided against it, and booked – for the first and only time on my journey – a sleeper instead. Ladies and gentlemen, I take my hat off and admit it: I mostly slept through Texas. And why not, with Louisiana and the Big Easy on the horizon?

Prior to Katrina, my only real awareness of New Orleans was Paul Simon praying for someone to take him to the Mardi Gras in the city of his dreams in a pronunciation which I have already learned is much-mocked: 'It ain't Noo Or-LEENS, honey, it's N'Awlins,' said the female conductor when I showed her my ticket. Over dinner as we trundled across the dry, dull endless scrub that makes up most of Texas I met Clarence who came from there but was going back. Not without regrets: 'I lost plenty. Folks, mostly. My grandmother. She died. She was in her nineties, she wouldn't leave. She didn't have no means to anyhow. Lots of poor black folks didn't. The government just didn't care.'

Other people did, though, like Harrison and Joanne, a stocky middle-aged couple dressed in what I at first take for a uniform: a dark maroon shirt and trousers on the man and a dress the same colour for his wife, who is also wearing an old-fashioned bonnet-style hat. And then I'm struck by the resemblance to the travelling Amish. I'm not far wrong. I get talking to them and Harrison explains that they're Mennonites, a religious grouping closely related to the Amish. The both live in Kentucky but have been travelling down to New Orleans for three weeks out of four for the last two years, to help with reconstruction work. They live in a hostel and work as carpenters. Both of them. Helping out after natural disasters, he told me with one of those surreal gentle smiles that religious people sometimes spook me with, is something the Mennonite community considers a social obligation.

Arriving in New Orleans even years after the 2005 cataclysm that was Hurricane Katrina it's not hard to see why people here still think that central government doesn't give a damn, and why volunteer workers are so needed and appreciated. The little wooden houses alongside Louis Armstrong International Airport are poignant testimony to the essential fragility of so much of the globally envied American way of life. These are homes that would have had refrigerators, colour TVs, heating and air-conditioning, but in the wake of a hurricane – three years on – look like the hovels on the edge of Harare, Zimbabwe, trashed and looted, where they have not been plain blown away.

Three-storey brick houses along the railway line still lie derelict, without doors or windows, skips piled high with rubbish lined up outside. On the left is the great bulk of the newly restored and refurbished Superdome, the sports arena that was turned into emergency housing for 30,000 residents unable to flee the hurricane. On the right, the damaged buildings of a furniture warehouse and a depot for a dairy company based in Houma, a small town further out into the Gulf swamps and even more vulnerable. The adverts painted on the brickwork are for 'creamery butter': 'American Beauty since 1892'. The windows are smashed, broken air-conditioning units lie on the ground next to an old school bus, its distinctive yellow smeared with graffiti, mattresses piled on its roof, ripped blue plastic tarpaulins strewn across the ground next to a tiny two-man tent. Obviously still in use. It is not an optimistic arrival.

The station has the feel of a railway in wartime: busy with people jostling one another, faces lined and drawn, tired. Out front I climb into a taxi – I have no enthusiasm for tramping these streets – and all of a sudden I know why this city is still called the Big Easy: it's behind the wheel, half the size of a butter mountain squeezed into a lime green tropical shirt and shorts, grinning broadly, sipping constantly from a quart-sized container of fizzy pop as he slides his ancient Dodge along the wide streets, before we crawl into the rectilinear warren of the Vieux Carré, the French Quarter, and with a hand wiped across his lips, a loud belch and a laid-back demand for 10 dollars – the meter in this cab was no more in the habit of running than its driver – deposits me on a corner outside St Peter House. Welcome to the edge of America.

You only have to look at Google Maps and see New Orleans from space to realise how insanely fragile this city's existence is. South Louisiana isn't really *terra firma* at all: it's a transition zone where the land bleeds into the sea in 10 thousand spidery veins. Most of the modern city is built on reclaimed muck – there is no bedrock for more than 50 feet down. This is the *bayou*: a unique word for a unique landscape where the vegetation – mangroves and cypresses growing out of the slimy algae-covered water – surreally extends the false impression that this is territory naturally inhabitable by life forms other than egrets and alligators. Even on the way north, inland, solid ground is the exception rather than the rule: the railway hugs the swampy coast of the great expanse of Lake Pontchartrain which when the weather turns, joins forces with the Mississippi to the south to roll over the levees or burst through them. It is uncannily, eerily wild and beautiful, the tarmac causeway across the lake a thin, straight concrete line in a world of weird contorted organic forms, pelicans with full beaks and trees with slime-covered branches that reach out like zombie arms. It is easy to see why there have been so many horror stories set in the bayou swamps.

The French built their little city in the early years of the eighteenth century on one of the very few bits of raised land – they sensibly referred to it as an island – in a rigid grid pattern with a wooden church and military parade ground – Place d'Armes – on the river frontage. A map made in 1770 by Captain Pittman of the British Army shows it with its fortifications: wedge-shaped wooden ramparts and 'a trifling ditch'. Incredibly, the rectangle within his map's walls is preserved almost perfectly today between Rampart Street and the Mississippi and Canal Street and Esplanade Avenue. This is the Vieux Carré – the old square – universally known as the French Quarter, even if many of its buildings date from the subsequent, brief, late eighteenth-century period of Spanish rule. And this is where I find myself standing on the balcony outside my room in St Peter House, a modest but beautiful little B&B in its heart, wondering what continent I'm on and in which century.

There are banana plants growing in the courtyard, and a smell of cigar smoke in the air, as I saunter – there's no other way to walk in New Orleans – up triple-named St Peter Street/Calle San Pedro/Rue St Pierre in the early evening savouring the tropical warmth in the air, admiring the intricate curlicues of the ironwork on the balconies. Hurricane? What hurricane? Up ahead is Bourbon Street, and I'm slightly apprehensive that the famed 24-hour party zone will either be Disney or down-and-out. To my surprise, it's neither, at least not exactly. It's loud, tacky, sleazy, relaxed and perversely exhilarating all at once, utterly self-conscious with its jazz bars and street-drinking culture, its strip joints and souvenir shops with a local turn on the tacky T-shirt motto: 'I drove my Chevy to the levee and the levee was gone.' Here a 'Hurricane' is a sticky sweet cocktail of light rum, dark rum, grenadine and passion fruit juices. A man with a sandwich board on the street is advertising Huge Ass Beers To Go. A man with a huge ass is drinking one next to him. There's a smell of garlic and gumbo in the air.

I pick a restaurant at random amid the clutter on and off Bourbon and sit down to a plate of Creole cholesterol with Karin Carpenter in my head singing about crawfish pie, jambalay, and filee gumbo. Until now I'd never known what 'filee gumbo' was – specifically the *filee* bit – it turns out to be a thickening agent made from plant leaves used as an alternative to okra. My plate of 'shrimp gumbo' – I have just about got used to the strange American habit of reversing our definition of prawns and shrimp size-wise – oozes rich tomatoey goo and I follow it up with a jambalaya of chicken and spicy sausage with tomatoes and celery and rice, and feel fit to burst. Time for a beer. Maybe even two.

Not a 'Huge Ass', though. Across the street is a bar with a jazz band playing Dixie and a beer called Abita on tap which I've never heard of. The guy next to me at the bar has, though. His name is Gary and he's in computers, lives in Houston but comes to New Orleans regularly on business. Not as regularly as he used to – 'before Katrina' – but enough to know that Abita is made by a microbrewery in Abita Springs 30 miles away. Their 'Amber' is the colour it says, rich and malty and full of flavour. And to round it off, Gary offers me a cigar, only he pronounces it 'see-gar', 'coz we're in Louisiana, man'. And we light up and lighten up and listen to the music. And have another beer.

And then we hit the cigar shop for a couple more. I've never really been a smoker – at least not of cigarettes – but a good cigar is an occasional pleasure, not least since I visited Havana a couple of years back. It is of course illegal for Americans to buy Cuban cigars – even if you're Arnold Schwarzenegger – but that doesn't mean you can't buy a cigar hand-rolled by Cubans, especially in New Orleans. At the Cigar Factory on Decatur Street they sit there in a line, speaking Spanish to one another, separating out the leaves – medium-leaf binders and long-leaf fillers – like I watched them do at the La Corona factory in Havana. The salesmen are locals, African-Americans with cigars firmly between their lips setting the right example to their customers, offering tips to choose between the robust Vieux Carré or the full-bodied Tres Hermanos. The tobacco can't come from Cuba either, so instead they use Nicaraguan, Honduran and Dominican. I'm sure a connoisseur could tell the difference, but I'm just a dilettante who's had a couple of beers and enjoys the taste, although perhaps not so much the Purito, which boasts a 'sweet dip', as if the end had been dipped in honey.

Puffing proudly Gary and I head for the Music Legends Park back on Bourbon, where a couple more Abita await us at the open-air bar along with bronze life-size statues of New Orleans jazz heroes. Did you know that 'Fats' Domino's real name was Antoine Dominique Domino? I didn't. He stands there in bronze effigy with a keyboard fixed to his fingers, alongside trumpeter Al (Alois) Hirt and clarinettist Pete Fountain, born Pierre Dewey

LaFontaine. I had somehow never quite realised the French input into the jazz gene pool.

There's a real-life jazz trumpeter too and a fine skat singer, and it's easy to sit back and soak in the music in the warm air, the heady mood dulled only slightly by a few drops of rain from a heavy night sky. As the rain made its presence more tangible we migrate to one of the premises of the anomalously named Bourbon Street Blues Company, where there's a rock band playing. It would be easy to say New Orleans ought to be about jazz and blues, but that would be like saying that Liverpool ought to be about nothing but the Beatles. Even nearly half a century later. What New Orleans – and certainly Bourbon Street – is about is hedonism: eat, drink and be merry for tomorrow... And let's face it, there are not many cities where that is a more appropriate motto. That's what they celebrate with those famous jazz funerals that have origins in Dahomey and Benin. That's what Mardi Gras is all about, 'Fat Toosday' as the locals say.

Places like the Bourbon Street Blues Company – and just about anyone else that has one – rent out balconies in 'the Quarter' to the rampant partygoers that congregate for the annual celebration of excess. There used to be a whole district of town given over to making the elaborate costumes and masks and the shops are still full of extravagant feathered affairs for a giveaway price, for one simple reason: today the vast majority are made in China. Only the elite 'carnival tribes' – that uniquely New Orleans fusion of Black African and Native American culture with a hint of paganism and a wash of Franco-Spanish high Catholicism – still make their own. The best do the rounds of their own neighbourhoods before joining the main parade, with their traditional exotic names, from Yellow Pocahontas, the Northside Skull and Bones Gang or the Krewe of Grotesque and Outlandish Habilments. The cheap Chinese masks are worn by people like me, and Gary here, and just about everybody else in the Bourbon Street Blues Company tonight: out-of-towners, just here for the beer. And the music.

My normal local back in England is a quiet rural pub with neither piped music nor jukebox, where I will stand happily for hours at the bar revelling in good conversation, traditional English ale and quietly savouring the smoking ban. So what the hell am I doing here with a fat cigar in my mouth, drinking lager from a bottle and going 'yeehah' to a mega-loud rock band fronted by a feisty female singer with a ciggy in one hand and a beer bottle in the other singing a cover version of 'The Summer of '69' in homage to an era that vanished long before she was born.

'Hey, man,' calls Gary, 'you really gotta try one of these,' and before I can say 'Yes', 'No' or 'What the hell you goin' on about', there's a black girl in boots jumped on to the table in front of me, her head tilted back so she can hold in her mouth a test tube full of bright red liquid. I'm staring in amazement at this act, wondering what comes next when I find out: she crouches down to my height, pulls my head over towards hers and as Gary yells, 'Open wide, feller', I do what he says and she leans over, cradling my head in her ample cleavage and empties its contents down my throat. 'Now you've got to give her three bucks,' says Gary, beaming with red-nosed intoxication, and hands her a 10-dollar bill saying, 'That's for him, one for me and one for you!'

She virtually straddles his chest to empty the second test tube – bright blue this time (as far as I could ever make out they're all just vodka-based with a dash of colour and maybe flavour) – into Gary, while seconds later he takes a blue one and, rather less expertly, returns the compliment to our waitress, who's now almost supine on the table. Gary has done this before. More than once. So, I soon perceive, have most of the blokes in here, and I'm relieved to say more than a few of them are my age. The 'test-tube shooters' come out whenever the senior bar staff judge the 'party mood' to be right. It's a strange form of sexual intercourse, a suggestive interchange of fluids – but not bodily ones – that as a soft-porn experience is probably one step down from lap dancing. Yes, it is a transaction in which sex undoubtedly plays a part, but then so is employing a barmaid with a low-cut top.

Two more shooters, another Abita and I'm not worrying about the political correctness of any of it. I've lost sight of Gary in the mounting crush indoors and wander out, away from Bourbon Street's commercial hedonism down the strangely quiet gaslit backstreets. The moon is scudding behind dark clouds and as the raindrops get heavier my mind is running scenes from *Interview with the Vampire* to Sting's 'Moon Over Bourbon Street'. Risqué, ridiculous, wildly over the top. Just like the real thing.

Next morning the rain is pelting down as I make a dash for the Café du Monde at the end of Decatur Street. It's 10:30 a.m. but it feels like dusk with rain thumping off the rooftops, guttering overflowing and spilling like waterfalls onto the streets and into fast-filling drains. Even without giant waves washing in from the lake or the mighty Mississippi spilling over the levees, it is easy to imagine New Orleans suddenly being washed away, especially here on the river's edge. The rain is bouncing off the striped canopy as I dash for cover and coffee.

The Café du Monde is a New Orleans institution, and has been since 1862, opening whenever possible 24 hours a day, seven days a week, except for Christmas Day. In the middle of Katrina it stayed open to midnight until damage to the kitchens forced the staff to close down – it took two months to repair the damage. With the rain forcing people to take cover, I have to wait a while to find a seat at a table, and even longer to get served. American waitresses may live on their tips but those at the Café du Monde either do more than well out of the tourists – or just as probably – do very badly indeed. Whichever it is, the service is about the slowest I've had in America. Then again, maybe that's just New Orleans sleepiness.

But the coffee, when it comes, is as good as its reputation: a rich, strong brew flavoured with chicory and traditionally served here 'au lait', 50–50 with hot milk. It comes, if you're doing the Café du Monde thing – which I am – with *beignets*, which in New Orleans at least they manage to pronounce properly. In France a beignet is a doughnut which can be sweet or savoury, ring-shaped or just a ball of deep-fried dough. The New Orleans variant – specifically at the Café du Monde, is a small square deliciously light doughnut dusted with icing sugar. Served three at a time. Don't ask me why. If you ask for a beignet, you get three. If you ask for another, you get another three. It's tempting.

The French Market area, which is where the Café du Monde is located, right on the riverfront where the original city docks would have been 200 years ago, at the moment is in a state of transition. The farmers' market is still being repaired after Katrina – and still was when Gustav hit – and although there is a daily flea market, the permanent shops are definitely on the twee side: if you want teddy bears, collectible dolls or handmade sweeties, this is your place. The shop names say it all: Pets Are People, A Tisket A Tasket, Artichoke Gallery, Aunt Sally's Praline Shop. You know a retail outlet in America is precious if it calls itself a 'shop' instead of a 'store'. The French Market ought to be New Orleans's Pike Place but it looks increasingly more like 'Old Sacramento'. Which is a shame.

But this is where I'm picking up the city tour. Most cities do bus tours to show off their prettiest attractions. In New Orleans – with the prettiest areas for once remarkably better seen on foot – they do a bus tour of the disaster areas. It's going to take a couple of hours though so I pick up a little something for lunch. That sentence doesn't work so well unless you've seen New Orleans' favourite 'little something', a sandwich called a *muffuletta*. This competes with the 'po-boy' for the claim to be New Orleans' classic takeaway. The po-boy – originally 'poor boy' – is a long sandwich made from a French-style baguette, and in New Orleans unlike anywhere else in America, or Britain for that matter despite our supposed love affair with the 'French stick', they have proper baguettes, with hard crusty exteriors and light airy centres. The 'po-boy' is literally stuffed with food which can be anything from cooked oysters to beef. But the *muffuletta* is something else again: simultaneously delicious and a challenge to the human digestive system.

It is made with a Sicilian-style circular flatbread, split down the middle and stuffed – and I mean stuffed – with a salad of marinated olives, celery, capers and peppers, topped with layers of Italian salame, then layers of ham, then layers of mortadella, then layers of cheese. Now you can – and people do – argue for ever about the exact nature of each of these ingredients: does it have to be provolone cheese or can you use emmental, is mozzarella an essential too (as well as the provolone), does it have to be Genoa salame or can you use Napoli, should the ham be air-dried or moist? But I can tell you now: the absolute defining thing about a *muffuletta* is its size. This is the most mouth-challenging monstrosity ever to have been loosely defined as a sandwich, although perhaps in those terms exactly as the inventor intended: an entire meal in a piece of bread. In fact, two whole meals. Possibly even a dinner party.

I'm still staring with wonder at the thing in my hand, contemplating just the physical difficulty of squashing it enough to fit a corner between my teeth, as I board the bus for an experience that is soon leaving a completely different taste in my mouth. We start off by driving through the Garden District which was originally virtually a rival city to the Vieux Carré: this is where the English speakers moved in when the United States took over the territory from Napoleon. The 'Louisiana Purchase' actually cleared the way for the whole US expansion westwards as far as the Rockies and what only warfare finally defined as the Mexican border, but at the time the only real prize anyone cared about was New Orleans itself, the city that guarded access to the vast Mississippi waterway system.

The white American gentry were not keen to mingle with the mixed race, multilingual Creole community so they built their own grand villas in a separate little grid system a short walk away. It is a district even today of sedate grandeur with magnificent gardens on display in contrast with the French Quarter where the intimate courtyards are hidden away from the street. There is a rich smell of tropical blooms in the air: azaleas, magnolias and other bright flowers I can't even begin to name. The trees have knobbly gnarled trunks like something from a fairy-tale jungle. The houses have stained-glass windows. And some of them are still missing bits of roof.

Which is a lot better than the Lower Ninth Ward. This was – and is, to the extent that it is populated at all – the poorest part of New Orleans. The houses here are not just missing bits of roof: some of them have no roofs at all. In fact some of them aren't doing too well for doors and windows either. In more than a few places they aren't even houses any more: just tracts of urban wasteland, as if in the wake of a nuclear holocaust. It is as if Katrina happened just yesterday, not a few years ago. The guide fills in the missing details: holes cut in roofs were made to get people who were stuck in their attics out when the floodwater rose above window level: in places here it reached 15 feet. Some had to smash holes in their own roofs from the inside to get out and sit on them to wait for the rescue helicopters.

Graffiti on one wall reads, 'Fix the Ninth Ward, not Iraq.' More than one of my fellow tourists – all Americans – snaps a photograph of it. It is the first overtly negative comment on the war I have seen. The Iraq War is unpopular primarily because of the cost in American soldiers' lives and the waste of billions of dollars. It is hard to imagine what the response would be if, as in Britain, the war was not so much seen as a response to terror at home but a direct cause of it

Still there is no doubt in New Orleans how George W. Bush's legacy will be perceived. From down here, in a quarter built well below sea level, you have to look up at the levees. They have been patched with concrete and reinforced by the US Army Corps of Engineers, but I still wouldn't be happy to move in to a property here. Nor would most of the residents. According to the guide, more than 12,000 were evacuated, most of them permanently. We pass the dowdy offices of a law firm with a sign in the window touting for class action business: 'Hold the corps to account'.

Even in the more affluent suburb of Gentilly it's a depressingly similar story. Many of these homes were little touched by the hurricane, but they look as if they're in a war zone. When the well-do-do fled in their cars, the looters moved in. But it wasn't the immediate few days of chaos that did the damage but the long and badly managed process of getting the city back to normal. Many of the affluent white population haven't come back and in the meantime their houses have been gutted by the poor left behind. Doors have been smashed in with axes, not to rescue people but to 'liberate' their belongings. It puts a grim reality behind the black humour on one of the T-shirts down Bourbon street: 'I stayed in New Orleans for Katrina and all I got was this lousy T-shirt, a Cadillac and a plasma TV. Worse still is the damage to the physical infra-structure: the rising price of metals on the global commodity market has made it worthwhile for thieves to rip out the copper wiring from the walls. Given that here too most of the property is wooden rather than European-style stone or brick, the result is houses that look as if they've been literally ripped apart.

Even the Central Business District is far from back to normal. The Super-dome may have had a major renovation but it still looks like it could be wel-coming refugees as much as rival teams. Along Baronne Street the five-star Le Pavillon, a member of the Leading Hotels of the World group, has a plaque on the wall next to the door proclaiming 'only spirits could have foreseen that this unprepossessing locality would become the centre of the great city of New Orleans'. The only word that still seems apt is 'unprepossessing locality'. This is definitely a part of town to get a cab around late at night.

The rain is still pouring down as I get off the bus back at the riverfront. The Mississippi looks swollen and vaguely threatening, a great lazy force of nature against which the elegant little houses of the Vieux Carré seem insubstantial, though they are the ones that have best weathered the storms. To get out of the rain, I head for the contrasting huge mall archly labelled Shoppes at Canal Place. It is full of smart stores, big brands, and no customers. Saks Fifth Avenue occupies three floors which is two more than the number of potential buyers inside. Shiny new cars sit parked on the polished marble of the hallways: a Range Rover and a little Mazda convertible. Buy both and be prepared for what the weather throws at you.

Further on, Riverwalk Shopping is all but empty save for a few bums, the food court virtually abandoned. One of the bums, a bloke of indeterminate age with frazzled hair and a lumberjack checked shirt hassles me for some change 'for something to eat'. I give him literally what change I have in my pocket, a less than princely 81 cents. He thanks me politely and to my astonishment actually uses it to buy food, of a sort: a 35-cent pastry and two bags of crisps. Not exactly a *muffuletta*.

On a wet day in Britain a mall like this would be heaving with compulsive consumers partaking in the national sport: shopping – but here the staff out-number the customers. I find myself wondering how the economics of it all work out and then I see an ad at a fast-food stall, the sort of ad I have seen all over town but the first with a price on it, bilingual of course: 'Help Wanted/Se Necessita Ayuda $7 per hour'. Do the sums (as the Americans don't quite say): that's about £4 an hour, barely two-thirds the British minimum wage.

I know that this is the home of capitalism, the sink or swim society, but I can't help thinking that Marx or Lenin would have said that if ever a country was ripe for revolution it was this one. All the images they used to show children in the Soviet Union about why America was evil are actually more real than even I had imagined: winos, bums, beggars, people sleeping on streets and tens of thousands of those lucky enough to be in work struggling to get by on wages that are little better than slavery. What they didn't show children in the Soviet Union of course was the big cars, the movie stars, the rows upon rows of homes with swimming pools, the malls stuffed with every luxury, the Wal-Marts with every necessity at rock bottom prices, the endless fast-food stores offering more than you could (or should) eat, for next to nothing. And those were enough for the Russians to get rid of Marxism-Leninism for good.

The difference between western Europe and America is that here the feeder chain is longer and if the sky's the limit for the successful then it also goes very low indeed. Pond life here has to struggle to subsist, particularly in the service industries. If you work well you'll get good tips, the logic says, and if you get good tips, it also says the company can afford to pay you less than a living wage and if it had to pay you more then it wouldn't employ you at all and the only tips you'd get would be cigarette ends on the pavement. It works, after a fashion. It's almost certainly why the quality of service is higher than in Europe, but there are times when it feels cruel.

I'm in this slightly melancholic, rather depressed mood as I enter the Crescent City Brewhouse, for a much-needed pint of good cheer. And almost immediately I'm cheered up by the man behind the counter: a huge black man shucking oysters and whistling quietly to himself. I order up a brew – a classic Pilsner in the Czech style but perhaps just a little too gassy – and ask him what he makes of New Orleans these days. He gives a smile that would be rueful if it weren't beaming, and says, 'N'Awlins has had it rough but we'll come through. Those of us that's still here and ain't goin' nowhere.'

Having seen the areas left uninhabited, I ask if the city's population has seriously fallen, and he gives me a look like I've walked in from Mars. 'You kiddin? Way back, way way back, in the sixties, N'Awlins had three quarters of a million people. Today it ain't much more than one third o'that. People's comin' back but they're still not much more than half what there was before Katrina. And this city's had a lot of trouble for a long time.'

I tell him I saw almost as much destruction in the more wealthy parts of town, and he confirms what the guide told us: 'It's mostly the richer folks who've gone and won't be back. Up in the areas like Gentilly and so near the lake, where the levee broke, you see houses up there half a million dollars and more, easy, but those folk all worked for companies who pulled them out, transferred them to new jobs in Denver or Houston or somewhere, and they ain't comin' back. They've got their kids into new schools and they won't do the upheaval again.

'Those houses are all owned by the insurance companies or the government or whoever but they're all boarded up, just sitting there for the looters, not that there's much left. All the obvious stuff went long ago, but they're still at it, rippin' out the air-con units, pulling the wiring out of the walls for the copper.'

Does he see a future for New Orleans? 'Oh, sure. Things get bad, then they get better. Life's like that. Drink up your beer, there's children sober in Africa.' And he goes back to whistling, and shucking oysters. 'There's always hustles goin' on in this town, y'know. You seen them guys on Bourbon go up to some fat boy and look down and say, "Man, I bet you 20 bucks I can tell you where you got them shoes", an' he say, "No way, he can know where I got my shoes", so he say, "Okay, shoot," and this wise guy says, "Man, you got 'em on yo' feet".' And he rolls with laughter. 'Y'know I've even seen someone give 'em the money. I guess that's just N'Awlins, for ya.'

I guess. But outside, the storm atmosphere is building, flags are flapping wildly rattling their poles, the clouds dark and brooding, as if at any moment they might unleash another tropical wave, or worse.

It's starting to feel like time to move on.

Like Paul Simon says, you can wear your summer clothes in New Orleans. Just check the weather first.

NEW ORLEANS TO MEMPHIS

TRAIN: City of New Orleans

FREQUENCY: 1 a day

DEPARTS NEW ORLEANS, LOUISIANA: 1:45 p.m. (Central Time)

via

Richmond, LA

McComb, Mississipi

Brookhaven, MS

Hazlehurst, MS

Jackson, MS

Yazoo City, MS

Greenwood, MS

ARRIVES MEMPHIS, TENNESSEE: 10:00 p.m. (Central Time)

DURATION: Approx 8 hours, 15 minutes

DISTANCE: 406 miles

20

Walking in Memphis

THE KING would have crooned it had he still been alive. The Boss did just as good a job. Bruce Springsteen, Cher, almost anybody who's anybody has done a cover of Marc Cohn's 'Walking in Memphis' tribute to one of modern music's most sacred sites.

It's running through my head now but I very much doubt if any of them felt the way I feel, arriving in Memphis at what seemed the relatively reasonable hour of 10 o'clock on a cool, rainy night and stepping out of Central Station – a deserted echoing monument to the better days of railways – into a darkened urban landscape. A street sign proclaimed Main Street but it sure as hell didn't look it.

There are not many cities more sung about, from Chuck Berry's 'Long distance information, get me Memphis, Tennessee,' to Bob Dylan's quixotic 'Stuck Inside of Mobile with the Memphis Blues Again,' and a thousand others before and after. The Mississippi city has three prime claims to fame: as the 'home of the blues', as the chosen home of Elvis Presley, and as a shrine to black Americans' civil rights movement: the place where Martin Luther King was assassinated. There are not many places more important in the history of the fission and fusion between white and black culture in modern America. Right now, however, Memphis looks as if both had cut a deal and deserted it.

The motel I had booked online was billed as the 'Downtown/Graceland Super 8', which I had a sinking feeling was going to turn out to be a misnomer. Especially as if this is Main Street, downtown is distinctly downbeat. There's a line of shops all closed and unlit, a dimly glowing yellow sign that said 'Taxis' but with none in sight, in fact not a vehicle of any kind in any direction, or a human being. If there's anybody walking in Memphis tonight, which I doubt, they aren't doing it on Main Street.

And then, surreally, like the Knight Bus in a Harry Potter film materialising on a London street, there's the ching of a bell and out of the dark, clanking and clattering along tarmac-embedded rails I hadn't even noticed, emerges a magnificent ancient tram, at least a century old, all polished wood and glowing brass, with its driver, a solemn-looking black man with a peaked cap and greying beard standing rigidly erect at a brass wheel set horizontally atop a metre-high column. The tram comes to a screeching halt and he turns to look at me as if I and not he was the unnatural apparition.

Needless to say, he hadn't a clue where the Super 8 Downtown/Graceland was to be found. I have a feeling I'm going to need one of Harry Potter's wizards for that. But he does have a suggestion: Beale Street, the real heart of downtown Memphis. There's sure to be a cab driver there. 'Hop on board,' he says. And so feeling like I've just entered an alternative universe I climb on board his pristine, brightly lit and spotlessly empty vintage tram for a free ride clanking along ancient rails through the empty streets of Memphis.

Beale Street isn't empty. It's awash with neon. The tram driver, as if he actually were one of the Hogwarts wizards, points with an impish smile, opens the doors and says, 'Mind how you go.' And then he's gone again, an illuminated figure in an incongruous antique conveyance disappearing passengerless into the night. I stare after him for a second, not quite sure what has just happened.

But there I am, my feet not 10 feet off of Beale as in Cohn's song but right on it. I stop to take it in. Beale Street is what most people mean when they say 'Memphis', when they don't mean Graceland, that is. Behind me in a park in the dark stands a cast-iron statue of Elvis; ahead of me, stretching gently downhill in a glare of patriotic red, white and blue neon, a strip of bars, restaurants and music venues, and to the right, a row of low-flung Fords, decorated in a black-and-white checker pattern that at first makes me think they might be police squad cars, until I thankfully realise they were that elusive American urban commodity: taxis.

Reassured that there will be a means of conveyance to get me to wherever the vagaries of online reservations had booked me a room to lay my head, I decide I may as well feed it first – albeit not quite as Grace Slick's dormouse said – with a few beers and a burst of the blues.

The most striking thing about the establishments down Beale is their similarity to one another. The restaurants all offer 'bar-be-cue ribs', the bars all offer music and beer. I settle on the Rum Boogie Café simply because having walked to the end of the busiest section of the strip it seems as good as any other and had an intriguing selection of guitars hung on the wall. These appear to be signed by, if not actually donated by, just about every guitar hero you can think

283

of starting with Memphis's own original rockabilly star Carl Perkins. It's easy enough to imagine ol' Carl hanging his axe here back in the late fifties. Maybe even Elvis too, but Billy Joel? Isn't he the Piano Man? And did Sid Vicious really give them an acoustic? If ever there was a kid with a slim grasp of the word 'acoustic' in any form, it has to be Sid. I ask the barman for an answer to that question at the same time as I ask for a pint of Blue Moon wheat beer. I get the latter but I'm not really sure about the former. 'Sure thing,' he says, with a smile and shrug. He either doesn't know or doesn't care. Maybe both.

My beer comes in a 'Big Ass' plastic glass but it's good and so is the band: an old-fashioned rock-blues quartet, two of whom, on guitars and drums, look like superannuated beatniks, complete with berets, beards and shades, while the upfront harmonica player has a Blues Brothers trilby hat. The vocalist is a fat guy twirling a double bass and hauling out heartfelt lyrics in a far-flung rangy voice to the obvious appreciation of the 'house musician', a black trumpeter with a sparkly boater and a mean line in pumped-up riffs.

And then just before they launch into their next number he comes to the mike and announces: 'Folks, we got a couple of real special guys here tonight.' I'm looking round me to see which incognito stars of the music world I've failed to recognise – not Jimmy Page and Robert Plant surely, or Paul and Ringo going to take a little turn on bass and drums – but he's pointing to a couple of blokes with cropped hair and T-shirts knocking back beers by the bottle at a table in the corner. I don't recognise either of them. 'Two of our brave boys,' the bloke with the trumpet continues, and all of a sudden I have an inkling of what is to come, 'just back from Iraq.' The crowd breaks into spontaneous applause. All except for me. Because I'm standing up, of course, and holding a plastic glass of beer. And wondering. Just wondering.

It wouldn't happen in Britain. Not never. Just not now, not for this war. Here are no such doubts. My country right or wrong? Or just respect for 'our boys' fighting foreign wars. Everywhere I have been, from the quiet worried looks of the mothers in Montana, to the garish rolling martial legends on the slot machines in Reno to the heroes' welcome here in the bars on Beale Street, the war that was supposed to be finished more than three years ago is as omnipresent as the Stars and Stripes. No questions asked. Certainly not of the serving troops.

As the band take to the stage again and resume their blues-based rock'n'roll an older man with a lean aquiline face and white hair swept back and flowing down below his shoulders for all the world like an ageing hippy, a surviving grandfather from the flower power summer of love, stands up and invites the young soldiers to his table, snaps his fingers at a waitress and orders a round of beers. I catch just a snatch of conversation, one syllable that explains all, "Nam', uttered with a grave face by the older man. The young ones shake his hand and call him, 'sir.' And he laughs and high-fives them, and they pick up their beers and clink them in mutual celebration. Of survival. So far.

It's moving in a macabre sort of way, and at the same time uncomfortably sobering. Time to go. Time for bed. Outside, I clamber into the back of the nearest available Ford and almost faint in a warm fug that would have done credit to a bear's hibernation den. The bear is still in it, wrapped in half a dozen overcoats and a woolly hat despite the equivalent of six hair dryers on maximum heat blasting from the dashboard; he turns a broad face rimmed with a knotted fringe of grizzled hair towards me, blinks as if surfacing from a long dormancy and says, 'Where you headin', man?' Miraculously, he does know where the Super 8 is: back past Central Station.

'Man, you could almost'a walked it, if there was anywhere to walk,' he growls amiably as we pull under the freeway overpass and past the inevitable swathe of deserted parking lots, 'but then you never know the hell where these places is.'

By now though I think I'm beginning to. I recognise it straight away when he deposits me outside a bleak five-storey block next to the freeway and what appears to be a derelict school. The room is at least clean and comfortable and five storeys up, with a soft-drink vending machine – out of order but humming menacingly – in the corridor. And a panoramic view of the freeway. And the derelict school. But standing on the balcony looking out at the bleak landscape in the rainy night, I feel a mild sense of elation. After all tomorrow morning, I'm going to Graceland.

Graceland, Memphis, Tennessee. I'm going to Graceland. Paul Simon sings me to sleep.

It's still raining the next morning, however. And I'm still in the Super 8, neither downtown nor anywhere near Graceland. And with not much idea of how to get there other than by taxi, until the Asian hotel manager suggests that for little more than the price of the cab and the entrance fee he can get me on the list for a local tour company whose fee includes a collection service.

Forty minutes later, after a circuitous tour of other Memphis hotels, we're bouncing off the tarmac onto a piece of concrete hard-standing by a small office building with a sign that reads 'Blues City Tours', then below, as if an afterthought, 'and Hand Car Wash', which makes me wonder how good the tour business is. But the driver is drawling: 'Right next door, folks, is the show-room of Madison Automobiles, where Elvis bought his first Cadillac back in 1956.' We're obediently getting our cameras out when he adds, 'Obviously they're not here no more. They moved out east.' And not recently either. The building he's referring to is an empty shell with peeling paint and a 'To Let' sign that might well have been there ever since Elvis left the building.

As we pile off one bus and wait to get on to another, I notice one young woman complaining vocally about 'being flipping messed about' in the unmis-takable tones of 'estuary English'. Wholly atypically I find myself doing that very American thing: asking where she was from. Before long we're discuss-ing – as you only do on distant neutral ground – whether supporting Charlton Athletic or West Ham requires the most blind devotion, not to mention in her case, the unspeakable awfulness of having a boyfriend who supports Man-chester United. 'He's from Trinidad,' she adds by way of mitigation. I nod; not many Manchester United supporters actually come from Manchester.

'Y'know, though,' she continues, staring into what looks like the middle distance, 'Trinidad, like, that's a Third World country an' all, but you never get nuffin' like that.' And I follow the direction of her gaze and notice that oppo-site the shuttered shell that had once been Madison Automobiles is a line of derelict buildings with graffiti scars and broken windows. 'It's a bit grim round 'ere,' she says. This is a girl from the East End of London. She knows what she's talking about. But she's got a point. From what I've seen of Memphis so far – which admittedly isn't much – beyond Beale Street's bars it's not exactly as vibrant as I'd been expecting.

Never mind, I tell myself. Graceland will be different.

It is, but only just. And it takes rather longer than I expect to get there, partly because we've gone via the airport where the driver gets out and starts unload-ing baggage. At this point I notice that the woman fussing about getting off the bus in a hurry has a ticket in her hand marked 'Blues City Tours – and Hand Car Wash – and Airport Shuttle'. Enterprising folks, clearly, but it's not pleasing another woman, middle-aged with hennaed hair who has been broadcasting at some volume that she's from Denver, Colorado, and this is her seventh visit to Graceland. She's complaining that this detour – which, to be frank, is what back in England we'd call 'taking the piss' – will mean she will only have three and a half hours to spend at the shrine. For wholly different reasons, I'm also a bit peeved by her revelation: three and a half hours seems way more than enough time to spend on the memorabilia of a dead rock star. Even the 'King's'.

The 'Graceland Visitor Center' is on the opposite side of the road to the mansion itself. In the snaking queue through the cinema-style entrance lobby I make up my mind to opt for the 'Platinum Tour' which is going to give me access not just to the mansion but also Elvis's two custom airplanes and Elvis's Automobile Museum and something mysteriously called Elvis After Dark. Only now I realise I could even have stayed at Heartbreak Hotel, a 'fashionable boutique hotel' according to the brochure but right now, on a damp autumn day, it looks as concrete and boxlike as the Super 8.

First there's the queue for the shuttle bus. It only goes across the road, but then the road is a 10-lane highway, and if you're not on the shuttle, you don't get past the gates. Before we even board, there's a photographer inviting us to queue up to get our 'souvenir' picture taken against them: the famous Graceland image with their wrought iron motifs in the shape of Elvis with guitar and music notes spinning off from it, all set against a blue sky with the word Graceland dancing in the clouds. Which is a hell of a lot different from the reality; the sky is grey and the gates are small, small enough to climb over easily were it not for the 24-hour security men patrolling the grounds, and the paintwork has dulled with age, while the brickwork of the walls on either side has been defaced by adulation: 10 thousand scrawled, chalked and scraped signatures. All intended as homage, but collectively like so much urban graffiti. We pass straight through, onto hallowed ground and the home of the King rises to meet us.

To call Graceland 'tacky' would be a cheap remark, in the same way as to call it 'cosy' would be missing the mark in an altogether different dimension. As rock stars' homes go, it really is *sui generis*, a one-off, very much a product of its time, place and the boy who bought it. For Elvis Presley was still very much a boy, just turned 22 and already a global icon but still a kid from Hicksville, USA when he bought the 'mansion' that would become his lifelong home and indeed pass into legend after his death. Graceland is as famous as Elvis, an icon in its own right, sung about almost as much as Memphis. (Even as I write this I come across yet another incidental proof of its iconic status: Microsoft Word spellcheck doesn't even query 'Graceland'. Try adding 'land' to almost any other girl's name!) Elvis Presley's home is the second most frequently visited residence in the United States, and rising up the charts; the first is the White House. Security concerns that have forced stricter controls on fewer visitors there mean that the King's palace is well on the way to becoming number one.

And yet the word 'palace' hardly fits. Indeed, I use inverted commas around the word 'mansion' deliberately. The house isn't exactly modest but as rock star retreats go, it is really rather small. Madonna wouldn't house her servants in it. There are stockbroker homes all over Surrey that are grander by far than the most famous house in rock and roll history. In fact, there are a couple of places just across the road behind the Visitor Center, that are bigger and better-looking, albeit with less land. Even so, the Elvis spread isn't exactly George Bush's Texas ranch: just 14 acres south of Memphis in an area that was a lot less developed in 1957 when he moved in. That's another thing I hadn't quite expected either: 'moved in' is exactly what he did. Unlike the palatial homes of many another rock star, Graceland wasn't built to order or even substantially altered to the great man's requirements. And then there's the killer: for all the magical resonance just the word 'Graceland' has acquired over half a century of legendary status – a state of grace, a tranquil haven, an island of domesticity amidst the storm-tossed ocean of rock'n'roll celebrity – the name wasn't even chosen by Elvis. In fact, he didn't bother to give his home a name at all. For all the King was concerned, it might have remained No. 3245 Acacia Avenue or whatever it was called before it became Elvis Presley Boulevard. The previous owner, a Mrs Ruth Moore, gave her house the name that was to become a global icon. She named it after her favourite aunt. Aunt Grace. Elvis never even knew her.

Walking up to the front door, it's hard not to notice that you are forced to look up at the house simply because it's built on a small hill. Even on Elvis's doorstep, the house is distinctly unprepossessing: an exaggeratedly large white stucco portico attached to what in Surrey would be considered an unremarkable, slightly pretentious, 'detached home'. The walls on either side of the portico are covered with stone cladding, the sort you see on those 1960s bungalows that squat like scabs on the outskirts of attractive English villages. When the house was built in 1931, it was all the rage. It occurred to me that the walls behind it might even be wooden. I was not allowed to check. It would be easy to call it vulgar, but it's really just embarrassing.

As, of course, is everything inside. Although it is perhaps fair to debate how much of that you can blame on Elvis and how much on the seventies as a decade. The King succumbed like the rest of us to leather sofas in unsuitable pastel shades, polystyrene ceiling tiles and shag pile carpet. It is the shag pile carpet in particular – taken to the rock star extreme of being laid not just across the floor but across the ceiling too – that gave Elvis's 'den' its nickname, 'the Jungle Room'. But there's no 'pretty little thing waiting for the King', just some dated furniture: exotic hardwood, South Pacific-style stuff that you might find in a Polynesian-themed restaurant. Americans today call this sort of style 'Tiki'. It looks like something the set builder for Peter Jackson's *King Kong* might produce if he ever went into interior design.

The Jungle Room is in the basement, however. The ground floor layout immediately through Elvis's front door, I was surprised to note, almost exactly mirrored that in the much more modest Crosby family home in Spokane: dining area one side, 'lounge' on the other, with stained-glass lights above the broad double doorways. The tour is mercifully 'self-guided' which means you get an audio guide to hold to your ear and press set buttons when you get to specific locations. Standing between the two front rooms, for instance, with the formal table set for six beneath the ballroom-sized chandelier on one side and the battery of white brocade sofas next to the glass, knick-knack-covered coffee table on the other, we have Elvis's daughter Lisa-Marie telling us how when they had guests in, her father would spend hours upstairs in front of the mirror before making a grand entrance in some outrageous costume bedecked with jewellery: 'You'd hear clanking.'

I know, of course, this is sort of a 'rhinestone cowboy' thing – it goes with the spangled capes and the jewel-encrusted jumpsuits and such – but then Lisa Marie adds that upstairs was 'special' and the Graceland commentary cuts in to say that that is why the upper storey is closed to the public, because it was Elvis's 'private' area. And I'm thinking, what could be up there that's more private than everything else on display down here: is there some secret that the world must never know about Elvis? Could it possibly be that 'the Pelvis' was gay? Not on the evidence of his overt enthusiasm for women, though his wife Priscilla would later claim he was not particularly sexually active during the five years of their marriage. Bisexual maybe? Don't even go there: there are enough conspiracy theories about Elvis to fill several books many times longer than this one. That's the thing about Elvis: the legend not only lives on, it has a life of its own.

All the same I'm still bemused by how unawesome Graceland is. The kitchen could be my mother's, circa 1982 (she was always a bit behind the times) and actually looks as if people used to cook in it, which given the Presley family's down home eating habits, maybe Elvis himself would rustle up one of his special treats, even if most meals were left to the chef, Mary Jenkins. When he was in hospital with colon problems, she brought him sandwiches made with sauerkraut and 'wiener' sausages (that must have flushed him out!).

Bizarrely it is the pool room alone that might aspire to taste, providing that is, if you like the style made famous by Liberty of London – all brightly coloured leaded lights hanging over the pool table and tightly ruffled swathes of drapery covering every inch of the walls and ceiling, as if it were an art nouveau attempt to recreate the fabulous tent of some oriental despot. By contrast the 'media room' may have been cutting edge when it was assembled but today looks like it could have been put together from a second-rate jumble sale: the three CRT televisions installed across one wall, a mere 30 years on, look about as modern as a butter churn. Elvis had three because he had heard that President Lyndon Johnson prided himself on watching all three of the then main US network news programmes at once. It is an interesting definition of the level of intellectual sophistication both men aspired to.

Outside the house the four-car garage has been turned into an exhibition of personal items, including a grotesque, greying white fur bed (what is there upstairs that could be more embarrassing than that?!), guitars, and the great man's reading desk. Elvis was, the audio commentary is keen to tell us, a voracious reader, whose taste was both wide-ranging and intellectual. As proof, laid open on his desk is a copy of the Warren Report into the assassination of President Kennedy. And German writer Hermann Hesse's heavyweight allegorical novel *Siddhartha*, open at Chapter 8: 'The Coming Aquarian Age and the Emancipation of Women'. Yeah right, I bet Elvis the Pelvis read it every day! There are scribbles in the margin that you can't get quite close enough to read properly; call me a cynic, but I can't help feeling that if I could they would say 'who you kiddin'?'

Outside is another memento of Elvis's leisure time activities that seems more in keeping with the man: his firing range with a human silhouette peppered with holes and a collection of hand guns and rifles. I'm not suggesting Elvis was some kind of homicidal maniac, at least not any more than any of his peer group pals. Owning a gun and indulging in regular target practice go with the territory in which this typically 'white trash' southern poor boy grew up. That was part of the potency of the Presley magic: only someone from his background could have fused black and white music so successfully. This is no place for a detailed analysis of the Elvis phenomenon – God knows there are enough of them out there – but even three decades after his death Elvis remains a huge force for popularising American culture on a global scale. Think of the impersonators: Chinese Elvis, Indian Elvis. Back then, in the late 1950s at the height of his fame, his conscription into the army and service in occupied Germany only serving to seal the most enduring image post-war Europe already had of the US GI: 'Overpaid, oversexed and over here.'

The Trophy Room next door is the predictable floor to ceiling collection of gold, silver and platinum discs, enough to put poor old Bing's impressive display to shame. There are also posters and mementos of the 31 – mostly lamentable – movies he appeared in and a poignant quotation: 'I wanted to do drama but ended up in light comedy.' The truth was, of course, that there was no way Hollywood was going to let him do anything but sing, though it is tempting to wonder how he would have compared given a real chance to compete with Marlon Brando in *On the Waterfront* or James Dean in *Rebel Without a Cause*. On the face of his actual movie performances the answer is badly, but then he was never really given a chance. All Hollywood wanted was endless repeats of the song-packed light-hearted formula that had made millions in *Blue Hawaii*. The last chance came in 1976, a year before his death, when Barbra Streisand wanted him to play the role eventually taken by Kris Kristofferson opposite her in *A Star is Born*. Elvis was interested but a deal fell through because his greedy agent Col. Tom Parker demanded he get top billing over Streisand. It was asking too much too late. A shame, really.

For all the tat, with Graceland's modesty comes the indisputable impression that compared to many trophy homes owned by global icons, this really was a family home, albeit a family home for a wild boy who made it good and indulged himself and his family. Amongst the more moving 'exhibits' are the swings in the garden, untouched since his daughter Lisa Marie used to play on them, as she testifies in your ear when you push the relevant button on the audio guide. There is also the tragedy of the fact she was just nine and her parents already divorced when her father died. But until the end she still came to stay with him frequently. Elvis kept ponies for her in the paddock behind the house. The little kidney-shaped pool – far removed from the grand swimming pools of movie stars, or even the exercise pools of the modern middle classes – has a shallow end suitable for a small child.

Presley was just 42 when he died, a victim of success and excess in equal measure, addicted to junk food and prescription medication. His tomb, forever festooned with flowers and wreaths from his bizarrely ever-growing legion of fans, is one of the chief draws at Graceland. I had imagined the so-called 'Meditation Garden' to be a little grave in a wooded glade in a quiet corner of the estate, a place perhaps with a headstone and maybe a solitary cherub, smothered of course in flowers, where fans would go and stand silently, their heads bowed, and then move on. It would be a bit crowded, of course – this is Elvis – but it would be a place of quiet reflection, a last resting place. Marc Cohn may suggest he hovers around his tomb. I don't think so.

For a start, Elvis wasn't buried at Graceland at all. Not first time around anyhow. He was buried next to his mother, who had died 17 years earlier during his spell serving in the army in Germany, in Memphis's Forest Hill cemetery. But within weeks of Elvis's death – and after an apparent attempt to disinter and steal the body – his father Vernon decided that in the interests of the above-mentioned security, mother and son should both be reinterred at Graceland. Next to the swimming pool!

Why Vernon chose a spot on a patio next to a circular fountain just a few feet away from the pool I do not know. I suppose he was getting on and didn't want to walk far – the grave is only a few yards from his 'office'. Vernon himself would later be buried there, as would Elvis's grandmother, while a small plaque commemorates the star's twin brother, Jesse Garon Presley, who died at birth, and is buried in their home town of Tupelo. What the world would have done with a duplicate Elvis Presley is hard to imagine, but we conspiracy theorists can't help believing his manipulative manager would have been at least sorely tempted to keep 'Elvis' alive a while longer.

On his tomb his middle name is spelled Aaron, though in real life it was Aron, but that was possibly a misspelling on his birth certificate. Elvis had spoken of wanting to 'correct' it to the biblical version, and they did so when he died. I have always vaguely assumed 'Elvis' was a made-up name – and that he was really called Trevor or Dennis or maybe something macho-embarrassing like a 'A boy named Sue' or John Wayne being called Marion – but no, it would appear, however improbably, that Elvis was a family name. He was called after his father – Vernon Elvis Presley. As a name 'Elvis' has virtually no pre-Presley etymology. I have no idea if it was a common boy's name in southern US – or any other – families in the 1950s, but the Presleys certainly changed its status forever.

To call your child Elvis today would be an act of extreme cruelty akin to mutilation at birth. Which is not to say that people don't do it. I suspect worryingly large numbers do, though I have never met an adult Elvis myself. But then there are adult men around today – in their forties – who bear a large number of the names of the England 1966 World Cup winning football team. And my mother worked in a nursery school where there was a child referred to as Graham Wilson, but whose full name was Billy Graham Ian Paisley Harold Wilson. He should almost certainly have been taken into care immediately after his Christening.

The other Presleys had odd names too. His grandmother was Minnie Mae Presley, his mother was Gladys Love Presley and he had an aunt called Delta, not to mention Uncle Vester (who sounds like he belongs in the Addams family).

Overlooking this curiously kitschy little family plot is a life-size statue that certainly appears to be Jesus Christ, even though there is but one word engraved on its stone pediment: Presley. Nice touch, Vernon. Those who proclaim 'Elvis is God' may do so tongue-in-cheek but the exponential growth of the legend and the multimillion global industry spawned since his sad and somewhat sorry death has been a miracle only matched by the success of those who believed the same thing of Jesus Christ and set out to spread the word.

The Elvis industry grows and grows. When Elvis died the estate was costing half a million dollars a year just to maintain and his daughter's inheritance had shrunk to just $5 million, half what a top English football player now earns in a year. But her mother Priscilla was inspired to hire professionals to capitalise on the legacy. She became chairman of Elvis Presley Enterprises and oversaw the transformation of the old family home into a major attraction. The trust is now worth well in excess of $100 million. In 2005 Lisa Marie sold 85 per cent of the business and, although she still owns the property and her father's possessions, she turned over management to entertainment company CKX, fittingly the ultimate parent of the *American Idol* television show. There are currently plans to redevelop the entire area on a 100-acre site either side of Elvis Presley Boulevard, to tear down the lacklustre Heartbreak Hotel and replace it with three new hotels. His ghost goes marching on.

By after little more than 90 minutes of Graceland, I'm afraid to tell true fans out there, I'd had just a little bit more than my fair share of Elvis. I've now been into Elvis's Automobile Museum, seen the pink Cadillac – and the purple one – admired the prototype 1971 Stutz Blackhawk and Priscilla's much-loved 1970 Mercedes roadster. I'd walked on and off the two planes with their time-warp 'luxury' accommodation and managed not to spend several thousand dollars on a replica diamante-studded jumpsuit. A glance into the Elvis After Dark experience reveals it to be essentially just more memorabilia, much of it perfectly ordinary seventies tat, including 'the actual Monopoly set' Elvis used to play with. By far its most interesting exhibit is a 25-inch television with a gunshot hole right in the middle of the screen.

According to some of the star's surviving friends – and the official Graceland line – the TV is there because 'Elvis just shot up things' from time to time. But this particular television has its own legend. The story is that it used to belong to the International Hotel in Las Vegas and was in the room used by Elvis when he was playing there in 1974 and on came the singer and actor Robert Goulet, famed for playing Lancelot in the Broadway musical *Camelot*.

When Elvis was conscripted into the army in the fifties he had been forced to leave behind local girl Anita Wood with whom he exchanged passionate love letters from Germany. Or did at least before he bumped into Priscilla, the daughter of an air force officer serving there. Goulet allegedly added his own postscript to one of them saying he was 'taking good care' of Anita while Elvis was away. Even 15 years later it seemed, just seeing Goulet's face on TV was enough to get the King reaching for his six-shooter.

But then by that stage Elvis was already killing himself on a daily basis. I was disappointed to find that on the day of my visit none of the Graceland eateries was offering, as I had been assured they did, the King's favourite – and possibly terminal – meal: the fried banana-peanut butter sandwich. Here, however, for the delight of those of you who want to live a bit of rock history – the bit where you die an early death of heart failure (ideally on stage) – is the recipe from *The Presley Family Cookbook*, written by his Uncle Vester. So here you go – the food of kings:

You need: two slices of white bread, two tablespoons of smooth peanut butter, one small ripe banana (mashed), 2 tablespoons of butter. Spread the peanut butter on one slice of bread and the mashed banana on the other, press the slices gently together. Then melt the butter in a pan, or if you prefer the genuine Elvis variation, melt some bacon fat instead! Place sandwich in the pan and fry on both sides until golden.

Consume with a glass of buttermilk.

Count the cholesterol.

That last bit was my own advice. Elvis would apparently consume a dozen of these at a single sitting. As the natives around here say: go figure!

Personally, I'd consumed enough Elvis for one day. I headed back into town, having found the Blues City Tours driver who was easily open to persuasion to drop me downtown, even though he was sceptical that I could really have had my fill after barely two hours at Graceland. I also declined his offer of a supplementary tour of Sun Studios, the legendary recording venue where the King first laid claim to his crown.

This might seem a bit dismissive, but when I tell you that all there is to see nowadays is a tiny two-storey building surrounded by vacant parking lots, unused except for tours that on their own attract so few punters they make it a condition of the 'free' shuttle bus from the city centre to Graceland that you stop and 'do' Sun Studios on the way back. I had had enough of the 'as brochured' Memphis and wanted to see a bit more of the real city. That seemed initially at least to mean back to Beale Street. I was gradually beginning to realise that almost everything else in Memphis could be summed up in those two words: Beale Street. I was about to find out that apart from Beale and Graceland, there really isn't anything much else at all.

Back in the 1850s Beale Street, as now, led down to the Mississippi, only then it ended in docks crowded with steamboats, the main means of transport on the country's major thoroughfare. Memphis was a cosmopolitan frontier town filled with Jewish, Italian, Greek and Chinese immigrants to mix with the Anglo-Americans and a burgeoning African-American community, most of whom were then still slaves but less than a generation away from freedom (though more than a century from true equality). The fact that Memphis was so important to the black civil rights struggle is particularly poignant given that the city's early growth was due almost entirely to its flourishing slave market. The slaves, of course, and later the supposedly free black families who lived on in the area, were there primarily to pick the cotton and, spurred by the arrival of the railroad in 1857, in the early years of the twentieth century some 40 per cent of the entire world production of cotton was traded here. By 1900 the city had its own opera house to cater for the 'gentry' arriving from the east coast to build up commerce, not to mention finishing schools for their daughters. Memphis was giving itself airs, but it was also bringing in a mixed bag of gamblers, bootleggers and street conjurers. In short, Beale Street had absolutely every ingredient necessary to become a cauldron out of which would come some of the most vibrant, poignant music the world had ever heard.

The man they still revere as the 'father of the blues' is someone I should probably be ashamed to admit I'd never heard of. If I'd thought of it at all, I had probably just assumed that that line in 'Walking in Memphis' that begins 'WC Handy' was a bizarre reference to Memphis's otherwise little-known reputation for public convenience provision. Thanks to a plaque outside a little wooden house down past the busy bit of Beale, I now know better: William Christopher Handy – always known as WC – was born in 1873 in a log cabin in Florence, Alabama, still preserved there. His grandfather had been a slave, his father a preacher. Handy became a handyman, DIY carpenter, painter and plasterer. In his spare time he took up playing the cornet and then a guitar which led to a row with his father who called it a 'sinful thing' – and he had never even dreamt of how Elvis would play it.

In 1909 Handy, by then married and making money playing and teaching music, moved his family to Memphis and wrote a song for the mayoral candidate which he named after him, 'Mr Crump'. He later changed the tune and renamed it 'Memphis Blues'. It set the standard for the 12-bar blues we still know today and which would eventually give birth to rock'n'roll. From then on he composed prolifically, producing 'Beale Street Blues' – which laid the foundations of the street's claim to fame – and 'St Louis Blues'. His music was picked up even by white jazz bands and 'St Louis Blues' became an RCA movie starring Bessie Smith. Handy lived to the ripe old age of 84, dying in 1958, but still too soon to see the black people of Memphis win the same rights as their white fellow citizens. Handy's little wooden house has been preserved and there is a statue of him in WC Handy Park as a counterpoint to the statue of Elvis on Elvis Presley Plaza at the other end of the Beale Street strip, two demigods of modern American – and therefore world – music.

The only trouble with all of this is that it makes Memphis seem a lot more interesting a place than the city itself in these early years of the twenty-first century actually is. At the corner of Beale and Main Street, beyond Elvis Presley Plaza and a good hundred yards from the end of the actual 'entertainment strip' there is a Hollywood-style gold star set into the pavement commemorating the Grand Opera House which stood there from 1890 until it burned down in 1923, and paying tribute to the nearby New Orpheum Theater which replaced it in 1928 and still stands there following an expensive renovation in the 1980s. The star in the street proudly proclaims, 'For over a century this corner has been the entertainment centre of the Mid-South "where Broadway meets Beale". It is a proud boast, and a terribly, woefully idle one. There is nothing there but a half-empty parking lot, an underused tram stop and the Orpheum itself which may once have hosted Cary Grant and Andy Williams but is today little more than a nostalgic shell.

Modern Memphis has suffered Buffalo's complaint. The city has been not so much eviscerated as had its heart ripped out and is struggling in vain to retain a memory of its soul. Admittedly my enthusiasm is not helped by a slanting icy rain but with the best will in the world I want to find a vibrant city centre and have so far found only the ghost of one. Opposite the Orpheum I board a tram, one of the fabulous antique conveyances that so miraculously rescued me from depression outside Central Station the night before.

The word 'tram' is, of course, wrong. They are locally referred to as 'the trolley' although their movements are controlled both by guide rails on the ground and the overhead power cables. These are the 'streetcars' that Tennessee Williams, in a New Orleans context, named 'Desire'. Metropolitan areas all over America are experimenting with their reintroduction, restoring and redeploying beautiful examples of an ancient, efficient and colourful mode of public transport. But not as such. In almost every case they are tourist attractions and nothing more. Memphis is a case in point. The trolley runs in a loop around a large chunk of the so-called city centre including a 'scenic' portion along the Mississippi riverfront. I never saw more than six people on one. And none of them are natives. We tourists are only there for the ride, which is just as well, because there is nothing much to see. Downtown Memphis is a mess: the stop by Elvis Presley Plaza is the trolley's highlight. From there it runs by faceless buildings, hotel convention centres, office blocks and the inevitable surfeit of parking lots, before turning in a wasteland of petrol stations and warehouses to roll along the Mississippi under a crowded confusion of highway flyovers with an unused and all but unusable stop next to the Memphis Pyramid.

Ah yes, the Pyramid. Well, a city called Memphis in honour of the capital of ancient Egypt would have to have one, wouldn't it? That was certainly what the city fathers thought when they invested in building the third-largest in the world, smaller only than the original Great Pyramid of Giza and the high kitsch Luxor Hotel in (where else?) Las Vegas. When it opened in 1991, ahead of the Vegas theme-park monstrosity, the 32-storey stainless-steel structure was hailed (by its sponsors) as one of the wonders of the modern world. It isn't, though, and in fact never was, even though its glistening silver shape does indeed incongruously dominate a cityscape that otherwise ignores it. What it was, was a 21,000-seater arena for the Memphis Grizzlies basketball team who shared it with the local university side. Apart from basketball the only event of any note it ever served was a concert in 2002 on the 25th anniversary of Elvis's death. In 2004 the Grizzlies deserted it for the newly built – and architecturally wholly nondescript, if potentially less embarrassing – FedExForum. The university team followed them. Since then the city's landmark architectural achievement has lain empty, a white elephant in the shape of a silver pyramid marooned on the muddy shores of the Mississippi.

I get out of the trolley and walk around it – not as easy as it might be given that it lies literally on the wrong side of the tracks. The wind blows old programmes and out of date brochures around crevices in the concrete understructure. The glass doors are dirtied and verging on the opaque, the lobby within slowly decaying, the whole thing a spectacular monument to municipal folly and the American fad for the 'next thing' leaving the last decade's obsession to slow decay. There is continual municipal speculation about finding a new use for it. But everyone I ask thinks they'll probably just knock it down.

Along the railroad track a bit further on is a placard to mark the site of long-gone Poplar Street station from which John Luther 'Casey' Jones drove the

Cannonball Express for the last time on a cold morning in April 1929. Further down the line outside Vaughan, Mississippi, a faulty set of points left the train on a collision course with freight cars. Rather than jumping off to save his life, Casey stayed in the cab slowing the train to minimise the impact. He was the only fatal casualty. He remains America's best-known hero of the railway era, but probably only because he died in a place where they valued any excuse to write a song and 'The Ballad of Casey Jones' ensured his immortality. Some railway historians reckon he had been going too fast anyhow.

Just up the road is a more poignant if equally bleak memorial to another, rather more significant, American hero. At first glance it seems, as so often in America – a country that we think of as embodying the future – like stepping into a time warp to the 1960s: a drab, nondescript motel that looks eerily like the Universal Studios tour set from *Psycho*. The faded turquoise pillars outside support the sign that in big letters on a one-time illuminated sign proclaims 'Lorraine Motel', the latter word with each letter picked out in red on big white circles. The building itself is long and low, two stories with turquoise panels between the rooms, and net curtains pulled behind thin balconies. On every room save one.

On 6 April 1968 (April is a particularly cruel month in Memphis) civil rights leader Martin Luther King, at the height of his fame and the peak of the campaign for equality for American blacks, had come to Memphis to support black sanitation department workers striking for equal treatment. At just after 6:00 p.m. King went out onto the balcony of room 306 and was shot in the head. President Lyndon Johnson declared a day of national mourning but it was not enough to stop rioting engulfing more than 60 cities including Memphis where the National Guard were called out to impose order.

Two months later an escaped white convict called James Earl Ray, who had broken out of jail in Missouri a year before the assassination, was arrested travelling out of London's Heathrow Airport under the name Ramon George Sneyd. He was extradited to the US, taken to Tennessee and charged with King's murder. He pleaded guilty but later insisted he did so only to escape the death penalty. He was sentenced to 99 years, escaped briefly in 1977, but was recaptured and spent the rest of his life trying to withdraw his guilty plea, alleging conspiracies and demanding a retrial, to the extent that even King's own son came round to supporting him. He died in 1998 aged 70, still in prison, still insisting on his innocence. No murder in American history other than that of President John F. Kennedy has been the subject of more suspicion and conspiracy theories, involving groups as disparate as white supremacists, rival Black Power groups and the US government itself. With Barack Obama leading the Democrat race for the presidency as I write, it seems all at once poignant, symbolic and ominous.

As a powerful centre of black culture it was logical that Memphis would play an important role in that civil rights struggle, of which Obama's rise is the most obvious, startling product. Next to the motel is the national Civil Rights Museum, a pointed memorial to decades of injustice, but which is not free from controversy, being considered by some blacks as more of a 'gesture institution' than a real apology. The unrest, of the 1960s and early seventies particularly, also played a role in bringing the city's musical heyday to an end, as the conflict exposed, bled and eventually upended the melting pot that had created it.

And without the music there really isn't much left of Memphis. The local visitors' magazine recently challenged a group of travel writers to come up with the things that made Memphis *truly unique* (their italics). Apart from Graceland, their list included the following:

1. Chucalissa Archaeology Museum, where Spanish conquistador Hernando do Soto first spotted the Mississippi and called it Espiritu Santo. (Well, actually, even the museum admits nobody knows where that was but it must have been somewhere around here. They have a few pottery shards.)
2. Mud Island. (Exactly what it says on the label: a muddy sandbar in the Mississippi, with a bit of a park on it.)
3. Sun Studios. (The only tourist attraction that has to bribe people through its doors.)
4. The Lorraine Motel. (A monument to a murder, and possibly a miscarriage of justice.)
5. The Pyramid. (An empty sports arena awaiting demolition.)
6. The Peabody Hotel Ducks.

Okay, I have to give them the last one: if only on the grounds of trying. The Peabody itself is an architecturally nondescript 1920s monolith of plush luxury hotel rooms. Sometime back in the 1930s the general manager returned from a hunting trip with some live tame decoy ducks which began frolicking in the lobby fountain to the amusement of guests. The incident turned into a tradition of duck-keeping on the hotel's top floor and a daily routine, worked up by a circus animal trainer, of taking them down in the lift and rolling out a red carpet to the fountain for them to have a splash. This being Memphis someone decided the lobby band needed a musical accompaniment and broke into the 'King Cotton March'.

Bear in mind that the 'King Cotton March' is remarkably similar to its composer John Philip Sousa's 'Liberty Bell March', which became globally famous as the theme tune to *Monty Python's Flying Circus*, and you can see why this bit of choreographed surreal circus has become such a hit. We Brits are supposed to love such meaningless traditionalised wackiness – look at the House of Lords – but I can't help seeing this as less of an eccentricity and more of a marketing gimmick. Especially now that other Peabody hotels in Orlando, Florida, and Little Rock, Arkansas, have adopted the 'tradition'. That's right, folks, you can tell it's a Peabody by the marching ducks, just like you can tell a McDonald's by the golden arches.

The Memphis Peabody does have one other claim to fame: the fact that it was the setting for a crucial scene in John Grisham's bestselling thriller *The Firm*. What they don't boast of quite so much is that when it came to making the movie, they kept the name but chose another location for the shoot: one with a better view of the river than you can get from any of the Peabody's rooms.

Where were we? Oh yes… there's one more item on the list:

The Gibson Guitar Factory.

I also have to give them something here: there are few guitar makes more famous than the Gibson, and in particular the iconic Gibson Les Paul. Les himself, however, comes from Wisconsin where he was born in 1915, and was the man who designed and built – back in 1941 – perhaps the world's first solid body electric guitar. In terms of men who changed the world, you'd have to put old Les – 92 in 2008 and still playing – right up there on the list. No less than Keith Richards of the Rolling Stones has paid him the following inimitable compliment: 'We must all own up that without Les Paul, generations of flash little punks like us would be in jail or cleaning toilets.'

Les of course never had much to do with the guitar that bears his name. He simply signed a contract in 1950 that allowed them to use it. Apart from a minor tweak he had no input whatsoever in design. Les just sat back and took the royalties, while Gibson went on to sell the guitars all over the world. I should also point out that Gibson is in fact based in Nashville, Tennessee, not Memphis, and that the factory here is a recent addition. But they do make guitars and if factory tours are your thing… But I'd had enough at Harley Davidson.

Right now I've got other things on my mind, food for example. Deprived of my peanut-butter-banana heart-attack special, I'm going to try another local treat that in the long term could probably be just as lethal but in the short term sounded a sight more tasty: 'Memphis famous barbecue ribs.' In Memphis uniquely 'ribs' are always pork, and the best were reputed to come from the Blues City Café, where else but on the corner of Beale Street. The tables are spartan, diner-style, the chefs behind the counter smiling round-faced black men who clearly enjoy their work, the waitress a sour-faced white girl who clearly hates hers. She takes my order with the thinnest-lipped smile I have ever seen on someone with even the remotest hope of getting a tip – perhaps it's my accent. We Brits – our reputation goes before us. But within just a few minutes she comes back with a cold beer and the finest, largest plate of melt-in-your mouth pork ribs smothered in just slightly smoky spicy sauce it has ever been my good fortune to survive.

If you are used to counting either calories or cholesterol, you need not so much a pocket calculator as a Cray supercomputer in Memphis. Other delights on offer include the fattest 'French fries' I have ever seen, 'southern fried catfish', deep fried burgers (!!), much of it washed down – if you can call it that – with thick milkshakes. Some of the food, like my ribs, is undoubtedly genuinely delicious, but all of it – and I am no gym-going vegan health fanatic – is potentially as lethal as Glasgow's very own deep-fried Mars bar. And I bet that as soon as they discover that on Beale Street, they'll be adding barbecue sauce and claiming they invented it.

By now the weather was turning colder again and the drizzle was as incessant as ever, making me wonder if I've somehow become a rain god, as Douglas Adams would have put it, dragging a wave of atmospheric depression and persistent precipitation in my wake. Now I know why Marc Cohn's lyric has him touching down in the Land of the Delta blues in the middle of the pouring rain. Maybe this weather is more common than I'd thought. Cohn may have been 'blue as a boy can be', but I don't even have a first-class ticket.

Time to pay Memphis's music scene a final visit. I wander out onto Beale, stopping briefly to cross the street to the bizarre anomaly that is A. Schwab's 'variety store': est. 1876, motto: *If you can't find it at A. Schwab's, you don't need it.* Well, it might have been true in 1876 and maybe for half a century or more afterwards, but nowadays it ought to read 'If you can find it at A. Schwab's you probably don't need it'. Bare boards, goods piled in cardboard boxes, Schwab's looks wholly unreconstructed: a place to pick up a pair of overalls, a mop, an odd button or some out of date underwear. By which I mean underwear that is past its sell-by date: long johns or fleecy knickers. Schwab's is so unreconstructed that you just know somebody has gone to an awful lot of trouble to unreconstruct it: almost certainly the same somebody who orders in the mojo candles and the Beale Street souvenirs that you can't help suspecting sell more than the knickers. Schwab's nearly closed in the 1970s when Memphis was at its lowest ebb and just beginning to rethink itself. It might have been better if it had closed; it would certainly have been more honest. The conservationists succeeded, however, in preserving it, right down to the 'nickel candy machines', which will still spit out a (very small) piece of gum in exchange for a five-cent coin. It's still owned by a Schwab – third generation which in US terms makes them almost a historic dynasty – but again I couldn't help feeling he was, like the shop, preserved for the tourist industry rather than for any more practical purpose.

Back outside I crossed the road to the first bar with a band playing a little place called The Blues Hall with a long wooden counter and a small quartet knocking out a few passable tunes on acoustic instruments at the end. It was only when a door opened in what I had thought was the wall and I was blown away by a replacement wall of sound that I realised where I really was: back in the Rum Boogie Café. The Blues Hall, it turned out, was effectively the same place as the Rum Boogie next door, linked by internal doors. What looked like a series of independent bars competing with one another in a vibrant music scene, I was beginning to realise, is really just a rock'n'roll theme park.

A conversation with the barman in The Blues Hall revealed that they have been joined at the hip for years. Or what seems like years. The Rum Boogie has in any case only been going since 1985, so in part answer to my earlier question, if its collection of signed guitars is in any way genuine, it can only be because the owners have collected them rather than been given them in homage to any legendary reputation. Carl Perkins, incredibly enough, may still have been going strong in 1985, but both Elvis and Sid Vicious had plucked their last string years earlier.

More than a slight disillusionment has crept into my mood here that even a couple more beers and a more than adequate standard of music – in both bars – can't quite compensate for. I feel surprisingly sorry for Memphis. It's a city that's outgrown itself, in the way a wild but winsome teenager might settle down to become a boring middle-aged suburbanite. It's worse than what happened to Elvis as he became a podgy ballad-crooning travesty of the weasel-hipped rock'n'roller: as if he'd survived and gone on to be a sad old man stripped of the glories of his past and then in his declining years some nostalgia wave had swept back to buy him a nice new rocking chair and say, 'Never mind, granddad, you're a national icon now.'

Memphis has been saved from total decay at the cost of its heart and soul. It has suffered the same wasting disease as so many other American cities and not even such shiny nostalgic prosthetics as 'the trolley' can substitute for the loss of vibrancy and purpose. On top of this, like a replica rhinestone cowboy's cape, its musical history has been dusted down and Disneyfied, Beale Street resurrected as Mickey Mouse's Main Street. The music is still here but it's being played rather than made. Memphis has become a tribute act to itself. If that isn't enough to give you the blues, I don't know what is.

MEMPHIS VIA NEW ORLEANS TO WASHINGTON DC

TRAIN 1: City of New Orleans
DEPART MEMPHIS: 6:50 a.m.
ARRIVE NEW ORLEANS: 3:32 p.m.
DISTANCE: 406 miles

TRAIN 2: The Crescent
DEPART NEW ORLEANS, LOUISIANA: 7:10 a.m. (Central Time)

via

Sidell, LA	Greenville, SC
Picayune, Mississippi	Gastonia, North Carolina
Hattiesburg, MS	Charlotte, NC
Laurel, MS	Salisbury, NC
Meridian, MS	High Point, NC
Tuscaloosa, Alabama	Greensboro, NC
Birmingham, AL	Danville, Virginia
Anniston, AL	Lynchburg, VA
Atlanta, Georgia	Charlottesville, VA
Gainesville, GA	Culpeper, VA
Toccoa, GA	Manassas, VA
Clemson, South Carolina	Alexandria, VA
Spartanburg, SC	

ARRIVE WASHINGTON DC: 10:10 a.m. (Eastern Time)
DURATION: approx 27 hours
DISTANCE: 1,152 miles

21

Ghosts in the Machine

IT WAS 2:20 in the morning when I woke to find a large Cuban prodding me gently in the backside and saying, 'Excuse me, ma'am.'

I get this a lot. I think it's to do with the hair, which was probably all he could see given that I was sprawled across two seats with my eye mask on and blanket pulled up over my face. He wanted to sit down. On top of me, apparently. Or at least in half the space I was occupying. The train had been full enough when we set off and I had a shrewd idea it was going to get worse, when I saw the conductor coming round and counting empty seats. But I knew there was one carriage at the rear of the train that was totally unused for no obvious reason and hoped that by feigning unconsciousness – or possibly death – I could persuade anyone from attempting to sit next to me, especially if they were large and female. I had by now developed a healthy paranoia – or you might just call it a survival instinct – about huge women with arses the size of Ecuador squeezing a small proportion of them into their allotted seat and the rest over me. It wasn't the way I wanted to go. I didn't want to be squashed by some outsize bloke either but on this train it was the ladies who were carrying all the weight.

The Cuban was actually quite petite as travellers on The Crescent go – he only needed a seat and a half – and he was clearly no more enamoured of having to sit next to me than I was to him. What had happened to the idea of underused American railways? By now I was coming round to seeing the advantages of flying. Getting from Memphis to Washington DC isn't easy by train: it means either going back up to Chicago or back down to New Orleans. I had opted for the latter. Part of my original plan had been to continue all along the Gulf Coast and maybe even down into Florida, but since Katrina that has been impossible: even three years later the tracks along the coast have not been repaired.

So instead it was back on the City of New Orleans, which wasn't such a chore – initially – as this was, after all, the train that inspired my whole odyssey, ever since my first hearing of Woody Guthrie's son Arlo's evocative rendering. The train itself was, regrettably, less romantic than I had envisioned, there only being two Amtrak models and I was more than used to both by now.

Arlo Guthrie of course didn't write the song that became his greatest hit. The music business mythology, which Guthrie has propagated, says he was having a drink in the Quiet Knight bar in Chicago in 1971 when one of the regular performers, a singer-songwriter called Steve Goodman, came up and asked if he could play a song for him. Guthrie, who got pestered like this all the time, said Goodman could buy him a beer and he would listen to him sing for as long as it took him to drink it. It was the best beer of his life. Goodman's nostalgia-tinged poignant elegy to the American railroad era moved Guthrie so much he asked to record it and the result was an instant hit that won him two Grammy awards, and secured his financial well-being for the rest of his short life. Goodman had been diagnosed with untreatable leukaemia in 1969 and died in 1984, aged just 36. In notes on a posthumous collection of his work his wife Nancy praised his ability to 'extract meaning from the mundane,' precisely the magic trick performed in 'City of New Orleans', with its references to freight yards and rusted automobiles. It has since become an anthem not just for the train but the city too, played by Guthrie among others at fund-raising events for the victims of Katrina, a piece of good magic Goodman could not have anticipated.

But it's the second side of the triangle on this journey that is starting to get to me. The Crescent service up through the old south, Alabama, Georgia and the Carolinas, is the most packed train I have been on outside the south London commuter network. And this trip is overnight and over a thousand miles long. And I'm stuck next to a large Cuban playing salsa music at 140 decibels on his iPod.

By now I'm getting annoyed by this big empty carriage at the end of the train, and storm down to see if there is still space. There is. All of it. Still empty. With an eye to a showdown I find the conductor who must have seen me coming because he's wearing protective glasses over his spectacles.

'Excuse me, sir,' I try, using my best newly learned American polite warm-up. 'Could you tell me if there's any reason why all these seats are still empty.'

He looks surprised. 'Yessir. It's because we've got about another 60 people getting on this train.'

'Oh,' I said, still wondering if he was trying a flanker, 'and when's that supposed to be.'

'Starting at Lynchburg,' he replied without a blink behind his doubly protected eyes. So that's that.

I return to my seat and a new round of eardrum-threatening iPod wars: the shuffle god blesses me with Joni Mitchell singing 'Woodstock'. I can only pray to God there won't be half a million more boarding this train.

Just as I'm nodding off the conductor comes to check our tickets, and the Cuban tells him – for no other reason I can imagine than to evoke my sympathy – that he only has one lung. It works too, even if I can't understand why the product of a lifetime puffing Partagas Coronas means I have to spend the night listening to a tinny second-hand rendition of 'Guantanamera'. I get up and go to sulk myself to sleep on a bench in the brightly lit, noisy café car, thankful at last of my eye mask and the artificial fibre mock-Indian blanket I'd picked up on Albuquerque platform.

As a result by the time we crawl into Washington DC's – yes, you guessed it – Union Station, I'm all but wrecked. More than 10,000 miles on trains around this vast inland empire is an experience both exhilarating and exhausting. By the time I've caught the metro to the university district south of Georgetown where I've booked a room, all I want to do is make immediate use of its bed.

But it's incredible what 15 minutes' catnap in a room that isn't crammed with other people and shaking from side to side can do, and before I had dared hope I'm ready to take on the world, or at least the White House.

Not that you can. Not these days, at least. It used to be possible with little more effort than an hour or so of queuing and the self-control to stand behind the braid rope rather than run over and bare your buttocks on the big desk in the Oval Office. But the 'war on terror' has put a halt to all that – no bare-cheeked terrorists here – just as the IRA long ago put a halt to small boys being photographed on the doorstep of Number 10, Downing Street. Necessary security, you understand, nothing at all to do with the self-important hubris of one George W. Bush.

Instead, like the natives, I am reduced to staring through the gates of 1600 Pennsylvania Avenue, as are the hordes of visiting American school kids. This is a pity because I have done what they no longer can – when I was their age I was in there (though my parents wisely kept me in line and my trousers on) – and instead they are reduced to sitting on the steps of the monument to General Sherman (the man the tanks are named after), while their earnest teacher gives them a lecture on the history of the White House, focusing – to my amusement very largely on 'when the British burnt it down'. This was a long time ago – 1814, to be exact – in a war the Americans confusingly call the War of 1812, even though it lasted from 1809 to 1814; it is a big factor in their history, although British readers will almost certainly scarcely be aware of it, as it was little more than a few minor colonial skirmishes in the much greater conflict of the Napoleonic Wars.

One of the prime reasons for it was that the British attempt to enforce their continental blockade against Napoleon meant they declared American ships which violated it subject to attack. They started the war, with an attack on Canada, and insofar as there was a winner at all basically lost it, giving up the maritime issue, though with the defeat of Napoleon this was soon no longer an issue. And the US benefited indirectly from the British blockade which was an issue in persuading Napoleon to sell the loose package of land referred to as Louisiana, which, as we have seen, along with the railroad gave birth to the continental United States. It was also the war in which the 'Star-Spangled Banner' was penned, so in modern times those 'bombs bursting in air' would have to be labelled 'friendly fire'. Nothing new there. But the remarkable thing about hearing this teacher tell his kids about it, is to what extent the British are still portrayed as the baddies.

We know Hollywood does this all the time – witness Mel Gibson films *passim*, and the absurd *U-571* which had the American, rather than British, navy capture the U-boat with the Enigma machine code book on board – but it is a funny old fact of life over here; villains have English accents. The Americans call them 'British accents' of course, even though they would never classify a Northern Irish, Scottish or Welsh accent as such, because 'Britain' deep down in the psyche still somehow represents the 'evil empire' they escaped from in 1776, even though – at least partly in gratitude for much-needed help in 1941 – we have been their obedient martial servants for the last half century. It seems a little unfair.

But then I can forgive quite a lot for a seat at the bar in Old Ebbitt's Grill. This Washington institution just across the road from the White House comes highly recommended by a friend who used to be Washington correspondent for *The Sunday Times*. Although George W. wasn't in the habit of popping over for lunch – and nor will his successor be, if the Secret Service have their way – I bet he often wished he could have done. Several of their nineteenth-century predecessors did, although the last sitting president known to have dropped by was Theodore Roosevelt, and that was before the First World War. The place boasts the stuffed head of a walrus he's supposed to have shot. But the lesser politicians still come to gossip over secluded tables in its clubby, mock-Victorian atmosphere.

If I really wanted a take on the election campaign this would have been the place to hang out in the hope of either running into or eavesdropping on a member of the Obama or McCain campaign team. But I'm not here to listen out for hot tips in politics; I'm here to eat crab cakes. Ebbitt's is a hot favourite for Sunday brunch which means there's a queue for tables. But there's just one of me and there's a space at the bar, where before long I'm tucking into the most mouth-wateringly melting Maryland crab cakes, one of America's genuine culinary gifts to the world. You can almost forgive them McDo and KFC – just for the chance to taste one of these succulent little patties of white lumpmeat from crabs fished from Chesapeake Bay. Washed down with a spicy Bloody Mary and it's a match for any cuisine the 'cheese-eating surrender monkeys' can throw at them.

I find myself seated next to an affable bloke in late middle age and a striking, athletic-looking young woman. She looks athletic for a reason: she is an athlete, here to participate in the annual Marine Corps Marathon tomorrow morning. Despite the name, which suggests it is run solely by crop-headed young men carrying backpacks and rifles, this is an amateur marathon run in their honour, which originally began and ended at the national Marine Corps Memorial, the famous bronze of the flag-raising on Iwo Jima island. Jena has high hopes of beating a personal record and her father wants to watch her do it. That's why they're in here: stocking up on the carbs first.

I have faster-moving objects on my mind for the minute. The Smithsonian Institution on the National Mall, that great green parkway that stretches from the odd obelisk that is Washington Monument to the great white dome of the Capitol, imitated by so many of those state 'capitols' across the continent, is one of the world's truly great museums. But unlike most, what makes it superlative is not the collection of really old stuff but the really rather recent stuff. Of all the 19 museums which make up the Smithsonian in total, there is absolutely nothing quite like the National Air and Space Museum on the Mall: for a start there aren't many other places on earth where you actually can touch the moon. Or at least a part of it.

I have a vivid memory of being allowed to stay up late – through the night – as a child to watch the 'historic' scenes of Neil Armstrong stepping out of Apollo 11's lunar landing model, and curiously even more of television's tame

Oxford historian, AJP Taylor, controversially dismissing it as 'the non-event of my life'. All these years later, it's hard to say Taylor was totally wrong, but I still feel a frisson at being able to go up to and almost touch (it is covered in a Perspex shell) the command module they came back to earth in, its exterior still bearing the char marks of re-entry. The iPod god can play REM's 'Do You Believe They Put a Man on the Moon' if he wants, I'm not even giving him a chance. The only thing I still find astonishing is how small the craft were.

And that goes for the other icons of the development of flight hanging over my head: Charles Lindbergh's Spirit of St Louis, the first aircraft to cross the Atlantic, the Bell X-1, in which Chuck Yeager back in 1947 became the first man to break the speed of sound, and the SpaceShipOne, the first privately-funded spacecraft, paid for by Microsoft co-founder Paul Allen, which in 2004 won the X-prize for carrying three people to space (defined as 100 kilometres above the earth). These – and I have to pinch myself as I look up at them – are not models; these are the real things! And most remarkable of all is that all three of these aircraft, each of which defines a milestone in human flight, are not just much, much tinier than I had imagined, but are incredibly similar in size, human in scale.

Two other objects against the far wall are far more sinister and yet, united here, strangely reassuring: a Pershing (yep, him again) missile and a Soviet SS-20, the two weapons of mass destruction that became totems for either side, poised against each other from the Urals to Greenham Common. In my days reporting that parlous stage of the superpower conflict, when Yuri Andropov and Ronald Reagan turned their backs on one another and the doom-mongers had the clock ticking down to nuclear Armageddon poised at five minutes to midnight, I lived with these two tall strangers day and night, without ever having seen either. And now here they are, the SS-20 a gift from the Kremlin, a powerful token of reconciliation that the men in power in Washington and Moscow today would do well to remember.

Yet there is one more set of rooms that contain objects with even more evocative power, even if they are gathered together here only as part of a temporary exhibition. Entitled Treasures of American History, this is an inspired one-off bringing-together of items that show how in a very real way this mighty country is not just a military but a cultural icon for the world. What treasures of any other nation would resonate so widely across the globe as the original Barbie dolls, Kermit the Frog and Dorothy's red slippers from The Wizard of Oz. It says a lot for the curator and for America's sense of itself that they can put these together with Thomas Jefferson's Bible, Abraham Lincoln's top hat and a buckskin coat belonging to General Custer, the dress worn by Jackie Kennedy at JFK's inaugural ball and, of course, the compass used by Lewis and Clark on their mission of continental exploration.*

There was, however, an oversight. It is addressed on the building almost next door: a strange, almost organic structure in curving natural limestone. The National Museum of the American Indian was an afterthought, not even imagined until a quarter century after the Museum of National History was established. The idea didn't come until 1989, the building until 2004, and for all its interesting architectural quality – designed by Canadian architect Douglas Cardinal (of mixed Métis and Blackfoot Native American origins) to echo natural stone eroded over centuries by wind and water – is how little is actually on display.

The museum collection contains over 800,000 objects and 125,000 photographs. But there is precious little to be seen, beyond some simplified storytelling and superficial references to religion, culture and art, more than one would have expected from the Mayan and other Central American 'Indian' civilisations. Obviously the mostly nomadic, hunter-gatherer tribes of the Great Plains have left less in terms of objects, but wandering around a display that on an intellectual level is less satisfying than the average waxworks, I feel only disappointment at the scale of opportunity missed. I have a friend in England who has learnt Navajo and spent weeks at a time on a reservation: he has told me more in a drunken conversation in the pub than I have learned wandering around a supposedly 'national' museum dedicated to this continent's oldest inhabitants. Is there somewhere here, for example, an attempt to discuss or place historically the ancient ruins I passed coming over the Rockies? Not as far as I can see. I leave with the feeling that this impressive building is nothing more than a fig leaf, for a display that might as well be called 'Injun Lite'.

But then the 'Indian wars' – the euphemism for what is now widely recognised with embarrassment as near genocide – belong to a far more distant past than the wars of the twentieth and twenty-first centuries. More than probably any other capital city on earth, Washington is a place of tokens and totems. It has never been the 'imperial city' that New York remains, not a capital in the same way as London or Moscow or Paris, or even Tokyo or Beijing. This is a political hothouse, a city of present-day intrigues and monuments to the past.

---

*These and other American icons are now once more on display at the nearby Museum of American History which has been reopened after major renovation.

None of them more important or compelling than the war memorials. In particular the 75-metre long, sunken wall of black granite etched with the names of 58,256 US personnel listed as missing or killed in the war that spluttered into life from 1959 onwards and came to its end with that humiliating airlift from the roof of the US embassy in Saigon on 30 April 1975. This powerful sombre monument – perhaps the first great war memorial to depict conflict as sacrifice and tragedy rather than heroism – both symbolises the scar it left on America's heart, and did much to heal it.

It also finally forced the authorities to recognise the dead of another battleground in South East Asia, one that was on the verge of being forgotten, the Korean War. Arguably a conflict still unfinished – there has never been a formal peace treaty and North Korea is with Iran the biggest bugbear in the eyes of the Pentagon and White House hawks – the relatively brief three-year war that was halted by armistice on 27 July 1953, cost – according to recent dramatically upgraded figures – more than 54,000 US lives. It was only after the construction of the Vietnam memorial that pressure from veterans of the Korean conflict finally forced the government to honour their fallen too, even then it did not see the light of day until 1999, 17 years after the Vietnam memorial.

It offers a stark contrast in design, yet is – almost incredibly – equally powerful: not a wall of names but a statuary group that in theory is more conventional but in reality is not. For these are not proud soldiers at the moment of victory, but grey ghosts stalking out of the shrubbery: men in full fatigues, 19 of them, though it is not easy at first to count them: fanned out across a triangle of low shrubs, advancing slowly, surreptitiously, warily. And on the granite wall behind them: sandblasted photographic images of others. This is no triumphant pageant either, but an army of the dead. As dusk falls and the subtle fibre optic lighting kicks in suffusing the scene with an eerie glow against the sunset, I can feel a chill wind down my spine.

I go back across to the dark scar of the Vietnam memorial. I have a question I want to ask of the serenely smiling young officer of the National Parks Service whose duty it is to stand guard and offer information to visitors: 'When will they build the next one?' 'Sir?' 'The next memorial? To Iraq?' He stands there impassively, the smile fixed but frozen on his face. It is not his fault, not his job, not his responsibility. And he is right, I am being unfair, but it is a question that had to be asked, for those guys in the bar in Beale Street, the one from 'Nam as well as the ones on leave from Baghdad, for the boys from Malta, Montana, and their brave mothers. I didn't expect an answer.

But that's what I get for wandering around war memorials at dusk, the night before Hallowe'en. On the way into town that evening, to try a few beers from the Capitol City Brewing Company's brewpub on New York Avenue – the first establishment brewing on the premises in the capital since the end of Prohibition in 1933, I am haunted by more ghosts. Real ones, this time, or should that be the reverse: the youth of Washington University kitted out in Hallowe'en party gear. Almost all of them under 21 and therefore by US law too young to drink, almost all of them carrying crates of beer or bottles of wine on their way to private parties. It lends a surreal air to the scene on the streets as I look out of the window over a pint of Pale Rider, emblazoned in honour of the season with a grinning Death's Head and the slogan 'Hell on Wheels'. Superheroes There are vampires, ghouls, mad axe men covered in blood, white-skinned Morticias from the Addams family, the occasional Batman and a lone Darth Vader (perhaps strayed from the pavement outside Sid Gruman's Chinese Theater). Superheroes, movie stars and intimations of mortality.

The next morning as I head for the station and the last leg of my continental tour, little more than a commuter run up to New York and JFK airport, they are all out there again. In their thousands, the fit, energetic youth of America, competing in the Marine Corps Marathon. It is nicknamed the People's Marathon, run in honour of fallen heroes of the most prestigious branch of America's awesome armed forces. In 2006 they ran a 'satellite event' in Iraq to allow serving soldiers there to take part. As I watch them pound past the marble monuments of Washington, this deliberately self-styled 'Athens of the New World' – these fit, muscular, self-confident young men and women, Jena from Colorado somewhere among them – I find myself filled with a curious mix of admiration and trepidation. And offer a silent wish: I hope to hell you know where you're going, because in the modern world, whether we like it or not, we're going with you.

22

All Hallows' Eve

HALLOWE'EN IN NEW YORK and the last pumpkins are spread on the cobbles of Union Square for the bustling farmers' market. I know how they feel: it is the end of my journey and I might yet turn into one. I have come full circle, with a few zigzags thrown in en route. The city that was steaming and sub-tropical little over a month ago is now basking in a bright but chilly early winter sunshine.

Reluctant to repeat my experience of the 'Y' I have managed to grab a room at a less-known but almost equally iconic Manhattan mini-institution, Hotel 17 in the Gramercy Park district just a stroll from Greenwich Village. It is a cosy, no-frills sort of place, resurrected from near dereliction and restored as an old-style New York home-from-home. There are no en-suite bathrooms in most rooms – compared with even the cheapest motel out in the sticks – but you risk bumping into a better class of clientele waiting for the shower. Madonna once stayed here and one of the pictures in her infamous *Sex* book was allegedly shot on the premises (I'm pretty sure I know which one). Woody Allen used it as a location for his 1993 film *Manhattan Murder Mystery* with Diane Keaton.

But then the whole of New York looks like a scene from a murder mystery tonight. The ghouls on the Washington metro were as nothing to the vast hordes of hobgoblins, Tellytubbies, Jedai Knights and mini-skirted NYPD policewomen with shackled male convicts in tow. The Hallowe'en Parade is the counterpart Celtic import to the St Patrick's Day Parade, at the opposite end of the year: tonight literally tens of thousands of New Yorkers have donned costumes from the truly frightening via the hilariously grotesque to the wholly whimsical to gather south of Spring Street in 'the village' and parade up Sixth Avenue to 23rd Street. But even these hordes are just the tip of the iceberg. There are children in fancy dress too – little devils and witches – but this is not primarily a night for them. Hallowe'en is an adult event, an innocent orgy of mild excess disguised as a Saturnalia of sin. This is America indulging itself, reimagining itself, letting its hair down and having fun. The Hallowe'en I remember from my Irish childhood – all bobbing for apples, making 'turnip lanterns' out of swedes (whoever had heard of pumpkins in 1960s Britain?) and damp squib firework displays in suburban back gardens – was nothing like this 'Volksfest' of saucy micro mini-skirts, beer and costume jokes at the expense of everything from popular culture to organised religion and national politics.

In the 1995-founded home of the Heartland Brewery on Union Square I sip a Smiling Pumpkin Ale alongside Jesus Christ, a 'Naughty Nun' and Pharoah, and watch as Wonder Woman, Little Red Riding Hood and Catgirl compete to take orders from Shrek, Darth Vader and that evil giant rabbit from Donnie Darko. But the hit of the night is undoubtedly the girls in glasses with their hair tied up in buns, 'Miss Wassila' beauty queen sashes and low-slung machine guns. A total unknown just a few months ago Sarah Palin is – at least in New York City – everyone's favourite Hallowe'en nightmare. I pass three versions of her on the way to the Gents, each one more willing than the last to pout and pose. Digital flashes fill the air as vampires and ogres jostle for a view of the scariest costume in town. Especially when she puckers up for a kiss with a particularly rubberised Barack Obama. More than a little of tonight's frisson comes from the fact that it is the final Friday before an election that everyone knows will be a watershed one way or another in American history.

Palin, the controversial Alaskan governor drafted in as running-mate for the elderly earnest John McCain, is anathema to most of these hip young New Yorkers but everyone knows she struck a chord out in the great heartland between the coasts that those here would call 'redneck country'. Union Square this afternoon may have been awash in Obama buttons and T-shirts displaying the unmistakable features of the charismatic young Chicago senator, but I know for sure that out there in Malta, Montana, they'll be voting McCain-Palin straight down the line. And what about the cowboys in Colorado?

With just a couple of days to go before the election, behind the fancy dress there is a tangible feeling of an America trying once again to reinvent itself. Right here and now there is both hope and uncertainty in the air. Will Barack Obama become the first black president? And if he does, will it really change the way the world feels about America and the way America feels about itself?

Four days later there is the first inkling of an answer as Obama's electoral victory resounds around the world. The rest is history. It just hasn't been written yet. One way or another, America has not reached the end of the line.

WASHINGTON TO NEW YORK

TRAIN: Northeast Corridor
FREQUENCY: regular trains through the day
DURATION: approx 3 hours, 30 minutes
DISTANCE: 225 miles

TOTAL MILEAGE COVERED: 10,825 miles

The Soundtrack

Here is what was playing on Peter's iPod.

New York, New York – Frank Sinatra
An Englishman in New York – Sting
Waitin' for My Man – Lou Reed
America – Simon and Garfunkel
All Along the Watchtowers – Jimi Hendrix
The Wreck of the Edmund Fitzgerald – Gordon Lightfoot
Does Anybody Really Know What Time It Is? – Chicago
What Made Milwaukee Famous – Jerry Lee Lewis
Swingin' on a Star – Bing Crosby
After the Gold Rush – Neil Young
All the Way to Reno – REM
You Picked a Fine Time to Leave Me, Lucille – Kenny Rogers
Year of the Cat – Al Stewart
Do You Know the Way to San Jose – Dionne Warwick
Cracked Actor – David Bowie
All I Wanna Do – Sheryl Crow
C'mon, Take Me to the Mardi Gras – Paul Simon
Jambalaya – The Carpenters
Moon Over Bourbon Street – Sting
Memphis – Marc Cohn
Heartbreak Hotel – Elvis Presley
Memphis Blues – W.C. Handy Preservation Band
City of New Orleans – Arlo Guthrie/Steve Goodman
Woodstock – Joni Mitchell

The Beers

VISITING AMERICA TODAY no longer means weak tasteless lager. All across the continent there are literally thousands of new microbreweries, and a few of the old ones have been reinvigorated too. Here are just a few that helped me wash away the dust of the railroad.

Heartland Brewery, New York City
(Founded 1995)
http://72.167.25.128/Heartland/media/heartlandbrewery.html

Red Hook, Seattle, Washington
(Founded 1982)
http://www.redhook.com

Lakefront Brewery, Milwaukee, Wisconsin
(Founded 1987)
http://www.lakefrontbrewery.com/

Yuengling, Pottsville, Pennsylvania
(Founded 1829)
http://www.yuengling.com

Salt Lake Brewing Company, Salt Lake City, Utah
(Founded 2004)
http://www.squatters.com/

The Pike Brewing Company, Seattle, Washington
(Founded 1989)
http://www.pikebrewing.com/

Wynkoop Brewing Company, Denver, Colorado
(Founded 1988)
http://www.wynkoop.com/

Phantom Canyon Brewery, Colorado Springs, Colorado
(Founded 1993)
http://www.phantomcanyon.com/phantom.html

Grand Canyon Brewing Company, Williams, Arizona
(Founded 2007)
http://www.grandcanyonbrewingco.com/

Abita Brewing Company, Abita Springs, Louisiana
(Founded 1986)
http://www.abita.com